PAINTER™ 6
f/x & Design

Sherry London
Rhoda Grossman

CORIOLIS

The Coriolis Group, LLC
14455 N. Hayden Road, Suite 220
Scottsdale, Arizona 85260

480/483-0192
FAX 480/483-0193
http://www.coriolis.com

Library of Congress Cataloging-In-Publication Data
London, Sherry.
    Painter 6 f/x and design / by Sherry London and Rhoda Grossman.
        p. cm
    ISBN 1-57610-611-X
    1. Computer graphics. 2. Fractal design painter.
I. Grossman, Rhoda. II. Title.
T385.L6492 2000
006.6'869--DC21   00-021571
                                              CIP

Printed in the United States of America
10 9 8 7 6 5 4 3 2 1

President, CEO
Keith Weiskamp

Publisher
Steve Sayre

Acquisitions Editor
Beth Kohler

Marketing Specialist
Patti Davenport

Project Editor
Melissa D. Olson

Technical Reviewer
Nancy Wood

Production Coordinator
Meg E. Turecek

Cover Designer
Jody Winkler

Layout Designer
April Nielsen

CD-ROM Developer
Michelle McConnell

 CORIOLIS

Other Titles For The Creative Professional

Adobe ImageStyler In Depth
by Daniel Gray

Adobe InDesign f/x and Design
by Elaine Betts

CorelDRAW 9 f/x and Design
by Shane Hunt

Flash 4 Web Animation f/x and Design
by Ken Milburn and John Croteau

GIMP: The Official Handbook
by Karin Kylander and Olaf Kylander

Illustrator 8 f/x and Design
by Sherry London and T. Michael Clark

Looking Good In Print
by Roger C. Parker

Looking Good On The Web
by Daniel Gray

Photoshop 5 Filters f/x and Design
by T. Michael Clark

Photoshop 5 In Depth
by David Xenakis and Sherry London

To Rhoda—friend and partner. You've made this a lot of fun.
We need to do this more often!
—Sherry London

To my high school adviser who told me I was too smart to be an artist.
See, I wasn't that smart.
—Rhoda Grossman

ABOUT THE AUTHORS

Sherry London is an artist, writer, and teacher—exactly what a college aptitude test predicted. She was a contributing editor for *Computer Artist* magazine (before that publication's untimely death), and she has written for *Pre, MacWeek, MacUser,* and the combined *MacWorld/MacUser* magazine. She currently writes for *Electronic Publishing* magazine. Sherry has taught Photoshop and prepress in the continuing education department at Moore College of Art and Design in Philadelphia. Currently, she teaches QuarkXPress, Adobe GoLive, and Flash at Gloucester (N.J.) County College. She has spoken at a number of conferences, including the Thunder Lizard Photoshop Conference and the Professional Photographers of America convention. She has written a number of books on programs such as Photoshop, Painter, Illustrator, FrontPage, and After Effects.

Rhoda Grossman is a digital painter with a background in cartooning, caricature, and fine art. As principal of Digital Painting, she creates illustrations for print and the World Wide Web. Rhoda teaches Painter, Photoshop, and computer media fundamentals at the Center for Electronic Art in San Francisco and at Foothill College in Los Altos Hills, California. A member of the Graphic Artists Guild and the San Francisco Society of Illustrators, Rhoda is an advocate for the fair treatment of artists in the marketplace. She is the author of *Photoshop Effects Magic* and co-author of *Painter 5 f/x* (with Sherry London and Sharron Evans). For samples of Rhoda's artwork and her cartoon autobiography visit **www.digitalpainting.com**.

ACKNOWLEDGMENTS

To the technical staff at MetaCreations, thanks for your help. Also, thanks to the PR and product management team at MetaCreations.

To the folks at Coriolis:

- Melissa Olson, thanks for the handholding.

- Thanks to Meg Turecek, for the production expertise.

- Jody Winkler and April Nielsen, thanks for the cover and interior design.

- As for Mariann Barsolo and Beth Kohler, acquisitions editors, thanks for acquiring us.

To the Foothill College students who contributed their art to the book and the CD-ROM, we are honored to be the first to publish your work. Keep on painting!

To John Webster, thanks for the use of your beautiful photographs.

Thanks to Pauline Thomas Troia, Anthony Troia, Adam Thomas, Carole Watanabe, and Ida Levy for the use of your faces.

And a big hand to Max, Tessa, and all the ZEUM kids who contributed their art and their hands.

We are grateful, once again, to attorney Roy S. Gordet for sharing his expert knowledge of copyright law.

Most of all, thanks to Mark Zimmer, Tom Hedges, John Derry, and others from the company formerly known as Fractal Design for inventing Painter in the first place.

—*Rhoda Grossman*

In addition to the folks who Rhoda thanked, I'd like to add:

- Elizabeth Mitchell, senior technical specialist at MetaCreations, for your support, advice, and inspiration.

- Kelly Loomis, 7rings.com, for an exciting Web site and for being so willing to share your expertise.

- Ed Scott, for the use of the wonderful photos he took in China.

- Margot Maley, Waterside Productions, for being there for us.

—*Sherry London*

Contents At A Glance

Chapter 1   Basics

Chapter 2   Brush Effects

Chapter 3   Send In The Clones

Chapter 4   Paper Textures

Chapter 5   Patterns

Chapter 6   Collage

Chapter 7   Animation And Scripts

Chapter 8   Web Effects

Chapter 9   Dynamic Effects

Chapter 10   Text Effects

Chapter 11   Esoteric Effects

Chapter 12   Fine Art Techniques

TABLE OF CONTENTS

Introduction xix

Chapter 1
Basics 1

Welcome To Painter 6   2
What's New, Pussycat?   2
    Palette Pleasers   2
    Brushes All In A Row   3
    Material Things   4
    Objects   4
Floaters, No; Layers, Yes   4
    Layer It On   5
    Project: Creating Fruit Layers   5
    Working With Layers   7
    Project: Manipulating And Moving Layers   8
    Layers, Layer Editing, And Masks   9
    Project: Creating Objects   11
Other Painter "News"   14
Getting Organized   14
Getting Customized   15
    Customize Your Libraries   16
    Customize Your Icons   17
    Regrouping Variants   18
Painter 6 And Other Programs   19
    Painter For Photoshop Users   19
    Poser   20
    Project: Life Drawing Practice   20

Chapter 2
Brush Effects 23

Getting Acquainted With Brushes   24
    Jump Right In!   24
    Project: Refrigerator Art   24
    Project: Using The Look Designer   25
    Methods Without Madness   26
    Project: Testing! Testing!   26
    More Brush Controls   27
Just A Dab   27
    Project: Anatomy Of A Brush   27
    Input Variables   29
    Project: Express Yourself   29

Project: Theme And Variations For Piano   30
New Dabs   31
Project: Consider The Source   32
New And Improved Categories   33
Different Strokes   33
Project: A Rake's Progress   33
Bristle Basics   34
Project: Bristling With Excitement   35
Held Captive   36
Project: Taking Prisoners—Creating A Captured Dab   36
Different Layers   38
Deeper Is Better   38
Project: Thick, Thicker, Thickest   38
Wetter Is Better   39
Project: Water Color Still Life   40
Meanwhile, Back At The Palettes   42
Oil's Well   42
Project: Smear And Blend   42
Keep On Plug-In   43
Project: Changing Leaves   43

Chapter 3
Send In The Clones **45**

Basic Techniques   46
Chalk Cloner   46
Project: Pastel Drawing   47
Project: Scribbling A Clone   49
Project: Using The Melt Cloner For A Watercolor Look   50
Project: Oil Painting   51
Project: Colored Pencil Drawing   52
Soft Cloner And Straight Cloner   53
Project: Selective Reverting   54
Project: Selective Elimination   55
Project: Two-Point Cloning   57
Project: Sunflowers And The Van Gogh Cloner   58
Advanced Cloning   60
Making Watercolor Cloners   60
Project: Watercolor Study   61
Project: Watercolor Wash   63
Project: Felt Marker Sketch   64
Project: Still Life And The Impressionist Cloner   66

Chapter 4
Paper Textures **69**

Anatomy Of A Texture   70
What's The Value? How Paper Textures Texture   73

Textures By Design: The Make Paper Command   77
    Project: Engineering The Texture   77
        Phase 1: From Triangles To Black Satin   78
        Phase 2: Reengineering The Texture   80
        Phase 3: Making The Crinkly Texture   81
        Phase 4: Express (Texture) Yourself!   82
Repeat It Again, Sam   85
    Project: How Textures Repeat   86
    Project: Texture Tango   88
        Go Water Buffalo!   89
        Floating Color   91
        Toning A New Texture   92
        Crackle Multiplied   93
Rhoda's Text-ures   94
    Project: It's Greek To Me   94
    Graphics With Impact   95
    Impastable Text   96
    Project: Bulging Paper Text-ures   96
    Project: Randomizing Textures   98

Chapter 5
Patterns 101

A Pattern Primer   102
    Language Of Pattern   102
    Creating Rectangular Repeats   103
    Project: Single Motif Repeats—Part 1, The Block   103
    Painter's Offsets   104
    Project: Single Motif Repeats—Part 2, Using The Offset Slider   105
    Motif-Based Drops And Bricks   106
    Project: Single Motif Repeats—Part 3, Half-Drop Repeat By Hand   107
    Project: Single Motif Repeats—Part 4, Creating A Diaper Pattern   110
        Building The First Double-Repeat   111
        Building The Vertical Double-Repeat   113
        Creating The Final Pattern Tile—Start Loop   114
        Finishing Up   117
    Linked Motifs   118
    Project: Linked Motif Pattern   119
Painted Patterns   121
    Using The Pattern File   121
    Project: Fire And Confusion—Pattern Process   122
        Playing With Fire   122
        Dry Brush And Image Hose   125
Photographic Patterns   127
    Project: A Simple Seamless, Endless Repeat   127
Learning To Love Lines   129
    Project: A Four-Way Repeat   129

Patterned Prose   132
   Project: Text In A Shape   132
Primitive Pennies: Putting Patterns Into Practice   134
   Project: Counterfeiting Coins   134
      Ancient Coin   136
      Coin Paper   136
      Scaled Litmus   137
      Many Patterns   137
      Dissolving Coins   137
      Difference   138
      High Pass   138
      Blue Gold   139
      Embossed Color   139
      Color High Pass   139
      Masked Litmus   139
      Soft Litmus Mask   141
      Double Circle   141
      Stone Circle   142
      Masked Patterns   142
   Project: Kimono My House   144

Chapter 6
Collage   **147**
E Pluribus Unum   148
   Project: Hands On Collage   148
   Twenty-One Flavors   151
   Project: Surrealist Poster   153
   Seamless Blends   158
   Project: Mystery Novel Cover   158

Chapter 7
Animation And Scripts   **163**
Animation Basics   164
   Project: Toon Man Walking   164
      Moving The Background   165
      Combining The Background With The Cartoon Character   166
Experimental Animation   167
   Project: Photo-mation   168
Abstract Animation   169
   Project: Neon Spiral   169
   Project: Recorded Stroke Effects—Purple Heart   170
   Project: As The Worm Turns—Caterpillar Convention   171
Scripting Movie Effects   173
   Scripting Basics   173
   Project: A Script To Invert Color And Distort   174
Rotoscoping   175
   Consider The Source   175

Project: Muybridge Child Running   176
  Style 7.20: A. Negative Space   177
  Style 7.20: B. Gradient Color   177
  Style 7.20: C. Inverted Gradient Color   179
  Style 7.20: D. Fiber Clone   179
  Style 7.20: E. Van Gogh Clone   180
  Style 7.20: F. Van Gogh Clone Inverted And Distorted   180
Splicing Movies Together   180

Chapter 8
Web Effects   183

Painter And The Web, A Brief Introduction   184
Color For The Web   185
  File Formats For The Web   186
  Painter And The 216 Web-Safe Colors   186
Color Sets   188
  Project: Creating A Small Web-Safe Color Set   189
Graphic Techniques For Low Color   191
  Creating Low Colors Through Posterization   191
  Project: Using The Posterize Using Color Set Command   192
  Project: Posterizing The Image, Part 1   193
  Project: Posterizing The Image, Part 2   193
  Using Some Current Gradient Effects   195
  Project: Using Pop Art Fill   195
  Project: The Gradients|Express In Image Command   197
  Project: Creating A Graphic Print Brush   198
    Creating The Graphic Print Brush   198
    Using The Graphic Print Brush   199
    The Graphic Print Brush, Continued   199
Patterns And Texture   200
  Project: Developing A Background Pattern   201
The Illusion Of Depth   202
  Project: The Great Emboss   203
    Come To The Masquerade   203
    Adding Surface Texture   204
    Finishing Up   205
  Buttons And Interface Items   205
  Project: Swan Song   206
Image Maps   209
  Project: A Road Is A Road Is A Road (And Is Also An Image Map)   210
Images Sliced, Diced, And Rolled (Over)   214
  Project: Slicing Up An Image   216
    At First Slice   216
    A Chance To Dice   218
    Recombinations   219
    Setting Slices   221
    Exporting The Table   222

Chapter 9
Dynamic Effects 227

About Dynamic Layers   228
Creating Rice Paper   228
   Project: Burning Your Bridges With The Burn Dynamic Layer   228
   Growing A Paper   230
   Project: Growing Things With The Growth Command   230
   The Liquid Lens—Or How To Make Pudding From Paper   234
   Project: Mixing Up Some Liquid Pulp   235
   Textures To The Rescue   236
   Project: To Texture Twice   236
   Controlling The Burn Dynamic Layer   238
   Project: Making Deckled Paper   238
Heavy Metal   240
   Learning Liquid Metal   242
   Project: A Touch Of Liquid Metal   243
   Project: Drawing An Abstract Painting In Metal   247
Bevel World   248
   Project: A Beveled Ornament   248
      Beveled Liquid Metal Topping   248
      Building A Beveled Base   249
Dynamic Layers And Masks   252
   Project: Masking An Effect   252

Chapter 10
Text Effects 255

Vector-Based Text   256
   Staying In Shapes   256
   Project: Strokes And Fills   256
   Project: Font Stylin'   257
   Making A Commitment   259
   Project: Esoterica Fills   259
   Project: Image Fills   261
   Project: Quick-And-Dirty Marbling   263
   Project: Me And My Shadows   265
   All Together Now   267
   Project: Alphabet Sampler   267
Dynamic Text   269
   Project: Flaming Type   271

Chapter 11
Esoteric Effects 273

Mosaics   274
   Creating Random-Image Mosaics   274
   Project: Creating A Mosaic Repeat Pattern   275
      Tiling Nothing   275

Creating A Background Tile   277
Repeat Pattern Déjà Vu   279
Creating Image-Based Mosaics   280
Project: Creating A Mosaic From An Image   280
Laying A Foundation   280
Color And Select   282
Putting It All Together   284
Marbling   287
Preparing A Base   287
Project: Meet The Blob   288
Creating A Get Gel   290
Project: Recipe For Marbling   290
What Can You Do With A Get Gel?   292
Project: Making A Tiny Rake   292
Creating Your Own Pattern   292
Project: Roll Your Own   293

Chapter 12
Fine Art Techniques   295

The Big Picture   296
Practice! Practice!   296
Learning To Draw With Painter   296
Project: Warm Up   297
Project: Shape Up   298
Project: Line Up   300
Project: What You See Is What You Draw   301
Project: Accentuate The Negative   303
Learning From The Old Masters   305
Tonality   305
Geometry   307
Project: Simplifying Shapes   307
Use Your Edge   308
Stealing From The Old Masters   309
Drawing On Reality   309
Project: Still Life Painting   310
Still Life Using Paper Cutouts   311
Room With A View   313
Life Drawing   314
Project: Imitation Of Life   315
Portraits   316
Project: Portrait Of The Author As A Middle-Aged Woman   317
Project: Self-Portrait Painting   320
Trace And Fill   320
Wet And Dry   321
Mixed Media   322

Index   323

INTRODUCTION

Welcome to our second book on Painter, the best natural media painting software in the known universe. Painter is now better than ever, and so is this book. We've rewritten most of it from scratch. The palettes and tools of Painter 6 are more efficiently organized than those of its predecessor, and the same goes for *Painter 6 f/x and Design*.

Painter 6 can satisfy both sides of your brain. You can approach it with a technical mind-set by delving into its underlying construction. Or you can simply plunge in and start painting, using the intuition and abandon you had when you were a child—before somebody told you that you weren't an artist or shouldn't try to be one. I had the opportunity recently to be an artist-in-residence at ZEUM, San Francisco's Center for Art and Technology for children. I spent several weekends introducing kids as young as 5 to Painter 6. Within minutes, they were using a WACOM tablet, drawing and painting from their own imaginations. They did especially well when their parents and I stood back and let them do their own thing. A good deal of refrigerator art was created, as well as more than a few items suitable for framing. Some of that art is included on the CD-ROM accompanying this book to inspire you to return to the creativity you may have misplaced while you were so busy growing up.

Who Wrote This Book

Sherry London and I bring more than 100 years of life experience to this book. Major chunks of our lives have been devoted to creating both digital and conventional art, as well as teaching it and writing about it. We divided up the chapters so we could each focus on our own special interests and areas of expertise. We've made no attempt to homogenize ourselves into a single voice, and we think you'll benefit from the variation in our points of view and the different approaches we take to present Painter techniques.

What's In This Book

BY
RHODA
GROSSMAN

We provide technical information when needed, but our focus is on results. You don't need to understand everything under the hood in order to drive a car skillfully. But you need to know the rules of the road, how to shift gears, and what kind of fuel to put in the gas tank. By the time you finish this book, your parallel parking should be just about perfect, and you'll even understand how to work all those little buttons on the stereo.

Automotive metaphors aside, each chapter contains theory and practice, in varying amounts. We have not squeezed every topic into a preset formula. Rather, we have allowed the topics to determine the nature of our presentation. But there is an underlying structure to the chapters and to the book as a whole. We provide a foundation and build on it. You will be developing basic skills and gradually combining them into advanced techniques.

Painter 6 f/x and Design is not meant to take the place of your *Painter User Guide*. If you provide the motive, we will provide the means and opportunity to go beyond the manual. With the user guide in one hand and this book in the other, you'll be able to accomplish much more than you could with only one of them. But because you only have two hands, you'll have to put both books down while you work.

Hands-on projects are provided to lead you through the complexities of Painter 6 features and effects, and to encourage your creativity. These projects have been developed for use in our Painter classes, so you'll get the benefit of a college course for a fraction of the cost of tuition. And you won't have to commute or find a place to park.

Sherry's expertise in fiber art makes the chapters on textures and patterns as complete an exploration of those topics as you'll find anywhere. My chapters on brushes, cloning, and collage are liberally sprinkled with insights from my experience in traditional fine art and illustration. One chapter is devoted entirely to animation. It offers you the opportunity to practice cloning and other Painter techniques in a different context—movement. The chapter on fine art is the equivalent of a basic course in drawing, painting, graphic design, and art appreciation.

The Color Painter Studio

Color versions of many of the chapter images are found in this book's Painter Studio. You can flip to the color images to compare your final results to ours. Wherever you see the paint brush symbol next to a caption in a chapter, you'll know that a full-color version of the image is waiting for you in the Painter Studio. The Painter Studio also features new images that showcase how Painter students have created exceptional solutions to the book's projects, as well as our own Painter effects.

The CD-ROM

The CD-ROM that accompanies *Painter 6 f/x and Design* is chock-full of goodies. You'll refer to it again and again for the files you'll need to complete the projects in this book. In addition, you'll find libraries, custom brushes, animations, and more. Browse additional artworks created by Painter students. Also, experience the work of children using Painter for the first time; their work will amaze and inspire you.

Technically Speaking

Painter works on Power Macintosh computers and on PCs running Windows 95, 98, or NT4. This book and its companion CD-ROM are cross-platform, too. When keyboard commands are mentioned, they are given for both Mac and Windows.

Before you start working, we recommend that you allocate as much RAM as possible to Painter and close all other applications. Depending on the muscle of your system, some computation-intensive effects might take a long time. If you don't want to invest in more megabytes or megahertz, try working on smaller images.

Who Needs This Book

There are almost as many ways to use this book as there are ways to use Painter. Professionals, students, and hobbyists will all find this book a useful resource. Fine artists, illustrators, graphic designers, and Sunday painters will learn exciting techniques for getting the most out of Painter 6. Read it like a novel. Use it as a handy reference. Practice the simple demonstrations to get a feel for the basics. Use the CD-ROM images and the how-to steps to learn advanced techniques. We hope you'll use this book for more than just propping up your WACOM tablet!

BASICS 1

BY
RHODA
GROSSMAN AND
SHERRY LONDON

This chapter gives experienced users helpful hints on working more efficiently with Painter 6, including ways to customize the Painter environment. We'll show you how to get organized so your Painter environment becomes your desktop artist's studio.

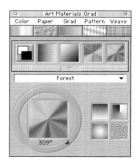

Figure 1.1
Painter 5's Art Materials palette combined five palettes in one place.

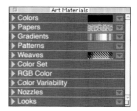

Figure 1.2
Painter 6's Art Materials palette allows you to view multiple palettes at one time and scroll between them.

Figure 1.3
You can show any of the subpalettes by clicking on the arrowhead at the left of the subpalette name.

Welcome To Painter 6

Painter 6 is an awesome program. It just keeps getting better. The biggest news in Painter 6 (and the difference that you'll notice first) is a totally redesigned screen layout that makes it easier to find Painter's commands. A second major happening is that floaters have been superceded by Photoshop-style layers. A third big development is that you'll see a new brush engine that controls the way that you paint. All these changes, and more, are covered in this book.

In this introductory chapter, we'll talk about the new interface, the new Layers palette and masking methods, and ways to customize your Painter installation. We make the assumption that you've either used a previous version of Painter or you are a somewhat experienced computer artist who understands the basics of creating computer imagery.

We'll also briefly discuss using other popular graphics programs in conjunction with Painter. We give Photoshop users special attention throughout the book and try to point out differences and areas of similarity.

What's New, Pussycat?

Painter 6 looks new when you launch it. Over the years, Painter has suffered heavily from "creeping palette-itis," an all-too-common disease brought on by too many features and not enough monitor space. The Brush features were the worst offenders. Painter 5 contained seven different palettes (eight, if you include the Controls: Brush palette) that dealt exclusively with brushes and painting options. In addition to those seven or eight palettes, you also had the Objects palette, the Art Materials palette, the Tools palette, and a few more for good measure.

Painter 6 has grouped all these free-floating palettes into three major palettes, plus the Tools palette, the Brushes palette, and the Controls palette. Finding a brush control is now much easier.

Palette Pleasers

Before you dive into the specifics of each of the palettes, we need to explain the basic "look" of the new palettes. Figure 1.1 shows the original Art Materials palette, and Figure 1.2 shows the newly redesigned Painter 6 version.

Common to all three of the major new palettes is the ability to display multiple subpalettes at one time. The Art Materials, Objects, and Brush Controls palettes are really "super palettes." They are palettes of palettes. Each embedded palette has an arrowhead to the left of the palette name that can be twirled down by clicking on it. Twirling down the arrowhead reveals the embedded palette as you can see in Figure 1.3.

If the embedded palette has a downward-pointing arrow at the right side of its name, that subpalette contains a menu of additional options and commands.

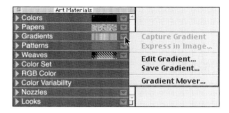

Figure 1.4
The arrow on the right of many
of the subpalettes contains a
drop-down menu.

Figure 1.4 shows the Art Materials: Gradients palette menu. As you can see, it gives you a number of additional possibilities. Throughout this book, you'll be told to click on the *Palette Name*: *Embedded palette* menu. When you see that type of reference, you're being asked to click on the arrowhead at the right of the subpalette name to reveal the drop-down menu. For example, if you're asked to select Art Materials: Gradients palette menu|Express In Image, you should click on the arrowhead to the right of the Gradients entry that's located in the Art Materials palette. It sounds a bit convoluted, but you'll easily get used to it (we've adopted the conventions used in the Painter manual).

The individual palettes themselves have not changed very much. For example, the Gradients palette looks just about the same (especially when the Painter 5 version is expanded to show the gradient types). In Painter 6, the six tiny previews of gradient type are new. In Painter 5, the previews were larger and arranged three by three.

One of the major benefits of the new system is that you can have multiple subpalettes open without taking over your entire monitor real estate. Because the palette scrolls, you can size it as needed for your monitor. Sherry is very lucky. She has two monitors attached to her Macintosh. She can paint on the 21-inch monitor and keep her palettes open on the 17-inch monitor next to it. If your monitor is smaller, Painter still takes up a lot of room for palettes, but you don't have to keep everything open. The new Art Materials palette takes up less screen room than the old one when all the subpalettes are closed.

One of the nice features of the new palettes is that you can see some of the critical settings even with the subpalette hidden. On the Art Materials palette, for example, you can see the current color, gradient, pattern, paper texture, and weave. You can also get to the menus with the subpalettes closed (you could in Painter 5, too, but many users found it counterintuitive to look at one palette while using the menu for a different palette).

Brushes All In A Row

The Painter 6 team has done an incredible job of streamlining the brush controls. In Painter 5, you had to search all over for the various controls that enabled you to customize your brushes. Now, they're all in one place—the Brush Controls palette.

Figure 1.5

The Brush Controls palette allows you to manipulate brush settings.

Figure 1.5 shows the streamlined Brush Controls palette. From it, you can set the General controls for the brush (the Method and Subcategory settings that previously needed to be set on the brushes palette itself). You can also set Size, Spacing, Angle, Bristle, Expression, Well, Cloning, and a number of other specialized categories for different types of brushes. In addition, you can control the Impasto (or depth) information as you paint. You should enjoy having control of your brushes at your fingertips—especially when Rhoda shows you what you can do with the brushes in Chapter 2.

Material Things

You just looked at the Art Materials palette. Some changes have been made to the items available on it. In Painter 5, the Art Materials palette contained subpalettes for Colors, Papers, Gradients, Patterns, and Weaves. These subpalettes are still part of the Art Materials category. However, instead of setting your color variability underneath the Colors palette, you'll set it in the Color Variability subpalette.

All your nozzles for the Image Hose can be selected in the Nozzles subpalette. If you're not familiar with the Image Hose, this invention allows you spray photographic (or painted) objects onto your image. It's a marvelous tool, and versions of it are available in other programs now. Painter was the first program to offer this feature, however.

You can store all your brush looks in one place now, too. The Looks palette is also found in Art Materials. Brush looks let you store a particular combination of brush, pattern, paper, and nozzle settings so that you can use it again at a later date.

Objects

Figure 1.6

The Objects palette in Painter 6 gives you access to Layers, Masks, Dynamic Layers, and several other subpalettes.

The Objects palette also existed in Painter 5. However, two of the critical elements have been renamed. Therefore, in place of floaters, you'll see *layers*, and in place of plug-in floaters, you'll see *dynamic layers*. (We'll talk about the reason for these changes in a bit.) Figure 1.6 shows the new Objects palette.

The Objects palette also contains the subpalettes for the Selection portfolio (which let's you drag selections onto your image) and the Image Portfolio (formerly the Objects: Floaters palette).

Floaters, No; Layers, Yes

We find it ironic that Painter's floaters, which were one of the first implementations of raster objects, should give way to Photoshop layers, which came a year or so later. Actually, the change to layers is welcome. Perhaps because Painter's implementation was one of the first ones, it was not as complex or all-encompassing as Photoshop's solution to the same problem.

What's the difference between a floater and a layer? A floater was an object of a particular size that moved freely above the canvas. The size of the floater could be changed, but it wasn't the same size as the image. A layer is the same size as the image in which it resides. It's the equivalent of a sheet of clear acetate placed over the canvas to keep paint from dripping on the background. Once the acetate has been painted, it can be moved anywhere in the image.

Adding additional space to a floater in Painter 5 was very tricky. Even though adding the space itself was easy, *using* the added space was not. When you look at an object in a floater (or in a layer as well), you're seeing a part of an image that isn't masked. Each floater had a mask, and even if you enlarged the floater, you couldn't see anything else that you painted on the floater unless you also revealed it in the mask. With layers, you can add a new one and paint in it immediately—without having to do anything special to it. The old mask brushes are gone—and not missed, either!

Layer It On

When Painter introduced floaters in version X2, it also introduced the Floater Portfolio. The Floater Portfolio was an image library from which you could drag stored images to your canvas as needed. When you dragged an image out of the Floater Portfolio, it became an ordinary floater that could be moved, manipulated, masked, modified, multiplied, and finally merged into the background. Although the "floater" terminology no longer exists, the Floater Portfolio is now the Image Portfolio library.

You can find ready-made images to drag into your compositions in Painter's Image Portfolio. You can use them just by dragging them onto your canvas. You can create your own image libraries, too. Layers give collage artists un-limited freedom to alter each item in an image, at any time, before committing themselves to the position, size, opacity, or other characteristics of these elements.

PROJECT Creating Fruit Layers

Even if you've used Painter before, you'll find this project us-ing layers beneficial. You should find it helpful for learning which features of floaters remain and what you need to do differently. In this project, you'll load a portfolio of fruit images, position them on colored paper, and (eventually in this chapter) manipulate them into a still life arrange-ment. You'll need to drag the FRUIT portfolio from this book's companion CD-ROM onto your hard drive before you begin this project. Here are the steps to follow:

1. Open the current Image Portfolio. It's the last entry on the Objects palette.

TOOLS AND THE IMAGE PORTFOLIO

It doesn't really matter which tool is currently selected when you drag an image from the Image Portfolio. After you drag an image onto your canvas, the Layer Adjuster tool becomes the current tool.

SELECTING A FRUIT

Figure 1.9 shows the cursor over the apple in the open Image Portfolio drawer. This works because the picture of the apple can't be seen when the drawer is shut (that is, the apple isn't one of the fruits shown in the five preview pictures above the drawer). The Objects: Image Portfolio preview bar shows either the first five items in the palette or the five most recently used items. If an image is on the preview bar, you need to drag it to your canvas from the pre-view bar. You won't be able to drag the images that are shown in the preview bar onto your canvas from the open drawer. They are, effectively, "grayed out." An easier way to select your image is to choose it by name in the drop-down menu at the bottom of the Objects: Image Portfolio palette.

Figure 1.7
You need to drop down the menu that contains the image name so that you can load the new library.

2. Select Load Library in the Image Portfolio palette's drop-down menu (shown in Figure 1.7) and navigate to the FRUIT portfolio that you copied to your hard drive.

3. Highlight FRUIT and click on Open, as shown in Figure 1.8. You'll see the fruit in the Image Portfolio.

4. Choose File|New to open a new canvas. Choose a width of 500 pixels and a height of 360 pixels. Choose a grayish-green paper color. (Consult your Painter User Guide if you need help selecting a paper color. Basically, you just click on the large color swatch on the New File dialog box and change the controls in the Color Picker until you produce the color that you want.)

5. Select the Image Adjuster tool (the pointing finger icon that's third from the right on the second row of the Toolbox).

6. Place your cursor over the image of the apple in the Image Portfolio palette, as shown in Figure 1.9.

7. Drag the image to the canvas, where it expands to its normal size. Repeat this step to place the pear, the peach, and the grapes in your image as well. Figure 1.10 shows the fruit placed onto your canvas. Each piece of fruit is now a new layer in the Objects: Layers palette.

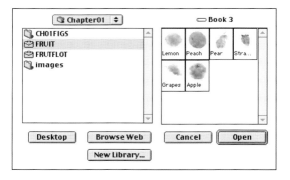

Figure 1.8
Selecting the desired portfolio on your hard drive loads it into the Objects: Image Portfolio palette.

Figure 1.9
Place the Layer Adjuster tool over the desired image in the Image Portfolio so that you can drag the image into your working composition.

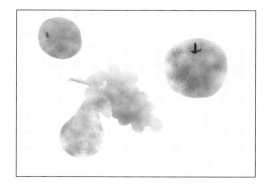

Figure 1.10
The fruit is moved to the canvas.

Working With Layers

Once you place an Image Portfolio item onto the canvas, you can make it active again by clicking on it with the Layer Adjuster tool or by clicking on its name in the Objects: Layers palette, as shown in Figure 1.11. You deactivate it by clicking on the canvas or on a different layer in the Objects: Layers palette.

You can group or ungroup layers by clicking the appropriate buttons on the Objects: Layers palette. When you group layers, the grouped layers move as one.

You can get rid of layers by dropping them to merge them into the Canvas layer. You can drop a single layer or group by clicking on the Drop button. You can drop all the layers at one time if you choose the Drop All option on the Objects: Layers palette menu. You can also undo any of the Drop actions.

You can merge two or more layers together without dropping them by first grouping them and then clicking on the Collapse button in the Objects: Layers palette. The layers merge into one, and it's as if the additional layer(s) never existed.

You can move the object in a layer around by dragging it with the Layer Adjuster tool. Move it in front of or behind other Layers by dragging its name to the desired position in the Objects: Layers palette list. If the Layer Adjuster tool is selected, you can also use the buttons that are on the Controls palette to arrange the layers. Figure 1.12 shows the features of the Controls: Adjuster palette.

Figure 1.11
The Objects: Layers palette is the central control station for all activities involving Layers.

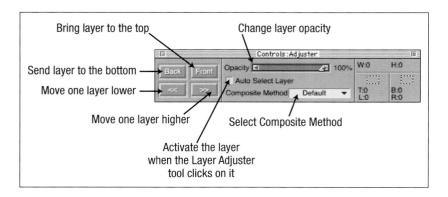

Figure 1.12
The Controls: Adjuster palette offers additional features for working with layers.

PROJECT Manipulating And Moving Layers

In this project, you'll move the layers around. You're going to change the size of the red apple, flip and rotate the peach, and alter the color of the grapes. Here are the steps:

1. Arrange your layers to match the layer order shown in Figure 1.11, and move the layer objects so that they're approximately in the positions shown in Figure 1.10.

2. With the apple layer active, choose Effects|Orientation|Scale. Type "125" or drag the handles on the bounding box to about that amount (see Figure 1.13).

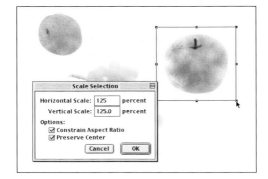

Figure 1.13

Enlarge the apple by typing the percentage of enlargement or by dragging a handle on the bounding box.

3. Select the peach. Choose Effects|Orientation|Flip Horizontal. Choose Effects|Orientation|Rotate and drag a corner handle to any position you want.

4. Select the grapes and choose Effects|Adjust Colors. Move the Hue slider to the left until the preview window shows red grapes. Be sure to have Uniform Color showing in the Using pop-up menu. Figure 1.14 shows the Adjust Colors dialog box.

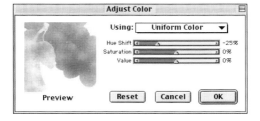

Figure 1.14

The Adjust Colors dialog box enables you to change the hues in your layer.

5. Change the red apple into a green one with Effects|Adjust Colors, shifting the Hue slider to the right this time. Change the name of this layer by double-clicking on it in the Objects: Layers palette list and typing "Granny Smith apple" in the Layer Attributes dialog box that appears.

Layers, Layer Editing, And Masks

Masking was not a pleasure in Painter 5. It's not a lot of fun in Painter 6, either, but it's better (a little). One of the major changes in Painter 6 is that you can actually make a selection in both a layer and a mask. The selection in a layer behaves mostly as you would expect. You can paint only within the selected area. You can fill the selection or apply effects. You can also delete the selection and remove it from the layer, replacing it with transparency.

An odd thing happens, however, if you try to move the selected area of a layer. When you move a portion of a layer using the Layer Adjuster tool, you get a *layer floating object* (that's what it says in the Layers palette). A layer floating object is an object that's in a "halfway" state. It isn't an independent layer, but it isn't exactly part of the current layer either. You can move it by itself, but if you try to move the object on the layer that produced the floating layer object, you move both the layer and the "floating" layer.

You can convert this layer floating object into a real layer, but it isn't obvious as to how that's done. Painter has no commands to do this on any menu that we can find. However, if you alter the location of the layer floating object in the Objects: Layers palette list (move it up or down), it then becomes a layer. Alternatively, if you try to apply an effect to this layer floating object, it disappears and becomes part of the original layer again.

If you're a Photoshop user—especially if you use masks a lot—you might find yourself both baffled with and annoyed at Painter's masking implementation. If you are more comfortable with Photoshop's masking, you might still prefer to create any major masking changes in Photoshop and then bring the image into Painter.

Although we're addressing this masking discussion towards Photoshop users, don't fret. If you've never used Photoshop, you probably don't miss the features that it adds anyway. In Photoshop, you can do anything that you want to a mask. With the exception of using filters that won't work in grayscale or other features that don't work on a grayscale image, you can use just about every feature of Photoshop in a layer mask or alpha channel.

Many of Painter's brushes work in masks, but many of them don't. In general, the simple brushes work. The Cloners seem to work but don't really clone. The Image Hose doesn't protest, but it quietly sprays the nozzle on your image rather than on the mask (but it paints the nozzle's image mask into the mask). The brushes with a Plug-In method actively protest and give you an error message. Several other brush types produce error messages as well. The Pens brush with the Pattern Pen or Grad Pen variants work beautifully in the mask to create wonderful semitransparent effects. Brushes that use a Build-Up method will paint, but because the Build-Up method builds up color toward black, the brush is useless for changing visible areas of the

PRESERVING TRANSPARENCY

When you paint in an empty layer or in an empty part of a layer with a regular brush, the mask is automatically updated to reflect the new areas in the layer. If you want to protect the layer so that only the object already in the layer is visible (and remains visible), you can select the Preserve Transparency checkbox in the Objects: Layers palette. This works just like the checkbox of the same name in Photoshop.

mask (which are black) to invisible areas (white). The brush simply doesn't work that way—white ink can never build up over black.

You can trick a mask into recognizing a selection, but it isn't worth the pain (even if you manage to see a selection marquee, the tools don't behave the way they do when they aren't used in a selection). The Fill command fills the entire mask with black, regardless of your current color. The Pattern Fill command also fills your mask with solid black. The Delete/Backspace key works. Also, Select|Invert works.

You can't use the Magic Wand in a mask (although it works in a layer). The Select|Color Select command sometimes works usefully in a mask. If you try to paint in a layer mask that has an active marquee, the marching ants are ignored and the tool paints wherever it pleases.

You can't place an image into the mask as you can in Photoshop. You can't load a layer mask as you can in Photoshop. You can't select (that is, *load*) the layer transparency as you can in Photoshop. You also cannot load the layer mask itself. In order to change the mask into a selection, you need to copy the mask first.

Here are the basic principles for working with masks:

- Areas in the mask that are black make the layer image opaque and visible.

- Areas in the mask that are white make the layer image completely transparent.

- Gray areas in the mask make the image in the layer semitransparent, depending on how close to white the shade of gray is.

- To change a layer mask into a selection, you need to first choose Copy Mask from the Objects: Masks menu and then save it as a new mask. You can then click on the Load Selection button in the Objects: Masks palette to load the new mask as a selection.

- The layer mask is specific to a layer, but any other masks that you create on the layer can be used anywhere in the image.

- You can load multiple masks by choosing the Add To Selection option in the Load Selection dialog box. (You can also subtract one mask from another or intersect one mask with another.)

- It helps to think of a mask as simply a different type of selection. The layer mask is a selection that is interactive (you can see its results immediately in the visibility of the image in the layer). Other masks are "selections-in-waiting"—areas that are waiting to be selected and can be combined with other masks into new selections.

- You can always create new user masks by selecting the luminosity of an image and saving it as a mask. You can copy this user mask into the layer mask to affect the visibility of the image in a layer.

Even though Photoshop and Painter have different ways of creating and using masks, Photoshop's ways are not always better. Painter still gets a lot of power from its masks. Even if Sherry is not always fond of them, you can learn to use masks to your advantage to control the visibility of a layer. Painter has some useful masking features, such as the sliders in the Color Select command and the ability to dynamically change the tolerance setting of the Magic Wand.

PROJECT Creating Objects

In this project, you'll work with some "previously prepared" fruit. Starting from scanned images, the fruit has already been processed and is in an impressionistic state, which can be effective to preserve some of that hand-picked quality. We've already prepared the apple, pear, peach, and grapes as finished, masked objects. (If you prefer a more traditional masking approach, feel free to tighten up on the masking.) Their masks are the same shape as the fruit. The strawberry and lemon, however, have pieces of a white background surrounding them. Their masks are rectangular, and you need to treat them differently. In the next project, you'll try out several ways of coaxing the image to part company from its background. Follow these steps:

1. Drag the strawberry and lemon images onto the canvas. As you can see in Figure 1.15, they each have a white background.

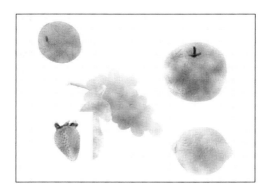

Figure 1.15
These Image Portfolio layers contain white backgrounds.

2. Select the strawberry in the Objects: Layers palette list. Open the Objects: Masks palette. Click on the Strawberry Mask entry in the Objects: Masks palette to select it. Leave the eye icon closed. This allows you to work on the mask while looking at the image itself (otherwise, you'll only see a black rectangle and you won't know where your strawberry starts and ends). Figure 1.16 shows you the

Figure 1.16
Select the mask but turn off its visibility (eye) icon.

Objects: Masks palette with the strawberry mask correctly selected (although in grayscale it's almost impossible to see that it's selected).

3. Choose the Large Chalk Brush variant of the Dry Media brush. With white as the foreground color, begin to paint away the background around the strawberry. It becomes transparent as you paint. If you accidentally mask out part of the fruit, switch to black and paint it back in. Change the brush size or opacity, as needed, and zoom in for better control.

4. Save the "fresh" strawberry to your Image Portfolio library so you can avoid the chore of masking out the background the next time you want to use the image.

5. Drag the lemon from the canvas back into the Image Portfolio library. You'll be prompted to name the library entry. Type "lemon" and click Yes when asked whether you want to replace the earlier version.

6. As a side effect, Painter removes the lemon from your image. (Bug or feature? You decide.) You can always drag it out again—after all, that's why you saved it.

7. In Painter 5, the steps that you just performed were the best way that you could remove the background from a floater. However, Painter 6 has a way to remove a layer's background that you might find much easier. Make the Lemon layer active.

8. Select the Flat Eraser variant of the Eraser brush. Simply paint out the white background of the lemon on the Lemon layer. When you're done, drag the lemon into the Image Portfolio to save it.

Why would you go through the hassle of doing steps 1 to 6 when you can simply erase the background (or draw around the lemon with the Lasso tool, choose Select|Invert, and delete the background)? The main reason to bother with the longer set of steps is that they are nondestructive. When you erase part of the lemon, it's gone forever. If you alter the mask of the lemon, you can fine-tune the visibility of your layer. Add white if too much is showing; add black if you removed too much. Only the mask gets changed—every single pixel on the image layer is still there. It's a very powerful feature—even if the Eraser or the Lasso are seductively easy choices.

Here are a few more how-to tips:

• To give a layer a more descriptive name, double-click its "generic" name in the Objects: Layers palette list and type a new name in the dialog box that appears.

- To create new image layer, select an image you want to make into a layer object using any of the selection tools. Click on it with the Floater Adjuster tool and it will appear as a new item in the Objects: Layers palette list.

- To save this item to the current portfolio, drag and drop the image into the Image Portfolio library on the Objects palette with the Floater Adjuster tool. Name it in the Save Image dialog box. Your new floater now appears as a thumbnail image in the current library.

Do you want more strawberries? Just keep dragging them in from the Image Portfolio library. It's a bottomless fruit cup. Better yet, create a copy of any fruit layer in your image by holding down Option/Alt while dragging the item to a new location.

Make each berry look slightly different from the others by changing size and position and adjusting some color variables. Try "ripening" one of them by darkening it a bit with the Brightness/Contrast controls. Figure 1.17 shows one finished arrangement. When you're satisfied with yours, save it as FRUIT.RIF in RIFF format to retain the layers.

Group the layers in your still life arrangement by selecting them all (Shift-click on each name in the list or use Select All in the Objects: Layers palette menu) and then click on the Group button. Painter names this Group 1, by default. You can still see the individual layers in the group when you click on the arrow to the left of the group name. Clicking on it again closes the group. Figure 1.18 shows the group open.

You can also create a drop shadow for the group. Select Effects|Objects|Create Drop Shadow to apply a drop shadow to the entire group. Figure 1.19 shows some specific settings for you to try. Figure 1.20 shows the finished example.

If you want to save this image so that you can edit it later, you need to save it in RIFF format. That's Painter's own file format.

Figure 1.17
(Left) Here's a still life with layers.

Figure 1.18
(Right) Group the layers in the image.

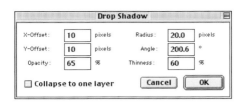

Figure 1.20
Here's the fruit composition
with shadows.

Other Painter "News"

The new news in Painter 6 is that in addition to the new Layers feature and the new palette arrangements, Painter 6 has gone back to basics and created some wonderful new brush types. Painter has a new rendered type of brush stroke, a new airbrush that mimics the real thing, and strokes that paint in multiple colors at one time. Rhoda tells you all about them in Chapter 2. Painter has a marvelous new Impasto control that replaces the Impasto dynamic plug-in (by the way, dynamic plug-ins are now called dynamic layers). The Impasto controls allow you to turn any brush into a brush that paints with texture and depth as well as with color. Painter provides an enormous category of Impasto brushes to go with the new feature. Again, Rhoda will tell you all about this in Chapter 2.

Sherry is the "pattern junkie," and Painter 6 has given her a lot of new toys as well. One of her favorites is the new Pattern Pen variant of the Pens brush. Figure 1.21 shows a fast sketch using three brush looks (found in the Art Materials: Looks palette) containing masked patterns. Sherry will tell you how to use and create patterns and masked patterns in Chapter 5.

Getting Organized

"A Place for Everything...and Everything in Its Place." Maybe it's a sign of creativity to have a messy desk, but we think a little "housekeeping" will help you find what you want quickly as well as streamline Painter's efficiency. (Having said that, of course, we also need to tell you that neither of us is likely to win an award for homemaking.)

You'll need some palettes more often than others. How can you keep them from crowding each other and covering up the whole screen? Mac users have

ABOUT GROUPS

When layers are grouped, they're all surrounded by a single bounding box. You can add a drop shadow to each element of the group quickly with Effects|Objects|Create Drop Shadow. If you ungroup them at this point, each item would still have its own drop shadow and be listed as "Item Plus Shadow." With the exception of rotating, scaling, and flipping, Drop Shadow is the only effect you can apply to an entire group of layers.

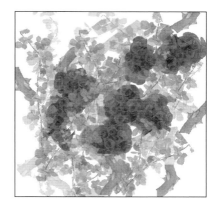

Figure 1.21
You can paint with pattern using the new Pen Pattern brushes.

a Window Shade feature—just double-click on the title bar to "snap" any palette (or document) open or closed. If you can see any part of a palette, you can click on it to bring it forward. When a palette is completely hidden, go to the Window menu and click it off and then on again. It will come to the front. There are also keyboard shortcuts for opening and closing each palette. You can keep the arrowhead pointing right on any subpalette to collapse it. Just twirl down the arrowhead when you want to reveal the entire palette again. The Arrange Palettes command in the Window menu lets you return to a nice, neat default configuration or any custom arrangement you've saved.

Suppose you want frequent access to both the Colors and Papers subpalettes. They share space in the Art Materials palette. You can twirl down the arrowheads next to both of them on the Art Materials palette and keep them both visible at all times (using the scrollbar on the Art Materials palette). On the other hand, if you expect to be working for a while with the same tool, color, and paper, you might want to hide all the palettes (Command/Ctrl+H). This keystroke will toggle the palettes back into view when you need them.

The new organization of palettes is efficient and sensible once you get the hang of it. However, previous users of Painter will have a few things to unlearn.

Getting Customized

Painter can adjust the sensitivity of your graphics tablet. Whenever you launch Painter, go to Preferences|Brush Tracking and make a stroke or scribble that's typical of your pressure and speed. Painter will adjust to your touch. This is also a good way to see whether your tablet's pressure feature is working. Painter won't remember this setting, so it's a good habit to begin each session with a trip to the scratch pad. If you want to increase or decrease Painter's sensitivity, for different projects or different areas of the same image, make adjustments in Brush Tracking as often as you need to. You might want to set a function key to open Brush Tracking quickly. Figure 1.22 shows this dialog box.

PHOTOSHOP USERS ALERT: COMMAND/CTRL+H

Photoshop users are accustomed to using the Command/Ctrl+H keyboard shortcut to hide the "marching ants" of a selection. Painter 6 provides a Hide Marquee option only in the Select menu; there's no keyboard shortcut for this. You can easily make a keyboard shortcut, however. Use Preferences|Function Keys to assign an F key to the Hide Marquee function.

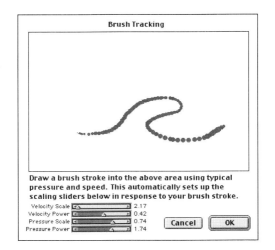

Figure 1.22
The Brush Tracking scratch pad
lets you set an average pressure
and speed.

Customize Your Libraries

You can create custom libraries of your favorite brushes, papers, and other materials. Eliminating redundancy and tossing out rarely used art materials will cut down on the time you spend rummaging around looking for the right tool. You might want to come back to this discussion after you've been working with Painter 6 for a while, and after reading the material on brush basics in Chapter 2.

When you're ready to put together your own libraries, open the appropriate Mover. There are Movers for Brushes, Paper, Gradations, Patterns, Weaves, and so on. Figure 1.23 shows the Paper Mover being used to gather together textures from a variety of libraries. Items in a library can be customized further by changing their names. You might be able to come up with a more descriptive name than Surface #37, for example.

Rhoda rarely uses Felt Pens or Crayons, so her custom brush library excludes them—she can always find them in the original library if the need arises. Figure 1.24 shows the Brush Mover being used to create a custom brush library. All the favorite standard brushes are included. The Gooey brushes from Painter 5 are the most recent addition to the library. (Because Painter 6 has

Figure 1.23
The Paper Mover dialog box
allows you to save and customize
your own paper libraries.

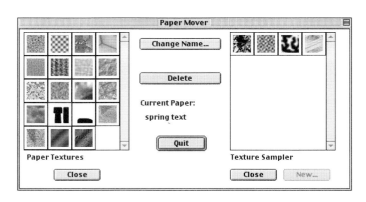

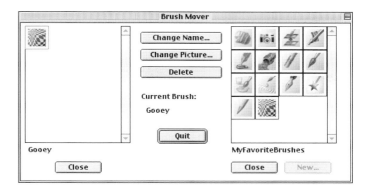

Figure 1.24
Use the Brush Mover to create custom brush libraries.

Figure 1.25
Deleting a variant removes it from the brush library.

simplified the brushes, if you have earlier versions of Painter and want the brushes that were no longer included, you can move them into a new library.)

When you've moved entire categories of brushes to your personal library and loaded the library, it's safe to eliminate unwanted variants in your loaded set of brushes. Use the Delete command in the Variant pop-up menu, as shown in Figure 1.25.

The Eraser group can afford to lose a few variants. Your Painter manual notes that the Bleach variants in the Eraser group differ from the Eraser variants only in that they always reveal white, regardless of the paper color. They also differ in their default opacity. The Bleach variants are set at 50 percent opacity, whereas the Erasers are set at 100 percent. If you work exclusively with white backgrounds, you might want to delete some of the Bleach or Eraser variants and adjust opacity and size when necessary. You might also want to delete some of the Bleach and Eraser sizes because it's just as easy to adjust size on the fly (Option+Command/Ctrl+drag).

You also might want to delete the Darkener variant in the Eraser category. Except for size and opacity, the Darkener is the same as the Burn tool, now found in the Photo Brush group. Similarly, the Dodge variant is just a very large eraser set to very low opacity.

When you've created a number of your own libraries and are sufficiently annoyed at seeing Painter's default libraries of papers, floaters, and brushes pop up every time you launch the program, it's time to go to Preferences| General and tell Painter which libraries you want to be the default choices. These will take effect the next time you open Painter. Proceed with caution here. If you mistype the file name, Painter fails to open and you have to reinstall the Painter settings. Renaming default libraries can be tricky, and parental supervision is suggested.

Customize Your Icons

Some of the icons on the Brush palette are more obvious than others. Some are so similar that there's a bit of a learning curve just to remember that the icon showing a brush over a ripple of water is *not* a watercolor brush! It's a group of distortion brushes.

SAFE SAVING

You're safer creating an alternate library and deleting unwanted items from it than you are to delete items from the default libraries. If you should need to acquire a brush tool that you got rid of, you can use the custom install to restore just the brush library. Remember to use the Brush Mover to save your brushes that have custom variants before reinstalling the program.

COPYING BRUSHES

The Movers in Painter 6 don't have a Copy command for transferring a brush from one library to another. All you do is drag and drop the icon you want to move.

READ THE FINE PRINT

You can avoid memorizing the icons by using the drop-down menu that lists the brush variants by name.

The icon for artist's styles (Van Gogh, Seurat, and so on) is a tube of paint. We thought we could improve on that, so Rhoda changed hers to a portrait of Rembrandt. Any image can be used to replace a brush icon, but keep it simple and use high contrast in order to recognize it at a glance. Rhoda dusted off her traditional markers, pens, pencils, and so on and scanned them to provide the image ALLTOOLS.tif on the companion CD-ROM. Use them, after making modifications if you like, to replace some of your default icons.

Here's how to make a different icon for any of your brush categories:

1. Open or create an image for your new icon. Select it with the rectangular selection tool while holding down the Shift key to constrain it to a perfect square. Figure 1.26 shows an image of scanned art supplies, with a portion selected to replace the Pens icon.

Figure 1.26
Scanned art supplies provide a convenient way to make new icons for your brushes.

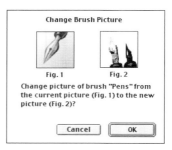

Figure 1.27
You can change to a different Brush icon using the Brush Mover.

2. Open the Brush Mover (found in the Brush drop-down menu on the Brushes palette) and click the category you want to change.

3. Click on Change Picture. The dialog box shown in Figure 1.27 appears. Click on OK. This cannot be undone.

Regrouping Variants

Because all the tools for making marks on a canvas are called brushes, we'll refer to variants of a given brush type as members of a group, such as the Pens group or the Loaded Oil variant of the Brush group. This helps avoid awkward references such as the Brush brush.

The number of variants is dizzying: Sable, Camel, Loaded, Wet, Dry, Cover, Penetration, Graduated, Rough, Fine, Wash, and Hairy (and in various sizes). Some of the names seem more descriptive than others. You might find it easier to locate your favorites if you divide some of the variants into more manageable (or different) groups. Painter has done a complete redesign of the brush library in Painter 6 to make it more manageable. Nonetheless, you might find that you prefer a different arrangement. One possibility is to group your variants by stroke type. For example, you might want to leave the Single-stroke brushes in the original group and create a new category for the Rake- and Multi-stroke brushes. Alternatively, you might want to break up the very large Impasto brush family into several small ones.

Painter doesn't provide a Variant Mover, but you can find a way around that. Just use the Brush Mover to copy the same Brush category twice. Give one of them the name "Rake/Multi" and delete all the Single-stroke variants from it. Then delete the Multi and Rake variants from the original Brush group so that only the Single-stroke variants remain. Finally, you can provide a new icon for the Rake/Multi group. It's a little involved, and if you're happy with the default organization of the brushes, just skip over this maneuver.

Painter 6 And Other Programs

Painter is compatible with a wide range of popular graphics applications. You can, for example, import EPS (vector) files from Illustrator or Freehand with the File|Acquire command. The EPS image appears as a layer in a new document, and you can use the Shape tools for vector editing. Painter auto-matically converts the shape to a bitmap (raster) image that behaves just like any other layer when effects are applied. To make Painter images acces-sible to other paint programs, save Painter files in TIFF or PICT format, unless you want to preserve layers as separate elements.

Painter For Photoshop Users

If you want to save layers and work on an image in Photoshop, save the image in Painter's Photoshop format. Painter's layers will appear as regular layers when you open the document in Photoshop. Painter automatically converts the mask into the Photoshop "white is selected" format.

As you've already noticed, we give tips to Photoshop users whenever we can. We encourage you to switch between the two programs, taking advantage of the best features of each: Painter's Natural Media tools and Photoshop's pow-erful selection capabilities, for example. Here are a couple of additional hints for making the transition from Photoshop to Painter, and back again:

- Painter doesn't have an "erase to saved" option per se. Make changes on a clone of the saved image. When you need to restore portions of the original, use the Soft or Straight Cloner.

- Painter doesn't have an 8-bit grayscale mode. You can turn a full-color image into shades of gray by using Effects|Tonal Control|Adjust Colors and moving the Saturation slider to 0 percent, or you can use Painter's Grayscale Color Set to create an image. To reduce the file size to 8-bit grayscale, convert the image mode in Photoshop.

- Be careful about applying composite methods that don't travel back and forth. Gel, Colorize, Reverse-Out, Shadow-Map, Magic Combine, and PseudoColor are Painter-only modes that aren't recognized in Photoshop. Color Dodge and Color Burn aren't understood in Painter. Flatten or drop any layers that have these proprietary composite methods or apply modes before you export the image.

- Painter can't understand Photoshop's adjustment layers or layer effects either (it ignores them), and the Photoshop format written by Painter doesn't allow you to keep any of Painter's dynamic layers active.

Poser

Traditional artists and students can benefit from teaming up Painter and Poser. It's an excellent combination for practicing life drawing skills. Poser allows you to model 3D figures and to create animations that walk and run.

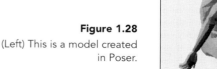 **Life Drawing Practice**

Here's one way to use Poser as an aid for life drawing (Rhoda provides other techniques in Chapter 12):

1. Create a model in Poser. Export it as a PICT or TIFF file.

2. Open the Poser file in Painter.

3. Use the File|Clone command and then, working in the clone image, choose Select|All. Delete the image from the clone.

4. Turn Tracing Paper on and use the "ghost image" as a guide for sketching.

The Poser image in Figure 1.28 is the Adult Male Body Type in the Automobile Pose in Poser's Classic Library. The drawing in Figure 1.29 is a combination

Figure 1.28
(Left) This is a model created in Poser.

Figure 1.29
(Right) Here's a sketch done in Painter from the Poser model.

of tracing with the Sharp Pencil variant, shading with Chalk variants, and "airbrushing" back some of the original Poser model with the Soft Cloner.

Commercial artists can benefit, also, by minimizing the time and expense of photo shoots to get "scrap" for illustrations or "comps." Here's another example of what you can do with Poser.

You can, for example, create a woman with ample proportions by combining two body types. Pose your model first, choose the lighting position and colors, and establish the camera angles. Poser's Flat Shaded Display emphasizes the planes of the form. You can get a full-figured look by adjusting the body part dimensions of a Female and a Sumo wrestler.

After the image is complete in Poser (and rendered and saved), open the image in Painter and clone it. You could use the Grainy Water variant of the Water brush, with a medium-rough paper texture to smooth the planes of the form. Hair and additional "accent" strokes can be applied with the Van Gogh Cloner. Chapter 3 provides a detailed discussion of cloning techniques.

Rhoda used this technique to create a "zaftig" nude for an editorial illustration for a magazine cover. The woman was flipped horizontally, the position of one leg was changed, and more smears with Grainy Water created a suggestion of clothing. The shadow was painted in with the Burn tool and a bit more smudging was done. Figure 1.30 shows a detail from the final image.

Figure 1.30
This is a detail from Rhoda's magazine cover.

Moving On

You've been introduced to some of the most versatile—and challenging—aspects of Painter 6. We invite you to return to this chapter as you develop a relationship with Painter. By the time you finish this book, you can expect that relationship to blossom from a nodding acquaintance to chummy familiarity.

The next chapter, on brushes, is really an extension of our "basics" discussion. Natural Media brushes are the foundation of Painter.

BRUSH
EFFECTS

2

BY

RHODA

GROSSMAN

Natural media effects are the core of Painter. You can create the look of wet or dry media, as well as thick paint or a thin wash, on smooth or textured surfaces. However, you won't stain your fingers with ink or have to endure the odor of turpentine.

Getting Acquainted With Brushes

The default Brush library consists of 15 categories. Most of them can be used to make traditional-looking marks on your canvas—Pencils, Erasers, Brushes, Dry Media, Impasto, Pens, Felt Pens, Liquid, Airbrushes, and Water Color. The other categories, especially Cloners and the Image Hose, contain tools for making marks that go beyond what's possible with traditional art materials. The capability of a brush to change your painting style and a nozzle that sprays fully formed images onto your canvas—these do not seem to have conventional equivalents.

It's useful to think of a brush category as a container. When you use Dry Media, for example, you must choose one of the variants in the category: Gritty Charcoal, Oil Pastel, Waxy Crayon (to name a few).

In this chapter you'll get familiar with Painter's brush families, and with the variables that give each brush its distinctive qualities. You'll examine each set of controls in a logical order, giving your left brain an opportunity to take in lots of technical stuff. But first, give your right brain a bit of fun.

Jump Right In!

Lots of people can drive skillfully without knowing much about what's going on under the hood of their car. Similarly, you can work successfully with Painter's brushes before you learn about such things as Squeeze, Jitter, and Damping. So—if you'll forgive a mixed metaphor—come on in, the watercolor's fine!

PROJECT Refrigerator Art

In this project, you'll scribble a little with as many brush variants as you can. The results might not be art, but a print will hold its own (especially if you use a magnet) on the fridge door. Here are the steps to follow:

1. Open a new picture (Command/Ctrl+N) that's about 500 pixels square, at 72 pixels per inch, using the default white paper color.

2. Close all palettes to keep from being distracted by the ones you don't need yet using Command/Ctrl+H (as in Hide).

3. Open the following palettes, found in the Window menu at the top of your screen: Tools, Brushes, and Color Set. The keyboard shortcuts for opening them are Command/Ctrl+1, 2 and 6, respectively.

4. Choose a brush category by clicking on its icon in the Brush palette, or you can find it in the pop-up menu at the lower-left of the Brush palette, as shown in Figure 2.1.

5. Choose a variant of the brush category from the pop-up list at the lower right of the Brush palette. In Figure 2.1 the current variant is Basic Crayons.

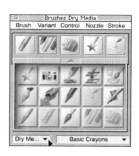

Figure 2.1
This is the Brush palette, with the cursor on the pop-up menu of brush categories.

6. Make a mark on the canvas. Scribble, draw, sketch, or scrawl.

7. Change the color by clicking on another swatch in the Color Set.

8. Repeat steps 5, 6 and 7 at will, using a different brush variant each time.

Some of your strokes might show paper texture. If you're using a graphics tablet, notice that some of the brushes are sensitive to changes in pressure. Observe what happens when you paint over strokes with another variant. Some strokes are opaque; others are translucent.

Note: You won't really need the Tool palette for now because the Brush tool is active by default, and it's the only tool needed for painting. However, it doesn't take up much space, and you might as well get used to looking at it.

PROJECT Using The Look Designer

The Look Designer (formerly called the Brush Look Designer) is shown in Figure 2.2. The Look Designer updates your stroke instantly when you change to a different variant or make alterations to the current variant. You can choose to show the stroke on a plain background or against stripes. The striped backgrounds are useful to show the effect of a smeary or distortion brush. Change the black stripes or one of the black swatches to a different color if you want by selecting the new color and clicking on the Set Colors button. Here are the steps to follow:

1. Choose a color in the Color Set or on the Color section of the Art Materials palette.

2. Open the Look Designer by clicking on the Brush palette pop-up menu: Brush|Brush Looks|Look Designer.

3. Choose a brush variant and make a stroke on the swatch. If the stroke doesn't show up, try switching to one of the stripe patterns. Strokes that don't add color but only smear existing pixels (for example, variants in the Liquid brush category) will have no effect on a solid-color area.

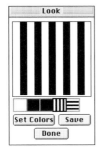

Figure 2.2
This is Painter's Look Designer.

The Look Designer has a couple limitations: You can't change its size, and you must close it (by clicking on Done) before you can make strokes on an open image. An alternative to the Look Designer involves making your own document for exploring brushes. I've included a file called BLT.tif (which stands for Brush Looks Tester) on the CD-ROM accompanying this book. It's much bigger than the tiny Look Designer and allows you to draw across different backgrounds with the same stroke. Whenever you have too many scribbles and strokes on your BLT, use Edit|Revert and the original image will reappear.

Figure 2.3 shows the BLT.tif image with strokes made by Chalk, Felt Pen, and Liquid variants. Notice that the Chalk stroke is the same opaque color on both the gray and white areas of the BLT. The Felt Pen, on the other hand, is darker on the gray area, due to its transparency. Finally, the Coarse Smear variant of the Liquid group shows up only on areas where there's some change in color, such as at the edge between the two solid colors and in the patterned area.

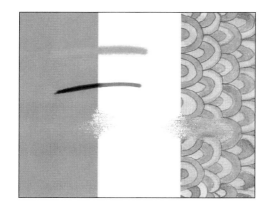

Figure 2.3
This is the Brush Look Tester with three test strokes.

Methods Without Madness

Method is the major factor determining the nature of a brush. The methods are Buildup, Cover, Eraser, Drip, Cloning, Wet, and Plug-in. Each method is divided into subcategories that determine whether the stroke will be sensitive to paper texture (Grainy), whether the edge of the stroke will be anti-aliased (soft) or not (hard), and so on.

PROJECT Testing! Testing!

In this project you'll continue exploring brush variants, but now you'll also examine some of the variables that give each one its special look and feel. Here are the steps:

Figure 2.4
The General section of the Brush Controls palette.

1. Open the General section of the Brush Controls palette, shown in Figure 2.4, so you can see the method and subcategory for each brush variant you use.

2. Open the BLT.tif image.

3. Choose a medium-light color and one of the Felt Pen variants. Draw a horizontal stroke across both gray and white areas of the BLT image. Notice that the stroke appears much darker over the gray background. Another stroke over the first one will darken the color even more. This is the way you'd expect markers to behave, and it's characteristic of the Buildup method.

4. Now try the Large Chalk variant of the Dry Media brush family and make a stroke with the same color. Observe Large Chalk's ability to cover the background tone. This opacity is what defines the Cover method.

5. Notice that the subcategory for Large Chalk is Grainy Hard Cover. *Grainy* refers to the ability of this variant to show paper texture. Open the Paper section of the Art Materials palette and switch to a different paper. Make another stroke with Large Chalk to see the difference paper can make.

Note: Plug-in is really a catchall for a wide variety of methods that have little similarity to one another.

6. Change the method of the Felt Pen variant by clicking on the Method pop-up menu and dragging to Cover. When you make a stroke with this altered marker, it will behave like chalk!

More Brush Controls

How a brush looks and behaves is also influenced by its size and shape, the type of stroke it makes, whether it adds color or just smears existing colors, how it responds to pressure or other input, and how much variability is permitted. Each default variant has had all those considerations determined for it. You can find out what those settings are in the appropriate sections of the Brush Controls palette, and you can change any of the settings to fine-tune your brush or create your very own custom variants.

The Size section of the Brush Controls palette, shown in Figure 2.5, has sliders for Size and Minimum Size. A third slider, Size Step, controls how smoothly the size changes occur. A larger percentage causes more abrupt changes in brush size.

The Preview box shows the diameter of the brushstroke. Click on the preview to toggle between the hard and soft view. In the hard view for a brush with size variation, there's a black center surrounded by a gray outer ring. The center shows the smallest diameter of a stroke, and the gray ring shows variation in size as a function of pressure or other input variables.

The soft view of the preview shows how the pigment is distributed in the stroke. A more graphic profile of this distribution is indicated in the six smaller squares to the right of the preview box. They represent the choices of shape for the tip of your brush.

Just A Dab

Many of Painter's brushstrokes are composed of a series of dabs whose characteristics can be manipulated. Most dabs are composed of one or more circles or ellipses, but any shape or even an image can be made into a brush dab.

PROJECT Anatomy Of A Brush

You'll examine several settings that give a brush its characteristic behavior, alter some of them, and then save the changes as a new variant. Here are the steps:

1. Open a new picture that's about 500 by 400 pixels at 72 ppi with a white background.

2. Choose the Calligraphy variant in the Pens category. Make several strokes on your canvas with a dark color (see Figure 2.6).

   Notice that the Calligraphy pen behaves like its traditional counterpart, making thicker lines on vertical strokes and much thinner lines

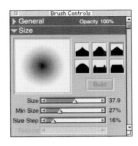

Figure 2.5
This is the Size section of the Brush Controls palette.

Figure 2.6
Here are some strokes made with
the Calligraphy pen.

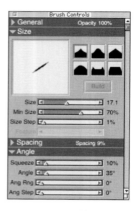

Figure 2.7
Here are the Size and Angle
controls for the Calligraphy pen.

on diagonal ones. Not surprising, when you look at the brush tip preview in Size controls. It shows a thin elliptical dab (see Figure 2.7). The angle of the dab (35 degrees) is indicated by a slider in the Angle section of the brush controls, also shown in Figure 2.7. What determines the thinness of the ellipse is the Squeeze setting (10 percent, in this case).

3. Move the Squeeze slider to the right and observe changes in the brush tip preview. At the maximum value of 100 percent, the brush has a circular tip. It's no longer a calligraphy pen.

4. Open the Spacing section of the Brush Controls palette. Move the Minimum Spacing slider all the way to the right and make another test stroke on your canvas. Now you can see individual dabs, such as the string of beads shown in Figure 2.8.

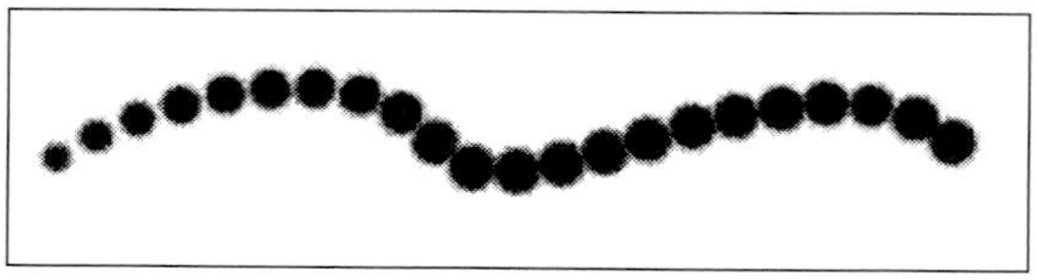

Figure 2.8
An increased Minimum Spacing
setting shows individual dabs.

5. Save this new brush as a variant in the Pens family. Use the Save Variant command in the Variant pop-up menu at the top of the Brushes palette. Type the name "Beads" in the Save As field, as shown in Figure 2.9. Beads is now in the alphabetical list of variants for Pens.

Look at the General section of the Brush Controls palette and notice that the subcategory is Grainy Hard Cover. Recall that a Grainy subcategory will respond to paper texture. That's fine for the Calligraphy

Figure 2.9
The current settings are saved as
a new variant called *Beads*.

pen, giving it the appearance of ink slightly bleeding into the paper at the edges of the stroke. However, you'll want your Beads pen dabs to have smooth edges.

6. Change the subcategory to Flat Cover and make a test stroke with the Beads variant.

7. Change the subcategory to Soft Cover and make another test stroke.

   Figure 2.10 shows the Beads brush with the Flat Cover and Soft Cover subcategories. Soft Cover makes the dabs too blurry, but Flat Cover makes the beads appear too close together. You've already increased spacing to the maximum, so what can you do? The next step handles this problem nicely.

Figure 2.10
This shows examples of the Beads variant with Flat Cover (top), Soft Cover (middle), and Flat Cover with Size decreased (bottom).

8. Decrease the size of the dab to about 10 so that there's just a tiny bit of space between the dabs, as shown in the bottom stroke of Figure 2.10.

9. Give your beads more variation in size. The Calligraphy pen you started with has a Minimum Size setting of 70 percent of the maximum. Move the Minimum Size slider to about 40 percent. Make another test stroke with varying pressure to your graphics tablet. It should look similar to what's shown in Figure 2.11.

Figure 2.11
The Beads stroke with more variation in dab size as a function of pressure.

Input Variables

How does a variant "know" that size is a function of pressure? For an answer, it's time to look at another set of controls. Open the Expression section (formerly called Sliders) of the Brush Controls palette, as shown in Figure 2.12.

PROJECT Express Yourself

You'll change the way brushes behave by selecting different input variables to control the expression of output variables. Follow these steps:

1. With the Beads variant you've been working with still selected, notice that size is a function of Pressure input. Choose Random from the pop-up menu of Controllers for size and make another test stroke.

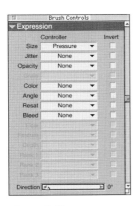

Figure 2.12
Here are the Expression controls.

EXPRESSION CONTROLS

The input variables, called *controllers*, are chosen from a pop-up menu for each of the expression variables. Expressions that are not available for the current variant are grayed out. The controllers include Direction and Velocity, which are especially useful for creating variations with a mouse. Source refers to the clone source or, in the absence of a designated source image, the current item in the Pattern library. Pressure is a natural way to make variations in size, opacity, and other expressions. Wheel, Tilt, and Bearing refer to options available with certain graphics tablets such as WACOM's Intuos models. Random input can create decorative results, depending on the variable linked to it.

2. Change the controller for Opacity from None to Random; then make a test stroke. Figure 2.13 shows the result of random input for size as well as for size and opacity.

Figure 2.13
Here's the Beads variant with random control of size (top) and both size and opacity (bottom).

3. Next, make the beads scatter around the path of your stroke. Open the Random section of the Brush Controls palette. Move the Jitter slider all the way to the right to get the maximum effect. Make a stroke, which should look similar to Figure 2.14. Your brush no longer looks like a string of beads, and you can save it as a new variant if you want.

Figure 2.14
Here's the Beads variant with random jitter added.

COLOR CONTROL

There are two ways to control color variation in Painter. In the Expressions controls *Color* refers to the variation between the primary (foreground) and secondary (background) colors. The kind of variability you see between dabs in the Piano Keys stroke, for example, is a primary color variation and is controlled in the Color Variability section of the Art Materials palette with separate sliders for Hue, Saturation, and Value.

PROJECT Theme And Variations For Piano

Brushes can change subtly or dramatically based on the relationships established in the Expressions controls. Some surprising looks can result from adjustments made there. You'll experiment with the Piano Keys variant in the F/X group. Here are the steps:

1. Make a new picture or continue working on your current canvas.

2. Choose a medium-value color and make a few Piano Keys strokes, or a couple of curves, in different directions.

The multicolor parallel lines are always perpendicular to the direction of your stroke. This indicates that angle is a function of direction. Expression controls show that the angle is indeed linked to the direction, with all other input variables inactive. Look at the soft view of the dab in the Size controls. It's a thin vertical line. The Color Variability section of the Art Materials palette has 15 percent variation in tonal value and 4 percent variation in hue. This is what gives the stroke a variety of shades within a more limited range of colors.

What happens to the stroke when you change some of these settings? Make a new stroke after each of the following changes, and compare your results to Figure 2.15. Reset the default values between your changes by using the Restore Default Variant command in the Variant pop-up menu. The top stroke was made with the default settings for Piano Keys.

3. Increase the variation in hue by moving the +/-H slider on the Color palette to the right. The results are shown in the second stroke.

4. Change the angle of the dab to 45 degrees, and the result will look like the third stroke in Figure 2.15.

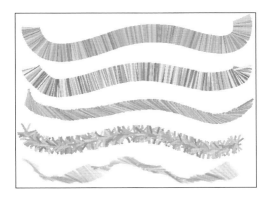

5. On the Expression controls, make Angle a Random function. This stroke looks like a Christmas tree decoration.

6. Using Expression controls again, make Opacity and Angle functions of Source. Now your stroke will have variations based on the luminance of the current pattern. Try changing to different patterns until you get an effect you like.

New Dabs

Painter 6 introduces a wide variety of dab types in addition to the old familiar ones—Circular, Bristle, 1-pixel, and Captured. The complete list of dab types is in the pop-up menu on the General section of the Brush Controls palette, as shown in Figure 2.16. Changing the default dab type can have an even more dramatic effect on the look of a brush than changing its method. Three of the dab types (Line Airbrush, Rendered, and Projected) allow you to assign a source other than color (or in addition to color) as the medium to paint with. The sources available for a Rendered dab are shown

---

BE CAREFUL WHAT YOU WISH FOR

In earlier versions of Painter all settings for a brush variant would revert to default values automatically as soon as a different brush was chosen. This is no longer true. Painter 6 remembers all the changes made to a variant, whether or not you want to keep them. If you want the original version of a brush back, you must use the Restore Default Variant command in the Variant pop-up menu on the Brushes palette. This can be annoying, especially if you share a computer with another Painter user. There needs to be a global command for returning all brushes to their default settings.

Figure 2.15
Experiments with the Piano Keys Variant.

Figure 2.16
This is the pop-up menu of dab types in the General section of the Brush Controls palette.

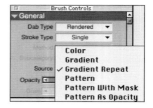

Figure 2.17

This is the pop-up Source menu available for some dab types.

in Figure 2.17. A Projected dab can have all but Pattern As Opacity as the source, and the Line Airbrush gives you a choice between Color and Gradient.

Consider The Source

Now you'll play with some of these new dab types that have choices for their source. You'll find a couple of likely candidates in the Brushes family: Graphic Paintbrush and Graphic Paintbrush Soft. Here are the steps to follow:

1. Open a new picture with a white background at 72 pixels per inch, big enough to give you plenty of room to experiment.

2. Choose the Graphic Paintbrush variant of the Brush group and a dark color.

3. Notice that the default source is Pattern As Opacity. Therefore, it's probably a good idea to choose an item in the Pattern library on the Art Materials palette. I used Picket Fence for the first stroke in Figure 2.18.

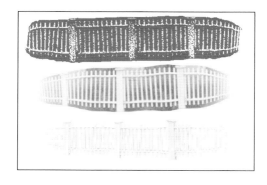

Figure 2.18

Here are some strokes made with the Graphic Paintbrush variant and different sources: (from top) Pattern As Opacity, Pattern, and Pattern With Mask.

SOURCE OF CONFUSION

The term *source* is already used in reference to an image that's designated as a clone source, or the current pattern (if there's no clone source image). Now you must use the same word to refer to choosing from different types of patterns and gradients as a medium for your painting. Maybe it's not so bad, considering you have to use the word *brush* to refer to several things: the item in the Tools palette that allows you to paint, the library of stroke-making categories, and one specific category in that library.

4. How does painting with Pattern As Opacity differ from painting with Pattern or Pattern With Mask? Switch to each of those sources and make a test stroke. The middle stroke in Figure 2.18 uses Pattern as the source, and the bottom stroke uses Pattern With Mask.

   Clearly, Pattern As Opacity lets you paint with the color of your choice, and the selected pattern determines the opacity of the stroke, with lighter areas giving less opacity. Using Pattern results in the actual pattern appearing, but Pattern With Mask eliminates the background behind the fence so that only the fence appears. Your results will vary depending on the pattern you work with.

5. Switch to the Checkers pattern and make a stroke with the Graphic Paintbrush.

6. Use the same pattern but switch to the Graphic Paintbrush Soft variant and make a stroke. The edges of this stroke are softer, as shown in Figure 2.19.

BE A BRUSH CONTROLS DETECTIVE

Can you find the variable or variables that give Graphic Paintbrush Soft a fadeout on the edges of the stroke? Looking at the General section of the Brush Controls palette is not much help. The only difference between the two variants is a few percentage points in the Grain setting. That wouldn't be enough to make such a noticeable difference. See if you can find the critical difference between them. I'll tell you the answer later.

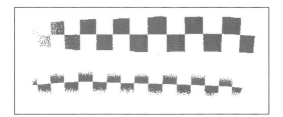

Figure 2.19
Here are some strokes made with Graphic Paintbrush (top) and Graphic Paintbrush Soft (bottom), using the Checkers pattern.

New And Improved Categories

The Dry Media category is new in Painter 6, but it simply combines the previous Chalk, Charcoal, and Crayon families. This reorganization is sensible and efficient. Photo and F/X brushes used to be in their own separate libraries, but now they are included as families in the default library. It's handy to have them more readily available. Some of the Gooey brushes from Painter 5 have been added to the Liquid group—another welcome change. The Airbrush group now has many more variants to choose from. And if you're wondering what happened to Piano Keys, it's now a member of the F/X family. Most exciting of all is the Impasto group, used for creating thick paint effects. It deserves and receives a special section later in this chapter.

Different Strokes

The General section of the Brush Controls palette has a pop-up list of four stroke types: Single, Multi, Rake, and Hose. The vast majority of brushes are Single stroke, made up of one row of dabs. Multi strokes have been almost completely removed from Painter's Brush library now that there are so many sophisticated dab types available. The Hose type is "native" to the Image Hose brush, but if you switch to it you can use any brush to paint with nozzle images.

 A Rake's Progress

Rake strokes such as the Scratchboard Rake variant of Pens or Depth Rake in the Impasto family are composed of several parallel strokes, like the tines of a fork. When Rake is the current stroke type, the Rake section of the Brush Controls palette is enabled, as shown in Figure 2.20. Examine the effects of the Rake controls by following these steps:

1. Open a new picture that's about 500 pixels square, with white as the background color and a resolution of 72 ppi.

Figure 2.20
This is the Rake section of the Brush Controls palette with default settings for the Scratchboard Rake.

2. Choose Scratchboard Rake from the Pens family. Also choose a dark color.

3. Make a stroke with the default settings of the brush to use as a standard of comparison.

4. Change one of the sliders to a different position and make another stroke on your test canvas. Return to the default values between each change by using the Restore Default Variant command in the Variant pop-up menu on the Brushes palette.

5. Continue to examine the effect of each slider or checkbox; then try some of them in combination.

Compare your test strokes to Figure 2.21. The vertical strokes, from left to right, include a default stroke, a reduced Contact Angle, and an increased Brush Scale. Next is a stroke resulting from enabling the Spread Bristle option. I liked the tapering effect, but the bristles were too close together so I reduced the number of bristles from 10 to 4 to produce the next stroke. The horizontal squiggle was made with Soften Bristle Edge turned on. The circular strokes show default values on the left and then the result of increasing Turn Amount to 100 percent.

Figure 2.21
Several rake strokes were made to test changes in the Rake Controls.

Bristle Basics

A brush variant that appears to be a Multi stroke type but is actually a Single stroke type is the Dry Ink variant of the Brush group. This is because the dab itself is complex, as you can see in the soft view of the brush tip (see Figure 2.22). Dry Ink has the Static Bristle dab type, so the Bristle controls are available.

WHERE DID IT GOGH?

In Painter 6 the Van Gogh variant of the Artists group is a Rake stroke, but earlier versions of Painter included a Multi stroke Van Gogh brush that had a more interesting look due to its capability of having bristles overlap instead of being perfectly parallel. Multi strokes can take a while to appear on your screen after you draw them, and they can be frustrating to wait for. If you miss the original Van Gogh variant, as I do, you can load the Painter brushes from an earlier version using the Load Library command at the bottom of the pop-up menu from the Brush categories. Better still, use the Brush Mover to create a custom combination of Brush families from Painter 6 and any other version you have. The Brush Mover is found in the pop-up Brush menu at the top of the Brushes palette. Alternatively, you can tweak the Rake controls for the Van Gogh variant. Increasing the Turn Amount can help, as shown in the figure. The leftmost squiggle was made with the old Multi stroke version. The center stroke shows the current Van Gogh rake with default values, and the stroke on the right has Turn Amount increased to about 100 percent.

Here are some Van Gogh strokes: (from left) the older Multi stroke version, the current Rake version, and the Rake with an increased Turn Amount setting.

PROJECT Bristling With Excitement

There are four sliders for controlling bristle characteristics. Thickness determines the diameter of each bristle without changing its number. When you move the Hair Scale slider to the left, the hairs get thinner but increase in number. Clumpiness controls variation in Bristle thickness. Scale/Size can produce subtle changes depending on the settings of the other sliders. In this project, you'll examine the effects of changing Bristle controls and create a new variant to add to your brushes library. Here are the steps:

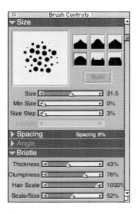

Figure 2.22

Here's the Soft view of Dry Ink, a Static Bristle dab type. It uses the default settings for Bristle controls.

1. Make a new picture or continue working on your current canvas.

2. Choose the Dry Ink variant of the Brush family and make a stroke with settings unchanged. Your stroke has a dry brush look because the bristles are fairly large and have a high degree of clumpiness.

   Keep the Size section of the Brush Controls palette open and, if necessary, click on the preview box to see the soft view, so you can observe changes in the brush "footprint" as you adjust sliders in the Bristle controls. Compare your results to Figure 2.23.

3. Reduce Hair Scale to 250. The bristles are much finer, and the brush has a wetter look.

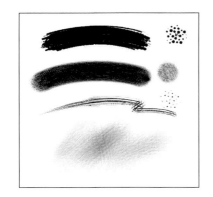

Figure 2.23

Here are some Dry Ink strokes and dabs, before and after changes to the Bristle controls.

4. Reduce Thickness to 21 percent. This gives you a loose "gap-toothed" stroke, because there's now more space between bristles.

5. Take Thickness down to the minimum, 1 percent. The bristles are so thin, they're scarcely visible. Even with black as the current color, strokes must be layered to build up tonality. (Hmmm...sounds like crosshatching to me.)

6. Save this variant as Crosshatch. Use the Save Variant command in the Variant pop-up menu on the Brushes palette.

Held Captive

Figure 2.24

Here's the Captured dab of the Impressionist variant.

Any stroke or group of pixels can be made into a brush dab by selecting it with the Rectangular Marquee tool and using the Capture Brush command in the Brush pop-up menu. Such brushes belong to the Captured dab type. The Piano Keys brush you worked with earlier has a Captured dab. You'll make some of your own before long, but first you'll look at another Captured dab brush that's part of the default brush library: the Impressionist variant in the Artists category. Enlarge it in the Size section of the Brush Controls palette and look at the Soft view of the dab element, as shown in Figure 2.24. The dab is roughly teardrop shaped and appears to have been made by smearing a small Dry Ink stroke.

PROJECT Taking Prisoners—Creating A Captured Dab

Figure 2.25

Here's the handcuffs icon for the new Captured brush category.

Before you actually make any Captured brushes, start a new Brush category to be the container for these unique variants. You'll name the new group Captured and use an icon that's unmistakable—handcuffs (see Figure 2.25). Follow these steps:

1. Open CUFFS.tif on the CD-ROM accompanying this book. Drag a Rectangular Selection marquee around the Handcuffs image, holding down the Shift key to constrain a perfect square.

MORE DETECTIVE WORK

A curved stroke made with the Impressionist variant is shown in the figure. Using what you already know about brush anatomy, can you predict some of the settings that determine the behavior of this variant? What input variable controls size and opacity? What is the angle range, and what controls its expression? Is there any Jitter assigned to this brush? By the way, the answer to the question, "How do Graphic Paintbrush and Graphic Paintbrush Soft differ?" is found in the tip profiles on the Size controls.

Here's a stroke made with the Impressionist variant.

2. Use the Brush|New Brush command. You'll be prompted to name your brush style. Type "Captured". Figure 2.26 shows the new category in your Brush library.

   You'll now make a leafy brush.

3. Use black on a white canvas. Draw a small cluster of three leaves with the Scratchboard Tool variant of the Pens family. This will become the dab element for your new brush.

4. Drag a marquee around your leaves with the Rectangular Selection tool.

5. Use the Capture Brush command in the Brush pop-up menu. Your leaves should now be in the dab preview in the Size section of the Brush Controls palette (see Figure 2.27).

Figure 2.26
The Captured category is now added to current Brush library.

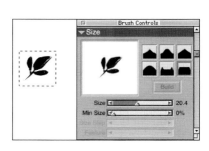

Figure 2.27
The leaf element is selected and captured.

6. Test your new brush. Make adjustments to the Size, Spacing, Expressions, and other controls to get the look you want.

Look at the leafy painting shown in Figure 2.28. In the Expression controls, I made Size a function of Pressure and Angle a function of Direction. I also set Opacity to Random.

7. Save your new brush using the Brushes|Variant|Save Variant command.

Figure 2.28
Paint with the Leafy variant.

> **Note:** The Wet layer and the Impasto layer won't be found in the Layers section of the Objects palette. Items in the Layers list (formerly called Floaters) correspond to the Layers in Photoshop. That is, they include pasted images, text, and elements in a composite that you're keeping separate while you work.

Different Layers

In this section, you'll examine the Impasto brushes in depth. *Impasto* is a good term in this case, because Impasto effects have their own special depth layer. The other brush family that has always had its own unique Wet layer is the Water Color group, and you'll work with those brushes later in this section.

Deeper Is Better

In Painter 5, Impasto was a Dynamic plug-in that left a lot to be desired. Prior to version 5, the only way to create the look of thick paint was by using a command to add texture based on image luminance. With Painter 6, Impasto has grown up!

> **Note:** The Impasto group has a variant called Graphic Paintbrush. Yes, that's the same name given to a member of the Brush category, which you worked with earlier. The Impasto version includes depth, as you might expect, but they both use Pattern As Opacity for their source.

PROJECT Thick, Thicker, Thickest

The Impasto layer is a "virtual" layer that contains the depth information for your painting. You can toggle it on or off with the Enable Impasto icon (the pink blob on the upper-right edge of the image window), as shown in Figures 2.29 and 2.30. Here are the steps to follow for this project:

1. Open a new picture at 72 ppi that's at least 500 pixels square (or bigger if your screen can accommodate it). Use black as the background color for a change. Click on the default white color swatch on the New Picture dialog box and move the value slider to the opposite end, so that all colors become black. Alternatively, type 0 in the Value field, and click on OK.

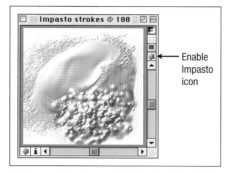

Enable
Impasto
icon

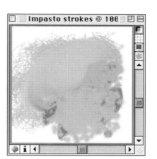

Figure 2.29
(Left) Here are Impasto strokes, with the Enable Impasto icon on, showing the depth layer.

Figure 2.30
(Right) Here's the same image with the depth layer turned off.

Figure 2.31
This is the Impasto section of the Brush Controls palette.

2. Make an abstract painting using a variety of Impasto brushes. Keep the Impasto section of the Brush Controls palette open while you work, observing changes in the settings when you switch to another variant (see Figure 2.31).

3. Turn the Enable Impasto icon off and on occasionally to see the difference between your thickly painted image and the flat version.

There are 32 variants in the Impasto group. Some of them apply both color and depth, and others apply only depth. You can adjust the amount of depth, alter the way depth is applied, and invert it to make a pit look like a swelling (and vice versa). If that's not enough control for you, there's a new menu on the Layers section of the Objects palette for determining how Impasto strokes will interact: Composite Depth. You can specify whether to add, subtract, replace, or ignore the depth information on other layers and the Canvas. Oh, yes, depth can also be manipulated by the usual gang of controllers (Direction, Velocity, Pressure, and so on) in the Expression section of the Brush Controls palette.

My favorite Impasto variant is Gloopy. Gloopy strokes can take a while to build up to their full depth because they are Multi strokes, but it's worth the wait. I used Gloopy to write the word *Chocolate* in rich browns (see Figure 2.32, which is also in this book's Painter Studio).

Figure 2.32
Here's some writing with the Gloopy variant of the Impasto brushes.

Wetter Is Better

Water Color brushes all use the Wet method and are automatically created on the Wet layer. All but one has the tip shape with greater density on the edges to produce the effect of pigment pooling at the edges of the brushstroke. The remaining variant is the Wet Eraser, required if you want to erase on the Wet layer. For this project, follow these steps:

Note: The Diffuse Water variant has some diffusion built in. If you'd like to add a diffuse effect to an area that has already been painted, select the area and press Shift+D. Repeat this "post-diffuse" command to increase the effect.

1. Open a new picture at a convenient size with white as the background color.

2. Choose Big Grain Rough or Hand Made from the Paper library. The Water Color brushes are of the Grainy subcategory, so this will enhance the traditional look.

3. Using a dark color, make a variety of strokes with the Water Color variants. Compare them to Figure 2.33. Notice that the Pure Water variant doesn't add color but rather smears or lightens other painted areas.

Figure 2.33
Here are some brush strokes made with Water Color variants.

4. Open the Water section of Brush Controls palette. There are two sliders: Wet Fringe and Diffusion. Move Wet Fringe to the right to increase the pooling of paint at the edges. It will act upon all the strokes currently in the Wet layer.

5. Move Diffusion to the right for a "wet into wet" look in the next stroke you make. The edges of the stroke seem to spread into the fibers of the paper.

Whenever you're finished with a Water Color painting or a portion of it, you may "drop" it into the Dry layer with the Canvas|Dry command.

REALISTIC WATER COLOR

The Wet Eraser should be used with caution if you want to imitate the look of a traditional watercolor painting. Follow a Wet Eraser stroke with the Fade command in the Edit menu to bring back some of the color. Alternatively, turn the opacity of the Wet Eraser down. Another good way to dilute color in the Wet layer is to apply strokes with the Pure Water brush variant.

PROJECT Water Color Still Life

The fact that the Wet layer is separate and transparent allows for some interesting possibilities. You can, for example, use a pencil or ink sketch in the dry layer as a template for a Water Color painting. Here are the steps you'll follow in this project:

1. Make a quick pencil sketch of a bowl of fruit or use the one provided on this book's companion CD-ROM (STILLIFE.tif). This still life is shown in Figure 2.34.

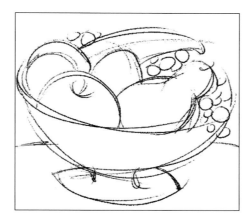

Figure 2.34
Here's the still life pencil sketch that will be the template for a Water Color painting.

2. Beginning with the Large Simple Water variant and appropriate colors, apply some light tints or "washes" over the apple, pear, bananas, grapes, and bowl. Don't worry about staying within the lines (see Figure 2.35).

Figure 2.35
Here's the pencil sketch with Water Color wash added.

3. Develop the forms with slightly darker tones and smaller brushes. Try Diffuse Water for shading. If the effect is too strong, use Edit|Fade to reduce your last stroke by any amount you like.

4. Finishing touches include adding (subtracting, really) highlights with the Wet Eraser and fading each one a bit.

5. Save your work in RIFF format to keep the Wet layer separate from the pencil sketch. Now select All and press the Delete key. Only the Pencil sketch disappears, as shown in Figure 2.36.

Figure 2.36
Here's the still life with the pencil sketch deleted.

Depending on how detailed your painting is, it may look better with some of the pencil lines remaining. Remember, you can fade the deletion (if that's the last thing you've done) to bring back the sketch at any opacity. Alternatively, using any of the regular Eraser variants, you can erase parts of the pencil sketch on the Dry layer.

Meanwhile, Back At The Palettes

In this section, you'll use another section in the Brush Controls palette to adjust the "smeariness" of a brush and return to the General controls for a more thorough look at the Plug-In method and its many subcategories.

Oil's Well

Conventional oil pastels have a slightly sticky and smeary quality, unlike the more powdery nature of chalk. Make some scribbles with the Oil Pastel variant of the Dry Media family and compare them with marks you make with some of the other Chalk variants in the group. What gives Oil Pastel its special look? The answer is in the Well controls. Resaturation, Bleed, and Dryout in various combinations control how smeary a brush is and how quickly it fades out.

PROJECT Smear And Blend

In this project, you'll alter the settings in the Well controls to adjust the smeariness of a brush. Follow these steps:

1. Open the Well section of the Brush Controls palette and the Brush Look Tester document (BLT.tif) or any image that has both white and patterned areas.

2. Use a light color and scribble across both white and patterned areas with the Square Chalk variant, as a basis for comparison. Notice that the Bleed value for this Chalk variant is 0 and Resaturation is 100 percent.

3. Switch to the Oil Pastel variant and make a similar stroke. Your stroke picks up some of the colors it's drawn over and smears them a bit. Notice that the Bleed value for Oil Pastel is 58 percent and Resaturation is 21 percent.

4. Reduce the Resaturation value to about 5 percent and make another stroke. This change makes the brush much smearier.

5. Increase Bleed to the maximum (100 percent) and reduce Dryout (measured in pixels) to about 20. This will make the brush run out of color quickly. Now it hardly applies any color at all but works nicely as a smear tool.

Compare your test strokes to Figure 2.37. By reducing Resaturation and Dryout to the minimum and increasing Bleed to the maximum, you can make any brush into one that adds no color but pushes existing pixels around.

Keep On Plug-In

There are many exciting brushes using the Plug-In method, mostly in the Liquid, Photo, and F/X categories. As you explore these variants, keep in mind that you can turn any brush into a Plug-In type just by changing its method and subcategory.

PROJECT Changing Leaves

Find the Leafy brush you made earlier in the chapter or load the Captured Brushes library to use my Leafy brush. Now, follow these steps:

1. Create a new, white canvas and make a few strokes with the Leafy brush to see how it behaves normally.

2. Now change the method to Plug-In, and the subcategory to Bulge.

3. Select a rectangle on the canvas and fill it with the Vines pattern from the default Pattern library. Use your new Leafy Bulge brush to make strokes on the Vines pattern, dragging some of them out into the white area. Figure 2.38 shows the default leafy strokes, a pattern fill, and some Bulge strokes.

4. Make another pattern-filled rectangle. I used Wavy Water from the Painter 5 Pattern library.

5. Switch the subcategory of the Leafy variant from Bulge to Hue Brush and make some strokes on your new pattern. These strokes will create leaf-shaped areas of color change, leaving the light and dark values unchanged.

6. Finally, switch the subcategory to Horizontal Crease and make more strokes in your pattern fill.

Note: Dryout is similar to Photoshop's Fadeout control, and it provides a good way for mouse users to imitate gradual pressure reduction.

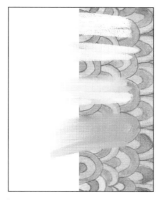

Figure 2.37
Here's the Oil Pastel variant with different settings in the Well controls.

Figure 2.38
Leafy brush is turned into a
Plug-In variant.

The bottom two rectangles in Figure 2.38 show the Wavy Water fill before and after the application of Hue Brush and Horizontal Crease brushwork.

Moving On

You've learned the basics for using and altering Painter's brushes. As you continue through this book, expect to gain even more familiarity and expertise with brushes. You'll gradually learn which ones work best for you, and you'll customize Painter's libraries to accommodate your work habits and personal style. In the next chapter, you'll explore a unique set of brushes that enables you to re-create any photograph as a painting.

SEND IN THE CLONES

3

BY

RHODA

GROSSMAN

Imagine having a set of brushes for changing a photo into a Van Gogh painting, a pastel drawing, or a pencil sketch. These are just a few of Painter's amazing Cloner brushes.

Basic Techniques

Cloning techniques have been part of Painter since the earliest version of the program. Cloner brushes make up a versatile set of tools for manipulating images and re-creating photographs or artwork in a variety of styles. Unlike filters, which have a global effect on an image or selection, Cloners let your right-brain influence the creative process. If you want to use a global approach, use Autoclone, but you'll miss out on the primary purpose of Cloner brushes—applying a style with your own brush strokes.

Painter 6 offers 15 Cloner variants that enable you to re-create an image using styles ranging from delicate to painterly to bizarre. You'll get acquainted with most of them in this chapter and learn tips and techniques to make the most of them.

Here are the essential steps in re-creating an image as a clone:

1. Open the Source image, which must remain open until you're finished cloning.

2. Choose File|Clone. A copy of the image appears.

3. Decide whether to delete the copy or add cloning strokes over it.

4. Select a Cloner variant.

5. Make brush strokes on the clone until the source image reappears in the new style.

What if you close the source image accidentally during a session or you want to quit Painter and continue working later or your cat manages to step on Command/Ctrl+Q while you're in the kitchen? Luckily, it's easy to reestablish a cloning relationship. Open the source image again (and your clone painting, if needed) and use File|Clone Source. You'll see a list of all open images. Choose the one you want to be the clone source. Any open image can be the designated clone source. This makes it easy to clone from one image into another.

Chalk Cloner

The Chalk Cloner is a good choice to begin practicing your cloning techniques. You can get results quickly with broad or scribbled strokes. The paper texture you select will strongly influence the outcome, because the Chalk Cloner belongs to a Grainy Subcategory. Delete the copy before you begin making cloning strokes. This will enable you to allow some areas of white to show through, thus enhancing the natural look. You can add paper texture to the white areas later with Effects|Surface Control|Apply Surface Texture|Using Paper.

TO DELETE OR NOT TO DELETE

Most clone paintings look best if you delete the contents of the clone copy and work on a blank canvas. Areas of white paper showing through can enhance the effect. You might need to use the Tracing Paper feature to help guide your strokes. Tracing paper allows you to see a lighter version of the source image while you are working on the clone. Command/Ctrl+T toggles this function on and off, or you can click on the Tracing Paper icon at the top of the vertical scrollbar. A notable exception to the delete "rule" is the Van Gogh Cloner. Bits of canvas showing through are not very attractive, so paint on top of the copy. Tracing Paper is not needed.

PROJECT Pastel Drawing

You'll begin with a scanned family photo and create a traditional-looking pastel drawing. Here are the steps to follow:

1. Open the image you want to work with. I'll use IDA.tif, which is included on this book's companion CD-ROM (see Figure 3.1).

2. Use File|Clone to make a copy of the image. Select All and delete the copy.

3. Turn Tracing Paper on to help guide your strokes (see Figure 3.2).

Figure 3.1
(Left) Photo of Ida.

Figure 3.2
(Right) The clone image has been deleted, and Tracing Paper is turned on.

4. Select the Chalk Cloner variant and choose a paper texture. Figure 3.3 shows some practice strokes made with Ribbed Pastel, Halftone, and Big Grain Rough. I like the look of Painter 6's new Big Grain Rough (see Figure 3.4).

5. Make strokes on the clone, toggling tracing paper on and off as needed.

Figure 3.3
(Left) Testing a paper texture. From left, Ribbed Pastel, Halftone, and Big Grain Rough.

Figure 3.4
(Right) Big Grain Rough paper is selected.

Figure 3.5
A sketchy vignette.

Note: The natural tendency is to focus on more interesting parts of an image. You see sharper detail in the center of the visual field and gradual blurring toward the periphery. You can draw the viewer's eye to particular areas of the image by varying the amount of detail in your painting according to what is important.

The quick sketch in Figure 3.5 was done with a few scribbles and a light touch. Paper texture is quite apparent. Notice that strokes are looser and sparser the farther they are from the center of interest. This might be a preliminary stage in the work or the finished product, if you like a casual vignette effect.

I frequently begin a Chalk clone by enlarging the size of the brush. This results in less detail and is a great way to rough in the basic forms and tonalities. The larger the brush, the less detail that comes through. Change the brush size on the fly quickly with Command+Option+drag or Ctrl+Alt+drag. Figure 3.6 shows Ida's portrait cloned with a larger Chalk Cloner.

It follows logically that with a smaller brush size, more details result. Figure 3.7 has details added with the default-size Chalk Cloner. I also softened the edges of the drawing with the Coarse Smear variant of the Liquid brushes. Yes, you can switch between cloning and "normal" painting tools during a cloning project.

Figure 3.6
(Left) The Chalk Cloner was used with an enlarged brush.

Figure 3.7
(Right) Detail has been added, and the edges have been softened.

PROJECT Scribbling A Clone

The scanned seashell shown in Figure 3.8 is provided on the CD-ROM that accompanies this book. You'll use this image for practicing several cloning techniques. Here are the steps to follow for scribbling a clone:

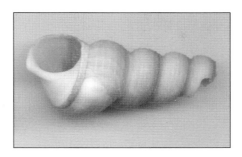

\ **Figure 3.8**
The scanned seashell.

1. Open SHELL.tif.

2. Use File|Clone to make a copy of the image.

3. Select All and delete the copy.

4. Turn Tracing Paper on.

5. Choose the Fiber Cloner.

6. Use circular scribbles to paint the clone, starting inside the shell and working outward.

Figure 3.9 shows the finished Fiber clone of the seashell. The nervous lines of the Fiber Cloner give the image energy. Notice that most of the background has been left blank. Circular scribbles were also used to make the Furry clone in Figure 3.10. Once again, the background was left alone to emphasize the prickly edges of the furry strokes.

Another new cloner that gives good results using the circular scribble technique is Splattery Clone Spray. Figure 3.11 shows the seashell created with the stippled look produced by that variant. I used a light touch to fade out into the background.

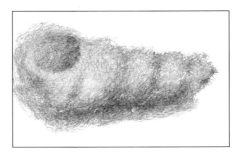

\ **Figure 3.9**
Fiber clone.

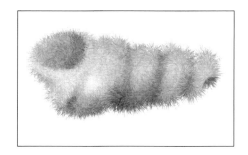

Figure 3.10
Furry clone.

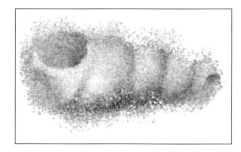

Figure 3.11
Splattery Clone Spray effect.

 ## Using The Melt Cloner For A Watercolor Look

With a little practice you can fake some watercolor effects with the Melt Cloner. Use SHELL.tif as the source image again. This time you'll abandon the scribble technique and follow the contours of the shell:

1. Repeat Steps 1 through 4 in the previous project, "Scribbling A Clone."

2. Choose Melt Cloner and enlarge the brush so that the basic form can be laid in quickly, as shown in Figure 3.12. (This is the same approach I took in the pastel portrait of Ida.)

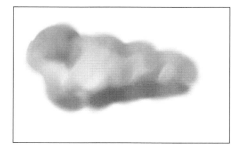

Figure 3.12
The Melt clone in progress.

3. Use Restore Default Variant on the Variant menu. This smaller brush size is perfect for stroking in a few details, such as some of the striations on the shell.

4. Apply Big Grain Rough paper to the finished painting (Effects|Surface Control|Apply Surface Texture|Using Paper). You can select Big Grain Rough in the Paper palette before you apply the effect, or choose it while the Apply Surface Texture dialog box is open. See the finished Melt clone in Figure 3.13.

Figure 3.13
The finished Melt clone.

Oil Painting

The Oil Brush Cloner has changed markedly in this version of Painter. It uses a Camel Hair dab for a rich, "brushy" look, and it has impasto qualities built in to produce the textured effect of natural bristles loaded with thick paint. A glance at the Impasto settings shows that Oil Brush Cloner paints with 10 percent depth. You can adjust the amount of depth on the Brush Controls|Impasto Palette.

The Oil Brush clone of the seashell in Figure 3.14 was created in the following way:

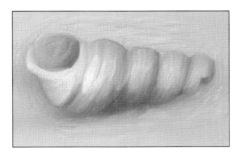

Figure 3.14
The Oil Brush clone on a smooth surface.

1. Open and clone the image SHELL.tif. Do not delete the copy.

2. Select Oil Brush Cloner and paint following the contours of the shell.

3. Feather out the strokes toward the edges of the image. This can be done with either the Depth Smear or Depth Equalizer (both variants of the Impasto family).

WHAT'S IN A NAME?

I think Raw Silk paper should be called Canvas. If you agree, you can change its name by using the Paper Mover. Find the Paper Mover in the Paper pop-up menu. Choose Raw Silk and then click once on the Change Name button. Type the new name and select Quit. Figure 3.16 shows the dialog box for changing the name of an item in your library.

Your painting will look as if it's painted on a smooth surface. If you want to achieve the look of paint on canvas, apply Paper Texture as you did for the Melt clone, but this time use Raw Silk. Figure 3.15 has had the Raw Silk texture added.

Examining my textured version, I felt that it had lost too much of the impasto look. Rather than go back and repaint it with stronger impasto depth (you can if you want to), I undid the Paper Texture effect. I repeated the Apply Surface Texture command but switched from Using Paper to Using 3D Brushstrokes. This strengthened the depth of my brushwork. Now, I could apply the "paper formerly known as Raw Silk" and the brush strokes would still hold their own.

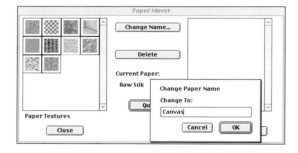

Figure 3.15
The Oil Brush clone on canvas.

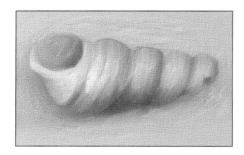

Figure 3.16
The Paper Mover dialog box.

REPEATING A COMMAND

The last Effects command you used appears at the top of the Effects menu, for quick access if you want to repeat it. Easier still is using the keyboard shortcut for repeating the previous effect: Command/Ctrl+forward slash (/).

PROJECT Colored Pencil Drawing

Pencil Sketch Cloner, like Chalk Cloner, uses a Grainy Subcategory, so choosing the right paper texture is important. Traditional pencil sketches are often built up of lightly sketched layers, called *crosshatching*. That's an excellent way to work with the Pencil Sketch Cloner.

You'll practice using layered overlapping pencil strokes in the more interesting areas of a drawing, allowing portions of the paper to show where there's less detail. Using the seashell image once again, follow these steps:

1. Open SHELL.tif. Clone and delete it.

2. Select Pencil Sketch Cloner and turn on Tracing Paper.

3. Sketch in the basic shape of the shell. Overlap strokes at various angles in the areas that are darkest in tone. You can tilt the drawing to work more comfortably. Use the Rotate Page tool as needed.

4. Develop the drawing with fewer strokes in the parts of the image that are lighter in color. Allow strategic areas of the paper to remain white. Figure 3.17 shows the drawing at an early stage.

> **Note:** If you're working with a mouse instead of a graphics tablet, you still have some control over pressure applied to a stroke. Use the Opacity slider in Brush Controls| General. This will enable you to emulate variation in pressure between strokes.

Figure 3.17
The pencil sketch in progress.

5. Apply a subtle paper texture to the finished drawing (Effects|Surface Control|Apply Surface Texture|Using Paper).

Handmade or Regular Fine paper are natural choices for the last step. If the texture looks too heavy, use Edit|Fade to reduce the effect. Figure 3.18 is the final stage.

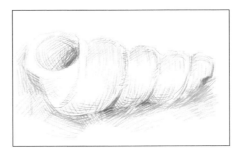

Figure 3.18
The finished pencil sketch.

Soft Cloner And Straight Cloner

Soft Cloner and Straight Cloner enable you to duplicate parts of the source image exactly. The Straight Cloner restores the original at 100 percent opacity, whereas the Soft Cloner can be used to "airbrush" the original pixels back in gradually. Why would you want to clone a source image without adding a different style? Here are three possibilities:

• To bring back portions of the source image that you want to clone differently or leave unchanged.

• To paint parts of one image into another.

- To duplicate a portion of an image in a different location within the same image. Your Painter 6 manual calls this *offset* or *point-to-point cloning.*

PROJECT Selective Reverting

Let's use the Soft Cloner for bringing back part of the source image. Users of Photoshop 4 might recognize this function because it's similar to the Erase To Saved feature. Here are the steps:

1. Open the photo ADAM.tif, provided on this book's companion CD-ROM (see Figure 3.19).

Figure 3.19
The photo of Adam.

2. Choose the Clone command (File|Clone) and apply some filters or effects to this copy (called Clone of Adam).

   I used Glass Distortion (see Figure 3.20). The background was pleasing, but I wanted to undo the effect on Adam's face.

3. Using the Soft Cloner, gently stroke parts of the original image back (see Figure 3.21).

Figure 3.20
Adam distorted.

Figure 3.21
Adam reverted.

PROJECT Selective Elimination

Another use for the Soft Cloner is retouching. For example, you might want to eliminate portions of a photo by cloning parts of the same image (or a different image) over it. Removing an ex-spouse by cloning a tree over him or her comes to mind. The photo of Carole in a field of sunflowers is ideal for practicing this kind of cloning (see Figure 3.22). You'll paint flowers over Carole until she's completely gone. Here are the steps:

Figure 3.22
Carole and sunflowers.

1. Open the CAROLE.tif file on this book's companion CD-ROM. Do not make a clone copy.

2. Choose the Soft Cloner variant.

3. Press and hold the modifier key (Macintosh: Control/Windows: Shift) while you click near the center of the large patch of flowers on the left. You'll see the number 1 next to a green spot, indicating the source pixel (see Figure 3.23).

Figure 3.23
This detail of Carole and sunflowers shows that the source pixel has been established.

4. Place your mouse or stylus on Carole at the same height (vertical position) as your source pixel.

5. Paint.

Brush strokes won't show, so use any kind you want. Notice the crosshairs moving around the flowers as you work, showing the source pixels as you apply them over Carole. With some luck you can create a seamless field of flowers in one stroke. Actually, you can use many strokes, because they're automatically aligned with your first source pixel. If you need to patch up some areas of the flowers to eliminate every trace of Carole, repeat Step 3 and change the source pixel(s).

PROJECT Two-Point Cloning

Painter 6 includes a group of cloners that resize, rotate, mirror, shear, and/or distort the source as you paint. Each of these cloners has an "x" prefix. The "x" has no special meaning, but it serves to group these variants together at the bottom of the alphabetical list. Painter 5 veterans will recall that these were named Super Cloners, and they came in their own separate library.

In painting flowers over Carole, you needed to specify only one point for the source pixel. The "x" cloners can be called *multipoint cloners*. They require that you indicate two or more points for the source pixels. The same number of points must be placed as destination pixels.

As a variation on the previous exercise, let's add several smaller copies of Carole to the sunflower field.

1. Open CAROLE.tif. Do not make a clone copy.

2. Choose the xScale Cloner.

3. Press and hold the modifier key (Control/Shift) while you click on the top of Carole's head. You'll see the number 1 next to a green spot, indicating the first source pixel.

4. You must indicate another point for reference. Press and hold the modifier key and then click at the bottom of Carole's dress to establish point two. A yellow line appears between the two points. The length and angle of that line are the variables used for changing the original pixels.

   When using any of the multipoint cloners, you need to establish the correct number of points for the destination pixels. This requires the Shift+Control keys on both Macintosh and Windows computers.

5. Press and hold Shift+Control. Click on the two places shown in Figure 3.24.

Figure 3.24
Click on the two destination points indicated. The yellow line shows the size of the clone.

6. Paint some strokes in the area designated for the smaller copy of Carole. Work carefully near the bottom of Carole's dress so that you can create the illusion that she's surrounded by flowers.

7. Switch to the xRotate and Scale variant. Repeat Steps 3 and 4.

8. Choose a spot for the new copy of Carole. Press and hold Shift and the modifier key.

9. Click to establish point 1 for the destination.

10. Click so that point 2 is at an angle to point 1.

11. Paint some strokes in the areas designated for the smaller, tilted copy of Carole. Figure 3.25 shows several Caroles at different sizes and angles.

Figure 3.25
Several Caroles at different sizes and angles.

Sunflowers And The Van Gogh Cloner

The Van Gogh Cloner is virtually identical to the Van Gogh variant in the Artists Brush family, except for the fact that color and value data come from the source image. Unlike with the other cloners, though, color and value information does not update as you drag your stylus or mouse. Instead, the source pixel you click on at the beginning of a stroke determines the color for the entire stroke.

The photo of sunflowers in Figure 3.26 is provided on this book's companion CD-ROM. It was taken in the south of France, not far from where Vincent Van Gogh painted similar still life arrangements. Therefore, the choice of cloning variant is clear. Van Gogh strokes will be added on top of the photo. This will allow you to get the look of thick paint covering the whole canvas quickly. Here are the steps:

1. Open SUNFLOWR.tif.

2. Use File|Clone to get a copy of the image. Do not delete the copy.

3. Choose the Van Gogh variant of the cloning brushes. Using short strokes that follow the direction of the forms; paint over the flower petals and leaves.

Note: Because the colors and values of a Van Gogh Cloner stroke are unchanging, short strokes are recommended, especially in areas with detail. The fact that a slightly different placement of the stylus or mouse could produce a very different stroke also means that you'll seldom get the same result twice.

Figure 3.26
Sunflowers on a chair—the source image.

4. Paint over the vase. Again, follow the shape of the form using strokes with a variety of lengths.

5. Paint over each of the cobblestones. They already have slight variations in color, and the Van Gogh effect is wonderful. Change the size of the brush tip to correspond to the changing size of the cobblestones. One or two strokes per stone should do it.

6. Paint the chair.

   The seat of the chair will require paying close attention to where you begin each stroke. If your stroke seems too light or too dark, don't bother to undo it—just try again. The frame of the chair is so dark you might not see much variation in the strokes. Try increasing the Value (light to dark) variation by moving the V slider in the Color Variation section of the Art Materials palette. Figure 3.27 shows my finished Van Gogh clone of sunflowers. Well, nearly finished.

7. Enhance the look of thick paint by applying a surface texture to the entire image (see Figure 3.28). Use Effects|Surface Control|Apply Surface Texture|Using Image Luminance. Experiment with the Shine and Amount sliders and with the Light Direction buttons.

8. If you like the effect, save the change. If you think the effect is too strong, use Edit|Fade. Alternatively, you can use Undo and try again.

Note: Before you click on OK to apply an effect to your image, see how it looks in the Preview window. When you place your cursor over this window, it will become the Grabber Hand cursor and allow you to drag to another area of the image.

Figure 3.27
Van Gogh clone of sunflowers.

Figure 3.28
Van Gogh clone with
surface texture.

Advanced Cloning

So far you've been using Cloner brushes straight from the can. Now you'll customize some of the cloner variants and change some noncloning brushes into cloners.

Making Watercolor Cloners

Figure 3.29 is a photograph of a door in a little French town. You'll find the file, DOOR7.tif, on the CD-ROM that accompanies this book. Use it for practicing watercolor techniques. The Water Color Cloner, new in Painter 6, makes a scatter of drips that quickly diffuse, as shown in Figure 3.30. This is not a useful

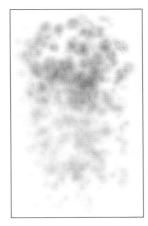

Figure 3.29
(Left) Door7 is the source photograph.

Figure 3.30
(Right) Diffuse splatters made with the default Water Color Cloner.

tool for re-creating the look and feel of the photograph. However, an array of brushes are available in the Water Color family that will serve the purpose. All you have to do is turn them into cloners. Just choose the watercolor variant you want and enable Clone Color in the Color palette (see Figure 3.31). When Clone Color is checked, the color picker fades, as a reminder that you can't choose colors while you use cloner brushes. Any brush can be transformed into a cloner by checking Clone Color in the Color palette.

Watercolor Study

A "study" lies somewhere between a rough sketch and a detailed rendering. Follow these steps for creating a watercolor study:

1. Open DOOR7.tif.

2. Select File|Clone.

3. Select All and delete. Turn Tracing Paper on.

4. Choose the Simple Water variant of the Water Color family.

5. Click on the Clone Color checkbox in the Color palette.

6. Make a few strokes to rough in the basic colors and tones (see Figure 3.32).

7. Reduce the size of the brush and paint on the darkest lines, to develop the forms of the door and the chair. You might also want to adjust opacity on the Controls palette.

8. Switch to the Wet Eraser variant. Resize as needed. Continue to develop shapes and depth by removing color from the lightest areas. Figure 3.33 shows the painting developing clearer forms.

Figure 3.31
With Clone Color checked, the current brush is a cloner or acts like one.

CLONE METHOD VS. CLONE COLOR

As an alternative to enabling Clone Color in the Color palette, you can change any variant's default method to Cloning in Brush Controls| General. Results can be quite different, depending on the variant you select. Try both techniques and choose the one you prefer.

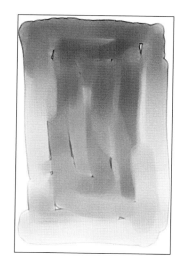 

Figure 3.32
(Left) Door7 is shown at clone stage #1.

Figure 3.33
(Right) Door7 is shown at clone stage #2.

If the Wet Eraser removes too much color, use Edit|Fade after each stroke. Better yet, turn the opacity of the tool down in Brush Controls|General.

9. Zoom in to paint more details with even smaller sizes of the Simple Water and Wet Eraser brushes. Adjust the Opacity setting as needed.

10. Use the Round or Flat Water Blender tool to smooth out any harsh transitions. Remember to enable Clone Color first. Does your finished painting look something like mine in Figure 3.34?

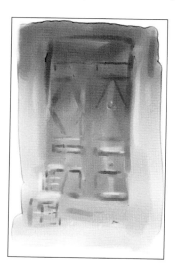

Figure 3.34
Door7 is shown with the clone finished.

PROJECT Watercolor Wash

Wash refers to the use of transparent layers of watercolors applied to a line drawing, usually pen and ink. The key to this technique is the fact that Painter has separate wet and dry layers. Use DOOR7.tif again, repeating Steps 1, 2 and 3, in the previous project.

Now create a "line drawing" that will serve as the detail layer. Actually, it's an emboss (see Figure 3.35). Follow these steps:

Figure 3.35
The clone embossed with the source image.

1. Use Effects|Surface Control|Apply Surface Texture. The critical setting is Using Original Luminance, the light and dark values of the clone source.

2. Choose Simple Water and enable Clone Color on the Color palette.

3. Paint. Your strokes will automatically appear on the Wet Paint layer, leaving the embossed (dry) canvas untouched. Set opacity low to create a thin wash effect. Increase opacity and decrease brush size as you develop the painting. Figure 3.36 shows a few large Simple Water strokes (with Clone Color on) over the emboss.

4. Use the Pure Water Brush variant at low opacity to clean up excess paint around the edges.

> **Note:** The emboss serves to guide your strokes, thus eliminating the need to toggle Tracing Paper on and off.

To enhance the painting, you might want to reduce the strength of the emboss, as shown in Figure 3.37. I deleted the emboss and used the Fade command to bring it back at about 50 percent. The "wet paint" was undisturbed.

Figure 3.36

(Left) Large Simple Water strokes on the emboss.

Figure 3.37

(Right) More detail on the Wet Paint effect; emboss is faded to 50 percent.

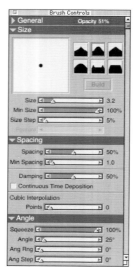

Figure 3.38

The default settings for Felt Pen Cloner.

Note: The Opacity setting can be altered even when the General controls are closed. Adjust the percentage by simply dragging to the left or right of the current number.

PROJECT Felt Marker Sketch

The default size of the Felt Pen Cloner is small and round. That's fine for details but not for laying down broad strokes. In this project, you'll alter the size, shape, and ink distribution of the Felt Pen Cloner to imitate traditional techniques more closely:

1. Select the Felt Pen Cloner.

2. Open the following controls: Size, Spacing, and Angle. Figure 3.38 shows the default values for the Felt Pen Cloner.

3. Increase the size of the brush to about 16. Choose the ink distribution profile that's on the left in the bottom row. This will give your marker a gradual dryout effect from the center to the edge of a stroke.

4. Change the round brush tip to an elliptical shape by moving the Squeeze slider in the Angle controls to about 50 percent.

5. Test your new brush by beginning a Felt Pen clone of your old friend the seashell. Open SHELL.tif. Select File|Clone and delete the contents of the copy.

   You might find it more comfortable to work with the canvas rotated. Use the Rotate Page tool or the keyboard shortcut for rotating the page (Option+spacebar+drag or Alt+spacebar+drag). Figure 3.39 shows the image ready for a right-handed user. The copy was deleted and Tracing Paper is on.

   If your strokes are too heavy, reduce the Opacity setting. I changed Opacity to 20 percent.

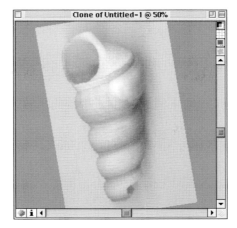

Figure 3.39
The page after being rotated.

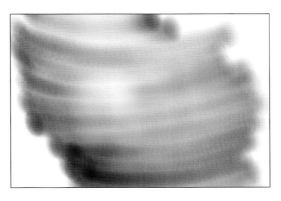

Figure 3.40
Magnified detail of test strokes.

A magnified view of my test strokes reveals the individual dabs that compose each stroke (see Figure 3.40). Even at actual size, this could spoil the effect. Reduce the spacing to make a smoother stroke. Figure 3.41 shows all the changed settings. At this point, you've made enough alterations to justify saving this brush as a new variant.

6. Save the variant by selecting Variant|Save Variant. Name it Big Dry Felt Pen Cloner.

7. Use Big Dry Felt Pen Cloner to paint the seashell image. Use parallel strokes that overlap slightly, following the contours of the shell. Add a second layer of strokes to accent some areas.

8. Use the default Felt Pen Cloner to draw a few details, such as the scalloped edges. Figure 3.42 shows the finished sketch.

Figure 3.41
The altered settings are saved as Big Dry Felt Pen Cloner.

Figure 3.42
The finished Marker clone sketch.

AN ALTERNATIVE TO TRACING PAPER

Fading the clone until it's barely visible provides a way to avoid toggling back and forth with Tracing Paper. Delete the contents of the clone as usual; then use Edit|Fade. Bring back just enough of the image to serve as a guide. Unlike Tracing Paper, which shows you 50 percent of both the source and the cloned image, this method lets you see your painted strokes at full strength.

PROJECT Still Life And The Impressionist Cloner

The Impressionist Cloner has been changed considerably for this version of Painter, but it's still lots of fun. This variant uses a captured dab that's rounded at one end and feathered out at the other. In previous versions of Painter, the Impressionist Cloner had a simple elliptical dab shaped like a grain of rice. This new-and-improved variant still comes with built-in variations in Value (luminosity).

You'll do another version of the sunflower arrangement, this time with a customized Impressionist Cloner.

1. Open SUNFLOWR.tif.

2. Use File|Clone to make a copy. Select All and delete.

3. Use Edit|Fade to undo the delete action just enough to be able to see a ghost image. Figure 3.43 shows the Fade dialog box and the image at 15 percent opacity.

Figure 3.43
The cloned copy is faded to 15 percent.

SEND IN THE CLONES

You could make a respectable Impressionist painting of the sunflower still life using the default settings for the Impressionist Cloner. However, I recommend making some changes:

1. Choose the Impressionist Cloner.

2. Reduce Spacing in Brush Controls to 15 percent to get more paint for each stroke.

3. Use Expression controls to make Angle a function of Direction.

4. Add a thick-paint effect by using these settings in the Impasto controls:

   - Draw To|Color And Depth

   - Depth Method|Original Luminance

   The amount of depth is up to you. I used 25 percent.

5. Paint.

Figure 3.44 shows a detail of the sunflower clone made with the default Impressionist Cloner, and Figure 3.45 shows the same portion of the image cloned with the new Impasto Impressionist Cloner.

> **Note:** Painter 6 remembers the changes you make to a variant. You can restore the default settings at any time. If you like the new cloner you just made, save it with a different name, such as Impasto Impressionist Cloner.

Figure 3.44
Default Impressionist clone.

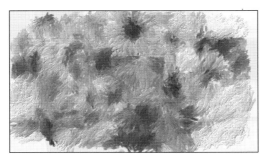

Figure 3.45
Impasto Impressionist clone.

Moving On

This chapter explored the power of cloners to re-create existing images in a variety of natural styles, and a few not-quite-natural ones. You learned how you can clone any part of an image to another part or to any other image. See Chapter 12 on fine-art techniques for more cloner effects.

You also practiced applying a few texture effects. The next chapter will examine texture in greater depth.

PAPER
TEXTURES
4

BY

SHERRY

LONDON

*Artwork created on the computer doesn't have to
look flat. This chapter looks at the structure of a
texture and how it differs from a pattern. You'll learn
how to create, capture, and use paper textures.*

Anatomy Of A Texture

One of the major complaints about computer art—and photography—is that if you touch it, it's flat; it has no tactile surface. One of the hallmarks of computer-produced artwork before the creation of Painter was that it, too, was flat.

Painter has changed the flat appearance of computer artwork to one that can mimic the look—if not the feel—of traditional art. It can at least *look* like it has a feel. Painter uses paper textures to create this "visual feel." You can use any of the paper textures that come with Painter, or you can easily create your own.

What is a texture? A simple answer is "something that looks like it would feel a certain way if you touched it." Words that can be used to describe the way a surface feels are hard, smooth, soft, rough, raised, lumpy—well, you get the idea. These words describe what's commonly meant by a *textured surface*.

There's another meaning, however, for the word *texture* that's more common if, for example, you want to purchase wallpaper for your house. A textured wallpaper design—as opposed to a *patterned* wallpaper design—is one in which the repeat of the pattern is not obvious and the surface plane has nothing that catches the eye.

Let's look at that definition more closely. In order to understand it, you need to understand the other terms involved—pattern and repeat. A *pattern* is formed when a specific motif (design element) or group of motifs is repeated at regular intervals across a surface. The individual unit that's repeated is called a *repeat unit* or a *pattern unit*.

Picture a small, yellow circle. By itself, it's a design element. Depending on the amount of space you leave around it, you can create a repeat unit of many different sizes. Figure 4.1 shows two versions of the same circle motif repeated with different amounts of white space.

You can also repeat the circle motif so that it's not in straight rows. This is known as a *drop repeat*, and you'll learn much more about this type of repeat as well as other repeat forms in Chapter 5. Figure 4.2 shows you a half-dropped circle repeat.

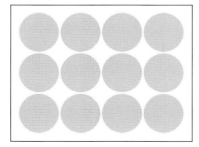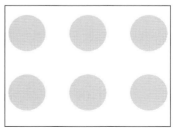

Figure 4.1
These two circle motifs show different white space amounts.

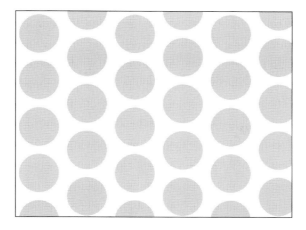

Figure 4.2
This is a half-dropped circle repeat.

You can also create a "grouping" of the motif and then repeat that grouping. Depending on the arrangement of the elements in the group, the resulting pattern may look very random. It's this element of seeming randomness that begins to define a texture. Figure 4.3 shows a random-looking pattern made from a number of circles. If you look carefully at the largest of the circles in the image, you'll be able to identify the repeat unit and see that it does re- peat itself along a regular grid.

Finally, if you were to take that random grouping and change the color so that it did not stand out—so that it looked embossed—the pattern would become a texture in the sense that the term is used in wallpaper design—and in Painter. Figure 4.4 shows the embossed version of Figure 4.3. You can see that it looks as if it would *feel* raised were you to touch it.

When you create paper textures in Painter, you can use patterns that have either obvious or subtle repeats. Painter gives you a variety of ways in which to display the paper texture in your image. Some of the brush methods are particularly sensitive to paper texture. If you paint with a grainy brush, or if you choose the Apply Surface Texture command using Paper Texture, you

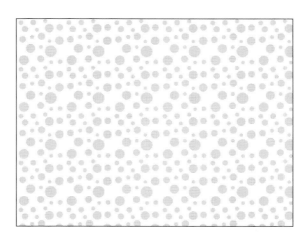

Figure 4.3
This is a pattern composed from a grouping of circles.

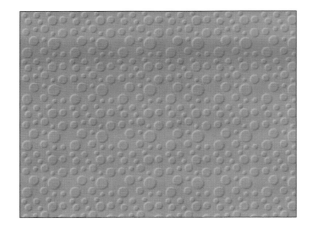

Figure 4.4

An embossed texture stands out from the background of the canvas.

would see your paper texture quite strongly. Figure 4.5 shows a quick Chalk clone of a photograph. I exaggerated the texture so that you could see it clearly. Notice that where I adhered most strongly to the original image, the texture is much less visible. I don't recommend using this strong of a texture on an image in general, but this example allows you to see how texture can interact with your brush stroke while you're painting.

Painter gives you tremendous control over the surface of your image. You can make your paintings look totally smooth, or you can create them over totally outrageous textures that become part of the design of the image. Painter comes with a large variety of paper textures. You can purchase additional paper libraries, and you can create your own. You can open and close new libraries using the Paper Mover, located under the Paper menu in the Art Materials palette.

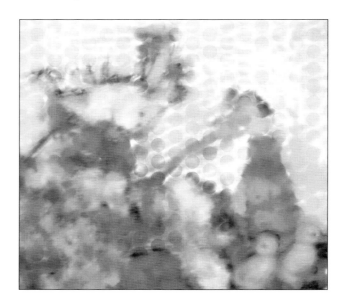

Figure 4.5

This Chalk clone of flowers uses a very large paper texture.

What's The Value? How Paper Textures Texture

What is it that makes a paper texture show texture? The *values* of the texture itself (that is, the gray tones in the texture) determine how much paint a paper texture "absorbs." It would be nice to tell you that anything white repels paint and anything black in the texture absorbs it—but that would be a lie. It's much more complex than that.

The texture that appears on the canvas when you paint is the result of the interaction of the following items:

- The brush
- The brush method and subcategory
- The values in the texture
- The scale of the texture
- The contrast and brightness settings of the texture
- The Grain setting in the Controls: Brush palette
- The Invert Grain setting in the Art Materials: Paper palette
- The Opacity settings and your stylus pressure

Here's a fast test that shows you how white and black can work in a texture.

1. Create a new document (Command/Ctrl+N). Make it 400 by 400 pixels with white as the paper color. The resolution does not matter.

2. Set your primary color to black in the Art Materials: Colors palette.

3. To test the way that gray values affect paper texture, you need to create a paper texture that's mostly black. This probably won't be a good or useful paper texture, but it will be one that illustrates the behavior of white and black in a texture. To start, select the Rectangular Selection tool in the Tools palette.

4. Press the Shift key to constrain the selection to a square and watch the Controls: Selection palette. Drag the selection until the W: and H: fields on the dialog box both show 20, as shown in Figure 4.6. Release the mouse button first and then the release the Shift key.

5. Fill the selection with the current color (Command/Ctrl+F).

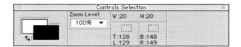

Figure 4.6
The Controls: Selection palette shows width and height amounts.

Figure 4.7
The Save Paper dialog box allows you to save a selection as a paper texture.

6. Zoom into the square that you selected as closely as you can (you can magnify it to 1200 percent). Choose Select|None. Use the Rectangular Selection tool and start at the top-left corner of the black square. Press the Shift key and watch the Controls: Selection palette as you drag. Try to release the mouse button when the width and height of the selection are both 22. Again, release the mouse button before you release the Shift key. The purpose of this step is to add some white around two sides of the black selection.

7. Save this area as a paper texture (on the Art Materials palette, choose Paper|Capture Paper). Name the texture "Mostly Black", set the Crossfade to 0, and click on OK. Figure 4.7 shows the Save Paper dialog box.

8. Mostly Black is now the current paper. If you look at its preview in the Paper palette, you'll see that you have large black squares surrounded by tiny white outlines.

9. Create a new document, 400 by 400 pixels. Set the paper color to a light yellow. You're going to try out the texture.

10. Select a bright blue as your primary color.

11. Click on the Brush tool in the Tools palette and select the Square Chalk variant of Dry Media brush (Chalk, Crayons, and Charcoal are called *Dry Media* in Painter 6). Change the subcategory to Grainy Flat Cover. Mentally divide your canvas into quarters across the width and in half across the length of the image (you'll put four texture samples across the width of the image and only two rows of texture samples). Paint an area in the upper-left quadrant. The "paint" is absorbed only by the areas that are white in the original pattern (that is, the "cracks").

12. Change the subcategory to Grainy Soft Cover and paint the next top quarter area. The paint won't react at all to the texture.

13. Change the subcategory to Grainy Edge Flat Cover and paint the next area. Now, the areas that are black in the Mostly Black texture absorb the paint and white areas repel it.

14. Try the Grainy Hard Cover Method subcategory. It uses the texture exactly as the Grainy Edge Flat Cover does.

15. Click on the Invert Grain box in the Art Material: Paper palette and then repeat Steps 10 through 13 using the bottom half of your image. As expected, you've achieved the reverse of your first actions. Figure 4.8 shows the practice image that you've created. The "regular" textures

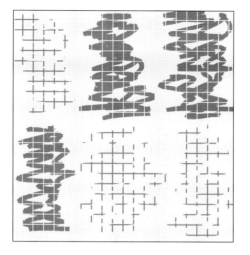

Figure 4.8
The top row contains the "regular" Mostly Black paper texture, and the bottom row contains the "inverted" Mostly Black texture. The examples are (from left to right) of the Grainy Flat Cover, Grainy Edge Flat Cover, and Grainy Hard Cover subcategories of the Square Chalk Dry Media brush variant.

are on top, and the "inverted" textures are on the bottom. Grainy Soft Cover is not pictured (it doesn't work at the same setting).

16. Uncheck the Invert Grain box on the Art Materials: Paper palette.

17. To see how the Method category affects the texture, clear the image (Edit|Select All, Edit|Clear). Repeat the exercise, changing the method to Buildup and then cycle through all the subcategories that contain the word *Grainy* (there are three). Place these examples along the top half of the image.

18. Select the default variant of the Charcoal brush. This brush also uses a Cover method. Cycle through the four Grainy subcategories and put them along the bottom of the image. Figure 4.9 shows the three Buildup textures and four textures created with the Charcoal brush. Notice the difference in the Cover textures between using the Chalk brush and the Charcoal brush.

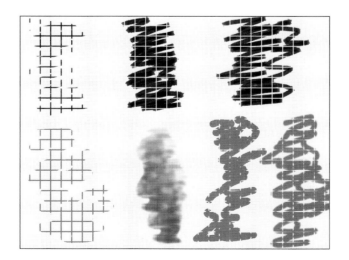

Figure 4.9
Top row: Three Buildup methods in Chalk. Bottom row: Four Cover methods in Charcoal. I turned the grain setting up to 100 percent on the Grainy Soft Cover.

Table 4.1 Methods and Grainy subcategories for brushes.

Buildup	Cover	Eraser	Drip	Cloning	Wet	Plug-in
Grainy Soft Buildup	Grainy Flat Buildup	Soft Grain Colorize	Grainy Drip	Grainy Hard Cover Cloning	Grainy Wet Abrasive	Add Grain Brush
Grainy Edge Flat Buildup	Grainy Soft Buildup	Grainy Hard Drip	Grainy Soft Cover Cloning	Grainy Wet Buildup		
Grainy Hard Buildup	Grainy Edge Flat Buildup					
	Grainy Hard Buildup					

Table 4.1 lists the various methods and the Grainy subcategories that they contain. These are the methods and subcategories that you can assign to a brush if you want to create a brush that reacts to the underlying paper texture.

The Wet method brushes are the only brushes using Grainy subcategories that do not show texture the way you would expect. Try out the various combinations to see how they react to texture.

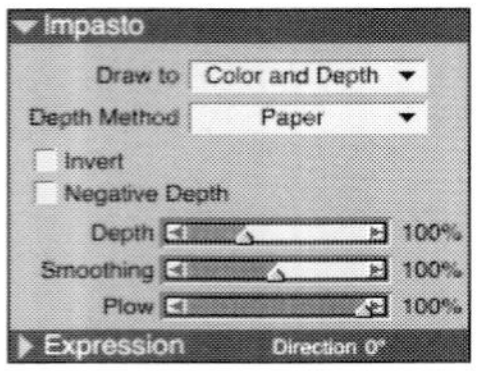

Figure 4.10 shows the new Impasto brush controls. Impasto—which in Painter 5 was a Dynamic Plug-in and had to be specifically applied as an effect to a floater—is now an integral part of any brush. You can add amazing depth to any of your brushes by setting the Impasto controls to Depth or Color and Depth. You can then instruct the controls to use the paper texture as the Depth method.

Now that you know how the textures react to black and white, can you predict how they will react to shades of gray? Figure 4.11 shows the same brush strokes as Figure 4.8 (the Grainy Cover subcategories with regular and inverted textures). The only difference is that the paper texture used is a 25 percent gray circle on a 75 percent gray square. The surprise in this roundup is that the Grainy Edge Flat Cover subcategory only shows texture along the edges—on textures that are basically gray, it cannot show the full texture.

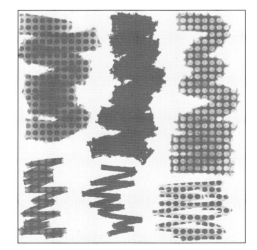

Figure 4.10

The Impasto settings allow you to use the paper texture to create depth effects with your brushes.

Figure 4.11

The Grainy Cover subcategories are displayed using a gray-on-gray texture.

So, what have you learned? The values within the texture exert a large influence on the way the texture appears on the painted canvas. You can achieve a sharper texture if you have both black and white values in the texture, and you can create a more subtle one if the texture contains close shades of gray.

Textures By Design:
The Make Paper Command

It's fun to use paper textures. It's even more fun if you create your own. Although you can make a texture of anything, Painter has a Make Paper command that gives you a jump-start on creating textures. In this project, you'll generate a paper texture and then modify and recapture it a few times until it becomes exactly what you want it to be (with suggestions, of course, about what I want to see the texture become).

Let's look at the Make Paper command first. Figure 4.12 shows the controls.

As you can see, you have a fairly large supply of basic elements from which to choose. You can create lines, circles, halftones, ellipses, triangles, and several other shapes as well. In addition, you can change the spacing and the angle of the element. It would probably take you a few years to explore all the possibilities of this texture editor. What's more, you can create totally original textures based on the Make Paper-generated ones by overlapping textures in an image using compositing methods and saving the resulting images as new textures. Let's work through an example.

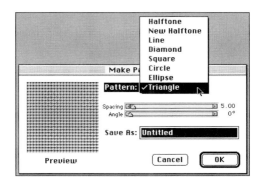

Figure 4.12
The Make Paper dialog box and controls give you a large number of paper texture possibilities.

PROJECT Engineering The Texture

This segment of the project shows you how to generate a texture using the Make Paper command. Here are the steps to follow:

1. Create a new document (Command/Ctrl+N) of 400 by 400 pixels, white paper color, and 72 dpi.

2. Open the Make Paper Texture dialog box (from the Art Materials palette, select Paper|Make Paper).

Figure 4.13

Triangle paper texture.

3. Select Triangle from the Pattern drop-down. Set the Spacing field to 20 (or as close as you can get it) and the Angle field to 24 degrees. Name the texture "20-24 Triangle" and click on OK. The texture is added at the end of your current Texture library list and is immediately available for you to select. Figure 4.13 shows the new paper you created.

4. Select the new paper texture to make it the active texture by choosing its name from the drop-down texture list.

Phase 1: From Triangles To Black Satin

This sounds much sexier than it is! Let's take the texture that you just created and apply it to a blank image using the Apply Surface Texture command (which is another way to use the paper texture in your image). The texture you'll create resembles black satin squares and quilting, and it can become the basis for further experiments. Follow these steps:

1. Use the new, blank document that you created earlier.

2. Select Effects|Surface Control|Apply Surface Texture. The dialog box shown in Figure 4.14 appears. You need to match the settings as precisely as you can, which can be a challenge because you cannot type the values into the slider controls (at least you can't on the Mac). See Table 14.2.

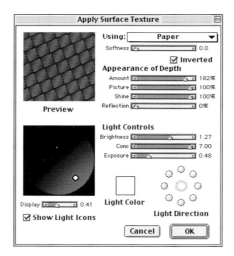

Figure 4.14

The Apply Surface Texture dialog box enables you to add texture to your entire image evenly.

Make sure that you place the light icon where it's positioned in Figure 4.14. It's on the intersection of an imaginary line that goes from the top-left to bottom-right corner and a line that goes from the midpoint of the bottom edge of the image to the midpoint of the right edge of the image.

Table 14.2 Settings For The Apply Surface Texture Command.

Parameter	Value
Using	Paper
Softness	0
Inverted	On
Appearance Of Depth:	
Amount	182%
Picture	100%
Shine	100%
Reflection	0%
Light Controls:	
Brightness	1.27
Conc	7.00
Exposure	0.48
Display	0.41

3. You now need to capture a segment of the image as a new paper texture. Choose the Rectangular Selection tool. Magnify the image to about 300 percent so that you can easily see the details of the texture.

4. Click on the intersection of four squares and drag the marquee to the right until you find another intersection of four squares. Then drag the marquee toward the bottom of the canvas until you locate another intersection of four squares that lines up with the marquee. The idea is to try to find a "natural" repeat in the image. Depending on the angle of your original Make Paper command, this repeat can be tricky or impossible to find. Figure 4.15 shows the enlarged texture surrounded by a marquee.

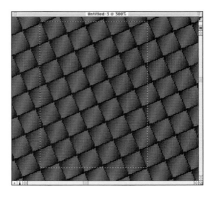

Figure 4.15
You need to select an area of the paper texture that seems to repeat.

5. From the Art Materials palette, select Paper|Capture Paper. Name the texture "Satin Squares" and set the crossfade to 2 or 3, unless you've really found a true repeat.

6. Click on OK to close the dialog box and save the paper.

Phase 2: Reengineering The Texture

In this project segment, you'll use the paper texture that you just captured to create another paper texture so that you can modify *that* one so that you can modify—well, you get the idea. Remember, you're making progress! Here are the steps:

1. Create a new document (Command/Ctrl+N) that's 400 pixels by 400 pixels and choose White as the Paper setting. The resolution can be left at 72 dpi.

2. Select the Square Chalk variant of the Chalk brush. Change the subcategory to Grainy Flat Cover. Set the Opacity field on the Controls: Brush palette to 75 percent. Set the Brush Size field to 30. Build the brush if the dialog box appears (it usually won't in Painter 6 because most brushes are now built automatically).

3. Choose black as your primary color.

4. Brush across the image from left to right, overlapping the brush strokes a little as you apply each subsequent row. Take care not to overlap them too much; otherwise, the texture will become much too dark. Fill the entire image in this manner. You'll get better results if you don't try to be perfect, however. Figure 4.16 shows you how the image should look.

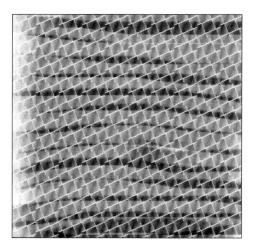

Figure 4.16
Apply the texture with overlapping brush strokes.

5. Select the entire image (Command/Ctrl+A).

6. Choose the Layer Adjuster tool, press the modifier key (Option/Alt) and click inside of the selection. This copies the image into a new layer.

7. Choose Effects|Orientation|Rotate and rotate the layer 45 degrees.

8. Click on the name Layer 1 in the Objects: Layers palette. Change the Composite mode of the layer in the Objects: Layers palette to Multiply. Click on the Drop button at the bottom of the Objects: Layers palette.

9. Choose the Rectangular Selection tool and select approximately the largest rectangle you can that only includes the area of the image that was multiplied (and is consequently darker), as you can see in Figure 4.17.

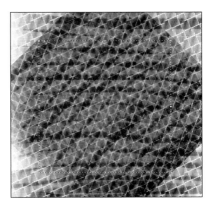

Figure 4.17
Make a new selection that only includes the multiplied area.

10. Choose Effects|Tonal Control|Equalize. Set the black point at about 92 percent and the white point at approximately 42 percent, as shown in Figure 4.18. By equalizing the texture with these settings, you create additional white and black pixels and make a stronger texture statement. This is an excellent way to create a texture with sharp contrasts from one that originally contained a lot of gray.

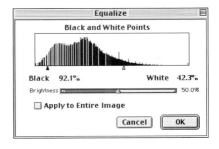

Figure 4.18
Equalizing an image sets the white and black points of the image to adjust the values of the image.

11. From the Art Materials palette, select Paper|Capture Paper. Choose a Crossfade setting of about 16. I named the texture ME1 (that's short for "Multiply Equalize," but feel free to call it whatever you prefer).

Phase 3: Making The Crinkly Texture

This is where you finally get to make the texture that you'll use as surface texture for a real image. This last texture-by-design uses the Apply Surface Texture command again to create the texture. Here are the steps:

1. Create a new document (Command/Ctrl+N) that's 500 pixels square, white paper color, and 72 dpi.

2. Change the scale of the texture to 65 percent using the slider or by typing the number directly.

3. Select Effects|Surface Control|Apply Surface Texture. Figure 4.19 shows the settings. They're basically the same as the settings you used to create the Satin Squares texture, but the light is in the exact center this time. Also, do not check the Inverted box. Change the Brightness field to 1.01, the Exposure field to 0.55, the Display field to 0.88, and then click on OK. Figure 4.20 shows the result.

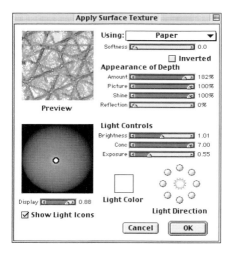

Figure 4.19
Use these settings in the Apply Surface Texture dialog box.

Figure 4.20
This is the final crinkly texture that results from your experiments.

4. Choose the Rectangular Selection tool. Press the Shift key to constrain the tool to a square selection and then select an area approximately 200 by 200 pixels in the Controls: Selection palette.

5. From the Art Materials palette, select Paper|Capture Paper. Set the Crossfade field to about 7 and name the texture "Crinkly".

Phase 4: Express (Texture) Yourself!

Now that you know how to create a texture using the Make Paper command, and you can massage it in a number of ways to create another texture that's totally original, it's only fair that you get a chance to try out the texture in a real image. After all, if a texture falls where no one can use it, is it still a texture? Philosophy aside, let's use the texture in a very simple manner, but one that you haven't tried in this chapter yet. The Express Texture command lets you apply the paper texture and turn your image into a grayscale at the same time. Here are the steps:

1. Open the file TWOGOATS.PSD that is on this book's companion CD-ROM.

2. Select the entire image (Command/Ctrl+A).

3. Choose the Layer Adjuster tool, press the modifier key (Option/Alt) and click inside the selection. This creates and floats a copy of the image.

4. Choose the Liquid brushes on the Brushes palette. Choose the Bulge brush, but change the subcategory to the Add Grain brush on the Brush Controls: General palette. This really makes a different brush, but it's an easy—and known—point from which to start. Check Figure 4.21 to make sure you're tracking along with me.

5. Change the Grain setting on the Controls: Brush palette to 30 percent. This is an odd brush in its use of grain. The larger the setting, the more grain it shows.

6. Brush in some grain on the goats and the rocks in Layer 1. Don't try to get even coverage. Brush more grain where you want it. If you're using a pressure tablet, start lightly and work up to build an interesting variation on the texture. You can also get excellent results by varying the scale of the texture and by changing the Contrast setting as you apply the texture.

7. Let's complicate this painting a bit. Choose Effects|Surface Control|Express Texture. Figure 4.22 shows the dialog box. Set both the Contrast and the Grain fields to 131 percent. Set the Gray Threshold field to 108 percent. These settings worked for me. If they don't look pleasing in your image, change them. I tried to get a coverage that kept the gray values and the midtones. The Express Texture command lets you apply the paper texture and turn your image into a grayscale image at the same time. Figure 4.23 shows a close-up of the image.

Figure 4.21
Use the Liquid brushes and choose Bulge. Then change the settings on the Brush Control: General palette.

CONTROLLING TEXTURE

In a feature that's new to Painter 6, you can change the Paper texture contrast and brightness using the sliders on the Paper palette. In this example, you might want to experiment with changing the contrast to 45 percent if the texture applies too strongly to your image. If you lessen the contrast, you'll create less depth to the texture.

Figure 4.22
The Express Texture dialog box allows you to apply texture as it changes your image to shades of gray.

Figure 4.23
The goats are now in grayscale, and you can see the changes in texture.

8. Click on the name Layer 1 in the Objects: Layers palette. Change the Composite mode of the layer to Multiply. The color comes back, although the image is a bit too dark.

9. You can add some more spice to the image and cut down on the darkness a bit by adding a new layer and fiddling—even though the "fiddles" are not playing a texture tune. Turn off the visibility icon next to Layer 1 in the Objects: Layers palette. Select the canvas.

10. Repeat Steps 2 and 3 to create another layer. Choose the Dry Ink variant of the Brushes brush. Set the brush's opacity to about 85 percent. Select the Clone Color checkbox in the Colors palette so that the brush uses the colors that are in the image.

11. Use this Dry Ink brush to alter Layer 2 and make it look more impressionistic. I brushed over the image at an angle from the bottom-left to the top-right corner. I used uneven short strokes and a brush size of 35 but kept the angle fairly consistent. I tried to preserve some of the coloring as I cloned; the detail is almost impossible to preserve and doesn't matter in this case anyway—it's only the color that really causes a change.

12. Make sure that Layer 2 is the top layer in the Objects: Layers palette (it should be anyway and will be highlighted to show that it's selected). Change the Composite mode to Pseudocolor. Turn on the visibility icon for Layer 1. Figure 4.24 shows the image in grayscale, and it's shown again in color in this book's Painter Studio.

The CD-ROM for this book contains a second "ending" version of this exercise (TWOGOATSIMPASSTO.RIF). As a variation, I used the new Impasto setting in the Brush Controls palette. I changed the Draw To setting to Color and Depth and the Depth method to Paper. I then set the Depth setting to 92 percent (nothing sacred about this number; it's just the one I happened to use). I then used the same settings for the Dry Ink brush as before. I made a

Figure 4.24
You've created textured goats.

change to the order of the layers, however, from Step 12, and placed the Impasto layer (Layer 2) above Layer 1 and gave it a Composite Depth setting of Replace when I changed the Composite method to Pseudocolor. As a final touch, I reopened the original TWOGOATS.PSD image and made that my clone source (File|Clone Source). I created a new layer and used the Cloners brush with the Soft Cloner set to a Grainy Hard Cover subcategory (a Grain setting of 24 percent and an Opacity setting of 20 percent). I painted onto this layer very softly but covered most of the layer. Because cloning onto a layer doesn't seem to align exactly, as a final step, I moved the layer (with the Layer Adjuster tool) into register with the goats. I had no need to change the Composite method because the layer was already very transparent.

Repeat It Again, Sam

Somewhere in the depths of the last exercise, I used the cryptic statement "find a natural repeat." I didn't feel much like clarifying the statement then, but I do now. Every paper texture is also a pattern, if you use the definition given at the start of this chapter of a pattern as a motif that repeats across a plane. When you either capture a paper or make a paper, you're creating a pattern—a repeating unit of pixels.

You can use this knowledge to create textures that have no seams—no way for you to know where one unit of repeat starts and another one begins. You did this without knowing it when you created the black-and-white grid texture. You did this knowingly—if not successfully—when you tried to find the repeat unit in the black satin squares.

One of Painter's really wonderful features is its ability to create seamless patterns in a special file type called a *pattern file*. If you've ever used Adobe Photoshop to create patterns, you've probably used the Offset filter. This filter allows you to see how a pattern will wrap and repeat. Painter does not have an offset filter. Instead, it creates a pattern file that automatically wraps an image onto the left side of the document when your brush goes off the right side, and it paints on the bottom of the image when your brush goes off the top.

PROJECT   How Textures Repeat

In this project, you're going to get a preview of Chapter 5 and use a pattern file to create a texture from a photograph. You'll be shown how to make sure that the texture is seamless as it's being created. Here are the steps to follow:

1. Open the file RHINO.PSD from this book's companion CD-ROM.

2. Choose the Crop tool and create a marquee around the largest rectangular area of texture that you can find, as shown in Figure 4.25.

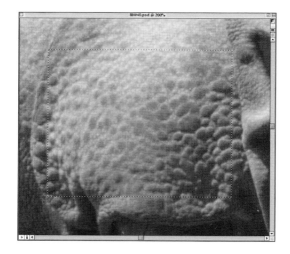

Figure 4.25

Make a rectangular selection around the most heavily textured area using the Crop tool in RHINO.PSD.

3. Click inside of the selected area to crop the image. Save the image as TEXTURE.RIF.

4. From the Art Materials palette, choose Pattern|Define Pattern. A checkmark appears next to the option on the Pattern menu. This means that you can now create a seamless pattern.

5. Press the Shift key and the spacebar at the same time. Move the cursor into the pattern file. The cursor becomes a hand. Keeping the two keys pressed, drag the image until the seam appears in the center, as shown in Figure 4.26.

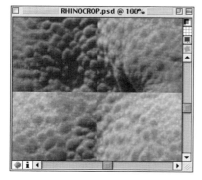

Figure 4.26

Notice the hard seam in the center of the rhino pattern.

6. Select the Soft Cloner variant of the Cloners brush. Choose Restore Default Variant from the Variant menu on top of the Brushes palette to change the brush (which you used earlier in this chapter) back to its original settings. Change the brush size to 4.0.

7. Press the Control key on the Mac or the Shift key on Windows to place the point from which the cloning occurs. You may clone from anywhere in the image. Try not to apply much coverage to the ends of the hard seams that touch the edges of the image window. Move your cursor over the seam line in the center of the image and start to paint. You'll need to stroke over an area several times in order to cover the underlying seam. If you seem, instead, to be creating a seam, stop, undo the last brush stroke, and reposition the clone source. You can increase your brush size up to about 30 and lightly brush over the seams after your first pass. (You might also want to zoom in on the image to see it better.)

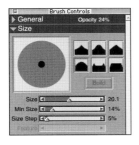

Figure 4.27
Select the Dull brush profile.

8. When you have the seam mostly covered, switch your brush to the Straight Cloner variant of the Cloners brush. Turn the opacity on the brush down to 75 percent in the Brush Controls: Size palette. Select the Dull brush profile, as shown in Figure 4.27.

9. Paint the center seam area again. The strokes will be more highly defined than your first pass, but because of the Dull profile brush tip, they will blend into the background. You can move the center of your pattern as you did in Step 5 so that you can check for any unintentional hard seams. Figure 4.28 shows the completed pattern file.

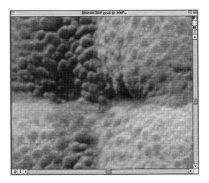

Figure 4.28
The completed rhino pattern has no seams.

10. This pattern will be used to create a paper texture, and paper textures need to be in shades of gray. The rhino pattern is still in color. Therefore, choose Effects|Tonal Control|Adjust Colors. Figure 4.29 shows the dialog box. Select Using: Uniform Color and move the Saturation as far to the left as possible. By lowering the Saturation, you create a grayscale image (or as close as Painter allows in an RGB environment).

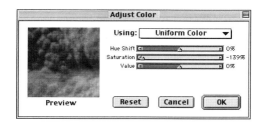

Figure 4.29
The Adjust Color dialog box
enables you to desaturate your
image to remove all color from it.

11. Now, you need to equalize the image to make a more pronounced texture. Select Effects|Tonal Control|Equalize. Set the black point to about 90 percent and the white point to about 30 percent (see Figure 4.30). Click on OK.

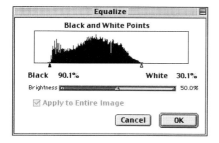

Figure 4.30
Equalizing the image creates a
more pronounced texture.

12. Select the entire image (Command/Ctrl+A).

13. Finally, choose the Art Materials palette's Paper|Capture Paper menu selection. Set the Crossfade to 0 and name the texture "Rhino". You'll put it to good use in the Texture Tango exercise that follows.

PROJECT Texture Tango

You've just created a rhino texture, and it's all dressed up with nowhere to go. Let's put it to good use and explore ways in which you can combine textures and use a number of different methods of applying textures in one image.

When you combine textures and texturing methods skillfully, you create an image that has artistic integrity and generates excitement. When you combine too many textures and methods just because you can, you run the risk of creating a sampler. It's a fine line. As a fiber artist and stitcher, I should probably not denigrate samplers. However, they're really my least favorite form of embroidery art. When they're well done, they do hold together, and they have a lot of historical interest. However, when I use the term in a pejorative manner, I'm really referring to the tendency of a new stitcher to use, in one piece, every stitch that he or she can do. That's never good art—unless the person only knows one stitch!

That's the end of my rant. This exercise combines a number of methods of applying textures, and uses two basic textures. This is enough to create a divertissement on a theme, and not enough to create texture *mal a la tête*. Again, I will not claim that you're creating fine artwork in this project. It's meant to spark your own creativity, while remaining nothing more than a good teaching vehicle.

You'll clone this texture into the image of a water buffalo, brush in a varying amount of detail, and then add surface texture. You'll then add three layers. One localizes a texture to a rectangular area, a second adds textured color through a mask, and a third adds a transparent texture on top of an area of the image.

Go Water Buffalo!

To begin, follow these steps:

1. Open the image WATERBUF.PSD on this book's companion CD-ROM.

2. Clone it (File|Clone).

3. Select the entire image (Command/Ctrl+A). Press the Delete or backspace key or choose Edit|Clear to remove the image from the clone.

4. The image is cloned in stages. Choose the Chalk Cloner variant of the Cloner brush. Change the Grain setting in the Controls: Brush palette to 10 percent and change the Brush Size setting to approximately 50. In the Brushes palette, select the Brush Controls: Size palette and change the brush tip to the Dull profile. Make sure that the Rhino texture is the current paper.

5. Drag the brush unevenly across the document until you fill the entire image with the fairly spotty background texture. Figure 4.31 shows you how the image should look at this point in the exercise.

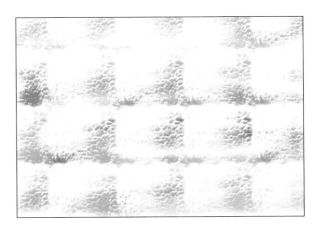

Figure 4.31
The background image for the water buffalo doesn't look like much yet.

6. Turn on the Tracing Paper (Command/Ctrl+T) so that you can see where the water buffalo is located. After you start to draw, you might find it easier to turn off the Tracing Paper once you've located the

water buffalo. I turned it off after I found the buffalo, because it allows me more freedom to explore "out of the lines."

7. Continue to use the Chalk Cloner brush but reduce the size of the brush and the opacity of the brush (to less than 50 percent). Turn the Grain setting up to about 16.

8. Brush in some of the areas around the water buffalo's face and body. Work lightly and build up more detail in key areas, such as the eyes and mouth. You'll leave less texture as you fill in detail, but that's okay. Try to achieve a smooth blend from detailed areas to less-detailed areas to the background. Avoid leaving sharp edges.

9. Continue to reduce the brush opacity and increase the grain to cover over some of the deeper areas of texture with image detail. Using the Chalk Cloner, you won't see sharp detail in any case. This just builds a color undercoating for the image. My final settings on the Chalk Cloner were a 76 percent opacity and a 49 percent grain. Soon after my first texture pass, I also reduced the texture contrast (in the Art Material: Paper palette) to 50 percent. I used a large brush to fill in some of the areas of background texture. Figure 4.32 shows the slightly-more-in-focus water buffalo.

Figure 4.32
You can now see some detail in the water buffalo.

10. Switch to the Straight Cloner variant of the Cloner brush. Change the subcategory to Grainy Hard Cover and change the Grain setting on the Controls: Brush palette to 12. Change the brush opacity to about 57 percent.

11. Brush in the finer details of the water buffalo's face and horns.

12. Select Effects|Surface Control|Apply Surface Texture. In the dialog box that appears, select Using: Paper, and set an Amount of 50 percent,

Picture: 100 percent, and Shine and Reflection of 0 percent. Place the light coming from the upper-middle left, as shown in Figure 4.33. Figure 4.34 shows the image after surface texture has been applied.

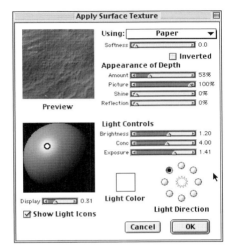

Figure 4.33
Apply Surface Texture settings.

Figure 4.34
The water buffalo with surface texture applied.

Floating Color

You were promised three layers. Here's the first of them. This layer covers the entire image and it colors the underlying image through scribbles in the mask. Here are the steps:

1. Select the entire image (Command/Ctrl+A). Choose the Layer Adjuster tool, press the modifier key (Option/Alt), and click inside of the selection. This creates a copy of the image in Layer 1.

2. Choose the Felt Marker variant of the Felt Pens brush. Change the Composite method in the Controls: Adjuster palette to Pseudocolor.

3. Select black as your primary color.

WHAT DOES PSEUDOCOLOR DO?

Pseudocolor method translates the layer's luminance into a hue, which can cause some unique coloring to appear. In this exercise, you'll create a mask to limit the areas where you want the pseudocolor effects to show.

4. Click on Mask in the Objects palette. You'll see an entry for RGB-Layer 1 and its mask. Click to select Layer Mask. Click on the visibility icon next to Layer Mask to turn it on (by opening the eye).

5. The mask is solid black, which means that the entire layer is visible. Select Effects|Tonal Control|Negative. This makes the mask totally white, so that only the areas that you draw in the mask are visible.

6. Turn the mask visibility icon back off, but leave the mask selected (that is, active). You can now see the image again. Figure 4.35 shows the mask that I created. Draw one that's similar to mine—or draw in yours over whatever areas you feel could benefit from added color. I also changed the primary color from black to gray over the course of drawing the mask (to create areas of semi-opacity in the layer), and I changed the opacity settings as well. The areas that I highlighted with the mask were the left side of the water buffalo's face, his neck area, and parts of his flank.

Figure 4.35
This is the mask for the full-image layer.

Toning A New Texture

The second layer for you to create adds a different texture to an area on the water buffalo's body. It's merged with the base image by controlling the opacity. Here are the steps:

1. In the Objects: Layers palette, select Canvas. This means that you're working in the original image.

2. Choose the Rectangular Selection tool.

3. Draw a marquee from the top of the image to the bottom and enclose the area between the water buffalo's two sets of legs.

4. Press the modifier key (Option/Alt) and click inside the selection. This creates a copy of the selected area as Layer 2 and places it above Layer 1.

5. Choose the Halftone 3 paper texture (it's one of the papers that installs along with Painter) in the Paper palette and set its scale to 200 percent.

6. Choose Effects|Surface Control|Apply Surface Texture. Leave the light where it was from the previous project, but change the Amount setting back to 100 percent and the Shine setting up to 38 percent. Figure 4.36 shows the image layer with the textured layer.

Figure 4.36
The finished layer shows the effects of the adding surface texture.

Crackle Multiplied

The final layer in this image uses a slightly different technique to apply another dose of texture to the image. This is a way to apply just the texture—without any image in it—to a part of an image. The principle is that you apply the paper texture to a plain white surface and use the Multiply Composite mode to blend the texture into the image. Multiply mode darkens the image based on the gray values in the layer. Any areas of black in either the layer or the underlying image become black; areas of white in either the layer or the underlying image take on the other color—white drops out and becomes transparent. Here are the steps:

1. In the Objects: Layers palette, click on New to create a new layer. This will be Layer 3.

2. Set your current color to white.

3. Choose Effects|Fill|Current Color (or Command/Ctrl+F) to fill the layer with white. Change the Composite Method setting to Multiply. The white layer looks as if it has disappeared.

4. Choose the Crackle paper texture on the Art Materials: Paper palette and leave it at its default settings.

5. Choose Effects|Surface Control|Apply Surface Texture. Use the same settings as you did in Step 5 in the previous project, "Toning A New Texture." Figure 4.37 shows the final image.

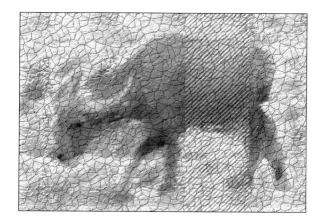

Figure 4.37
Surface texture is added to a layer filled with white and Composite Method is set to Multiply.

You ought to be able to think of many uses for this technique. You don't need to apply the texture to the entire image; you could have just selected areas to fill with white and then changed the Composite method to Multiply. Another slant on this is to vary the scale of the texture as you apply it to different locations. Depending on the nature of the starting image, you may be able to successfully use more textures than I did. However, if you're going to stylize a photograph, you do need to exercise some care not to overcrowd it.

Rhoda's Text-ures

My co-author, Rhoda Grossman, contributes the next set of techniques for this chapter. She likes to use text to create paper textures.

PROJECT It's Greek To Me

You can create a series of random letters in Courier or in any other font that you prefer. If you capture this text as a paper texture, it becomes useful for "greeking in" type for rough layouts of brochures or for other graphic design projects. Here are the steps to follow:

1. Select the Type tool. Notice that the Controls palette automatically changes to the appropriate options for text. I've used Helvetica Bold for this example and set the font size to 8 points.

2. Create a new document (Command/Ctrl+N) that's 200 pixels square. Set the paper color to white.

3. With black as the primary color, select the Text tool and type some gibberish into the document. Keep the type in a rectangular area. You can press the backspace or Delete key to remove the letters that you don't like so long as you haven't moved the text-insertion point. Painter creates a shape for each letter.

4. When you're satisfied, drop the type into the document by selecting the Drop All option in the Objects palette's Layers menu.

5. Drag diagonally with the Rectangular Selection tool to select the area in which you've placed the type.

6. In the Art Materials palette, choose Paper|Capture Paper. Set Crossfade to 0 or to a low number. The texture should be virtually seamless. Name the new texture in the dialog box that appears.

Test your new texture with any Grainy Method brush, such as Large Chalk. Figure 4.38 shows the Helvetica texture applied with Square Chalk.

You may use any color, and you may also change the size with the Scale slider on your Paper palette. Just above the Scale slider is a checkbox for inverting the texture (that is, coloring the background while leaving the letters white). Figure 4.39 shows three more examples of greeked-in text using different brushes.

Graphics With Impact

You can also use font textures for graphic impact—not just to show where type is to be placed. Figure 4.40 shows several textures that Rhoda created from type, each for a particular project.

The top-left example was created using the font Dear Teacher. It conveys a humorous, childlike feeling. To get the text at an angle, you'll need to rotate the type before selecting the area for capture (and after dropping all the shape layers from the type into the image). In the center is a texture made from question marks in several different fonts. The top right shows a versatile "digital" texture. In the bottom row you see a texture using the Sonata font, consisting entirely of musical symbols. Finally, there's a number-jumble, which required a higher Crossfade setting than the others.

Figure 4.38
This large Helvetica texture is applied with the Square Chalk brush.

Figure 4.39
You can use paper textures to create greeked-in text.

Figure 4.40
These paper textures were created from a variety of novelty fonts.

Impastable Text

I can't leave the topic of "text-ures" without a short discussion of the possibilities of using the new Impasto features with paper textures in general and with text textures in particular.

The Impasto brush controls enable you to stroke paper texture into any brush—even if the brush's method and subcategory don't normally make it texture sensitive. This is a dynamite new feature. Figure 4.41 shows a sampling of regular brushes with the Brush Controls: Impasto palette set to Color and Depth using Paper. The top row (from left to right) shows the text in a regular and in an inverted paper texture using the Artists brush with the Impressionist variant and the Dry Media brush with the Waxy Crayon variant. The bottom row shows (from left to right) pieces of the Impasto brush with the Gloopy variant and the Water Color brush with the Broad Water brush variant (using very light pressure on the tablet).

One brush that works very well with the Impasto controls to add paper texture to an already-created image is the Bulge variant of the Liquid brushes. Because this brush doesn't use color; it adds wonderful texture to anything—especially with the Impasto Color and Depth setting using Paper. The short project that follows shows you how to create a repeating pattern from text as a paper texture and use the Bulge brush to paint the texture into an image.

\ Figure 4.41
The Impasto controls allow you to add paper texture to almost any brush.

PROJECT Bulging Paper Text-ures

Here are the steps to follow for this project:

1. Open the file LILY.PSD on the this book's companion CD-ROM.

2. Create a new file that's 200 pixels square with a white background. Choose black as your current color.

3. Choose the Text tool. I used Vag Rounded at 60 points and typed the phrase "SIMPLE TEXT" onto the canvas. You can use any font and phrase that you prefer. I just wanted something that would show up well in print.

4. Choose the Crop tool. Leave some space (as leading) above and (as word spacing) to the right of the text. Don't crop off any length to the file; instead, crop close to the left side of the text. Click the mouse inside of the selection to crop. Select all of the text shapes and drop the text to the Canvas. (In order to create a repeat, you need to reduce the canvas size of the image so that it is just a bit wider than the text string you created.)

5. Use the Rectangular Selection tool to select the text. Switch to the Layer Adjuster tool, press the modifier key (Option/Alt), and click in the selection to copy the selection into Layer 1.

6. Move the text that's on the layer so that it appears below the text on the canvas.

7. Choose Define Pattern from the Pattern drop-down menu on the Art Materials: Pattern menu. Select the Canvas layer. Press Shift+ spacebar and move the text in the canvas layer so that it wraps around horizontally.

8. Make Layer 1 active and click on the Drop button.

9. Select the two lines of text (drag the Rectangular Selection tool from the top-left corner of the image to the right margin directly below the second line of text—don't leave any additional space under the second line of text). Figure 4.42 shows the texture being captured.

10. Choose Capture Paper from the Art Materials palette's Paper menu.

11. Select the Brush tool and choose the Bulge variant of the Liquid brushes. Set up the Brush Controls: Imposto to use Paper as the Depth Method and Color and Depth in the Draw To settings.

12. Paint where you want in the LILY.PSD image. Try inverting the paper texture and using several different textures. Figure 4.43 shows my experiments.

CAPTURING PAPER AND LAYERS

Neither the Capture Paper command nor the Caption Pattern command "sees" the layers in an image. Therefore, you need to drop all layers when you want to create a selection that defines a new paper texture or pattern.

Figure 4.42

Capture the two lines of text for your pattern.

Figure 4.43

The Bulge brush works well with paper textures.

PROJECT Randomizing Textures

Before I let the subject of textures rest, there's one more thing that you can do with textures that I have not yet discussed. You can use them in a random fashion. Here are the steps:

1. Open the image DANCER.PSD on this book's companion CD-ROM. This is a stylized image of two Mexican dancers.

2. Load the Liquid brushes and select the Bulge variant of the Liquid brushes (I really like that brush). Change the subcategory to Add Grain brush. (Remember to set the Impasto controls to Color so that you get no impasto effect here—unless you want it, of course.)

3. Choose as your paper texture, the Mostly Black grid texture that you created early in this chapter.

4. Open the Brushes Controls Random palette and select the checkbox labeled Random Brush Stroke Grain, as shown in Figure 4.44.

5. In the Controls: Brush palette, change the opacity to 35 percent and the grain to 38 percent.

6. Stroke the texture onto the pants of the male dancer. Notice that instead of a grid, you get a variety of upright crosses. This is because of the random nature of the texture.

7. Select the Regular Fine paper texture and set the Scale to 300 percent. Paint the texture onto the shirt of the male dancer.

8. Select several other textures and apply them to various areas of the image. Turn the Random Brush Stroke Grain setting on and off for different textures. Figure 4.45 shows my version of the dancers. I used a slanted texture made from the Beesknees font very softly in the background of the image.

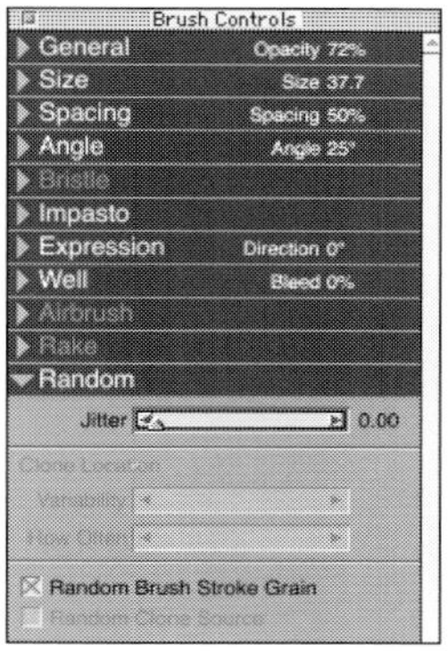

Figure 4.44
Painter 6 has a new palette that allows you to apply grain randomly rather than in a patterned manner.

Figure 4.45
The Mexican dancers now have random textures applied.

Moving On

This was a full chapter. You've learned how to create a texture either by capturing it from an area of an image or by designing the texture using the geometric functions built into Painter (Make Paper…). You should also understand how the gray values in a texture cause the texture to become either subtle or vivid, and you know how to use the Equalize command to make the texture contain the values that you want it to have. You've also seen how texture reacts to the various forms of grainy brush subcategories.

You've learned how to apply textures—either with the grainy brushes, the Add Grain subcategory of the Plug-in method, the Add Surface Texture command, or the Express Texture command. In addition, you've seen how you can make the texture repeat randomly and how you can use text for textures.

In the next chapter, you'll learn more about creating and using patterns. Chapter 5 builds on the skills you've learned here.

PATTERNS 5

Man has been called a "tool-making animal" who "thinks, therefore he is." It may be more appropriate to call man a "pattern-making and pattern-recognizing animal." This chapter covers a variety of pattern types and teaches you how to create and use patterns.

BY

SHERRY

LONDON

A Pattern Primer

Without the ability to recognize recurring events—which is, of course, the very basic definition of a pattern—you wouldn't have the assurance that day would follow night or spring would follow winter. Man is indeed a pattern-recognizing animal.

Painter makes it easy to create patterns. You've already seen in Chapter 4 how easy it is to create a repeat. The difference between a pattern and a paper texture is very simple: The paper texture lives in the Art Materials: Paper palette, and the pattern lives in the Art Materials: Patterns palette. Yes, I'm being somewhat facetious, but really, only surface differences and palette locations separate a pattern and a paper. The repeat mechanism is identical:

- Patterns in Painter can carry color information; papers cannot.

- Papers can produce surface depth alterations; Painter's patterns cannot (unless you convert them to papers).

- Papers can be crossfaded when captured; patterns can be offset. The processes of offset and crossfade are fundamentally different, as you'll see.

However, papers and patterns can use the same construction methods, and you can easily create *compound patterns* (my term) that are a mix of pattern and surface texture.

Language Of Pattern

Before you proceed, you'll need to master some terms first. A *pattern* is a unit that repeats (tiles) across a surface. When a pattern repeats in such a way that it's difficult to spot where the unit starts and ends, the pattern is called *seamless*. A seamless pattern is almost always the goal of pattern design (unless you design a pattern where the seam is part of the pattern itself). The pattern unit (repeat unit or tile) is created from a *motif*, which can be a shaped object or a rectangular group of pixels that has been arbitrarily designated as a pattern unit. The motif can also be called a *pattern generating unit*, because if you have one motif, you can use it to re-create the entire pattern. In Painter, as in Photoshop, the basic unit that can be defined or captured as a pattern must be a rectangle. It may contain other shapes, but there must be a discrete bounding rectangle whose interior can be repeated across a *plane* (a flat surface).

This chapter shows you a lot of tricks that you can use to create patterns. Painter allows you to offset patterns so that you can easily create brick and drop repeats, but the manual doesn't give you any hints on how to seamlessly repeat a motif if it has no white space around it (that is, if the background of the pattern motif isn't solid). That's okay, but a pattern tile that contains multiple copies of the motif (or of different motifs) can be more interesting than a tile that only contains one motif. Here, you'll learn how to construct a number of different types of patterns.

I'll draw on a varied background to show you these techniques. Much of my knowledge comes from my grounding in fiber art—I've designed needlework and knitwear for many years. Patterning is a subject that I know very well indeed. Textile patterns frequently use offsets to create interest (drop and brick repeats).

The simplest example of a pattern is one in which the pattern source is a single motif and the repeat is a simple copy, both vertically and horizontally. Simple motifs are the easiest type of pattern source because they appear against a plain background, which means they're inherently seamless. The search for seamlessness consumes most pattern artists; they struggle toward what sometimes can be a highly compromised and elusive goal. It's this search for seamlessness that will also dominate the discussion here.

A single motif is always seamless against a solid background, but the pattern it forms can be varied by the amount of blank space that you allow around it (the first project in Chapter 4 discusses this issue). It can also be varied by the placement of multiple versions of the motif against the background or by the offsetting of the motifs in Painter as the pattern is applied to the image. You'll now create some patterns using a single motif.

Creating Rectangular Repeats

The first pattern you'll create is the *block repeat*. In this repeat system, the pattern unit is duplicated along the horizontal and vertical axes in a straight line.

PROJECT Single Motif Repeats—Part 1, The Block

Here's how to create a simple block repeat.

1. Open the image BUTTERFLY.PSD from this book's companion CD-ROM. I created this image with help from the BladePro plug-in by Flaming Pear.

2. Select the entire image (Command/Ctrl+A).

3. Choose Art Materials: Pattern menu and select Capture Pattern. Figure 5.1 shows the dialog box. Click on the Rectangular Tile radio button and set Bias to 0. Name the tile Butterfly1. The pattern becomes the automatically selected pattern.

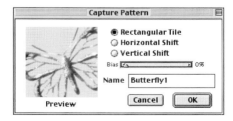

Figure 5.1

The Capture Pattern dialog box allows you to add your own patterns to the Art Materials: Patterns palette.

CLONE SOURCE AND
PATTERN FILL

You can only see the option to fill with a pattern if you've not defined a clone source for the image. If there is a clone source, the option will read Fill With: Clone Source.

4. Create a new document (Command/Ctrl+N) that's 900 pixels square.

5. Choose Effects|Fill; Fill With: Pattern. Figure 5.2 shows the first Butterfly1 pattern fill.

Figure 5.2

Here's what happens when you use the Butterfly pattern fill at 100 percent scale.

6. A truly wonderful feature in Painter is that you can change the scale of a pattern so that you can control the number of repeats. The butterfly is a bit large for a 900-pixel square image. Click on the Art Materials: Patterns palette. Change the Scale setting to 50 percent either by dragging the slider or by typing the value into the numeric field and pressing Return/Enter. Figure 5.3 shows the palette. Figure 5.4 shows the pattern image.

Figure 5.3

(Left) You have a number of options in the Art Materials: Patterns palette.

Figure 5.4

(Right) Here's the smaller Butterfly1 pattern fill.

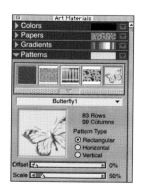

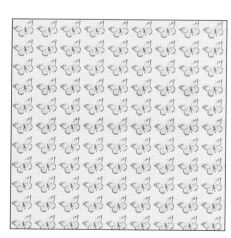

Painter's Offsets

The butterfly image has a very interesting shape, but the simple block repeat is somewhat boring. It's really not even interesting enough to use for wrapping paper, even though there might be other situations for which it would work nicely. A small rectangular block of the butterfly pattern could be a novel image on the front of a T-shirt. The pattern could also be a background behind a playful ad using a leisure-time theme (with a butterfly net in front).

However, to create additional interest, you can painlessly move the placement of the pattern units by changing the offset slider. No additional pattern capture is required. You'll try your hand at this in the following project.

PROJECT Single Motif Repeats—Part 2, Using The Offset Slider

In this project, you'll create a horizontal offset repeat (called a *brick repeat* in the textile world) and a vertical offset repeat (called a *drop pattern* in textile pattern design):

1. You may continue to use the 900-pixels-square image. If you've closed it, create a new file that's 900-pixels square.

2. Select the Butterfly1 pattern as the current pattern in the Art Materials: Patterns palette.

3. If the Art Materials drawer is open, close it and make sure you can see the pattern options, as shown in Figure 5.5. Set Scale to 50 percent and Offset to 50 percent. Click on the Pattern Type: Horizontal radio button. This setting will create a *brick* pattern—a pattern where the motifs in each row fall centered between the motifs in the row above it.

4. Choose Effects|Fill; Fill With: Pattern. Figure 5.6 shows the result. I surrounded one full repeat with a black line.

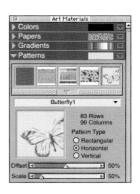

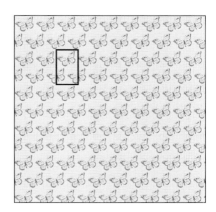

Figure 5.5
(Left) Set the Pattern offset to 50 percent and Horizontal.

Figure 5.6
(Right) Here's a brick repeat from the Butterfly1 pattern.

5. Change the Pattern Type setting to Vertical. Enter 50 in the Offset amount (even if it still says 50 percent) and press Return/Enter.

6. Choose Effects|Fill; Fill With: Pattern. Figure 5.7 shows the result (again, I surrounded one repeat with a black line). You've created a *half-drop repeat*—a repeat where the motif in each column appears centered between the motifs in the adjoining columns. This is the most common repeat type in both textile and wallpaper design.

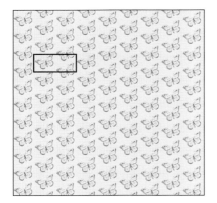

Figure 5.7

This is a half-drop repeat from the Butterfly1 pattern.

Now you know the basic building blocks of patterning. The rectangular (block) repeat, the brick repeat, and the half-drop repeat are the most common pattern algorithms in the world. Next, you'll take a slightly closer look at their anatomy.

Motif-Based Drops And Bricks

One of the main differences between the way Photoshop and Painter handle patterns is that Painter contains a way to automatically create drop and brick repeats, whereas Photoshop does not. Photoshop needs to have a rectangular selection defined and it will then blindly create a block repeat out of any set of pixels in the defined rectangle.

I mention this because if you understand how Photoshop creates a "dumb" repeat (no slur intended), you'll be able to take much better advantage of Painter's "smart" repeat. Look at the file that you just created—the one that contains the half-drop repeat of the butterfly. How would you define a rectangle that contains one entire repeat and *only* one entire repeat?

To begin, you need to determine what a repeat is. It's not the butterfly—if a single butterfly is the only object that you capture, you'll only produce a block repeat rather than the half-drop repeat. The butterfly, therefore, is your *pattern-generating unit*. With one butterfly, you can reproduce any pattern that uses the butterfly, but you'll need to recalculate the pattern method in order to do so.

How about two butterflies? Can two butterflies produce the entire half-drop pattern repeat? Yes, and I'll prove it. To begin, look at Figure 5.7 again. It shows a rectangle that moves from the left of one butterfly's wing in one motif to the same point in the next column that has a motif on that level (which is two columns over). The rectangle then stretches down one row to the top of the butterfly's wings in the row below (believe me, this is easier to *see* than to explain). If you look carefully inside the rectangle, you see one full butterfly and the bottom and top half of another. This is the 50 percent vertical offset that you set—the one that creates the half-drop repeat. Were you to copy this rectangle into Photoshop and define it as a pattern, it would re-create the half-drop pattern there.

You can use this knowledge to create a "manual" half-drop pattern in Painter. Here's how.

Single Motif Repeats—Part 3, Half-Drop Repeat By Hand

Pattern making has a deep mathematical component, so the instructions as you continue will become very precise. You need to be able to calculate and select to the *pixel* in order for the patterns to work.

In order to extract the exact repeat unit, you can magnify the image and find a "reference pixel" to use as the start point. You can also calculate in advance the size needed, in pixels, for the repeat. This project shows you a variety of methods you can use. First, here's the math you'll use to see how big the repeat must be:

- The Art Materials: Patterns palette should still show the definition of the Butterfly1 half-drop pattern (50 percent scale; 50 percent vertical offset). The palette also shows the size of *this* repeat (which uses only the scale amount to determine the pixel count). The palette says that the pattern is 83 pixels high by 99 pixels wide. That number is for only one butterfly.

- A half-drop pattern requires one motif row and two motif columns, as mentioned previously. Therefore, the butterfly half-drop repeat needs to be 83 pixels high (that is, one "row") and 198 pixels wide (two "columns"). That happens to be the exact size of the rectangle in Figure 5.7. Any selection of that size, anywhere in the half-drop image will be able to re-create the half-drop pattern. This is a major concept in understanding what makes a pattern repeat.

- If you want to "cut out" a rectangle that's exactly 83 pixels high by 198 pixels wide from the half-drop image, you have several ways to proceed. This method "proves" that any selection of the right size will re-create the pattern.

Here are the steps you'll follow for this project:

1. Create a new file that's exactly 83 pixels wide by 198 pixels high (File|New).

2. Select the entire image (Command/Ctrl+A). Press the modifier key (Option/Alt) and click inside the selection. This creates and floats a copy of the image. The image, in this case, is solid white.

CAPTURING A PATTERN

Step 8 is really unnecessary. You could have captured the pattern directly from the selection in the image. It's not necessary to select an entire file in order to capture a pattern—any repeating section will do. However, I wanted you to be able to see the pattern repeat, by itself, in order to look at its borders. Just know that you don't need to place the repeat into its own image. Having said that, I usually *do* place the repeat into its own image. Saving this file allows me to have a backup in case my Painter patterns ever disappear. It also allows me to use the file (if I don't save it in RIF format) as a pattern in Photoshop, which has no permanent pattern list.

PATTERN OFFSET AND CAPTURE PATTERN

The Bias slider establishes a default offset for the pattern based on the Pattern type. A Rectangular pattern cannot show a bias (or an offset).

3. Choose the Layer Adjuster tool. Drag the layer from the small image into the half-drop butterfly pattern image. Click on the butterfly image to make it active. Figure 5.8 shows the upper-left corner of the butterfly image with the layer in place.

4. If necessary, scroll the window so that you can see the upper-left corner. The layer will always appear there. Click on the layer in the Objects: Layers palette to make it active.

5. Drag the layer anywhere in the image.

6. Change the Composite Method setting to Multiply. The layer becomes (or seems to become) transparent because white "drops out" in the Multiply method.

7. Choose Objects palette: Layers menu|Drop And Select. The layer—which was the exact size needed to re-create the pattern—now becomes a selection and is also the correct size.

8. Copy the selection to the Clipboard (Command/Ctrl+C). Choose Edit|Paste|Into New Image. The copy is placed into a new image that's the same size as the selection. Figure 5.9 shows this new image, which is now the repeat unit.

9. Select the entire image (Command/Ctrl+A). Choose Art Materials: Pattern menu and select Capture Pattern. Name the pattern Butterfly2. Leave the Bias setting at 0 and the Pattern Type setting at Rectangular.

10. Make the half-drop butterfly image active (you might as well reuse it). Select None (Command/Ctrl+D). Choose Effects|Fill; Fill With: Pattern. The same half-drop pattern reappears, although the upper-left corner of the image has a different starting point for the pattern. Figure 5.10 shows the original left corner on the left and the left corner of the new pattern on the right. Notice that both contain the same pattern, however.

Figure 5.8
(Left) The white layer in the butterfly image shows the location of the repeat.

Figure 5.9
(Right) Copy the new pattern repeat unit from larger image.

Figure 5.10
The original (left) and new upper-left corners show the original pattern reconstituted.

11. You can easily get the exact tile that you need in case you want to move a half-drop or a brick repeat into Photoshop or another program that needs a Rectangular pattern with no offset (such as a Web browser). Click on the Butterfly1 pattern in the Art Materials: Patterns palette to select it. Change the Scale setting to 50 percent, the Pattern Type setting to Horizontal, and the Offset setting to 50 percent. This creates a brick pattern.

12. Select File|New. You need to double the height of your pattern (the "row" amount) and use it as the height in the File|New dialog box in order to create a brick repeat (a half-drop pattern doubles the width or column amount). Because this example uses a file that's 83 rows by 99 columns (that is, 83 pixels high by 99 pixels wide), you need to set a width of 99 pixels and a height of 166 pixels.

13. Fill the image (Command/Ctrl+F; Using: Pattern). Figure 5.11 shows that you have exactly one full and two half butterflies in the image. Were you to define this new file as a Rectangular pattern with no bias, you'd see results identical to selecting a horizontal pattern type and a 50 percent offset.

Figure 5.11
Here's the brick repeat unit.

This project may have seemed like a very convoluted way to get to the same place as using the Offset slider with a horizontal or vertical pattern type. In this instance, it was because of the white space that surrounds the butterfly. However, you should also have gotten a better understanding of what makes a pattern repeat properly. Instances exist—and the next project shows you one—where you cannot use Painter's offsets when you want to create a drop or brick pattern. This happens most often when you create a *diaper pattern*

What kinds of objects can you use with this patterning technique? You can use any object you want. The closer to square that the object is, the more the object will fill its space in the pattern. I'll show you some examples of this at the end of this project. You have two ways you can build the pattern tile. You can start with a canvas size that's square or you can space the first level of the repeat any way you want. In either case, you'll finish with a tile that's square, because I've had no luck with this technique when I try a tile that isn't finally square. Your choice of starting square or only ending that way has a major impact on your final pattern.

(which has nothing at all to do with wet infants). It's a pattern term with a respectable lineage and means a pattern that repeats on the diagonal. Essentially, a diaper repeat is one that both "drops" and "bricks."

PROJECT Single Motif Repeats—Part 4, Creating A Diaper Pattern

This project was nearly the end of me. I had seen a wonderful repeating pattern on a box of cookies, and I wanted to show you how to create it using a different motif. I could see the logic behind the repeat, but I could not seem to find a way to reproduce it. It took two solid days of curses and false starts before I found the best way—or at least *my* best way—to make this pattern. I would have given up in disgust if the final result were not as useful as I think it is. It makes a wonderful graphic statement and can be used as a background or as wrapping paper or fabric for almost any purpose. Best of all, the actual graphic "look" of the pattern changes dramatically based on the shape of the motif itself. The technique is not difficult—it was just very hard to figure out the first time.

This project creates a "double" diaper repeat. Instead of one motif repeated on the diagonal, the technique uses a grouping of four copies of the motif (although you certainly can use four different motifs if you prefer). The grouped motif repeats on the diagonal in both directions. Figure 5.12 shows a pattern similar to the one you'll create that uses arrows to create a pattern dummy. The patterns show the way the motifs face and interact with one another. Figure 5.13 shows the repeat unit needed in order to make this pattern work.

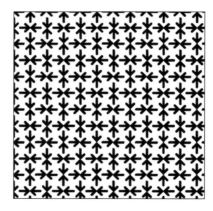

Figure 5.12
This pattern "cheat sheet" uses arrows to show you how the repeat will work.

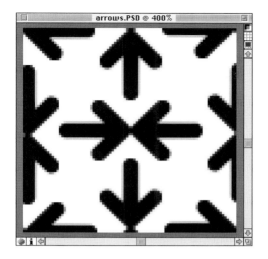

Figure 5.13
This single repeat unit for the arrow pattern is similar to the one you'll build (except you'll use a taxi as your motif).

Building The First Double-Repeat

Here's how to get started:

1. Open the file TAXITAXI.PSD on this book's companion CD-ROM. The driver of this London taxi wouldn't recognize it in its gaily colored and distorted disguise. The taxi is already in a layer for you with a transparent background.

2. Choose File|Clone. This creates a new file in which the taxi layer has been dropped onto the canvas layer. In "Photoshop-speak" you've created a flattened copy of the original. You need to have the taxi as a layer, but this at least gives you a new image of the correct size without any calculations. Choose white as your current color. Then, fill the image with the current color (Command/Ctrl+F). Alternatively, you could select the entire image and then choose Edit|Clear and then Select|None. Now you have a blank white canvas of the correct size. Use the Layer Adjuster tool to drag the taxi from the original into the clone. Continue to work in the clone image.

3. Make sure that the Canvas layer is selected. Choose Canvas|Canvas Size. Type the full amount of the image width in the Add: Pixels To Right field. In this project, you'll enter 150 pixels in this field, which doubles the width of the image. Choose Window|Zoom To Fit. Figure 5.14 shows the image in the enlarged file along with the Canvas Size dialog box.

4. Select the Layer Adjuster tool, press the modifier key (Option/Alt) and click on the taxi. This copies the taxi into a new layer.

PREPARING YOUR OWN STARTING POINTS

If you decide to use your own object for this patterning technique, change whatever image you use into a layer with a transparent background. It's easier to design this repeat if you don't have to contend with the white space behind the motif as you design. If you want your motif to repeat on a colored background, work the motifs against white until you have the final pattern built and then color your background last. You'll find that it's really easier to leave a white background.

ADD SPACE LEFT OR RIGHT?

If your motif is facing left instead of right, you should add the extra width to the left of the motif instead of the right.

Figure 5.14

The Canvas Size dialog box enables you to add space to any edge of the image.

5. Double-click on the highlighted layer in the Objects: Layers palette to open the Layer Attributes dialog box. Add the width of the original image (150 pixels) to the number in the Left field (enter "157" for this project). This moves the new object to its same relative position in the added image width (it's as if you simply doubled the image in your original file). While you have the Layer Attributes dialog box open anyway, rename this layer as Taxi2. Figure 5.15 shows the Layer Attributes dialog box and the position of the two images after you've made the changes.

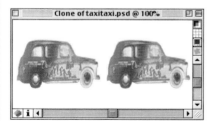

Figure 5.15

The Layer Attributes dialog box allows you to change the position of the copied taxi layer.

6. Choose Effects|Orientation|Flip Horizontal.

7. Your next step is to copy the two layers already in your image. Make the Taxi layer active by clicking on it in the Objects: Layers palette. Using the Layer Adjuster tool, press the Option/Alt key and click on the taxi in the image window to copy it to a new layer.

8. Make the Taxi2 layer active by clicking on it in the Objects: Layers palette. Using the Layer Adjuster tool, press the Option/Alt key and click on the taxi in the image window to copy it to a new layer.

9. Drag the topmost Taxi layer in the Objects: Layers palette to the top of the Layers palette list. Press and hold the Shift key and click on the Taxi2 layer directly beneath it in the Objects: Layers palette. Click on the Group button in the Objects: Layers palette to make a group of the two layers. Then click on the Collapse button in the Objects: Layers palette. This makes the two layers in the group into a single layer.

10. Double-click on this combined top layer and open the Layer Attributes dialog box. Rename the layer Double-Motif. Click on OK to close the layer.

Building The Vertical Double-Repeat

You're now going to create the vertical double-repeat. Figure 5.16 shows the arrows again. The figure shows the facing motifs at the bottom of the image and a rotated copy of the facing motifs at the top. It's this arrangement that you need to duplicate. Here are the steps:

1. Click on the canvas to select it because you cannot use the Canvas Size command when you have a layer active.

2. Choose Canvas|Canvas Size and add the width of the canvas to the Add: Pixels To Top box. In this project, add 300 pixels (the width of the image) to the top of the canvas. This gives you more than enough room to rotate your double-motif layer. Choose Window|Zoom To Fit.

3. Select Effects|Orientation|Rotate. Rotate the layer 90 degrees. Click on OK to close the dialog box.

4. The layer is already centered, because the Rotate command makes the object revolve around its center point. Double-click on the layer name in the Objects: Layers palette to open the Layer Attributes dialog box. Enter "0" into the Top field. This moves the layer to the top of the image while not changing its center location from left to right.

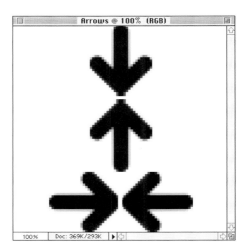

Figure 5.16
The vertical arrows give a preview of what you'll do in this part of the project.

This step is the second-most critical one for the success of the pattern (the *most* critical step was your decision of whether to start with a square image). The spacing that you use in this step is also a judgment call—I can't give you a rule for this that will *always* work. You need to move the rotated layer back toward the bottom of the image until the spacing between it and the first double-motif looks good to you. Depending on the shape of your motif, this may involve moving the rotated layer over the border of the bottom layer (Figure 5.17 shows what I mean by this— two rectangles are used around the two groups of motifs. You can clearly see the "virtual" rectangles around each motif group begin to overlap.)

5. Now, you need to move the rotated double-motif layer back toward the horizontal double-motif. You can move the rotated layer either by pressing the down-arrow key multiple times or by opening the Layer Attributes dialog box and trying various numbers (starting with 10) in the Top field of the Location area of the dialog box. I moved the double-motif layer down 40 pixels (so that the object starts at pixel 41).

6. Save your image at this point so that you can always return to it.

Creating The Final Pattern Tile—Start Loop

Because you used an "educated guess" to set the spacing in Step 11 of the "Building The First Double-Motif Repeat" project, it's always possible that you guessed wrong. After you build the pattern, you might not like it. Because of that, the following steps take great care to let you recover and go back to a "clean" starting point. A *loop* is a programming term for a series of instructions that may need to be executed more than once. I consider the remaining steps in this project to be a loop. You may need to come back to this point several times before you're satisfied with the results. That's why you'll clone your image and use the clone to produce the pattern rather than continue in your current file. Your original pattern file with the layers and the full number of pixels will be there for you if you need to back off and try again. Of course, I'll give you my idea of the "right" numbers for this example, but the patterning technique shown is one that I hope you'll use many times on your own.

Your first steps will be to clone and crop the image. You have two choices for cropping: You can crop the image with the Crop tool as close as possible to

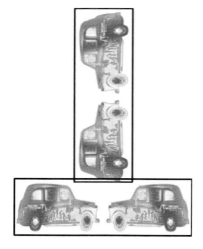

Figure 5.17
The rotated layer slightly overlaps the horizontal motif "rectangle" when it's moved into a good spacing relationship.

CROPPING BY THE NUMBERS

At the end of the last project, you moved the top layer down 40 pixels. You need to remove those pixels from the image so that the rotated layer is once again at 0 pixels from the top (or would be if there were still a layer in your image). If you don't remember the number of pixels down that you moved the image, you can open the Layer Attributes dialog box in your original image and see the value of the Top field. It's this number that you need to subtract from the Add: Pixels To Top field in the Canvas Size dialog box.

For this example, because you moved the double-motif layer down 40 pixels, you would enter the number "-40" in the Add: Pixels To Top field in the Layer Attributes dialog box.

If you select this method of cropping, you probably don't need to add "breathing room" to your image. You should already have sufficient space around it.

the motifs and then add some "breathing room" to the canvas size, or you can subtract from the top of the canvas the number of pixels by which you moved down the double-motif layer in the previous project. I'm going to explain the Crop tool method because it's a bit more complex. However, I'll show you in a sidebar how to use the Layer Attributes dialog box to crop.

1. Choose File|Clone. This drops the layers as it creates a new copy of the pattern-to-be.

2. Select the Crop tool. Drag a cropping marquee around the taxis in the image. If you don't get the crop marquee "right" the first time, you can place your cursor over any edge of the marquee and drag it to a better location. When you're satisfied with your cropping marquee (which should look similar to mine in Figure 5.18), you can execute the crop by clicking inside of the marquee boundaries.

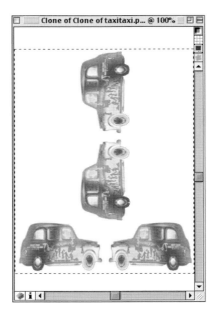

Figure 5.18
A crop marquee is drawn around the motifs in the image.

3. You need to add some breathing room around the image so that there's enough room for the full pattern to be created without overlap. I like to add 10 pixels to each edge at this step. Make the Canvas layer active and select Canvas|Canvas Size. Enter "10" in each field (Top, Left, Bottom, and Right). Click on OK to size the image. Choose Window|Zoom To Fit to view the image at the new size.

4. Now, you need to make the image square. Select Canvas|Canvas Size. In your head (or on a piece of paper if your math is as rotten as mine) subtract the smaller dimension in the Canvas Size dialog box from the larger dimension and divide the result by 2. If the number isn't evenly divisible by 2, you'll end up with two numbers that aren't the same (the larger number is one more than the smaller). See the sidebar "Squaring The Canvas" for an example. When you've resized your canvas, choose Window|Zoom To Fit to see the full image on your screen.

5. Choose Art Materials: Pattern menu and select Define Pattern. Nothing visible happens to your image, but it's now defined as a pattern file. This means that you can move the image within the file and it will wrap around. A pattern file also lets you paint in the image and have your brushes wrap around (but you're not going to do that in this project).

6. Select the entire image (Command/Ctrl+A).

7. Choose the Layer Adjuster tool, press the Option/Alt key, and click inside the marquee to copy the selection to a new layer.

8. Change the Composite Method setting on the Objects: Layers palette or the Controls palette to Multiply.

9. Press and hold the Shift key and the spacebar. The cursor turns into a hand icon. Drag the image down toward the bottom until the motifs wrap around to the edges of the image. As you wrap the image

SQUARING THE CANVAS

The largest dimension of my newly cloned image is 401 pixels. The smallest dimension is 314 pixels. Therefore, I need to subtract 314 from 401 (which equals 87 pixels).

I need to add a total of 87 pixels to the width of the image to make the width equal to the height (which, of course, makes the image square). I need to add the pixels so that the image stays centered. Therefore, one half of the total number of pixels needed must be added to each side.

I need 87 pixels, which divided by 2 equals 43.5 pixels. I can't add a half of a pixel to anything. Therefore, I'd need to enter 44 into to the Add: Pixels To Left field and enter 43 in the Add: Pixels To Right field. You need to do the math for *your* image because your dimensions might not be the same as mine.

around, you should be able to find a spot where the motifs don't overlap and where the spacing is pleasing to the eye. This will be your
pattern. (For the taxis, you should find a spot where a horizontal taxi
sits to the left and right of the two vertical taxis.) Figure 5.19 shows
you the final tile arrangement that I used.

Figure 5.19
The bottom layers of the motifs
are arranged so that they frame
the image window.

Finishing Up

Here's how to capture the pattern file to your Patterns palette:

1. Choose File|Clone to create a flattened copy of the pattern file (so you
   can easily go back and adjust the Define Pattern image if you don't
   like the pattern). Select the entire image (Command/Ctrl+A).

2. Choose Art Materials: Pattern palette menu and select Capture Pattern.

3. Create a new document (Command/Ctrl+N) that's 900 pixels by 900
   pixels. Choose Effects|Fill; Fill With: Pattern. Figure 5.20 shows the
   repeating pattern.

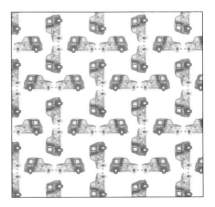

Figure 5.20
Multiple taxis crawl across the
finished image.

I hope you think the work was worth it. I really like this technique. The process goes much faster once you've worked through it a few times.

If you don't like the finished pattern, you have several places where you can
try again. You can add more space around the starting motif and make it
square before you begin (or crop close to the motif before you start to remove
unwanted space). You can return to the image that contains all the layers
and add or remove space there. Finally, you can return to the Define Pattern
file and change the positioning of the two layers in relation to one another.

The shape and angle of the motif plays a huge role in the final pattern.
Figure 5.21 shows the same instructions used with the butterfly motif that
you used earlier in this chapter. I included the layered motif on this book's
companion CD-ROM. It's called BUTTERFLYOBJECT.PSD. Notice how different
the pattern looks using the butterfly even when the instructions for building

**USING ADD PATTERN
TO LIBRARY**

You could, if you prefer, shortcut all of the steps in this last
set of instructions by choosing
Add Pattern To Library from
the Pattern drop-down menu
in the Art Materials: Patterns
palette. Again, I typically make
a new file for my complete
pattern just so that I have a
record of it and so that I can
use it in Photoshop.

Figure 5.21

The butterflies make an interesting pattern in this double-diaper technique.

it were the same. The difference in shape is the combination of the shape of the butterfly and the fact that it's at an angle rather than straight like the taxi.

The choice of a square or a rectangular starting image makes a huge difference in the final pattern as well. Figure 5.22 shows the project using a recolored and slightly rearranged statue of a jester that stands in the marketplace in Stratford-on-Avon, England (the birthplace of William Shakespeare). I included this image on this book's companion CD-ROM as well (JESTER.PSD). I used the instructions for a square starting image. Figure 5.23 shows the same motif worked as a rectangular image and made into a double-motif that's much closer than the first one. This version didn't become square until I was ready to prepare the Define Pattern file.

Figure 5.22

(Left) This motif of a jester from Stratford-on-Avon makes an interesting graphic statement. It began as a square file.

Figure 5.23

(Right) This is the same motif, but it started from a rectangular rather than a square starting file.

Linked Motifs

There's one more skill that you need to learn before you move on to a different type of source image for a pattern. Painter makes it very easy to create linking elements for motifs. You already created linked elements of a sort in the last project, where the motifs were spaced together so closely that using Painter's offsets on the pattern would cause seam lines and partial patterns to appear.

You can create greenery or chain links or whatever to attach the motifs together. This action, which is a major pain in Photoshop, is quite easy to do in Painter. The only decision that you need to make in advance is whether you'll want to offset the motifs at all, and if you do, whether you want a horizontal or vertical orientation.

PROJECT Linked Motif Pattern

Here, you'll create an example that will not be offset:

1. Open the BUTTERFLYOBJECT.PSD file on this book's companion CD-ROM.

2. Choose File|Clone. Then choose Select|All and press Delete/Backspace. Click on the original file to make it active. Choose the Layer Adjuster tool and drag the butterfly into the clone file.

3. Select the Paintbrush tool and the Image Hose brush with any of the variants. In the Art Materials: Nozzles palette, select the Ivy-2 nozzle. Choose Art Materials: Nozzles palette menu. Select Set Nozzle Scale and set the scale to 25 percent.

4. Select Art Materials: Patterns palette menu and select Define Pattern to create a file that can wrap around.

5. Click on the Canvas layer in the Objects: Layers palette to select the canvas. Paint with the Image Hose brush and let the ivy wrap off of one side onto the other. As you draw off of the left edge of the canvas, the brush will appear on the right edge. This ensures that your pattern will be seamless. Figure 5.24 shows the butterfly with ivy behind it.

6. Make the Butterfly layer active. Click on the Drop button in the Objects: Layers palette. (The Capture Pattern or Add Pattern To Library commands don't "see" the layers of the image.)

7. Choose Art Materials: Pattern menu and select Add To Image Library. This allows you to add a file that's already defined as a pattern directly to the library without having to make a selection. Name the pattern Butterfly Ivy.

8. Create a new document (Command/Ctrl+N) that's 900 pixels square. Fill the image (Command/Ctrl+F; Fill With: Pattern). Figure 5.25 shows the seamless pattern.

Figure 5.24
The Image Hose brush and the Define Pattern command work together to create a seamless tile.

Were you to change the pattern type, the image would no longer be seamless. Figure 5.26 clearly shows the seam that occurs when you try to make this pattern into a half-drop pattern (look in the center of the image). If you want to make a seamless half-drop pattern (vertical pattern type), make sure you

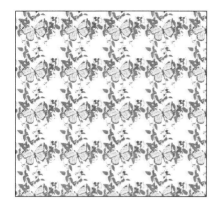

Figure 5.25
Here's the seamless, repeating butterfly and ivy pattern.

Figure 5.26
Here a wraparound pattern that's offset by 50 percent horizontally is no longer seamless.

don't spray any leaves on the side edges. For a seamless brick pattern (horizontal offset), don't place any ivy on the top or bottom edges. Figure 5.27 shows the butterfly as a half-drop repeat with the ivy only along the top and bottom edges. Of course, you can no longer apply it as a Rectangular pattern.

If you want to create a seamless half-drop or brick repeat of the butterfly and spray the ivy all over, you need to first create a half-drop or brick tile, the same as you did to create a rectangular half-drop or brisk repeat. Using that tile as a basis, select the background and spray away. When you redefine the pattern, don't set a bias (define the pattern as a rectangular pattern). Figure 5.28 shows the butterfly pattern as a brick repeat that's seamless but has ivy along all four sides. The two rows of butterflies are slightly different, but the image is totally seamless.

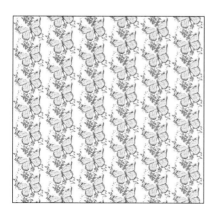 

Figure 5.27
(Left) You can create a seamless half-drop, wraparound repeat using the Offset slider if you're careful not to place the design along the side edges of the pattern.

Figure 5.28
(Right) Here's a pattern of seamless bricked butterflies.

Painted Patterns

Painted images are the second type of source image to discuss. When you use Painter's brushes, you have the choice of where to draw. You're not following any set formula that you must respect. If you're drawing flowers, you have the choice of where to put the flowers. If you're drawing boats, you can place them, within reason, where you want them to be.

This gives you a great deal of latitude in creating seamless patterns. It's always difficult to make a convincing seamless pattern of something realistic that contains an "up" and a "down," but it's certainly technically possible. If you want to create a seamless pattern that features a painting of someone rowing a boat down the Seine, you can.

Painter's pattern-making capability really shines, though, when you use it to create abstract, painterly surfaces. You can either begin with something on the canvas and modify it, or you can start with a blank slate. As you saw in the previous project, when you use a pattern file to create your pattern, your brushstrokes wrap around. In addition, you can manually move the canvas and make it wrap as well.

The pattern file has some limitations, though—and you've also seen some of these. The major limitation is that only the canvas wraps or can be scrolled. Layers don't wrap, nor do they show up in the pattern when it's added to the pattern library. Although it would be extremely convenient if you could place a layer over one part of the canvas and have it wrap across to the other side, Painter doesn't do that, so you need to accept this fact. However, you do have other ways to trick Painter into thinking that it's going to wrap a layer.

The other thing that's difficult about a pattern file (or about patterning in Painter in general) is that it's hard to be precise. Photoshop's offset filter allows you to control exactly how much the image will be offset. It's much more difficult in Painter to precisely offset an image by 50 percent (or by any other exact amount). The two different rows of the butterfly pattern in Figure 5.28 are a case in point. It would not have been nearly as easy to create the seamless pattern in Photoshop, but if you had, the two rows would have been identical. Therefore, you trade off ease of use for precision. When you can take artistic license, use Painter. When you must have a mathematically perfect pattern, use Photoshop—or figure out how to make Painter pattern precisely (there are ways).

Using The Pattern File

This section has two exercises. In the first one, you'll create a "controlled" image—one that starts from a known point (a *gradient*). The second project is an experimental "finger painting" (my term) that allows you to paint and then spray objects onto your pattern. These two exercises should help you to see what a pattern file can and can't do.

PROJECT Fire And Confusion—Pattern Process

In this project, you'll explore the pattern file by creating a gradation within the file and using a combination of the Fire brush and the Confusion brush to make several different seamless patterns. You'll finish up by using the Dry brush and an Image Hose on the seamless pattern.

Playing With Fire

The first seamless painted pattern you'll create starts with a gradation and uses both the Confusion and Fire variants of the FX brush. Follow these steps:

1. Create a new document (Command/Ctrl+N) that's 200 pixels square.

2. Choose Art Materials: Pattern menu and select Define Pattern.

3. Select the Painted gradient from the Gradient list in the Art Materials: Grad palette. Change the gradient angle to 309 degrees and the type to Radial (the right button on the top row).

4. Fill the image (Command/Ctrl+F; Fill With: Gradation, 50% Opacity).

5. Press and hold the Shift key and the spacebar. The cursor turns into a hand icon. Drag the image toward the bottom-right corner until the center of the gradation is in the lower-right corner (actually, it will be in all four corners). The lines that occurred at the edges of the image are now at the center cross of the image. This crossed line is called the *pattern seam line*, and it's this line that needs to be covered and eradicated in order to make a seamless pattern.

6. Fill the image again (Command/Ctrl+F; Fill With: Gradation, 50% Opacity). Repeat Step 5. There's still a seam.

7. Press and hold the Shift key and the spacebar. The cursor turns into a hand icon. Drag the image so that the lines formed by the gradations are positioned like a tic-tac-toe board on the image. Figure 5.29 shows this view.

Figure 5.29
The lines still frame the center of the pattern tile.

8. Fill the image again (Command/Ctrl+F; Fill With: Gradation, 50% Opacity).

9. Press and hold the Shift key and the spacebar. The cursor turns into a hand icon. Drag the image so that the newly created center is in the lower-right corner. Apply the 50 percent gradation fill again. Your image is beginning to look like folded paper.

10. Select the FX brush from the Brushes palette. Choose the Confusion brush variant. Brush over all the visible seams lines in the image and over all the edges. Let the brush cover the entire image, but with more attention to the "problem" areas. Scroll the image so that you can see the side seams and use the Confusion brush to cover over them. Keep scrolling the image and painting with the Confusion brush until the seam lines are gone.

11. Select the Fire variant of the FX brush. The variant will select the correct color for you. Place your cursor in the center of the canvas. Drag the brushstroke straight down until it's off the bottom edge and wraps around to the top. Drag the stroke to the bottom-right corner and off the canvas. Move the brush to the top-left corner and "scrub" the brush over the corner a bit; brushstrokes will appear in all four corners. Finally, drag the brush down toward the center of the image and release the mouse button.

12. Go over the areas that you've painted to make them a little bit darker. Change the color to green and paint in the areas that were not as yet colored with the Fire brush. Figure 5.30 shows the image.

Figure 5.30
This figures shows green and red fire on the gradation image.

13. Select the original fire color again (choose Brushes palette: Variant| Restore Default Variant). Let the brush lightly cover over some of the green areas. Allow some of the areas to "burn out" from the flame.

14. Use the Confusion brush again over the whole image and scroll as needed to make sure that there are no seams.

15. Alternate using the Fire brush and the Confusion brush until the image looks interesting to you and is seamless. (The Confusion brush has a tendency to blur out areas of the image that don't have much contrast in them. It's these areas that you need to fill with more flame.)

16. Choose Art Materials: Pattern menu and select Add Image To Library. Name the pattern Litmus 1 (because it looks like ink that has spread across a paper). Leave the Bias setting at 0.

17. Create a new document (Command/Ctrl+N) that's 1,000 pixels square. Fill the image (Command/Ctrl+F; Fill With: Pattern, 100% Opacity). Figure 5.31 shows my pattern.

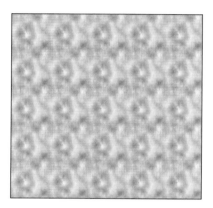

Figure 5.31
The Litmus 1 pattern is complete.

18. Return to the small file in which you built the pattern. Choose Effects|Tonal Control|Brightness And Contrast. Move the Brightness slider (the bottom slider) as far left as possible. Add this new pattern to your image library, just as you did the first one in Step 16.

19. Fill a large, 900-pixel-square image with the pattern to test it. Figure 5.32 shows this image. Notice that the square tiles are more apparent on this version than they were on the previous version. There's not really a seam, but the pattern features are definitely obvious—reducing the image brightness causes the seam areas to become more prominent. Even though you're working in a pattern file, there's no way to "wrap" an effect.

The starting gradient that you used in this example isn't seamless. Because of this, you saw a seam in the pattern as soon as you filled the image with the gradation. For your own entertainment, try the same project using the Painted gradient as a Linear gradation. Figure 5.33 shows my version—you'll see definite stripes, but the pattern has no obvious seam.

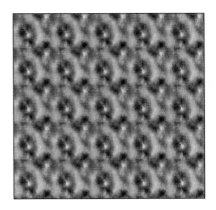

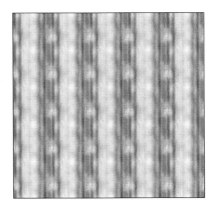

Figure 5.32
(Left) The low-brightness version of the Litmus 1 pattern shows a more obvious repeat, even though it's still seamless.

Figure 5.33
(Right) I developed this pattern from a Linear gradation.

In the course of writing this chapter, I created a huge number of variations on the Fire brush theme. In one version, I used the Graphic Brush variant of the FX brush to posterize the colors in the image. I've included this pattern tile for you so that you can work through the next project from the same starting point that I used.

You've already seen that brushes wrap in a pattern file but that effects do not, and you've also seen that it's not possible to make a layer wrap. That makes it tricky to add objects on top of a pattern file, although you can find ways to work around the problem. One excellent way is to place your objects inside a nozzle and spray them onto the pattern. Painter's manual has an excellent discussion on how to construct Image Hose nozzles. For now, though, you can simply use a nozzle that comes with Painter.

Dry Brush And Image Hose
In this project, you'll use the Dry brush and the Image Hose to create a seamless pattern:

1. Open the image GRAPHIC1.PSD on this book's companion CD-ROM.

2. Choose Art Materials: Pattern menu and select Define Pattern.

3. In the Brush list at the bottom of the Brushes palette, select Load Library. Choose the DryBrush library located on this book's companion CD-ROM. Select the New Paint Tools brush; then select the Dry brush variant.

4. Keep the colors moving vaguely in a horizontal direction as you brush off the canvas edges with the Dry brush. Try to create from this image an impressionistic landscape of mountains. Figure 5.34 shows my version of the pattern tile.

5. Choose the Image hose brush in the Brushes palette. Select the Small Random Spray variant.

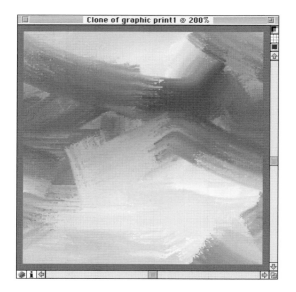

Figure 5.34
Here's my Dry brush
impressionist landscape.

Figure 5.35
The small forest pattern tile
is seamless.

6. View the Art Materials: Nozzles palette. Select the Small Forest nozzle. Spray your pattern tile lightly with trees. Figure 5.35 shows the tile.

7. Choose Art Materials: Pattern menu and select Add Image To Library. Name the pattern Forest Fire.

8. Create a new document (Command/Ctrl+N) that's 900 pixels square. Fill the image (Command/Ctrl+F; Fill With: Pattern). Figure 5.36 shows the repeating pattern.

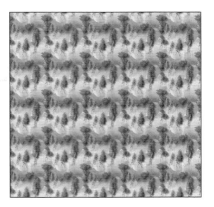

Figure 5.36
The forest fire pattern creates a seamless repeat.

Photographic Patterns

The possibilities for painted textures are endless, but you need to turn your attention to the most challenging and difficult of all of the pattern sources—photographs. The photograph presents a major test of your "seamless-making" ability because it's so arbitrary. However, there are ways to make a photograph behave. In this section, you'll look at tiling photos so that they're seamless. You'll learn a technique that works remarkably well for most photos and is quite easy. It also creates a somewhat offset repeat, but that's a side effect of the technique rather than an intentional action.

This technique does an excellent job of creating "endless" repeats—the miles of jellybeans, paper clips, or whatever that are frequently desirable as backgrounds. You'll use miles of swimming boys in this example—another photograph by Ed Scott from his China series. Because you're using Painter (Photoshop can do the straight photographic repeats just as well), you'll clone the image into a pencil sketch and create a repeat of the pencil sketch—artistic effects are Painter's specialty.

PROJECT A Simple Seamless, Endless Repeat

In this project, you'll take the image of boys swimming in a river, clone a pencil sketch of it, and make a seamless repeat. This technique makes an image seamless by using the Define Pattern command. Here are the steps:

1. Open the image BOYS.PSD on this book's companion CD-ROM.

2. Choose File|Clone to create a copy of the original.

3. Select the entire image (Command/Ctrl+A). Press the Delete/Backspace key to clear the image. Choose the Pencil Sketch variant of the Cloner brush and scribble a clone image into the canvas, as shown in Figure 5.37.

4. Choose Art Materials: Patterns palette menu and select Define Pattern.

Figure 5.37

Here's the pencil sketch clone of BOYS.PSD.

5. Hold down the Shift key and the spacebar and wrap the pattern around until the seam is roughly in the center of the image, as shown in Figure 5.38.

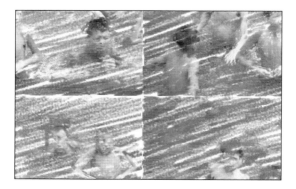

Figure 5.38

Wrap the pattern until you see the seam in the center of the image.

6. Choose Art Materials: Pattern palette menu and select Define Pattern again. This turns off the pattern wrap.

7. Start cloning over the seams in the image. Just watch carefully as you draw. Try to clone entire boys into the image and work primarily over the seams. Don't clone more than you need to and don't disturb the edges of the image window. Figure 5.39 shows my first "seamless" pass.

8. You can turn Define Pattern on again and wrap the image to check for seams. Keep alternating the wrapping and the cloning until you have a seamless tile.

9. Choose Art Materials: Pattern menu and select Add Pattern To Library. Create a new image that's 1,000 pixels square and fill the image (Command/Ctrl+F; Fill With: Pattern). Figure 5.40 shows the final image.

I've had incredibly good results from this technique with almost any type of original source material. The only caveat I have is that not every image looks good when it's repeated disembodied in space (for example, half of a person

TURNING DEFINE PATTERN ON AND OFF

Painter doesn't use the Clone brushes well on a pattern tile. The pattern tile confuses the cloning source. Therefore, by turning Define Pattern on only when you want to wrap the pattern, you can get the best of both worlds. If Painter shows you a funky cursor when you turn Define Pattern off and then try to use the Clone brush, select the original image in the File|Clone Source menu and the cursor should fix itself.

Figure 5.39
You make the image seamless by cloning over the seams and intelligently adding new figures to the image.

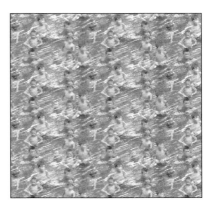

Figure 5.40
The seamless pencil sketch is shown in repeat.

who is not immersed in the water). You need to decide why you want to repeat something, because not all images lend themselves to the process.

Learning To Love Lines

You've spent a number of projects learning how to remove seams. However, sometimes seams are a wonderful addition to the overall pattern. An entire class of patterns exists that forms "naturally" seamless tiles or patterns where the seam itself is a design element. In this section, you'll look more closely at this class of patterns.

If you've ever studied a patterned tile floor, you've noticed that it has a four-way symmetry that allows it to repeat seamlessly. Painter can easily duplicate that tiled floor. You'll try an easy example first.

 ## A Four-Way Repeat

In this project, you'll create a four-way pattern using a simple linear gradation:

1. Create a new document (Command/Ctrl+N) that's 75 pixels square.

2. Click on the Gradation icon in the Art Materials palette. Select the Browns gradation from the list. Set the gradation type to linear by clicking on the first icon on the top row; then set the angle to 45 degrees.

3. Choose Effects|Fill; Fill With: Gradation.

4. Select the entire image (Command/Ctrl+A).Choose the Layer Adjuster tool, press the modifier key (Option/Alt) and click inside of the selection. This places a copy of the image into Layer 1.

5. Select the Canvas layer and choose Canvas|Canvas Size. Add 75 pixels (the image width) to the left of the canvas and add 75 pixels (the image height) to the bottom. Choose Window|Zoom To Fit to expand the window so you can see the full image.

6. Double-click on the top layer name in the Objects: Layer palette. This opens the Layer Attributes dialog box. Type "0" into the Left field to move the layer into the left corner of the image. It will fit exactly and will not overlap the original layer at all.

7. Choose Effects|Orientation|Flip Horizontal.

8. Click on the Drop button to drop the layer to the canvas.

9. Select the entire image (Command/Ctrl+A). Choose the Layer Adjuster tool, press the modifier key (Option/Alt) and click inside of the selection. This places a copy of the image into a new layer.

10. Choose Effects|Orientation|Flip Vertical. Change the Composite Method setting in the Objects: Layer palette or the Controls palette to Multiply. Click on the Drop button in the Objects: Layers palette to flatten the image. Figure 5.41 shows the single tile. Any pattern or image can be made seamless in this manner.

Figure 5.41
The four-way tile for the gradient is completed.

11. Select the entire image (Command/Ctrl+A).Choose Art Materials: Pattern menu and select Capture Pattern. Create a new document (Command/Ctrl+N) that's 1,000 pixels square. Fill the image (Command/Ctrl+F; Fill With: Pattern). Figure 5.42 shows the finished repeat.

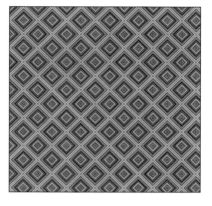

Figure 5.42

The four-way pattern shown in repeat.

The four-way repeat takes a gradation—or any other image—and makes its seam line totally invisible by moving and flipping the base element. Figure 5.43 shows a pattern-generating unit made by painting randomly inside of a 75-pixel square, and Figure 5.44 shows the pattern that the four-way repeat generated.

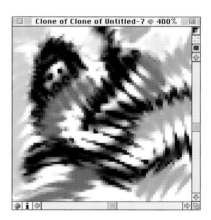

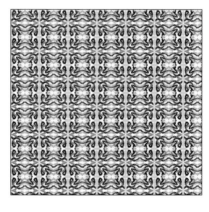

Figure 5.43

(Left) This is a nonsymmetrical four-way repeat pattern-generating unit.

Figure 5.44

(Right) The repeat made from the four-way nonsymmetric pattern is seamless.

You can find other "natural" repeats as well. A circular gradation will form a seamless repeat using just a plain block repeat. Figure 5.45 shows the Painted gradation applied circularly to a 100-pixel-square image and made into a repeat pattern.

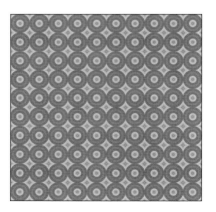

Figure 5.45

The painted gradation makes a wonderful repeat pattern.

You can create an interesting interlocked pattern from a spiral repeat. Follow the directions for the four-way repeat to produce the type of interlocking shown in Figure 5.46.

Figure 5.46
An interlocking spiral gradation in repeat creates a lot of excitement.

Patterned Prose

Elizabeth Mitchell, senior technical support specialist for Painter (and the technical editor of the first edition of this book), contributed this wonderful technique for adding patterns to text.

PROJECT Text In A Shape

In this project, you'll learn how to add a pattern to text and use the capability of Painter's shape feature to create an automatic outline for the text. Here are the steps:

1. Create a new image that's 900 pixels square (File|New).

2. Choose the Type tool.

3. In the Controls palette, select either an interesting typeface or a wide one. I used ICG Wonton. I set my point size to 300—you might need to experiment to find a good size for the font you select.

4. Type the letter "P" so that it's in the center of the image (if it isn't, you can move it afterward).

5. When you've typed the letter, choose the Layer Adjuster tool. The letter that you typed is displayed in the Objects: Layers palette as a Shape layer. Move it to the center of the image if necessary.

6. Press and hold the Option/Alt key and click on the letter with the Layer Adjuster tool to make a copy of the Shape layer. You'll have two letter-P shapes.

7. Close the visibility icon on the top Shape layer "P" to hide it for the moment.

8. Make the lower letter-P shape's layer active.

9. Choose Shapes|Convert To Layer. This changes the lower letter-P shape into a layer that contains the letter *P* in raster form. The Preserve Transparency checkbox near the top of the Objects: Layers palette should automatically be selected. If it isn't, select it now.

10. In the Art Materials: Patterns palette, make the diamond pattern you created during the four-way repeat project your current pattern. Fill the letter (Command/Ctrl+F; Fill With: Pattern). The Preserve Transparency checkbox keeps the fill to only the area occupied by the letter.

11. Make the top letter-P shape active. Turn its visibility icon back on. Choose Shapes|Shape Attributes.

12. In the Set Shape Attributes dialog box shown in Figure 5.47, uncheck the Fill checkbox and select the Stroke checkbox. Double-click on the Stroke color swatch to open the Color Picker. Select an orange color to complement your letter. (I used HSV 35, 87, 93.) Set Stroke Width to 15 and click on OK to exit.

13. Press the Shift key and click on the lower "P" layer and select both it and the "P" Shape layer. Click on the Group button in the Objects: Layers palette and press Command/Ctrl+G to group the two layers so that you can move them as one.

14. If you want, you can create additional letters in the same manner. Figure 5.48 shows the word *Pattern* created this way and then rearranged.

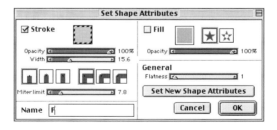

PATTERN FILLS ON A LAYER

The Fill command seems to behave oddly on a layer. In most cases, the strange preview that you might see is only an illusion. However, you cannot fill an empty layer with a pattern if you have the Preserve Transparency checkbox selected. Although this is obvious if you think about it, you might not notice the setting of the Preserve Transparency checkbox and wonder why the program isn't working. (I found this out the hard way, of course.) Also, if you're filling a specific area in a layer that does have Preserve Transparency on (such as the text shape), your preview is likely to be "viewing" some other spot in the image and showing you a blank white preview. The program is doing everything you told it to do—it just isn't looking at the spot you're filling. If you don't see what you expect to see, you can scroll the Preview box by clicking on it and dragging to a new location to preview.

Figure 5.47

You can set your shape attributes, such as Fill and Stroke, using the Set Shape Attributes dialog box.

Primitive Pennies: Putting Patterns Into Practice

You've experimented with a large number of ways to develop seamless patterns, but you've not yet done anything useful with the patterns that you've made. You need to remedy that. In the process, I also want to show you some tricks that might be less than obvious.

This project is really a series of tiny techniques with a put-it-all-together challenge at the end. My only regret will be that I won't be able to see *your* results to the challenge (unless, of course, you email them to me).

In the last section, I discussed creating "natural" patterns—one such natural pattern was the circular gradation that automatically creates a seamless pattern. That pattern, and the Litmus pattern that you created earlier in this chapter, form the basis for your experimentation. You already know how to create seamless patterns. By starting from these two common tiles, you can explore some techniques that you can use to add even more excitement to your patterns.

The first part of the project will show you how to overlap multiple patterns and scale factors as well as how to mix patterns and textures. The second half of the project challenges you to use these additional patterns to create a pleasing and unified image.

Counterfeiting Coins

Well, not *really*...there are laws against that. However, you'll manufacture and mint new varieties of "coins" (a baker's dozen of them) from the provided source images and use a number of techniques in the process. These should give you the urge to create even more variations. Here's my list of "rules" (for people who hate following any):

- *Variation Rule 1*—Get more mileage from your patterns by combining them using composite methods.

- *Variation Rule 2*—Any two seamless patterns when overlapped will form a third seamless pattern as long as one pattern has pixel dimensions that divide evenly into the other pattern.

- *Variation Rule 3*—You can turn patterns into paper textures and paper textures into patterns.

- *Variation Rule 4*—You can texture a pattern with a paper texture made from that pattern by using the Apply Surface Texture command Using: Paper.

- *Variation Rule 5*—You can mask a pattern file with a grayscale image of itself or of another pattern that has the same dimensions.

- *Variation Rule 6*—You can mask an image with a selection, and when you save the selection as a pattern, the mask is saved as well. You can then paint with that masked pattern using a pen or brush that respects the mask.

- *Variation Rule 7*—You can use the Apply Color Overlay and Dye Concentration commands to add subtle or dramatic color changes to an image without affecting the seams of the image if you apply the changes to the entire image.

- *Variation Rule 8*—You can use a pattern pen or create a brush that paints with the pattern as an alternative to using the pattern as a fill.

Each different technique in the project has its own project heading. Here are the first set of steps:

1. Open the files CIRCLE.PSD and LITMUS.PSD on this book's companion CD-ROM. These are similar to patterns that you created earlier in this chapter.

2. Load the COIN pattern library (COIN.PTL) from this book's companion CD-ROM (Art Materials: Pattern palette and select Pattern list menu|Load Library). This makes the COIN library your current pattern library. This is just a shortcut for you. The Litmus and Circle patterns are already defined for you. Figure 5.49 shows the variations. You might want to look at these in color before you start.

3. Clone both images before you start and use the clone versions as your "working" copies. You can leave the two original patterns open so that you can clone them again whenever you require a "clean" copy.

DRAG AND DROP WARNING

I repeatedly forget that Painter does *not* select the new image after I've dragged and dropped a selection into it. You need to keep this in mind as well; otherwise, you, too, will constantly be adjusting the image that you dragged *from* instead of the image that you dropped *to*.

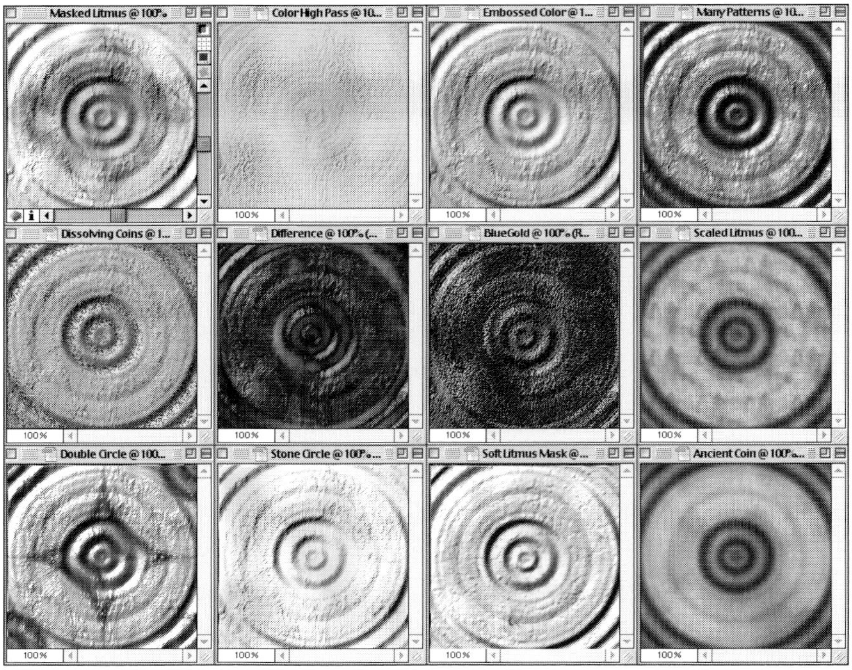

Figure 5.49
Variations of the Circle pattern in combination with the Litmus pattern.

PATTERNS AND LAYERS: A WARNING

Layers don't appear in captured patterns. There's no warning of this. If you capture a pattern and do not see the result you expected, don't blame Painter. Check first to see whether you've left a layer in the image. After you've done this a few times, you'll learn to drop your layers before you try to capture the pattern.

Ancient Coin

This subproject uses a Color composite method technique:

1. Make LITMUS.PSD the active image. Select the entire image (Command/Ctrl+A). Using the Layer Adjuster tool, drag the image into the CIRCLE.PSD image. Try out all the composite methods, but leave the layer in Color mode.

2. Choose Objects: Layer Palette menu and select Drop All. Select the image and capture it as a pattern. Name the pattern Ancient Coin.

Coin Paper

This is a "paper-from-a-pattern" technique:

1. Select the original CIRCLE.PSD image.

2. Select the entire image (Command/Ctrl+A). Choose Art Materials: Paper palette menu and select Capture Paper. Set Crossfade to 0. Name the texture Coin Paper. Now you have a texture from the original pattern.

3. Select|None.

Scaled Litmus

This is a project in scaling:

1. Click on the Art Materials: Pattern pattern. Make Circle your active pattern. Choose Art Materials: Pattern palette menu and select Check Out Pattern. A copy of the Circle Pattern appears.

2. Choose File|Clone to copy the pattern to a new file. Close the original. (This is just so you can see how to use the Check Out Pattern command.)

3. Make Litmus your current pattern. Set the pattern scale to 25 percent.

4. Use the Eyedropper tool to select the dominating light-gold color in the wide ring of the circle as your current color. (This is needed later in the project.)

5. Click on New in the Objects: Layers palette to create a new layer. Make certain that the Preserve Transparency checkbox is not selected.

6. Fill the layer (Command/Ctrl+F; Fill With: Pattern). Because Litmus is the same size as the Circle pattern, and 25 percent divides evenly into 100 percent, your tile is seamless. Change the Composite Method setting to Color. Select and capture the pattern as Scaled Litmus. This is an intermediate pattern, although you can certainly use it "as is" if you like it.

Many Patterns

This is a project involving texture. Follow these steps:

1. Scaled Litmus should be your current pattern. Check out a copy of the pattern and clone it.

2. Set your current paper texture to Pavement. Choose Effects|Surface Control|Apply Surface Texture. Use the default settings.

3. Make Coins your current Paper. Choose Effects|Surface Control|Apply Surface Texture, Using: Paper. Use the default settings again.

4. Select and capture the pattern. Name it Many Patterns.

Dissolving Coins

This is a composite method technique:

1. Make Scaled Litmus your current pattern. Check out and clone a copy of the pattern.

2. Create a new layer in the image. Your current color should be the gold that you selected earlier. Make sure that Preserve Transparency isn't selected. Fill the image (Command/Ctrl+F; Fill With: Current Color). This creates a layer of solid gold in the image.

3. Choose Effects|Surface Control|Apply Surface Texture, Using: Paper. Turn the Shine setting down to 0, but otherwise, use the default settings. Choose File|Clone, but don't work in the clone. The clone is for a later technique. Save the cloned file to disk and name it DISCOIN.RIF.

4. Change the Composite Method setting to Dissolve and set Opacity on the layer to 66 percent.

5. Choose Objects: Layers palette menu and select Drop All. Select and capture the pattern and then save it as Dissolving Coins.

Difference

This is another use for the Many Patterns pattern:

1. Make Many Patterns your current pattern. Create a clone of the "checked out" pattern.

2. Make the LITMUS.PSD image active. Choose Select|All. Choose the Layer Adjuster tool and drag the layer into the clone of the Many Patterns image.

3. Choose Effects|Tonal Control|Adjust Colors. Drag the Saturation slider all the way to the left to remove the color from the layer.

4. Change the Composite Method setting to Difference. Drop the layer; then save and capture the pattern. Name the pattern Difference. Undo the Drop command so that you have the layer back. You'll need it later. Save this step as DIFSTART.RIF.

High Pass

This creates another intermediate step:

1. Select File|Clone to create a clone of the Difference pattern.

2. Make Basic Paper your current paper. Choose Effects|Surface Control| Apply Surface Texture; Using: Paper. Use the same settings as before.

3. Select Effects|Esoterica|High Pass. Use a setting of 1.

4. Choose Effects|Tonal Control|Adjust Colors and set Saturation to 0.

5. Choose Effects|Tonal Control|Equalize. Set the black point to around 53 and the white point to about 43. You need to retain some gray values and enhance the detail in the image until you can see some of the original coin texture.

6. Change your Current Color setting to HSV: 48%, 60%, 65%. Select Effects| Surface Control|Color Overlay; Using: Image Luminance, Hiding Power.

7. Save this step as HIGHPASS.RIF. You'll return to it in a minute.

Blue Gold

This is an overlay technique:

1. Make the DISCOIN.RIF image active. It's the one you created in Step 3 of the "Dissolving Coins" project. Make another clone of it for later and work in the original.

2. Drag the top layer in the DIFSTART.RIF image into the DISCOIN.RIF image. Drop the layer.

3. Make the HIGHPASS.RIF image active. Choose Select|All. Using the Layer Adjuster tool, drag the High Pass image into the DISCOIN.RIF image.

4. Make the DISCOIN.RIF image active. Change the Composite Method setting to Overlay.

5. Drop the layer; then select and capture the pattern. Name it Blue Gold.

Embossed Color

This is another color composite technique:

1. Make the clone of DISCOIN.RIF active.

2. Drag the High Pass image layer on top of it.

3. Change the Composite Method setting to Color.

4. Drop the layer; then select the image and capture the pattern. Name it Embossed Color.

Color High Pass

This is an esoteric technique:

1. Make Gold Dye your current pattern. This is a "freebie" in the Coin library. Check out the pattern. Select File|Clone and close the original.

2. Apply Effects|Esoterica|High Pass; 3.

3. Select|All. Capture the pattern and name it Color High Pass.

Masked Litmus

Here's a masking and texture technique:

1. Make the LITMUS.PSD image active. Choose File|Clone.

2. Select Effects|Tonal Control|Equalize. Accept the settings that appear.

3. Select Objects: Mask palette menu and select Auto Mask; Using: Original Luminance. Turn off the mask visibility icon. Click on the Load Selection button; Choose Replace as the method in the dialog box.

> **SECOND NOTICE!**
>
> When Painter clones an image, the new image is always the active image. When you drag a layer into a different image, Painter does not make the "dropped into image" the active image. I'm constantly confused and consistently apply effects to the wrong document. You need to train yourself to *look* to see which image is active before you apply an effect.

4. Using the Layer Adjuster tool, click on the selection to float it. Do *not* create a copy. This selection "pulls" part of the color from the background image. Change the Composite Method setting to Difference.

5. With the layer selected, choose Effects|Orientation|Free Transform. Drag the lower-right corner handle until it's in the center of the image. Then, drag the entire object to the center of the layer. Figure 5.50 shows this image.

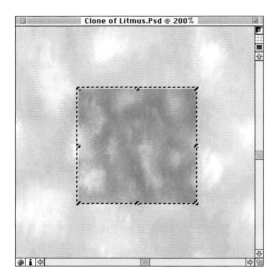

Figure 5.50
This shows the layer being scaled.

6. Select Effects|Orientation|Rotate and then rotate the layer 45 degrees. Use the Free Rotate command again, move the diamond to the upper-right corner, and drag the lower-right corner handle so that corners of the diamond shape touch the side edges of the background canvas.

7. Click on the Objects: Mask icon and select the layer mask in the Mask list. Choose Objects: Mask menu and select Feather Layer; 5.

8. Select the Canvas layer in the Objects: Layer palette.

9. Make the Pavement texture your current paper. Working in the canvas, choose Effects|Surface Control|Apply Surface Texture; Using: Paper. Use the default settings but change the Amount setting to 50 percent, Shine to 0 percent, and Softness to 1.3.

10. Make the Coin Paper your current paper. Working in the Canvas, choose Effects|Surface Control|Apply Surface Texture; Using: Paper. Use the same settings as before but bring the Softness setting back to 0 percent and the Amount setting back up to 100 percent. Save this file as MASKED.RIF.

11. Choose File|Clone. You'll come back to the MASKED.RIF image. Select and capture this pattern and save it as Masked Litmus.

Soft Litmus Mask

This is a variation on the prior theme:

1. Make the MASKED.RIF image active. Select the layer.

2. Choose Effects|Surface Control|Dye Concentration; Using: Image Luminance. Set the Maximum slider to 800 percent and the Minimum slider to 0 percent. This softens the color in the layer. Save this image as SOFT.RIF. You'll use it again.

3. Clone the image, select the clone image, and capture it as a pattern. Name the pattern Soft Litmus Mask.

Double Circle

This is a texture/pattern combination. You can combine pattern and texture, overlaying a pattern with a paper that uses the gray values of the pattern. If you offset the pattern before applying the texture, you get a different view. Here are the steps:

1. Make the CIRCLE.PSD image active. Choose File|Clone.

2. Choose Art Materials: Pattern menu and select Define Pattern. This turns the file into a pattern file that you can wrap.

3. Press and hold the Shift key and the spacebar. The cursor turns into a hand icon. Drag the image from the upper-left corner until the corner reaches the center of the image.

4. Make Coin Paper your current pattern.

5. Make the Pavement texture your current paper. Working in the canvas, choose Effects|Surface Control|Apply Surface Texture; Using: Paper. Use the default settings, but change the Amount setting to 50 percent, Shine to 0 percent, and Softness to 1.3.

6. Make the Coin Paper your current paper. Working in the canvas, choose Effects|Surface Control|Apply Surface Texture; Using: Paper. Use the same settings as before but bring the Softness setting back to 0 percent and the Amount setting back up to 100 percent. Turn Shine up as far as possible.

7. Select Art Materials: Pattern palette menu and select Add Image To Library. Name the pattern Double Circle.

Stone Circle

This is the last "standard" variation that you'll create. Follow these steps:

1. Create a new image that's 200 pixels square.

2. Make Coin Paper your current paper.

3. Make the Pavement texture your current paper. Working in the canvas, choose Effects|Surface Control|Apply Surface Texture; Using: Paper. Use the default settings, but change the Amount setting to 50 percent, Shine to 0 percent, and Softness to 1.3.

4. Make the Coin Paper your current paper. Working in the canvas, choose Effects|Surface Control|Apply Surface Texture; Using: Paper. Use the same settings as before but bring the Softness setting back to 0 percent and the Amount setting back up to 100 percent.

5. Drag the top layer from the SOFT.RIF image into the image. Choose Effects|Orientation|Rotate; -45 degrees.

6. Choose Effects|Orientation|Free Transform, move the square into the top-left corner of the image, and scale the layer until the layer covers the entire surface of the image.

7. Change the Composite Method setting to Shadow Map and set Opacity to 30 percent.

8. Select Art Materials: Pattern menu and select Add Image To Library. Name the pattern Stone Circle.

You now have 12 different pattern variations on a theme that you can use in the next project.

Masked Patterns

You were promised a "baker's dozen" of patterning techniques, so here's one more. In this project, you'll learn how to create a pattern with a built-in mask. I'm indebted to Liz Mitchell again for bringing this technique to my attention. Here are the steps:

1. Check out copies of your favorite three or four patterns of the dozen that you've just created, and then clone them and close the originals.

2. Make the LITMUS.PSD image active and choose File|Clone. This clone is your working image in which you'll build the masked pattern.

3. For each of the patterns that you've check out, make an irregular selection with the Lasso tool. After you create a selection, use the Layer Adjuster tool and drag the selection into the working image. Each selection appears as a new layer.

4. You may arrange the selections in the working image however you prefer. You can also click on the layer with the Option/Alt key pressed to make duplicates that can be moved separately. I finished this step with five layers from three patterns. Figure 5.51 shows my layered image before I built the mask.

5. Press the Shift key and click on all the layers in the Objects: Layers palette to select them. Group the layers (Command/Ctrl+G). Click on the Collapse button in the Objects: Layers palette.

6. Choose Objects: Layer palette menu|Drop And Select. All the "droppings" are selected.

7. Choose Art Materials: Patterns palette menu and select Capture Pattern. Name the pattern Masked. The pattern is added to the library and the selection is preserved.

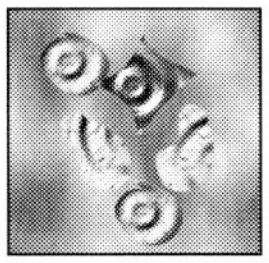

If you fill with this pattern, you'll not get a seamless pattern, as you can see in Figure 5.52. Although the base pattern (LITMUS) was seamless, when you save a selection, the pattern rectangle only includes the selected areas.

You can use the pattern, however, with a masked pattern brush. This is new to Painter 6, and Rhoda has discussed the pattern brushes in Chapter 2. You can use the Pen brush with the variant set to Pattern Pen, Masked, to try out this brush.

Create a new image that's at least 600 pixels square. Make the Masked pattern your current pattern and just randomly paint to see what happens. Figure 5.53 shows my "not terribly artistic" scribbling with the pattern pen masked brush.

Figure 5.51
You can drag selections from various patterns into your working image.

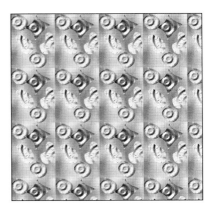

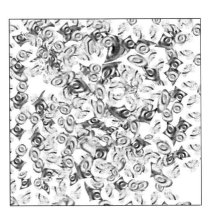

Figure 5.52
(Left) You might not want to use a masked pattern as a fill.

Figure 5.53
(Right) You can use the Pen brush with variant set to Pattern Pen, Masked, to paint with a pattern that contains a mask.

PROJECT Kimono My House

After the huge set of instructions in the last project, I think you need a break. The instructions for this project are quite short. You have a shape—a Japanese kimono shape—and all the pattern variations that you created. Your task is to develop a pleasing composition from these variations and place the patterns within the kimono however you like.

Here are some additional tips for applying the patterns:

- *Tip 1*—You can paint randomly with the pattern by using a pattern to fill an image and then designating that image as the clone source to the kimono. When you select a Cloner brush variant, select the Brushes palette menu|Controls|Random and click on Random Clone Source in the Advanced Controls: Random palette.

- *Tip 2*—You can also paint with the new pattern brushes. They will twist and distort the pattern as you paint. Of course, you can also paint with them in a clone source image and use a different Cloner brush to add them to the kimono image.

- *Tip 3*—You can save any pattern variant as a Paper texture and apply surface texture to the original pattern using Paper as the setting. Then you can resave the pattern using a different name. Use this textured pattern as your fill (or save it as a paper texture).

- *Tip 4*—You can apply both texture and/or a pattern from a clone source, which gives you very fine control over what appears in the image. You can even use the Super Cloners with the kimono.

Here are the steps to follow:

1. Open the image KIMONO.RIF on this book's companion CD-ROM. This image contains only a mask (defined in the Objects: Mask List palette). The mask should be visible as a red overlay. If it's not, click on the visibility icon next to the mask name in the Objects: Mask List palette.

2. Using the mask as your guide, decide which patterns you want to use and where you want to place them. Use the Rectangular Selection tool to choose an area on the image (it need not be precise). Click on the Load Selection button in the Objects: Masks palette. Load the New Mask 1 selection and click on the Intersect With radio button in the Load Selection dialog box. Your selection now conforms in shape to the kimono. You can fill the canvas or you can create a new layer by clicking inside the selection with the Layer Adjuster tool. If you select the Preserve Transparency checkbox before you fill with the pattern, the pattern will only color the desired area of the layer.

USING A LAYER FOR THE KIMONO

You can do all your painting inside a layer if you prefer. Load New Mask 1 as a selection and click inside of it with the Layer adjuster tool. This makes the entire kimono one layer. Select the Preserve Transparency checkbox on the Objects: Layers palette.

3. Fill the selection with any of the pattern variations. Change the scale as you desire before filling the layer.

4. Either drop all the layers or clone the image. The first option makes the image permanent. The latter option allows you to go back and fiddle with the image if you're not happy with your results.

5. Once your image is flat, you can continue to overlay patterns until you're satisfied. Figure 5.54 shows my "no-brainer" version. It's deliberately uninspired, though adequate, so that you can use your own creativity in this project.

You can, of course, paint with the patterns as well. Figure 5.55 shows the same example. This time, however, I used the Pen brush with the variant set to Pattern Pen and Pen brush with the variant set to the Pattern Pen, Masked, to paint on the kimono (with the mask loaded as a selection to keep my painting "within the lines"). You can change the size of the pen as you paint, which automatically scales the pattern with which you're painting. I also reduced the COIN paper to 25 percent scale and applied it as surface texture in the final step of the process to unify the composition.

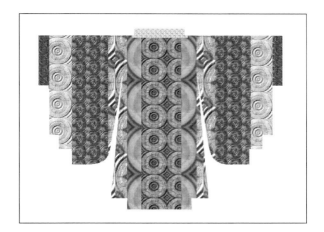

Figure 5.54
Kimono My House shows you a variety of ways to use the patterns that you created to fill selections.

Figure 5.55
The kimono looks quite different when it's painted, rather than filled in rectangular sections.

Moving On

It may be difficult for you to believe this, but there are a number of patterning techniques that I did *not* cover in this chapter. Exploring patterns can easily be a life-long journey, and the search for patterns can become an obsession. Look around you. Notice pattern. See how it's used and where it's used. Find unlikely places to use the patterning techniques that you've learned.

This chapter has shown you how to create simple block repeats, dropped and bricked repeats, and diaper patterns. You have not experimented with one-quarter drop (patterns that offset by only 25 percent) or random-drop patterns (where there are multiple offsets in the repeat), but you should have enough knowledge now to create and use them anyway.

You've explored a number of ways to make patterns seamless. You've even seen ways to use the pattern seams. In addition, you've learned many techniques for adding variety to the pattern elements that you created. I hope you'll never again (or almost never) simply drag a marquee around an area or object and call it a pattern. There's much more to it than that.

In the next chapter, Rhoda will teach you how to use Painter to create a variety of collages and collage effects.

PAINTER STUDIO

Turn to this section to see color images from selected projects. Follow the figure numbers back to the chapters to find step-by-step instructions. Additional images (those without numbers) are original to the Painter Studio. These images showcase exceptional solutions to the book's projects by Painter students as well as Painter effects created by the authors.

Chapter 1: Basics

In the first chapter, you meet Painter's new look, new brushes, and the new layers facility, which replaces the program's old Floater feature.

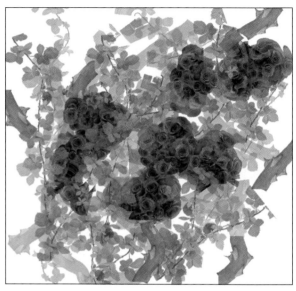

Figure 1.20

Use Painter's Image Portfolio to store the elements you want to reuse. Drag the elements into your image as layers and position and group them. Then, add a drop shadow to the entire group.

Figure 1.21

Painter 6 ships with a variety of Brush Looks, such as these roses, thorns, and brambles. Use the Pattern Pen, Masked, to paint the patterns onto your canvas. The pattern elements stretch, twist, and turn to conform to your brush strokes.

Figure 1.29

You can use Poser software to create the base models for life sketches. This image incorporates tracing with Painter's Sharp Pencil variant, shading with Chalk variants, and "airbrushing" with the Soft Cloner.

Figure 1.30

In this magazine cover detail, Rhoda Grossman used Poser to combine the body types of a woman and a sumo wrestler to produce a model that she cloned and manipulated in Painter.

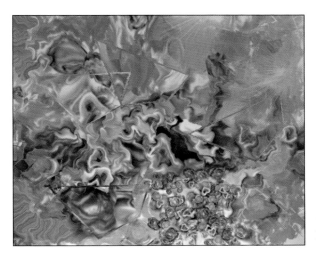

By experimenting with some of the new Image Hose features and a custom nozzle, Rhoda Grossman added distortions to this image. She used the new Shatter and Hair Spray variants.

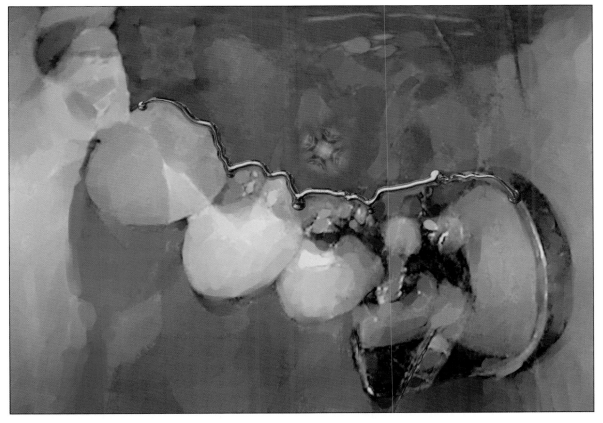

In an unusually intimate self-portrait, Rhoda Grossman scanned a print made during some reconstructive dental work and used several painterly techniques and filter effects on it. The Dynamic Kaleidoscope and Liquid Metal Layers were also used.

Chapter 2: Brush Effects

The figures on these two pages demonstrate some of Painter's Natural Media brushes as well as some brushes that do not have traditional equivalents.

Figure 2.32
Use the new Gloopy brush to write with chocolate.

Figure 2.15
Experiments with the Piano Keys brush show increased color variation, changes in dab angle, random dab angle, and expression as a function of source image luminance.

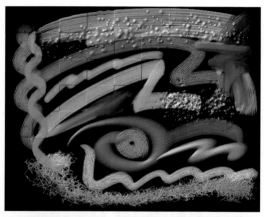

Figure 2.35
Use a sketch as a guide for painting on the Wet layer with Water Color brushes.

Painter's new Impasto brushes rely on a special depth layer. This Impasto painting shows the depth layer enabled (top) and disabled (bottom).

Figure 2.36
When the painting is finished, delete the Dry layer.

Vary the color in brush fibers by using Hue, Saturation and/or Value.

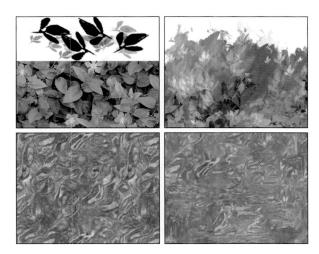

Figure 2.38
Create the Leafy brush from a captured dab, and then change it to a smeary brush and a brush for changing hue.

You can paint with a pattern or use the pattern as opacity input for painting with the color you choose.

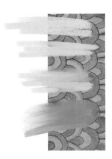

Figure 2.37
An Oil Pastel brush is made into a smeary brush by increasing the Bleed and reducing Resaturation.

Paint with a continuous gradient or with a gradient repeat to achieve a striped look.

The Pattern Pen can paint with or without the Pattern mask.

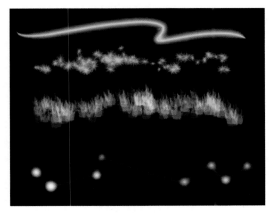

Many of the F/X brushes look especially good on a black background. Shown here are (from top) Neon Pen, Fairy Dust, Fire, and Glow with Continuous Time Deposition active.

The Impasto Pattern Pen is shown using the checkerboard pattern as the source of opacity. Pressure determines size.

Chapter 3: Send In The Clones

This chapter's cloning projects range from a series of seashell studies to renderings of photographs taken in Vincent van Gogh's neighborhood.

Figure 3.8 Re-create this scanned seashell as a painting in a variety of styles.

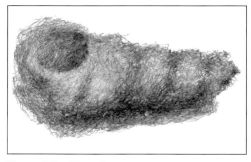

Figure 3.9 Fiber clone.

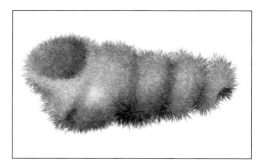

Figure 3.10 Furry clone.

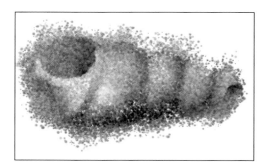

Figure 3.11 Splattery Clone Spray.

Figure 3.13 Melt clone.

Figure 3.14 Oil Brush clone on a smooth surface.

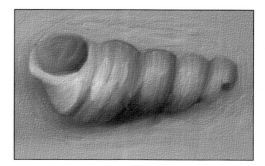

Figure 3.15 Oil Brush clone on canvas.

Figure 3.42 Felt Pen clone.

Figure 3.25
Use multipoint cloning to repeat part of an image at different sizes, angles, and locations.

Transform a photograph of a door into a watercolor painting by changing the default Water Color brushes into cloners.

Figure 3.29   **Figure 3.32**   **Figure 3.37**

Figure 3.26   **Figure 3.28**
A photograph of sunflowers on a chair is the source image for a painting that uses the Van Gogh Cloner.

Chapter 4: Paper Textures

You can make paper textures in many different ways and apply the textures to your images either with brushstrokes or by using the Add Surface Texture command.

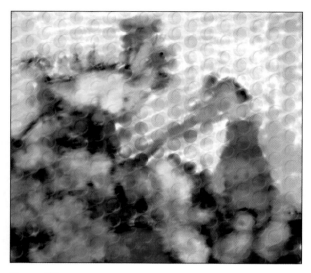

Figure 4.5
Paper textures can be very bold, as you can see in the circle texture shown here.

Figure 4.43
The Bulge brush works well with paper textures. In this case, a repeating text pattern is used as a paper texture.

Figure 4.32
Brush a paper texture created from a rhinoceros hide onto this water buffalo image.

Figure 4.36
Emphasize one area of the image with a different texture.

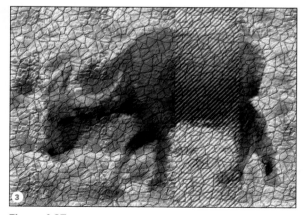

Figure 4.37
As a final addition to the water buffalo, add a third texture as an all-over effect to unify the image.

Figure 4.24

Create a paper texture by using the Make Paper Texture command and modify it repeatedly. Layer the textured images to create wildly textured variations on a theme.

Figure 4.41

Use text as paper textures. You'll find unlimited ways to work with these textures.

Figure 4.45

Take a photograph and create a stylized version using all of the techniques shown in Chapter 4.

Chapter 5: Patterns

Painter makes it easy to create patterns, and Chapter 5 teaches you how to create and use them. You'll learn a variety of new and unusual patterning techniques.

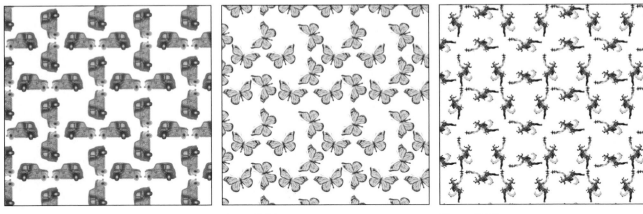

Figure 5.20   **Figure 5.21**   **Figure 5.22**

Arrange any element you want into a complex double pattern. The pattern can look completely different based on the shape and angle of the motif. These three examples use the same pattern arrangement, but you need to be knowledgeable to spot the repeats in the pattern.

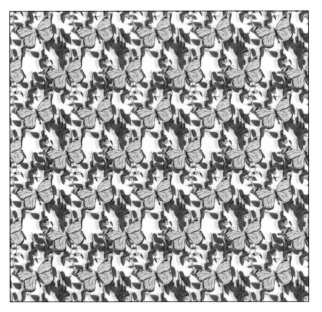

Figure 5.23

Change the spacing between the objects to create a different look, while still using the same pattern repeat system. Here, the jesters were moved closer together. The double-repeat of two adjoining motifs is more noticeable.

Figure 5.28

Create complex linked repeats in Painter by spraying imagery underneath a motif. Painter's wrap-around Pattern File makes this task simple.

Figure 5.30
Make a simple gradient seamless. Working in Painter's Pattern File, add brush strokes to change the gradient into a seamless, and more interesting, repeat unit. The repeat tile is not a sharply defined "object"; it is an amorphous painting that relies on color and placement.

Figure 5.31
Tile the repeat unit across a plane without showing seams. This type of pattern is difficult to achieve in other graphics applications, but Painter does it almost effortlessly.

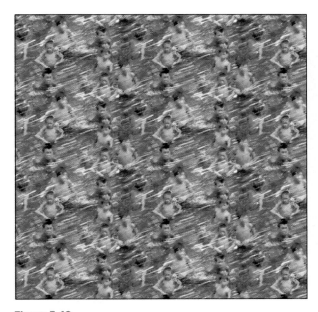

Figure 5.40
These boys began life as a photo taken in China by Ed Scott. Clone the image as a Pencil sketch. Then, define the image as a Pattern File, so you can clone over the image seams to make a seamless photographic pattern.

Figure 5.46
This seamless pattern finds a "natural" repeat by using a circular gradient to which the Twirl effect has been applied. It's made seamless by flipping the four elements that comprise the repeat, in the same way that tiles on a kitchen floor repeat without seams.

The three steps in the creation of seamless Painter pattern:

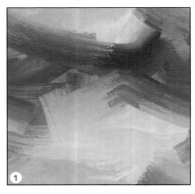

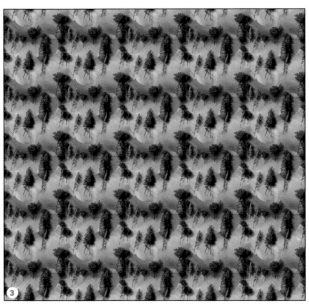

Figure 5.34
Use a dry brush to create the background of the pattern on the original tile.

Figure 5.35
Spray an Image Hose forest onto the pattern background in the next tile.

Figure 5.36
Work in a Pattern File to create a seamless tile. A Pattern File wraps the brush strokes as you paint and allows you to scroll the borders so they perform what Photoshop calls Offset With Wrap Around.

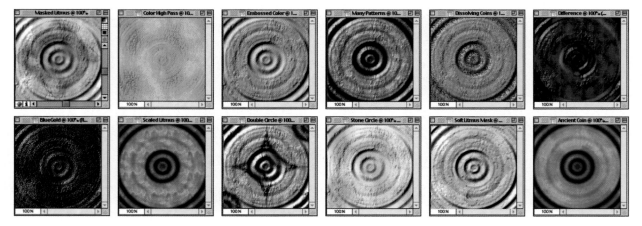

Figure 5.49
To create each of these variants on a circular gradient, take one element and change it. You have an almost unlimited range of pattern possibilities. These elements, although different, are related to one another and can be used harmoniously in the same composition.

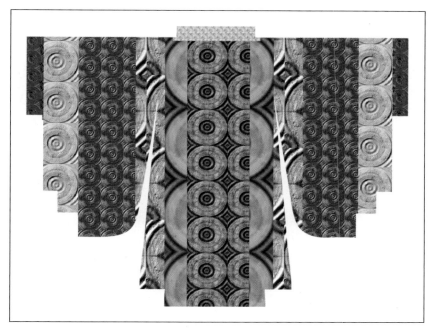

Figure 5.54

This kimono uses the pattern elements shown in Figure 5.49. Apply rectangular areas of the pattern to the outline of a kimono using the Fill With Pattern command.

Figure 5.55

Brush the pattern elements from Figure 5.49 onto the kimono using the Pattern Pen and the Pattern Pen's Masked brushes. The result is a more fluid and painterly kimono. Apply the circular motif paper texture with the Add Surface Texture effect to unify the composition.

Chapter 6: Collage

In Chapter 6's collage projects, you combine scanned objects and photographs in a variety of colorful ways.

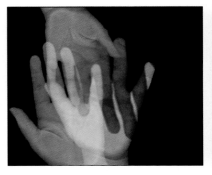  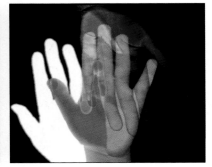

Figure 6.6
Use scanned hands to make a collage. Apply different composite methods to alter the way the layers combine.

Figure 6.7   **Figure 6.8**

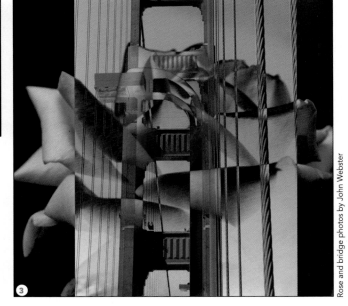

Rose and bridge photos by John Webster

Figure 6.9
Combine two photographs, which appear to have nothing in common, using composite methods. The art deco design of the Golden Gate Bridge (Figure 6.7) is combined with a rose in full bloom (Figure 6.8), using the Difference method to create Figure 6.9.

Background landscape photo by John Webster

Figure 6.18
Create a poster (such as this one for, perhaps, environmental conservation) from a collage of photographs and scanned objects.

Figure 6.20   **Figure 6.21**   **Figure 6.22**   **Figure 6.23**

Cats, rose, and house photos by John Webster are collaged in several ways to create a mystery novel cover. Using composite methods and manipulating transparency in the layer masks are the keys.

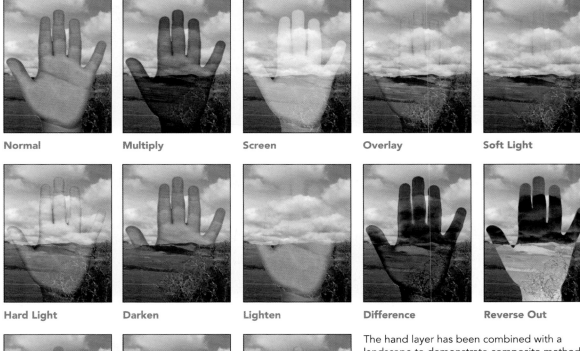

Normal   **Multiply**   **Screen**   **Overlay**   **Soft Light**

Hard Light   **Darken**   **Lighten**   **Difference**   **Reverse Out**

Saturation   **Color**   **Luminosity**

The hand layer has been combined with a landscape to demonstrate composite methods. Use these images as a guide for learning what to expect from each method. Results will vary, depending on the artwork you combine.

Chapter 7: Animation And Scripts

In Chapter 7, you create animations from brush strokes, apply scripted effects to movies, and make a movie sequence of still images.

Figure 7.16

Figure 7.17

Create a script to apply a series of commands to all movie frames. Here the smiley face is shown before and after a script makes the colors negative and adds glass distortion. You can apply scripted effects to still images, too.

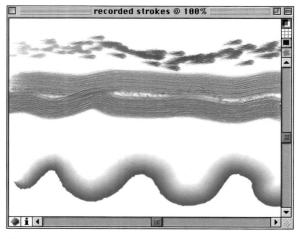

Figure 7.12

Record each of the brush strokes in the image window, and they are animated automatically.

Here's one frame from the animation based on Figure 7.12.

Figure 7.26
Make sets of Muybridge still photos, a woman dancing and a child running (below), into animation frame stacks. Use them as the source for rotoscoping, which allows you to draw, paint, or clone animations frame-by-frame.

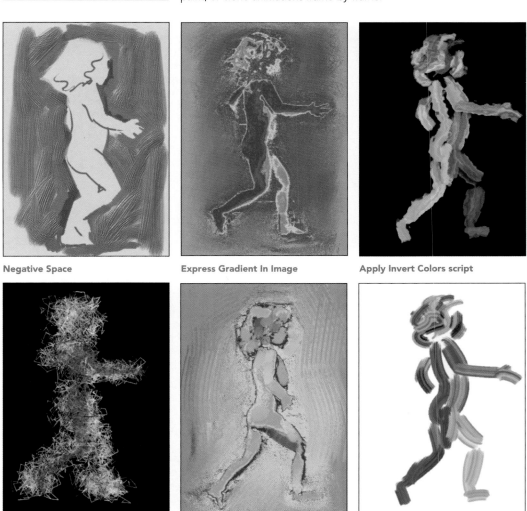

Negative Space

Express Gradient In Image

Apply Invert Colors script

Fiber Cloner

Smeary strokes in background

Van Gogh Cloner

Figure 7.20
A frame from the Muybridge running-child sequence shows the results of a variety of effects and techniques.

Chapter 8: Web Effects

A number of Painter features help you prepare images for the Web. In Chapter 8, you create images with very few colors, make embossed screen elements, and create screen links that change graphically when a mouse rolls over them.

Figure 8.7
This logotype is built with the help of the Posterize Using Color Set command.

Figure 8.8
Get a completely different look if you posterize the image first, and then posterize a second time using the Color Set.

Figure 8.11
The logotype contains even fewer colors when you apply a posterized gradient and a stroke to it.

Figure 8.14
The Gradients Express In Image command gives yet another look to the logotype.

Figure 8.16
Build your own graphic print brush to use the colors in the logotype.

Figure 8.27
In creating this plaque, you learn how to use the Bevel World dynamic layer command.

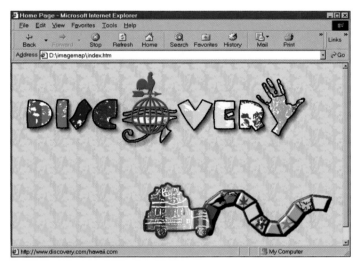

Figure 8.35
You can use Painter to create a complete Web page, including a patterned background, a logo, and an image map.

Figure 8.49
Create intricate tables to hold graphics, and then assign rollovers to these graphics with the Image Slicer dynamic layer.

Chapter 9: Dynamic Effects

Painter contains a number of dynamic layer effects that allow you to create effects and then modify them as often as you want without harming the image in any way.

Figure 9.2
The Burn dynamic layer lets you add distressed edges to images while retaining control over the shape, irregularity, color, and texture of the edge.

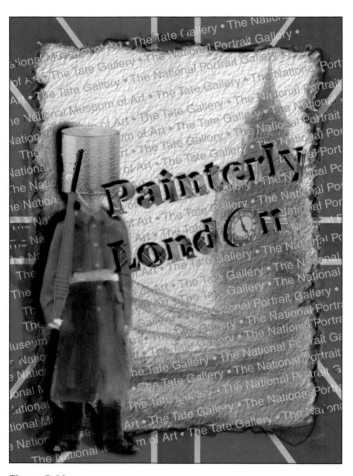

Figure 9.16
Sherry London used a watercolor image taken from photos of London, England, to create the burned edge on this postcard, which was part of Painter 6's prelaunch advertising.

Figure 9.15
You can also use the Burn dynamic layer to create effects that don't look burned. Apply the deckle on this sheet of rice paper with the Burn dynamic layer.

Figure 9.17

Kelly Loomis of 7rings.com created this delicate jewelry as linkware for the Web by using the Liquid Metal dynamic layer.

Figure 9.18

Create abstract shapes with the Liquid Metal dynamic layer, and then combine them with Bevel World layers to make wildly jeweled ornaments.

Figure 9.25

The Liquid Metal droplets reflect the following effects (from left): Standard Metal, Chrome 1, Chrome 2, Interior, and Clone Source.

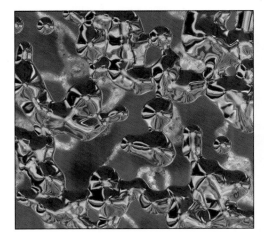

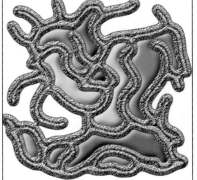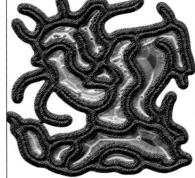

Figure 9.34

Finish your Liquid Metal imagery by adding embossed jewels. The jewels can be fashioned from the Bevel World dynamic layer (left), or you can use a third-party plug-in, such as BladePro from Flaming Pear (right).

Figure 9.27

The Liquid Metal dynamic layer can look like metal or water. Here, you make the droplets cling to the background image using the Rain button, but you can change them to reflect the interior view of the metal.

Chapter 10: Text Effects

In Chapter 10, you learn the basics of working with text in Painter 6. Then, you tackle a project to produce an alphabet composition that shows off your skills from A to Z. All the alphabet images on these two pages started with the same outline letter shapes.

Figure 10.13
Use the Neon Pen and Fire brushes to enhance text.

Figure 10.39
New Dynamic Text effects use colored shadow and Motion Blur.

Students at Foothill College in Los Altos Hills, Calif., created the solutions to the Alphabet project shown on these two pages. You'll find additional solutions to the Alphabet project on this book's companion CD-ROM.

© Laurie Aubuchon

© Roberta Faust

© May Madoka

© Carole Gleason

© Magda Elshimi

© Alyssa Sedmak

© Julie Wyeth

Chapter 11: Esoteric Effects

Painter contains a number of esoteric effects. Some of the effects resemble traditional craft techniques, such as mosaics and marbling.

Figure 11.10
Photographer Ed Scott took this picture in China. This image is used as the basis for creating mosaics.

Figure 11.14
In Painter, you can paint over any image and fill it with mosaics. You control the path, the size of the tiles, the colors, and the grouting.

Figure 11.18
Combine an image with a mosaic background, which you developed from a different image and made into a pattern. You can even make the pattern seamless.

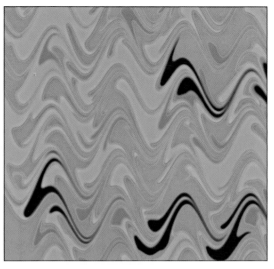

Figure 11.24
This image shows the first phase of the marbling process: creating a get gel (which means *to come and go* in Turkish).

Figure 11.27
Use the basic get gel and simulate the process of combing it with a fine comb to create a fanciful marbled pattern.

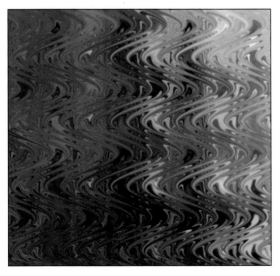

Figure 11.31
You can create and store marbling "recipes" so that you can use them on multiple images.

Chapter 12: Fine Art Techniques

Chapter 12's projects are based on traditional art school assignments. You practice eye-hand coordination, and work with basic shapes, such as blocks. The conventional still life is reinterpreted in some unconventional ways. You'll advance to sketching the human figure and finally to self-portraits.

Figure 12.4   **Figure 12.5**
A traditional study of a simple shape encourages you to see and render light and shadow.

Figure 12.28
Achieve the paper cutout style of this fruit still life by using color fills, applying paper textures, and adding drop shadows. Create the torn edge of the blue paper with the Dynamic Tear layer.

Figure 12.30
Rhoda Grossman created this gesture drawing by using a live model. With only a few minutes for this pose, she used the Oil Pastel variant and loose, rapid brush work.

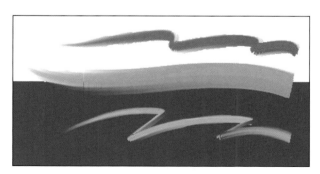

Figure 12.33
Painter's Sargent brush is named for painter John Singer Sargent.

Student Gallery: Cutout Paper

Rhoda Grossman's Painter students at Foothill College in Los Altos Hills, Calif., take the cutout paper assignment and run with it. This page and the next show samples of the imaginative work that can be done in this style. All work is copyrighted by the artists.

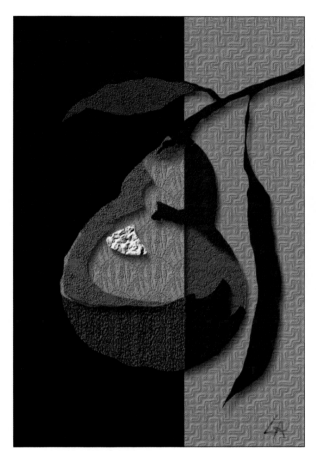

Pear
By Laurie Aubuchon

Landscape
By Buckley Duecker

Cat Resting On Blue Shawl
By Julie Wyeth

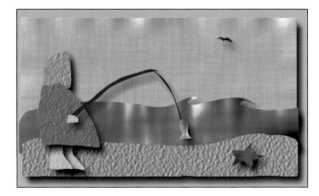

Girl Fishing
By Sheila Krakow

Bite The Hand

By William Bruner

Mice

By Roberta Faust

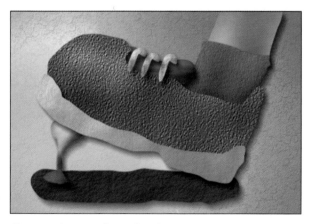

Chewing Gum Stuck To The Shoe

By May Nakayama

Self-Portraits

Chapter 12 provides several step-by-step techniques for creating portraits and self-portraits from reference photographs.

Figure 12.34
This project begins with a photograph reminiscent of a Rembrandt pose. The image's value and saturation have been adjusted.

Figure 12.37
Smudging with the Grainy Water brush on a clone copy of the image reduces detail and evokes a painterly look.

Figure 12.39
Paint the Impasto effect with the Smeary Varnish brush, one of Painter's many new brushes that function with a Depth Layer.

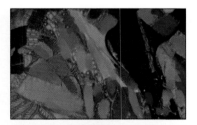

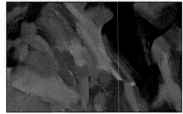

Figure 12.38
A detail of the colorful jacket shows some smudging strokes (top), and then the same section after adding Impasto effects (bottom).

Student Gallery: Portraits

Rhoda Grossman's Painter students used a variety of techniques in creating their self-portraits, including a hard-edge Trace-and-Fill style, Wet and Dry layers with Water Color brushes over a sketch, and mixed media techniques.

Judy McAlpin (Figure 12.40)

This line drawing was created with no breaks, so the Paintbucket could fill each section cleanly.

John Paga

Strong unrealistic colors were used in this drawing. The depth effects were made with Apply Surface Texture; Using: Image Luminance.

May Nakayama

Julie Wyeth (Figure 12.41)

Both artists used Wet and Dry methods. Lines were sketched with Pen or Pencil variants on the "dry" canvas. Then Water Color strokes, which automatically occupy a "wet" layer, were used. Either layer can be worked on without fear of harming the other layer.

Laurie Aubuchon (Figure 12.42)   **Tony Salguero**   **Nasser Ahmadiraof**

Students created these "mixed media" self-portraits by using some unexpected combinations of styles or effects.

Bill Bruner

The artist created a multiple self-portrait from a collage of photographs. He applied posterizing to reduce the number of colors, and then used Trace-and-Fill.

Sheila Krakow
This self-portrait has a simplicity and charm that manages to look "artless," although it was certainly well planned.

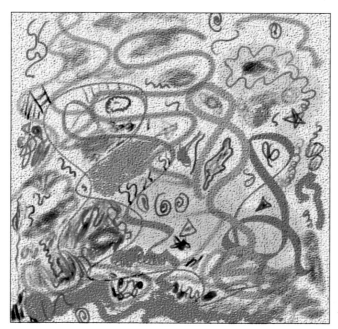

Kailin Lu
This seven-year-old artist used Painter and a WACOM tablet to create this in Rhoda Grossman's Cyber Studio at ZEUM, the Art and Technology Center for Children in San Francisco.

COLLAGE

BY

RHODA

GROSSMAN

Coming from the French word for "glue," collage traditionally refers to cutting and pasting bits of paper and printed matter into a composite. Painter allows you to do more than merely cut and paste. Using layers and masks, you can combine image elements seamlessly or blend them together in numerous ways to create a new image that's more than the sum of its parts.

E Pluribus Unum

That's the Latin slogan on the back of United States coins. It means "one out of many" or "money doesn't go as far as it used to." I'll use the first meaning, referring to the creation of one image out of many parts. The parts you'll need for these projects are on the CD-ROM that accompanies this book.

PROJECT Hands On Collage

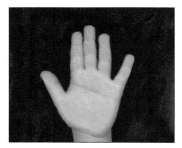

Let's make a simple collage of scanned images of children's hands. In the process, you'll use selection techniques, drag-and-drop maneuvers, and experiment with some composite methods. Here are the steps to follow:

1. Open the images MAXHAND.tif, shown in Figure 6.1, and TESSHAND.tif in Painter.

Figure 6.1
The scan of Max's hand.

2. Separate Tessa's hand from its background—use the Magic Wand tool to click on the black background. You'll see the "marching ants" surrounding the black area (see Figure 6.2). Use Select|Invert to reverse the selection so that the hand is selected instead of the background.

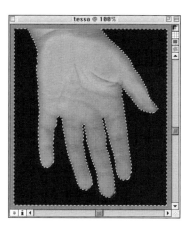

Figure 6.2
The black background around Tessa's hand is selected.

3. Use the Adjuster tool to drag Tessa's hand over to Max's hand and
    drop it. Tessa's hand becomes a new layer automatically. The new
    MAXHAND image is shown Figure 6.3.

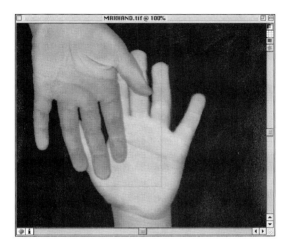

Figure 6.3
Dropping Tessa's hand onto
the MAXHAND image makes
a new layer.

Notice the thin, black horizontal and vertical lines showing on Max's
hand? These pixels came along with Tessa's hand as a result of my
forgetting a step in preparing for the Magic Wand selection. Of course,
I forgot on purpose in order to demonstrate how to avoid unwanted
pixel *schmutz* (as I call it).

UNWANTED EDGE PIXELS ON A LAYER

Look at the controls for the Magic Wand. The critical item for the moment is Anti-Alias, which is enabled by default.
Recall that anti-aliasing involves making a soft-looking edge, avoiding the dreaded *jaggies*, or the pixelated appearance of lines. You can't really soften pixels, so in practice this is accomplished by having a range of pixels whose colors
gradually blend into each other. For example, an anti-aliased black stroke on a white background will have some edge
pixels in varying shades of gray.

With regard to making selections, *anti-alias* means a soft-edged or slightly feathered selection. Pixels will be partially
selected near the edges. Therefore, with Anti-Alias enabled for the Magic Wand, your selection of the black background was only partial at the edges of the rectangular image window. When you inverted the selection, some of
those edge pixels were included with Tessa's hand. One solution is to disable Anti-Alias before using the Magic
Wand for removing an item from a solid background. Another is to use the Eraser tool to eliminate any unwanted
edge pixels.

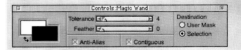

Magic Wand controls with Anti-Alias turned on.

Note: You can rename a layer by double-clicking on its name bar in the Layer list and typing any name you want in the Layer Attributes dialog box. This can help you avoid confusion when you have more than just a couple layers.

4. Use the Eraser variant to get rid of the black edges around the Tessa layer. Alternatively, delete the layer and redo Step 2 with Anti-Alias turned off in the Magic Wand controls.

5. Make another copy of the Tessa layer by holding down the appropriate modifier key (Macintosh: Option/Windows: Alt) and dragging the item to another location in the image. Notice your Layer list now shows two layers with the same name.

6. Reduce the size of the copy of Tessa's hand to about 80 percent. Use Effects|Orientation|Scale and type the percentage in the Scale Selection dialog box.

7. Repeat Step 5 so that you have a third copy of Tessa's hand. Use the original (full-size) layer.

8. Flip and invert the new layer, using Effects|Orientation|Flip Horizontal and Flip Vertical.

9. Arrange the layers so your image looks like the one shown in Figure 6.4.

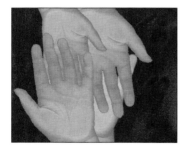

Figure 6.4
The hand collage has three copies of Tessa's hand with Max's hand in the background.

10. By default, all layers are fully opaque. Reduce the opacity of some or all of the layers by various amounts, using the Opacity slider in the Layers palette. The slider will adjust the opacity on the currently selected layer. One possible result is shown in Figure 6.5.

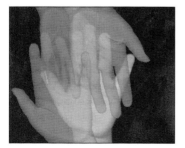

Figure 6.5
The hand collage is shown with layers at reduced opacity.

Twenty-One Flavors

There's more you can do with these hands, but first let's explore an exciting feature that has no equivalent in traditional collage—composite methods. When the Adjuster is the active tool, the Controls palette has a pop-up menu of 21 ways the current layer can be blended with the layers underneath it. Photoshop users will recognize most of these choices as *blending modes*. Your Painter 6 User Guide describes how each of the composite methods work, so I won't repeat that here. The visual examples in the User Guide leave something to be desired, so I've made a series of images using Max's hand as a layer on a landscape photo by John Webster. Take a moment now to examine composite method variations in this book's color Painter Studio.

Welcome back. The images in Figure 6.6 are all variations on the collage you've just made. Changing the composite method of a layer is a powerful technique. Even in grayscale, the differences are dramatic, but you should view them in color for the full effect. Here are the specific composite methods used in each of the variations (see whether you can figure out which layer was assigned each method, and try to produce the same effects in your collage):

• The left image in Figure 6.6 uses Screen, Lighten, and Multiply.

• The middle image uses Magic Combine, Gel, and Difference.

• The right image uses Reverse Out, Pseudocolor, and Hard Light.

One of the more fascinating challenges for a contemporary artist or designer is to take apparently divergent or unrelated elements and combine them effectively. Painter's composite methods can be the key to success. I chose two of John Webster's photographs that were as different as possible. His shot of the Golden Gate Bridge, shown in Figure 6.7, has bright saturated colors and the geometric lines of the Art Deco period. By contrast, the rose photo in Figure 6.8 has dark, muted colors and organic shapes. How can we put them together? In the imperative of a popular product for the feet, "Just do it!"

Figure 6.9 shows the bridge as a layer on the rose photograph. The composite method is Difference (one of my favorites). The Difference method subtracts

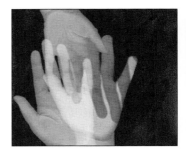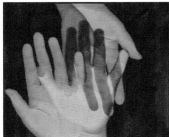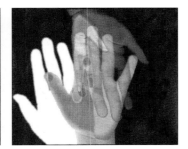

Figure 6.6
Three variations on the hands collage, using different composite methods.

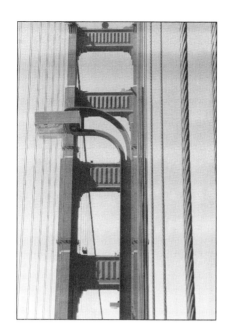

Figure 6.7
The Golden Gate bridge.

Figure 6.8
A rose.

Figure 6.9
A composite of the bridge and
rose using the Difference method.

one color from the other, depending on which color has a greater brightness value. This often produces surprisingly dramatic effects, as you can see. I cropped the image a bit, so the rose petals touch the edges of the picture. Sometimes it's just that easy!

PROJECT Surrealist Poster

Surrealism refers to the juxtaposition of realistically rendered images that could not actually occur in reality. The dreamlike paintings by Dali and Magritte are examples of this style. Your "handscape," used to demonstrate composite methods, will be developed into a kind of surrealist collage. You'll add more image elements, create drop shadows, and work with Painter's masks. Here are the steps:

1. Open HANDSCAP.rif and SCREW.tif. These images are provided on this book's companion CD-ROM.

   It won't be quite as easy separating the screw from its white background as it was getting the hands selected in the previous project. There are two areas of background to select, including the white inside the eye of the screw. Painter is supposed to allow you to add to selections in the way Photoshop does—by using the Shift key. I find this unreliable, though, so the following workaround might be necessary.

2. Select the outer background with the Magic Wand, as shown in Figure 6.10. Be sure Anti-Alias is turned off.

3. Use Save Selection in the Select menu. Click on OK in the Save Selection dialog box. The selection will be given the name New Mask 1 in the Mask list.

4. Select the portion of background inside the screw eye.

5. Use the Load Selection command, either in the Select menu or the Mask palette. Be sure to choose the Add To Selection button as the operation, as shown in Figure 6.11. Now the entire background is selected.

6. Invert the selection and drag the screw to the handscape collage. Give your new layer a descriptive name.

7. Open SHELL.tif. Yes, it's the same seashell you worked with in Chapter 3.

   The Magic Wand won't be much use for removing the shell from its background because they're so similar in colors and values. You'll remove the background in another way.

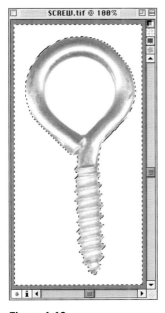

Figure 6.10
The screw's outer background is selected.

Note: The Save Selection command also appears as a button on the Mask palette. No surprise, if you think of masks as simply inactive selections.

Figure 6.11
The Load Selection dialog box is shown with Add To Selection as the chosen operation.

PHOTOSHOP PREFERENCES

Users of Adobe Photoshop might prefer to use that powerful program's elegant and sophisticated selection and compositing features to prepare an image for more enhancements in Painter. No problem. Just save the image in Photoshop format. When you open it in Painter 6, the layers will be intact.

8. Select all of the seashell image and drag it to the collage. Rename the new layer.

9. Resize the Shell layer to about 65 percent using Effects|Orientation|Scale.

10. Position the new items—shell and screw—so that the composite looks like Figure 6.12.

Figure 6.12
The screw and seashell are in position on the handscape collage.

Now it's time to eliminate the background on the seashell. You can simply use an eraser variant or paint on the layer's visibility mask. Every layer has such a mask automatically, and when the layer is active, its mask is available for manipulation. Masks need not be frightening except on Halloween. They won't seem so mysterious after a little examination.

Your collage has two layers with background pixels removed: the hand and the screw. Make either layer active by clicking on it with the Adjuster tool and open the Mask list on the Objects Palette. Make the mask visible by clicking the eye icon open. If you chose the hand layer, your image now looks like Figure 6.13. Black shows where pixels are fully opaque, and white indicates complete transparency.

Now activate the seashell layer and make its layer mask visible. This mask is a completely black rectangle, because the shell's background is part of the layer. All you need to do is make the background pixels white, by painting them with the brush variant(s) of your choice. You'll need to make the mask invisible again, of course, to see where to paint. Just make sure the mask is active (highlighted in the Mask

Figure 6.13
The layer mask for the hand
is visible.

list), as shown in Figure 6.14. Digital Airbrush or the Scratchboard
tool variant of the Pen tools are recommended for the next step.
Change the size of the brush as needed.

Figure 6.14
The Mask list shows that the mask
for the seashell layer is active.

11. Make the seashell layer active and click on its layer mask. Paint with
pure white over the background pixels to make them transparent. To
create the illusion that the screw is piercing the shell, paint two semi-
circles of white where the screw threads and the shell intersect (see
Figure 6.15).

Figure 6.15
The shell layer of the collage
is finished.

There's just one more major element to add: a bird perched on the
shell.

12. Open BIRD.tif, from a photo by John Webster. The file is on this book's
companion CD-ROM.

13. Use whatever selection techniques you need to separate the bird from its background. Then drag it to the collage. You could make a rough selection with the Lasso and then erase the unwanted background pixels later.

14. Select the seashell, screw, and bird layers by shift-clicking them in the Layer list on the Objects Palette. Then, group them by clicking the Group button below the list.

15. Select Effects|Objects|Create Drop Shadow. Accept the default settings.

    When you add a drop shadow to a layer, Painter automatically creates a group consisting of the layer and its shadow. Each can be manipulated independently. Just open the group and select either the layer or its shadow. You can easily nudge the shadow away from its layer, for example, to make the item appear to be farther away from the surface. Also, you can stretch the shadow out to give an item the appearance of 3D solidity. You'll practice these techniques in the next two steps.

16. Make a cast shadow for the bird. Open the group "bird and shadow" by clicking on the arrow to the left of the group's name on the Layer list. This allows you to select any part of the group. Select the shadow. Use Effects|Orientation|Flip Vertical. Then use Effects|Orientation|Distort to make the shadow appear to fall on the shell, as if light were coming from behind the bird. You might have to erase parts of the shadow or reduce its opacity to enhance the illusion.

17. The illusion of depth is spoiled by the screw shadow extending out beyond the hand. Erase that part of the screw shadow.

    Your collage should look something like Figure 6.16 at this point.

    Does it seem as though you're creating a poster on preserving endangered species? All you need is the message "Don't screw the environment!" And maybe you should make the bird look like he really means business.

18. Open MOUTH.tif and EYE.tif from this book's companion CD-ROM. Select|All of each image and drag them each to the collage. Position them as shown in Figure 6.17. Resize or distort as needed.

19. Erase unwanted parts of the eye and mouth layers. The finished collage is shown in Figure 6.18.

Figure 6.16
The collage shows all major elements and their shadows.

Figure 6.17
The collage detail shows the mouth and eye layers added.

Figure 6.18
The finished collage.

Seamless Blends

Unlike the hard edges of the layers in the poster you just made, many of the collages you see in print are composed of elements that merge seamlessly and fluidly with each other. The secret is working with the layers' visibility masks.

PROJECT Mystery Novel Cover

Your next assignment is to prepare artwork for a book jacket. Three photographs by John Webster are provided as source images. Here are the steps:

1. Open HOUSE.tif, CATS.tif, and ROSE2.tif in Painter. The files are available on this book's companion CD-ROM.

2. Select All and drag the entire CATS image to the HOUSE image, which will serve as the background.

3. Select All and drag ROSE2 to HOUSE.

4. Position your two new layers as shown in Figure 6.19. Reduce the opacity of each layer enough to see the background image so that you can begin to plan a composition.

Figure 6.19
The House with Cats and Rose2 layers, before blending.

5. Select the Rose layer and make the layer mask active. Use the Digital Airbrush to gently fade out the layer on the bottom and left so that it blends gently into the background.

6. Repeat Step 5 for the Cats layer.

7. Adjust the opacity of each layer. In Figure 6.20, my opacity is 85 percent for the cats and 75 percent for the rose.

Figure 6.20
The collage with layer masks manipulated for a seamless blend.

This collage could work well for a story about a house protected by cats—or maybe haunted by cats. Experiment to see whether you can make it look more eerie and mysterious. Experimenting with some composite method changes led me to the image shown in Figure 6.21. I switched from Default to the Gel method for the Cats layer. This made them merge more completely into the house and grounds. The composite method for the Rose layer was changed to Shadow Map, which darkened the sky considerably and minimized the cheery pinkness of the petals. A strange glow from the Rose layer remains on the façade of the house. This new version needed more tweaking in the layer mask to make different parts of the cats visible.

Yet another variation is shown in Figure 6.22. Using the Adjuster tool, I selected and moved the Rose layer so that its image appears in the lower foreground, and then I put the cats in the upper right area. I also applied

Figure 6.21
Another version of the collage with the composite methods changed.

Figure 6.22
The collage is shown with its layers in new positions and the colors of the house made negative.

Effects|Tonal Control|Negative to the canvas layer to invert the colors of the house. Additional changes to the visibility masks were made by using the Digital Airbrush at low opacity. Using white, I gently painted out some areas, and using black, I painted some areas back in.

There's literally no limit to the number of variations you can make to this image, even though it only has three elements. When you consider choosing from 21 composite methods, altering the visibility masks, changing the opacity, size, and position, and even applying special effects to one or more of the elements, the possibilities are endless. Some of my students have told me that they can become overwhelmed by so many choices. My advice to them—and to you—is simple: One variation at a time.

Just one more variation (I promise). To create the combination in Figure 6.23, I switched the Cats layer to the Gel method, making the white cat nearly

Figure 6.23
Another variation of the collage shows dramatic color changes.

invisible, although you can still see the dark parts of its face against the house. The deep magenta color of the rose is not a function of a composite method but rather the result of using Effects|Tonal Control|Adjust Colors to increase saturation and reduce value (brightness), along with shifting the hue slightly towards blue. I also used Adjust Colors on the house, after applying the Negative effect. The settings for Hue Shift, Saturation, and Value for both of these manipulations are shown in Figure 6.24.

Moving On

You've learned several techniques for combining two or more images successfully in a collage. You practiced using composite methods and working with the visibility masks for layers. I hope you can learn to manage the challenge of having so many possibilities available at your fingertips. And now for something completely different (but just as fascinating)—animation and scripts in Chapter 7.

Figure 6.24
The Adjust Color dialog box shows the settings for changing the Hue, Saturation, and Value settings of the Rose layer and the house.

ANIMATION
AND SCRIPTS

7

BY

RHODA
GROSSMAN

*Make traditional cartoon animations, create abstract
movies, or add special effects to existing movie clips.*

Animation Basics

Painter's animation capability is based on the model of traditional cel animation. Individual frames are literally stacked in perfect alignment, with an option for the number of translucent layers (called *onion skins*). You can create cartoon animations—line drawings whose motion can be simulated by making small changes from one frame to the next. Any image can be used as a background.

The File|New command gives you a choice between an image and a movie. In addition to the dimensions, resolution, and paper color, you also specify the number of frames. After you click on OK in the New Picture dialog box, you're given a dialog box for naming your movie and choosing a location for saving it. Then the New Frame Stack dialog box appears, with choices for the number of onion skins and the storage type. After that, Painter creates the frame stack and provides the Frame Stacks control panel, shown in Figure 7.1, for maneuvering between frames as well as playing and stopping your movie.

> **Note:** You can add blank frames at the end of your movie with the frame advance button in the Frame Stacks control panel. If you create a movie with only one frame and add more frames as you go, you can avoid the occasional false error message from Painter saying that there is not enough room on the disk to create the animation.

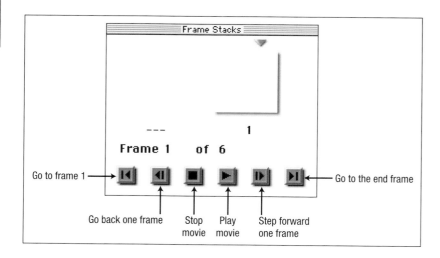

Figure 7.1
The Frame Stacks controls.

PROJECT Toon Man Walking

You'll make a simple animated loop of a cartoon guy walking. Use my primitive sketch, shown in Figure 7.2, as a model or create your own figure. Keep it simple. My guy has his hands in his pockets so that you don't have to work out the arm movements. Play the MANWALK movie on this book's companion CD-ROM to see my attempt at animating this fellow. The movements are about as primitive as the sketch, and small variations in his smile and the shape of his head add to the funky charm of the piece. Not too bad for five minutes of work. Now, here are the steps to follow:

1. Make a new movie that's 500 by 300 pixels at 72 dpi, with white paper and five frames.

Figure 7.2
The cartoon man animation starts with a sketch.

2. Choose five layers of onion skin.

3. Draw the man in the first frame, using a Pen or Pencil variant.

4. Turn on Tracing Paper and step forward to Frame 2.

5. Trace the head and upper body of the character and draw the legs in the next position. Repeat until you've completed all five frames.

   With Tracing Paper on and five layers of onion skin, you'll see a faint image of each preceding frame while you work on the current frame. By the time you get to Frame 5, shown in Figure 7.3, it should be easy to see whether any of the leg positions need to be redrawn in order to get a smoother animation.

6. Play the movie.

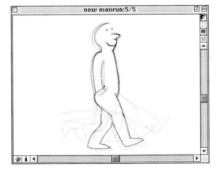

Figure 7.3
All five layers of onion skin are showing, with Frame 5 as the current frame.

Moving The Background

Your "manimation" is walking or running in place. He'll appear to move forward (from left to right) if you add a background that moves from right to left. If you want to use the FENCE movie provided on the accompanying CD-ROM as a background, skip to the next section, "Combining The Background With The Cartoon Character." Otherwise, create the FENCE movie yourself, as follows:

Note: When there's no image designated as the clone source, the Paint Bucket tool automatically uses the current item in the Pattern library.

1. Make a new image that's 650 by 300 pixels.

2. Use the Paint Bucket tool to fill the image with the Picket Fence pattern. The currently selected pattern on the Objects/Patterns palette must be Picket Fence, and the Controls|Paint Bucket settings must be What To Fill: Image, Fill With: Clone Source.

3. Select All and copy the image.

4. Make a new movie with the same dimensions (500 by 300 pixels) and number of frames (5) as the MANWALK movie.

5. Use Edit|Paste on Frame 1 of the new movie. The picket fence image will appear as a new layer. Align it with the left edge of the frame.

6. Use the Drop command in the Layer menu to flatten the image in Frame 1. Figure 7.4 shows Frame 1 with the Picket Fence layer pasted and aligned.

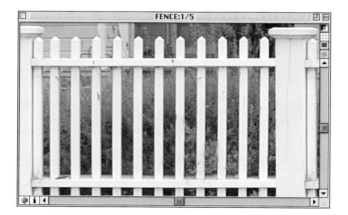

Figure 7.4
Frame 1 of the picket fence background.

7. Use the Frame Stacks controls to step forward to the next frame.

8. Paste the image again and move it slightly to the left of its position in the previous frame. Drop the layer.

9. Repeat Steps 7 and 8 until all frames are filled.

10. Play the movie.

Combining The Background With The Cartoon Character

For this part of the project you'll use the picket fence movie you just made or the FENCE movie provided on the CD-ROM that accompanies this book. You'll use cloning techniques to combine both movies (refer to Chapter 3 for cloning basics).

1. Open both the FENCE movie and the MANWALK movie.

2. Make the FENCE movie the active document and use the Set Movie Clone Source command in the Movie menu. This creates a frame-by-frame correspondence between the source movie (FENCE) and the destination movie (MANWALK).

3. Choose the Soft Cloner variant of the Cloners brushes.

4. Paint on Frame 1 of the MANWALK movie. Use a larger brush size for quickly filling in most of the frame, and a smaller size when you paint close to the man.

    Figure 7.5 shows Frame 1 finished. Notice that the bottom of the fence has an irregular edge with some white space remaining. This will give the illusion of snow on the ground so that the man will not be floating in space.

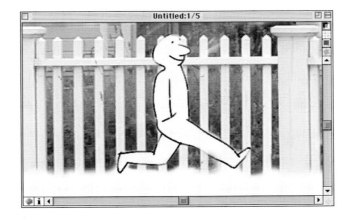

Figure 7.5
The background cloned into Frame 1 of the cartoon.

5. Go to Frame 2 of MANWALK. Frame 2 of FENCE will step forward automatically.

6. Repeat Steps 4 and 5 until all frames are complete.

7. Play the movie.

Experimental Animation

Animating with Painter 6 is not limited to traditional techniques. The power of Painter's effects and scripting capabilities give you many possibilities for experimentation.

Painter lets you open a series of single images as a frame stack. The image content can be anything. These images can be identical or vary in such a way that when played back they make a kind of flip-book animation. All the images must be the same size and numbered in order. In this section are several opportunities for you to practice creating and loading stacks of numbered files and animating them.

Figure 7.6

Here's the original photo
of Anthony.

PROJECT Photo-mation

Let's begin with the photo ANTHONY.tif shown in Figure 7.6.
Now, follow these steps:

1. Open ANTHONY.tif in Painter.

2. Use File|Save As to name the image Face01.

3. Repeat Step 2 until you have four identical images of Anthony—
   named Face01, Face02, Face03, and Face04.

4. Use File|Open and check the Open Numbered Files box. You'll be
   prompted to find the first and last images in the sequence. Name your
   movie when the Save dialog box appears and then click on OK in the
   Frame Stack dialog box.

   The frame stack will appear in a moment, along with the Frame
   Stacks controls. Now you're ready to apply some distortion effects to
   Anthony's face. Let's make him squint.

5. Begin on Frame 2 and use the Pinch variant of the Liquid brush to
   reduce both eyes slightly.

6. Step forward to Frame 3. Increase the amount of Pinch until the eyes
   are so tiny they're nearly gone, as shown in Figure 7.7.

7. Step forward to Frame 4. Use Pinch to make the eyes about the same
   size they are in Frame 2.

8. Play the movie.

Painter plays the frames as a continuous loop, so you should see the eyes
blinking and opening constantly. You can add additional distortions in a
similar way. How about using the Bulge variant on his nose or stretching out
his smile with the Thin Distorto brush? Open and play the ANTHONY movie

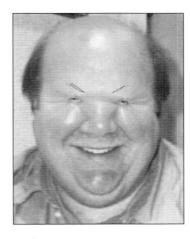

Figure 7.7
Anthony squinting.

on the CD-ROM that accompanies this book to see my friend with several facial tics. Imagine what I could do to somebody I don't like!

Abstract Animation

The content of an animation need not be recognizable objects or creatures. The style doesn't have to resemble something coming from Pixar or the Disney studios. Anything that changes systematically from frame to frame can be considered an animation. The subject of an animation can be movement itself. In this section, you'll experiment with that concept by creating movement with only a gradient fill. You'll also create movement by simply changing the tool used for making a recorded stroke. Finally, you'll explore Painter's new feature for animating a brush stroke.

 Neon Spiral

Let's create a short movie that gives the illusion of spinning toward or away from the viewer. Open and play the movie SPIRAL, which is on this book's companion CD-ROM, to see what you're aiming for. This sequence was created by filling each successive frame with a gradient. The trick is to move the angle of the spiral systematically between fills. Follow these steps:

1. Make a new movie of 12 frames that's about 400 by 300 pixels at 72 ppi. Use white for the paper color and choose the minimum number of onion skins (2).

2. Select one of the new glowing gradients: Orange Neon, Argon Tubing, Purple Gas, or Kryptonite Gas.

3. Change the default style of the gradient to a spiral or double spiral and set the angle ring to 0 degrees, as shown in Figure 7.8.

4. Use Effects|Fill on Frame 1, as shown in Figure 7.9.

Figure 7.8
The Argon Tubing Gradient is in a double spiral, with the angle ring at 0 degrees.

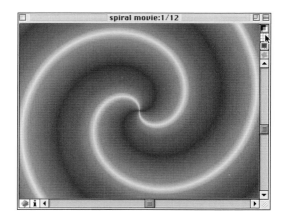

Figure 7.9
A gradient fill in Frame 1.

5. Rotate the angle of the spiral 30 degrees (360/12 frames).

6. Step forward to Frame 2 and repeat the Fill command.

7. Repeat Steps 6 and 7 for each successive frame.

8. Play the movie.

Your spiral should move smoothly if you used equal angle changes. Moving the angle ring clockwise will make the spiral appear to move toward you, and moving the angle ring counterclockwise will have the reverse effect. (It's just the opposite in the Southern Hemisphere, of course.)

PROJECT Recorded Stroke Effects—Purple Heart

Play the movie PRPLHART on the CD-ROM that accompanies this book. This animation's motion depends on random variation and inaccuracy rather than precision. You'll use Painter's Record Stroke and Playback Stroke commands to make a heart shape wriggle and jiggle. Follow these steps:

1. Make an eight-frame movie that's 200 by 200 pixels, with black as the paper color.

2. Choose the Van Gogh variant of the Artists brush family and a rich saturated purple in the Color palette.

3. Enable the Record Stroke command. It's in the Stroke menu on the Brushes palette.

4. On Frame 1, paint a single stroke shaped like a heart, similar to Figure 7.10. It's important that you paint the heart in one stroke, because the Record Stroke command can only record one stroke at a time.

5. Step forward to Frame 2 and turn Tracing Paper on.

6. Enable the Playback Stroke command in the Stroke menu on the Brushes palette.

Figure 7.10
A heart-shaped stroke made with the Van Gogh variant.

7. Click close to the pixel that corresponds to the beginning of your recorded stroke. The same heart shape will appear on Frame 2. Repeat this for all the frames in the stack.

8. Switch to the Turbulence variant of the Liquid brush family.

9. Return to Frame 1.

10. Continue using the Playback Stroke option, allowing the click point to vary slightly as you step forward and repeat for each frame. Figure 7.11 shows a frame after the Turbulence stroke is applied.

11. Play the movie.

> **Note:** Because there's hue and value variability built into the Van Gogh variant, each time you play back the stroke, it will be slightly different in brightness and color.

Figure 7.11
A heart-shaped stroke with Turbulence added.

As The Worm Turns—Caterpillar Convention

Painter 6 allows you to animate recorded strokes. The movie WORMS was made with a few simple strokes that were automatically animated with the Movie|Apply Brush Stroke To Movie menu command. Play the movie on this book's companion CD-ROM to see worms hurrying about their business. Then create a similar movie of your own.

1. Make a new movie of 10 to 12 frames that's 400 by 300 pixels in size, with a white background.

2. Make a new image with the same dimensions: 400 by 300 pixels. You'll use this canvas to record brush strokes that will be applied to the movie. You can discard this image after your animation is finished, or you might want to save it as an abstract painting that stands on its own. In either case, it will be useful to help you determine where to paint new strokes for the movie.

3. Choose the Grad Pen variant of the Pens family and make a selection from the Gradient Library. I used the two-point gradient with purple and white as the primary and secondary colors, respectively.

4. Enable the Record Stroke command, found on the Brushes Palette under the Stroke menu.

5. Make a long squiggly stroke from left to right along the bottom of the canvas.

6. Make the movie your active document and use the Movie|Apply Brush Stroke To Movie menu command. Now watch Painter automatically divide your recorded stroke into as many segments as needed to span the frame stack.

7. Play the movie.

Note: The Impasto Pattern Pen variant paints with the current pattern. Overlapping Waves works well for this project, but you can experiment with other choices.

8. Choose an Impasto variant for your next stroke. Good choices include Opaque Round, Round Camelhair, and Impasto Pattern Pen.

9. Return to the single image and use Record Stroke again. Make your stroke extend the entire width of the canvas again, but this time draw from right to left, higher up on the canvas.

Repeat Steps 6 and 7. Add a few more worms with other brush variants. I used the Impressionist variant of the Artists brush to make a whole swarm of tiny worms with one stroke. Figure 7.12 shows all the strokes I recorded, and Figure 7.13 has the Frame Stacks controls with a couple of frames from the WORMS movie.

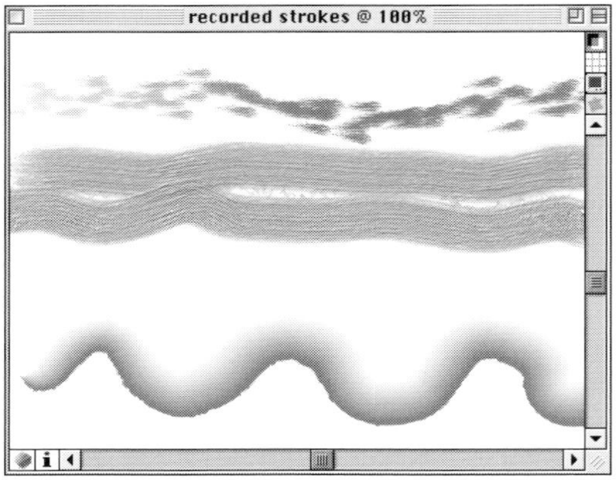

Figure 7.12
(Left) Strokes recorded to make the WORMS movie.

Figure 7.13
(Right) The Frame Stacks controls show the frames from WORMS.

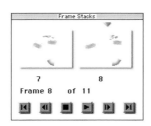

Animating recorded strokes works nicely with items sprayed from the Image Hose. Figure 7.14 shows a frame from the movie NOZFILM, which was created entirely with Image Hose nozzles. It's provided in the Movies folder on the accompanying CD-ROM.

Figure 7.14
A frame from the movie NOZFILM.

SAME STROKE, DIFFERENT BRUSH

You can repeat the same stroke using a different brush. This technique works especially well when Turbulence (a variant of the Liquid Brush family) is used as the second brush. For example, record a stroke with the Piano Keys variant of the F/X family. Use the Apply Brush Stroke To Movie command. Switch to the Turbulence variant, but do not record the stroke. Use the Apply Brush Stroke To Movie command again. When you play the movie, your Piano Keys stroke will be "turbulated."

Try this recorded stroke-repeat technique with the splattery variants: Leaky Pen, Spatter Water, and Fairy Dust. You can apply the same stroke over and over, with color changes if you want. The random scatter will give a rich layered look to the animation.

There is no limit to the number of strokes you can record and apply to a movie. Experiment with long and short strokes—fat, thin, straight, wiggly, spiked, sinuous, meandering, or random strokes. Change colors whenever you want to. Try some of the variants you seldom use or have never tried. The Nervous Pen is an excellent choice. This variant automatically makes a squiggly line. Increase the size to about 22 for a thick multistrand stroke that looks like the Fiber Cloner. The result of applying this stroke to your movie is a clump of lines that can vary from spidery to fluffy, depending on the pressure you apply to your graphics tablet.

Scripting Movie Effects

You can add one or more effects to a whole movie automatically by recording a script and using the Apply Script To Movie command.

Scripting Basics

Painter's script functions allow you to record every stroke in a painting for playback at any time. Script functions are located on the Object palette. Use the Record Script, Stop Recording Script, and Playback Script commands in the Script pop-up menu, or you can use the Record, Stop, and Play buttons, as shown in Figure 7.15. Let's practice making a script.

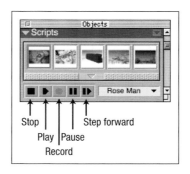

Stop   Step forward

Play Pause

Record

Figure 7.15

Button controls for script functions.

Note: The image size in Step 1 is just a convenient size; it was chosen arbitrarily. There's no need to worry about whether this size will be the same as the frame size of your animations.

Figure 7.16
Smiley face drawing.

Figure 7.17
Smiley face with the negglass script applied.

Figure 7.18
A frame from the WORMS movie after the negglass script was applied.

PROJECT A Script To Invert Color And Distort

You'll create a short sequence of commands to make colors negative and to add a distortion effect similar to looking through patterned glass. Follow these steps:

1. Make a new image that's about 300 by 300 pixels with white paper.

2. Choose any brush that can apply color. I used the Oil Pastel variant in the Dry Media family.

3. Select a bright red color and draw a big smiley face, similar to Figure 7.16. This will not be part of the script, but you need something to show the effects you'll record.

4. Enable the Record Script function.

5. Apply Effects|Tonal Control|Negative. This command inverts the color. Your drawing now has a bluish face on a black background.

6. Apply Effects|Focus|Glass Distortion, using Paper and the Refraction map option. Adjust the Amount slider, as needed, or change to a different paper to get the effect you like. Figure 7.17 shows my smiley face after Glass Distortion.

7. Stop recording and a Name The Script dialog box appears. I named it "negglass."

8. Make your caterpillar movie the active document (or use the WORMS movie on the CD-ROM that accompanies this book).

9. Select Movie|Apply Script To Movie. In the dialog box that opens, select the negglass script you just made and click on Playback.

Sit back and watch Painter automatically play back the script on every frame. Figure 7.18 shows one frame from the "postscripted" version of the WORMS movie.

PLAYING IT SAFE AND SAVING SPACE

You cannot undo the Apply Script To Movie command. Even when you're doing strokes and effects "by hand," when you go to the next frame, the previous frame is saved automatically. Therefore, make it a habit to save each version of a movie as a QuickTime/AVI file in order to keep from overwriting effects on movies you want to keep. Use Painter's Save As dialog box and accept the default Save Movie As QuickTime/AVI option. You must give the QuickTime/AVI version a new name in order to proceed. The Compression Settings dialog will appear. Accept default settings unless you have some reason to alter them. The QuickTime/AVI movie will be a tiny fraction of the size of your frame stack. After your save, you can continue working on the frame stack.

Another advantage of the QuickTime/AVI conversion is that the movie can be played by anyone with the proper movie player utility. However, double-clicking on a QuickTime/AVI version of your Painter movie opens it as a frame stack again, expanding to its original (uncompressed) size. You can continue working, using any of Painter's brushes and commands. Remember to save changes as QuickTime/AVI again, to conserve disk space.

Rotoscoping

Rotoscoping is a powerful, traditional technique for animating motion realistically. In the old days, before computers, it required shooting live action film of a subject engaged in the desired movements—say, a ballet dance. The film was developed and a projector capable of showing one frame at a time in perfect register (exact positioning) was focused on the animator's work table, where a stack of acetate cels, also in register, were ready for drawing. The animator advanced each frame in the rotoscope projector and sketched or inked the figure on the corresponding cel, thus, creating a cartoon version of the figure with no difficult "in-betweening" needed. The animator could change the figure to a completely different character, using the positions of body parts from the live action film for accuracy of motion. Remember the dancing hippos in the Disney movie? Rotoscoping the motion of a human ballerina was the secret of the hippos' graceful movements. Painter can emulate rotoscoping techniques.

Consider The Source

Painter's rotoscope capability is essentially a cloning activity. You designate a sequence of images as the clone source, and each frame of the sequence is linked to the corresponding frame of a blank movie that receives your drawing or cloning strokes. (Recall using a similar method when you added a background to your animated cartoon man, earlier in this chapter.) With Tracing Paper on, you can see enough of the source frame to draw on the blank frame that matches it. To enable the onion skins, click on the Tracing Paper icon on the edge of the image window or use the keyboard shortcut (Command/Ctrl+T).

PROJECT Muybridge Child Running

You'll create a series of rotoscoped animations using a sequence of photographs taken more than 100 years ago by the photographer Eadweard Muybridge. Figure 7.19 shows two frames from the Child series. The sequential photos provided on the CD-ROM that accompanies this book were scanned with permission from Dover's *Eadweard Muybridge: The Male and Female Figure in Motion* and prepared as a numbered series of digital files having exactly the same dimensions. Now, let's take the Child sequence and rotoscope the heck out of it!

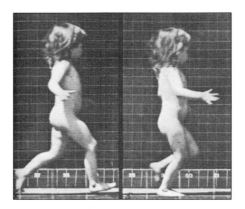

Figure 7.19
Two frames from the Muybridge Child sequence.

1. Load the Child images as a frame stack. Select File|Open and check the Open Numbered Files box. You'll be prompted to select the first and last images in the sequence. Navigate to the Numbered Files folder on the accompanying CD-ROM. Designate Child01 as the first image and Child12 as the last image.

2. After Painter creates the frame stack for you, use File|New to make a blank stack with exactly the same dimensions, resolution, and number of frames. You'll be prompted to name your new frame stack.

3. Make the Muybridge sequence the active document and enable Set Movie Clone Source in the Movie menu. This establishes each frame of the Muybridge photos as the clone source for the corresponding frame in your blank stack.

4. Make the blank stack active and turn Tracing Paper on.

   The hard part is deciding what brushes and techniques to use. Trace the edges of the figure with a pencil? Draw quick gestures with a thick brush? Use a different variant, color, and technique on every frame?

5. Draw or paint the figure in Frame 1, using whatever style(s) you like.

6. Step forward to the next frame. Painter automatically moves to the next frame in the Muybridge sequence.

Note: Find the pixel dimensions and resolution of any image by holding down the "i" at the lower-left corner of the image window.

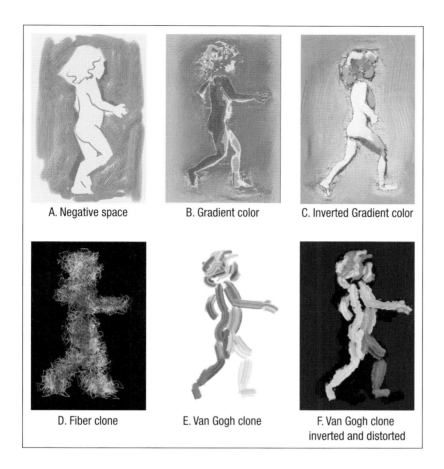

A. Negative space   B. Gradient color   C. Inverted Gradient color

D. Fiber clone   E. Van Gogh clone   F. Van Gogh clone inverted and distorted

Figure 7.20
Frames from the rotoscoped Child movies created with several techniques.

Repeat Steps 5 and 6 until you're finished with all frames. Then play your movie. Figure 7.20 shows several styles that might inspire you. Examine them in this book's Painter Studio. A brief description of the methods used to create each of the styles is provided.

Style 7.20: A. Negative Space

Using negative space refers to drawing what isn't there. The space around the figure in each frame was roughly filled in with a black Oil Pastel (Dry Media variant). Then a layer of warm brown was added with the Opaque Round variant of the Impasto brushes. Figure 7.21 and Figure 7.22 show the work in progress. As a finishing touch, just a few strategic lines were drawn with the Scratchboard tool to define the figure.

Style 7.20: B. Gradient Color

If you want to use Cloner variants to re-create the running child, you might want to add color to the frames first. Recall that Cloners use only the colors and values of the source image. My favorite way to add instant color to a gray-range image in Painter is to use the Express In Image command in the

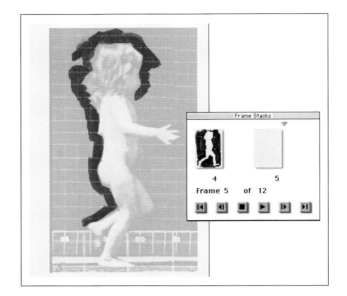

Figure 7.21
Frame 5 of Negative Space
rotoscope in progress.

Figure 7.22
Negative space painted with an
Impasto brush.

Gradient menu. You need to make a script to express the gradient colors in the entire movie. Let's re-create this movie step by step:

1. Open the original Muybridge sequence in the Child 1-12 folder as a frame stack.

2. Begin recording the script by clicking on the red Record Button in the Scripts section of the Objects palette.

3. Choose a gradient that has colors you like in the Gradient section of the Art Materials palette. I used the Bright gradient, consisting of greens and blues with a little purple.

4. Enable the Express In Image command, found in the Gradient pop-up menu. A dialog box appears with a bias slider that's used to determine the way gradient colors will be distributed in the image. Move the bias slider until the color distribution in the preview window is pleasing. I used 16 percent, as shown in Figure 7.23.

Figure 7.23
The Bias slider for the Express In
Image command.

5. Stop recording the script. Name it XpressGrad or something similar.

6. Undo the effect so that the colorized frame is grayscale once again.

7. Use the Apply Script To Movie command in the Movie menu. Find the XpressGrad script in the script library. All frames will automatically receive the gradient colors.

8. Save the new version as a QuickTime/AVI movie with a descriptive name, such as KIDGRAD.

9. Use smeary brushes from the Liquid group to smooth out the background and create fluid areas in each frame. You'll have to do this "by hand," rather than with a script, because each frame has a unique pose to be painted. I used Coarse Smear and Marbling Rake, as shown in Figure 7.24.

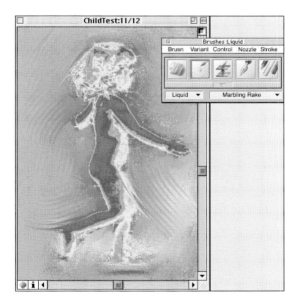

Figure 7.24
Marbling Rake strokes added to movie frames.

10. Save this version as a QuickTime/AVI movie with a different name, such as SMEARKID. Your current frame stack automatically saved the changes. It remains open and ready for more.

Style 7.20: C. Inverted Gradient Color

Make a script for Effects|Tonal Control|Negative and apply it to the previous movie. The cool green and blue colors turn to hot pink, orange, and chartreuse. This movie is called KIDGRAD2 in the Muybridge folder on the CD-ROM accompanying this book.

Other styles shown here are rotoscopes derived from KIDGRAD or its negative, KIDGRAD2.

Style 7.20: D. Fiber Clone

The Fiber Cloner is a new member of the Cloner family. Its strokes are composed of complex, energetic lines, similar to those of the Nervous Pen. Follow these steps:

1. Open KIDGRAD.

2. Select the Set Movie Clone Source command in the Movie menu to establish KIDGRAD as the source for rotoscope effects.

3. Make a new blank frame stack with the same dimensions and number of pixels. Use black for the paper color.

4. Select Fiber Cloner and turn Tracing Paper on.

5. Scribble over the girl in each frame. Allow the background to remain black.

DIFFERENT STROKES

The Van Gogh Cloner does not update color and value information throughout a stroke, as all the other cloners do. Instead, the color and value of the pixel you begin with remains for the entire stroke. Therefore, scribbling is not usually an effective technique. Shorter, deliberate strokes are recommended.

Style 7.20: E. Van Gogh Clone

With KIDGRAD still open, prepare to clone from it again as done in Steps 1, 2 and 3 in the preceding section, but use white paper for the blank frame stack instead of black. Then, follow these steps:

1. Select Van Gogh Cloner and turn Tracing Paper on.

2. Paint the girl in each frame using a few bold strokes that follow the contours of the figure.

Style 7.20: F. Van Gogh Clone Inverted And Distorted

This is similar to the previous style, but it uses KIDGRAD2 and black for the paper color of the blank frame stack. An additional script was made to apply the Effects|Focus|Glass Distortion command to the movie.

Splicing Movies Together

Several completed movies of the running child are provided on the accompanying CD-ROM. You can "splice" them together to get practice combining movies. Painter will allow you to combine movies only if they have the same frame dimensions. The number of frames doesn't matter. Here are the steps:

1. Open any of the Child movies.

2. Use the Insert Movie command in the Movie menu. You'll choose whether to add a movie at the end, the beginning, or between any frames you specify in the current movie. Then navigate to another Child movie to insert it.

Note: The Insert Movie command recognizes only frame stacks, not QuickTime or AVI movies. To change a QuickTime/AVI movie to a frame stack again, simply open it in Painter.

3. Repeat Step 2 until you've added all the segments you want.

Another sequence from Muybridge's motion photography is provided for your experimentation with rotoscoping. Figure 7.25 shows two frames from the Dancer series. Figure 7.26 is a frame from the movie JUNGLEDANCE on the CD-ROM that accompanies this book. Each frame was sprayed with the Image Hose loaded with the Jungle2 nozzle. Then the Fiber Cloner was used to sketch the figure.

Figure 7.25
Two frames from the Muybridge dancer sequence.

Figure 7.26
One frame from the movie JUNGLEDANCE.

Moving On

In this chapter you worked with most of Painter's animation features. You learned how to record and animate individual brushstrokes and how to script a series of effects to apply to a movie. You also practiced using the cloning techniques introduced in Chapter 3.

Your animation skills will serve you well in the next chapter, where you'll learn how to prepare animated GIFs as well as still images for the World Wide Web.

8

WEB EFFECTS

BY

SHERRY

LONDON

The Web has become such an important outlet for graphics use that Painter 6 contains a number of specialized tools that help you produce imagery with a lower number of colors. New since Painter 5 are Web brushes and a wonderful image-slicing plug-in.

Painter And The Web, A Brief Introduction

Everybody's doing it—getting online and surfing the Web. It seems to be the wave of the future, and you need to be able to swim—or else you might sink. If you haven't created your own home page yet, it's time to walk the plank. (I'll join you. Though I've created many Web sites, I haven't had time to create one for myself.)

You need to learn how to create Web graphics and get them online if you're going to be able to provide a full range of services to your clients, and Painter can help you with this. Keep in mind, though, it's only part of the solution of what to use for Web work—it's by no means the *complete* solution. It's much more of a solution now, in Painter 6, though, than it was in Painter 5.

This chapter explores some areas in the creation of Web graphics that are *unique* to Painter as well as areas where Painter has made a special attempt to provide Web benefits. This chapter is *not* about Web graphics, per se. That topic is much too broad to be covered in one chapter. Therefore, I'll assume you're already familiar with the basic concepts and constraints of creating graphics for use on the Web. That allows me to concentrate on showing you some tricks you can use in Painter to create eye-catching graphics.

If you need background on the Web or on creating graphics that are not Painter-specific, here are my favorite Web books:

- Lynda Weinman's *Designing Web Graphics* and *Coloring Web Graphics*

- David Siegel's *Creating Killer Web Sites*

- J. Scott Hamlin's *Photoshop Web Techniques* and *Interface Design with Photoshop*

If you do Web design, these books should be part of your library.

Now that you've heard the disclaimers, let's continue. Painter has special features, or it works in a special way, in several areas of Web graphic design. In Painter, you can convert an image to indexed color just by saving the file to an indexed color format such as GIF. This chapter discusses color indexing, color reduction, and Painter's color sets—and the commands that use them.

In Painter, you can create eye-catching graphics with a very small number of colors (and on the Web, fewer colors are better). This chapter looks at images built using the Posterize and Equalize commands and dynamic plug-ins; the Pop Art fill; the Color Overlay or Screen effects; and the Graphic Print brush.

This chapter also looks at ways in which Painter can be used to design Web elements. You'll create buttons and other interface items and use some of Painter's embossing techniques. You'll also work with the Bevel World and new Image Slice plug-ins.

In addition, this chapter briefly revisits the subject of patterns and textures. You'll see how the color constraints on the Web—and the need to add text to a Web page—impact your use of these elements. The chapter finishes by looking at how to create image maps (clickable links in a graphic) and embedded URLs. In Painter, you can also create animated GIF images. I'll discuss that topic briefly here. The process is similar to the animations Rhoda covers in Chapter 7.

Color For The Web

The biggest limitation on the Web concerns the use of color. There are two different, yet interrelated, Web issues: One issue is bandwidth and image size, and the other is hardware independence.

One of the major headaches in Web design is that you have no idea what hardware will be used to download and view graphics placed on the Web. Many people are still using 14.4 modems to access the Web, and after that, 28.8 modems are the most popular. Although DSL and cable modems are gaining in popularity, they're still not the norm. If your image loads too slowly, much of your audience will click their way somewhere else.

Most of the people who surf the Web are not artists. Many of those folks don't have 24-bit "true color" capability. They're using video cards that can only display 256 colors at a time—or even older cards with more limited color capacity. The browser that a person uses (as well as his or her hardware and operating system) determines what colors will be shown when only a limited number of colors are possible. If the person viewing your files has 24-bit capability, no colors in your image will be changed. It's only when the viewer

SELECTING GIF ANIMATION SETTINGS

Although you create a GIF animation exactly as you would create any other type of animation, you need to design the animation with the Web in mind. This means that you need to limit the size of the images, limit the number of colors used, and limit the number of frames of animation. You need to make your animation as small as possible. In addition, when you save your animation, you need to save it as a GIF.

The Save As GIF dialog box has a few settings that will concern you. In addition to determining the best color settings for your image and selecting transparency if you want it, you need to specifically set the Frame Delay, the Disposal Method, and the Looping.

The Frame delay sets the maximum frame rate for the animation. It's calculated in 100ths of a second. Therefore, if you set a frame delay of 25 ms, you're displaying 4 frames per second (100/25=4). This is the fastest rate at which the images would be displayed. If you fail to set a frame rate, the images display as fast as the computer can manage them—which could result in your carefully crafted animation whizzing by too fast to be seen.

The Disposal Method sets how the image is removed from the screen. You may leave this at Default. However, if your animation is transparent, you might want to select Background, so that the screen is fully cleared between frames.

Finally, if you want the animation to repeat, you need to select the Loop checkbox. Leave the Loop amount at 0 if you want it to repeat forever.

has fewer colors that the browser must step in and change the colors. There are 216 "standard" colors that will not be touched when a browser (Netscape, in particular) must reduce the number of colors to a specific set. These 216 colors are the same on the PC and the Mac. You can be confident that your designs will display properly if you only use these 216 colors in your images.

Not all images are happy in this 216-color palette, however. Save your full-color photographs as JPEG images instead. They will download faster as JPEG images and look better, as well. On the other hand, if you're creating original artwork for which you have a choice of palette, use the 216-color palette and take control of your line art or low-color work. Painter 6 uses the Netscape 216-color Web-safe color set by default.

You have only two ways to limit the number of colors in a file in Painter. One way is to create the file using very few colors (or apply Posterize Using Color Set, which reduces colors to the colors used in the current Color Set). The other way is to save the image in a format that reduces the number of colors (such as a GIF file format).

File Formats For The Web

GIF and JPEG are the most commonly used file formats for keeping file sizes low to enable fast transmission over a modem.

The GIF format is an indexed color format. (An *indexed color* file has 256 colors or less and contains a list of the specific colors in the file.) Painter enables you to create a GIF file with 4, 8, 16, 32, 64, 128, or 256 colors. The manual clearly explains the settings in the Save As GIF dialog box. The thing that's important for you to know is that there may be a large difference in file sizes between files saved with Dither on or Quantize To Nearest Color on. Dither mixes up pixels to give the impression of more colors than there actually are. It usually results in a better quality image. Unfortunately, dithering a file can add a lot to the file size.

When you save a Painter image as a GIF file, you won't see the changes reflected in the image until you close it and then reopen it. You don't lose the 24-bit color in your image until you actually close the image. This allows you to save the GIF image several times—dithered or not—and at various color depths to evaluate the file size before you make a final decision.

Painter And The 216 Web-Safe Colors

When you save a GIF file from Painter, a subtle shift in color can occur. If you're using an adaptive palette (which picks 256 or fewer colors from the original image), it probably doesn't matter. If the image that you want to save already has fewer than 256 colors and you want to preserve them exactly, you need to create a color set that contains only the colors used in the image. Then, when you save the file as a GIF and select the Color Set option, your colors are preserved.

The Web-safe colors—as well as any other colors used—will change in value by several numbers unless you save the file using the Color Set option. For example, a light coral on the 216 color list with an RGB value of 255, 204, 0 is saved by Painter in a GIF with an RGB value of 252, 204, 4. You can only save Web-safe colors if you use the Color Set option.

Painter 6 gives you better control over images saved as GIFs than Painter 5 did. However, you cannot see hex values within Painter (except when you have the Eyedropper tool selected, and then you can only see the hex value of the current color), and you cannot automatically create a color set from an existing image. Although Painter 6 is an improvement over Painter 5, it still doesn't give you total control. If you have Photoshop, you can save the file as a PSD image and convert it to indexed color in Photoshop using either Adaptive or Perceptual methods, or you can convert it to indexed color in deBabelizer with full choice over the specific 256 colors to be used. Either option gives you better control over the conversion (unless you use a color set).

You can interlace a GIF file to change its download/display behavior. An interlaced file downloads large, blocky pixels first and refines the image on subsequent passes. This makes it look as if the image is actually displaying faster than it really is. To interlace a GIF image, you need to check the Inter-laced box under Misc Options in the Save As GIF Options dialog box (see Figure 8.1). You cannot specify the number of passes in the Interlaced box.

You can also save an image as a JPEG file. The JPEG format was developed by the Joint Photographic Experts Group. This format holds 24-bit color but creates a smaller file size by using lossy compression. In lossy compression, as opposed to lossless compression, image data is actually destroyed and thrown away. The JPEG format creates blocks of color in your image and makes the image smaller by finding blocks of similarly colored pixels. It increases the resemblance of those pixels to one another, thus making the file easier to

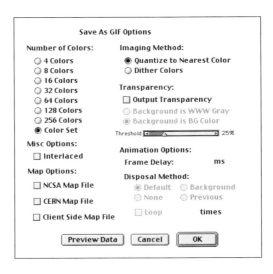

Figure 8.1
The Save As GIF Options dialog box allows you to save a GIF file from Painter.

compress. There are various degrees of data loss possible. The Best Quality setting removes only those areas that are really not visible at normal viewing distances. The highest compression settings produce noticeable image loss.

Some considerations must be addressed when working with JPEG images. The most important one is that you should not save any image in JPEG format until you no longer wish to edit it. If you resave a JPEG image, you cause more loss. (The only time when this is not true is when you save the image multiple times without closing it—your original image does not acquire the JPEG loss until the saved file is reopened.) JPEG is quite suitable for continuous tone photographs. It's much less suited to line art of solid-color images. The damage to those images is more noticeable, and the GIF format will do a much better job on those images.

GIF files have another advantage. They can have transparent areas where either a neutral gray background appears or the background behind the image is visible. This allows you to create shaped images for placement on a Web page. The transparency is determined by the selection in the image at the time the GIF file is saved. The image data in the selection area is visible, and the nonselected area becomes invisible. This means that if you use a single color as your image mask, you need to invert the selection before you save the file. You'll have the opportunity to try this later in the chapter.

Color Sets

Color sets are Painter's palettes. They're groups of colors already "premixed" for you to use. Their purpose is to let you easily and consistently select colors from a known source.

Color sets are similar to Photoshop's color tables, but Painter does not create one for a GIF image. There's no way to extract the colors from an image—even a 256-color one—and create a color set from it. You must either work with the ones that Painter provides (there are extras on the Painter install CD-ROM) or create your own from scratch. A new feature in Painter 6 enables you to force Painter to convert a GIF file to the colors in your current color set when you save it.

In this chapter, you'll be working for Discovery, a fictional client who wants you to create a Web site to help with their marketing efforts. Discovery is a nature-oriented travel group for children and teens ages 8 to 16. Parents join the program at various levels of "support" and receive, in return, a year's worth of activities for their children. These activities include day and night trips to a wild bird sanctuary, hikes along the ocean, and even trips to Brazil and Kenya to view vanishing species over summer vacation.

The first task you need to perform for this client is to develop a group of colors that will be used as the major accent colors throughout the Web page.

WEB EFFECTS **189**

You want to develop a palette of 10 to 16 colors that look appealing to children and will display consistently on all systems. You just happen to have an image of a barrel of hard candy, and if you could only borrow the colors in that image, you might be able to create a good Web site palette.

PROJECT Creating A Small Web-Safe Color Set

In this project, you'll create a color set from colors in the 216-color Netscape color set to find the nearest matches. Using these matches, you'll construct a 14-color subset of the Netscape palette to use as your color set for the Discovery project. Here are the steps:

1. Open the image CANDY.PSD from this book's companion CD-ROM. (This image is from my own collection, although it's certainly not one of my better efforts. However, the colors work.)

2. Choose Effects|Tonal Control|Equalize. Drag the white point left to 32 percent and click on OK. This brightens the colors in the image.

3. Create a new image to use as your "holding" area for your selected colors. A 400-pixel square image is fine, and it should have a white background.

4. You also need to select a brush to use to "save" (that is, apply) your colors into the holding file. Select the Brush tool. In the Brushes palette, select Load Library at the bottom of the drop-down brush selection menu. Load the WebMedia brushes as shown in Figure 8.2. You'll find this set in the Content Sampler folder that was installed with Painter 6 (or on the installation CD-ROM if you didn't perform a full install of Painter).

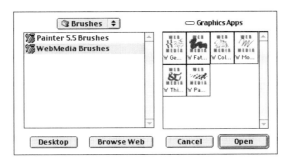

Figure 8.2
The WebMedia brush library contains brushes that were specially designed for the Web.

WHAT ARE WEBMEDIA BRUSHES?

Painter 5.5 introduced a new class of brushes to Painter, and Painter 6 has gathered these brushes into the WebMedia brush library. The WebMedia brush library contains brushes that are specially constructed to have aliased (or *jagged*) edges to reduce the number of colors in a stroke. These brushes are ideal for use on the Web because they do not alias colors to your image in an attempt to produce visually smooth edges. I urge you to try them out. They present you with wonderful possibilities.

Figure 8.3

Change the subcategory and opacity for the Colored Pencils WEB brush.

5. From the WebMedia brush set, select the W Monoline brush with the Colored Pencils WEB variant. Click on the arrowhead to show the Brush Controls: General palette. Change the subcategory to Flat Cover and increase the brush opacity to 100 percent, as shown in Figure 8.3.

6. Because this is a useful brush, save it as a brush variant (on the Brushes palette menu, select Variant|Save Variant and then name the brush "Flat Color WEB"). Remember to select the Colored Pencils WEB brush and choose Variant|Restore Variant so that the brush behaves as it was designed to. Select the Flat Color WEB brush.

7. Now you're ready to select your colors. Choose the Eyedropper tool. Locate a bright red in the image and click on it to make it the current color. Click on the Find Color button in the Art Materials: Color Set palette. Figure 8.4 shows the resulting dialog box. Leave the radio button set to Closest To Current Color. (The Closest To Current Color command selects a color from the currently selected Color Set.) Click on Search and then on OK. The nearest match to the original color appears as the Current Color. Select the Brush tool (with the Flat Color WEB brush) and leave a dab of color in the 400-pixel image.

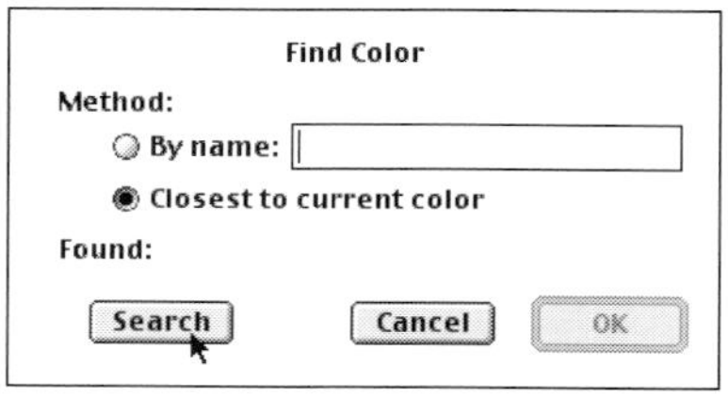

Find Color

Method:

○ By name: [   ]

● Closest to current color

Found:

[Search]   [Cancel]   [OK]

Figure 8.4

Find your selected color within the current color set.

8. Repeat Step 7 to find the following colors:

- A dark red
- A deep and a bright green
- A strong and a lighter yellow
- A strong and a lighter orange
- A deep aqua (The candy near the lower-left area of the bowl is good for this.)
- A dark brown (Pick a color from the candy diagonally above and to the right of the aqua one.)

Paint a dab of each selected color in your 400-pixel image. The colors can overlap.

9. You need three more colors, but these need to come directly from the color set because they aren't in the candy image. Pick a deep and a light purple from the color set and paint them into your 400-pixel image. Finally, select black (it's the bottom-right color in the color set) and paint it into your 400-pixel image as well. You should have 13 paint splotches (and the white background makes 14).

10. Twirl down the arrow next to the Art Materials: Color Set. Figure 8.5 shows the Art Materials: Color Set palette. Click on New Set button. The new color set appears as a tiny palette that you'll have trouble finding, but not to worry. The location of the color set becomes obvious when you add colors to it.

11. Click on each color in the 400-pixel image (with the Eyedropper tool) and then click on the Add Color button in the Color Set palette to add the selected color to the new color set. You may add the colors in any order you prefer, and you can sort the colors when you're done. Colors can be shown in "saved" order or by HLS (Hue, Saturation, Lightness), LSH (Lightness, Saturation, Hue), or SHL (Saturation, Hue, Lightness). To save the color set, click on the Library button in the Art Materials: Color palette. You're asked whether you want to save the current color set. Save it as SAFECNDY.TXT and then click on Cancel. This leaves the color set open.

You can now use the color set to choose the colors for your Discovery Web page designs.

Graphic Techniques For Low Color

In this section, you'll try a variety of techniques for simplifying the colorful photos that are embedded in the Discovery logotype. Some of the techniques work quite well for this purpose, and some will not. Regardless, they're useful to know and will work for other clients and other situations.

Creating Low Colors Through Posterization

I created the Discovery logotype from a combination of letterforms, clip art, and photographs. All the original files are on this book's companion CD-ROM. If you're in the mood, you can make your own logo photofill, but because the topic of this chapter is the Web—not cloning—I have provided one for you that's ready to go. It's called DISCOVERY.PSD.

Figure 8.5
The Art Materials: Color Set palette enables you to create and modify color sets.

 Using The Posterize Using Color Set Command

In this treatment of the logotype, you'll use the Posterize Using Color Set command to convert the image to the 14-color color set you created earlier. Here are the steps to follow:

1. Open the image DISCOVRY.PSD. It contains nature scenes from the four seasons embedded in stylized text. Figure 8.6 shows the starting image.

Figure 8.6

The Discovery logotype is used as the base image for the following indexed color techniques that use a low number of colors.

2. Choose File|Clone to create a copy of the image.

3. Choose Effects|Tonal Control|Posterize Using Color Set. Figure 8.7 shows the result.

Figure 8.7

The Discovery logotype after the Posterize Using Color Set command is applied.

Posterize Using Color Set is a command that's the equivalent of Photoshop's Image|Mode|Indexed Color; Using: Custom Palette command. It allows you to convert your image into fewer colors using the closest matches from your selected color set. However, the one difference is significant—you cannot specify a dither in Painter when you use this command. Therefore, the conversion is done using the Quantize method—each pixel in the image is converted to a color from the selected color set. The pixels may look like blocks of color because, when using a low number of colors, many of the middle tones, which give a photographic image its definition, are lost. This is not always the most attractive look.

For this example, the effect is not awful, but it's not wonderful, either. The scenes of the seasons in the original are not as sharply defined as they, perhaps, should be in order to identify the subject matter. When you change the colors, the cherry blossoms, mums, and the pumpkin as well as the snow-covered pine trees are no longer understandable shapes (although you had to look hard and long at the original to recognize the images anyway).

You could correct this by redesigning the imagery inside of the logotype (which is why the originals are all on the CD-ROM for you). If you want the Posterize

Using Color Set command to leave recognizable shapes, you need to enlarge some of the images that appear in the logotype so that they will hold their shapes when the entire image is simplified. The tulips are extremely iconic; the cherry blossoms are not. Even though the use of seasonal images is a good idea for this logotype, you probably need different flora or some iconic fauna (butterflies, birds, and so on) in order to make the design imagery clear.

Oh well, it's 4 A.M. and the client wants to see this Web treatment first thing in the morning. You'll need to try another way to simplify this image because a complete redesign is out of the question for right now.

PROJECT Posterizing The Image, Part 1

In this project, you'll see whether the Posterize command is an improvement as you try to develop a "designy" and semi-abstract low-color Web treatment for your client. Here are the steps:

1. Make DISCOVRY.PSD your active image. Choose File|Clone to make another copy.

2. Select Effects|Tonal Control|Posterize. At eight levels, the image looks just like it did before. Change the number of levels to 2. This results in a fairly attractive, stylized look, but it does not use the colors you wanted in the color set.

3. Apply the Effects|Tonal Control|Posterize Using Color Set command. The image is recolored using "your" colors. Figure 8.8 shows this image. The subject matter is no more identifiable than it was before, but posterizing the image prior to changing the colors to the desired color set makes for a more interesting design.

Figure 8.8
The posterized image is recolored with colors from the color set.

PROJECT Posterizing The Image, Part 2

When you posterize a color image into two levels, you do not produce a two-color image. Instead, you create an eight-color image—an image that contains red, green, and blue, and their secondary colors (magenta, cyan, and yellow) in addition to black and white. If you really want a two-color image, you need to remove the saturation from the image before you posterize it. Use the Posterize command again and apply a gradation made from the color set to add color to the image. This technique automatically creates a low-color image with the "right" colors in it. Here are the steps:

1. Make the DISCOVRY.PSD image active. Choose File|Clone.

2. Select Effects|Tonal Control|Adjust Colors and then reduce the Saturation setting to -139 (move the slider to the left). Leave the Using field set to Uniform Color, as shown in Figure 8.9.

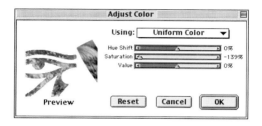

Figure 8.9

You can remove all the color from an image with the Adjust Colors command.

3. Select Effects|Tonal Control|Equalize and accept the default values offered. This automatically sharpens the contrast in the image by setting white and black points.

4. Choose Select Effects|Tonal Control|Posterize and set the levels to 2.

   If you see no need to equalize the image, a faster way to accomplish Steps 2 through 4 is to use the Effects|Surface Control|Express Texture; Using: Image Luminance command.

5. Open the image WEBGRAD.PSD. It already contains closely spaced stripes of the 14 colors in your color set or the 14 colors in my color set (if your colors differ significantly from mine, it's easy enough for you to create your own source image). Choose the Rectangular Selection tool and drag out a marquee that encompasses all the color stripes in the width but as few pixels in the height as possible. Twirl down the arrow next to the Art Materials: Gradients palette. Click on the arrow at the top-right of the Gradients palette and select Capture Gradient from the menu. Name the gradient *WebCandy*. Figure 8.10 shows the captured gradient inside of the Gradients palette.

Figure 8.10

The captured area becomes a gradient for you to use.

6. Create a new layer and keep it active.

7. Choose Edit|Fill; Using: Gradient.

8. Change the Composite Method setting to Screen. This makes the gradient "stick" to the black in the canvas layer.

9. Drop the layer by clicking on the Drop button in the Objects: Layers palette.

10. You're now going to create a stroke around the logotype. Make the original DISCOVRY.PSD image active. Choose the Objects: Mask palette. Choose Mask|Load Selection and load the selection in New Mask 1. Return to the clone document on which you've been working.

WEB EFFECTS **195**

11. Open the File|Clone Source submenu and make sure that DISCOVRY.PSD is assigned as the clone source.

12. Choose Select|Auto Select; Using: Original Selection. This loads the selection of the text outlines in DISCOVRY.PSD into the current image.

13. Select black (or a different dark color) in your color set as the current color. You'll use this to stroke the outline of the selection and give definition to the logotype.

14. Select the Colored Pencils WEB brush (remember to make sure that you've returned the brush to its original specifications). However, set the opacity to 100 percent.

15. Choose Select|Transform Selection to change the selection into a path-based selection.

16. Choose Select|Stroke Selection. The Colored Pencils WEB brush is aliased, so there should be no additional colors added to your image. Figure 8.11 shows the image.

Figure 8.11
The posterized logo has a low-color gradient and a stroke applied to it.

If you want to "play" with the Posterize and Equalize commands without immediately committing yourself to their effects, you can use the new Dynamic plug-ins located on the Objects: Dynamic Layers palette. There's one for Equalize and another one for Posterize. You can apply one "on top of" the other. An Alert dialog box will warn you when you need to "commit" a plug-in layer to an image layer (that is, remove the ability to modify the dynamic capabilities of the layer and render it to a regular layer).

Using Some Current Gradient Effects

Painter has two other low-color tricks up its sleeve. Both of them will work with the current gradient, which, in this case, is created from your limited color set. The effects that you'll now try are the Pop Art fill and Express Gradient In Image.

PROJECT Using Pop Art Fill

The Pop Art fill adds a very breezy, light-hearted look to the logotype. Pop Art fill, which is found in the Esoterica menu, uses either the image luminance, the current grad, or the original luminance of an image to apply a fairly coarse screen to the original image. You have a choice of two colors only, and the swatches use the Apple or Windows System Color Picker (with all the challenge of correctly specifying the desired color).

1. Make the DISCOVRY.PSD image active. Choose File|Clone to create a copy.

2. Write down the RGB or Hexadecimal values (choose the Eyedropper tool) for the two colors you want from your color set. (If you're working on a PC, you need the RGB value). I used the bright red and the deep yellow.

3. Choose Select|Auto Select; Using: Original Selection. This selects just the logotype.

4. Choose Effects|Esoterica|Pop Art Fill; Using: Current Grad. Set the scale to 25 percent. Figure 8.12 shows the Pop Art Fill dialog box.

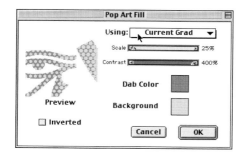

Figure 8.12
The Pop Art Fill dialog box.

5. Set the contrast to 400 percent. The Contrast slider controls the softness of the blend from one color to the other. At 400 percent, the edges are sharp and aliased, which is needed to limit the number of colors for the Web.

6. Select the two colors you want to use by clicking on each of the swatches, which opens the system Color Picker. Unfortunately, you need to enter the desired values into the system Color Picker (on the Macintosh, select the RGB or HTML picker—see the sidebar for more information). Figure 8.13 shows the resulting image.

Figure 8.13
You can use the Pop Art Fill command using Current Grad to create a cartoon look for your logotype.

This technique is very well suited to Web use because it produces a two-color image. It's also an excellent technique to use wherever you need to posterize an image into two colors because it gives a different look to the result. When

CHOOSING COLORS IN THE MACINTOSH SYSTEM COLOR PICKER

Painter uses the Macintosh Color Pickers when it needs a color selected during an Effects command. (Windows Painter also uses the System Picker, but the Windows System Picker always includes an RGB option.) OS 8.6 and above also have an HSV Color Picker (which is the same system used in Painter's Color palette), but the numbers are not compatible, so do *not* use it. You cannot use the HSL Color Picker, either, because you cannot specify the correct numbers to plug in there.

You need to use either the RGB Color Picker or the HTML Color Picker. The Macintosh System RGB Color Picker works on a scale of 0 to 100, although the normal RGB values range from 0 to 255. Those numbers, at least, can be converted. Because you're dealing with all Web-safe colors, only a few values exist. See the conversion chart.

Painter R, G, or B Value	Apple System Percentage
0	0
51	20
102	40
153	60
204	80
255	100

Conversion of 0 to 255 RGB values into percentages.

For example, if you need to select a color whose RGB value is 204, 51, 51, just enter 80, 20, 20 for the percentage RGB values in the Macintosh Color Picker.

you create a Pop Art fill using the current grad, you need to have a selection. Otherwise, all the image data is ignored.

PROJECT The Gradients|Express In Image Command

The Express In Image command in the Art Materials: Gradients palette's menu is another interesting method for controlling color in your image. This project shows it used by itself; the next project shows it used with the Graphic brush. Here are the steps to follow:

1. Make the DISCOVRY.PSD image active. Choose File|Clone to create a copy.

2. Choose Select|Auto Select; Using: Original Selection. This selects just the logotype.

3. WebCandy is your current gradation. Select Art Materials: Gradients|Express In Image command. The Bias slider controls where the gradient falls in the image (where it starts and ends). By dragging the Bias slider, you change the color mix of the image. Figure 8.14 shows the Discovery logotype created with the Bias slider near the left.

This makes for a very complex and colorful design, which still uses only 14 base colors. Setting the Bias slider in the middle creates almost an inverted color look to the logotype. Both looks are useable.

4. Actually, the gradient does add some additional colors as it softens the transition from one color to the next. To get back to your exact 14 colors, choose Effects|Tonal Control|Posterize Using Color Set.

PROJECT Creating A Graphic Print Brush

The Graphic Print brush in Painter 5 was one of my favorite brushes. Because this brush doesn't exist in Painter 6, you need to create your own custom brush that duplicates its functionality, but that's easy to do. When created, this brush adds another way to simplify and abstract color. The Graphic Print brush that you will create will have a plug-in method and use the Graphic Print subcategory. When you brush it over an area, it will add contrast to the area by softening the individual shapes while pushing light and dark areas further from each other in value. At its full strength, it reduces an image to black or white and the nearest major hue—red, green, blue, yellow, magenta, or cyan. You can picture the brush as a way to stroke your image with a variable amount of soft posterizing—the brush causes anti-aliased edges and large areas of soft blur as it works.

Creating The Graphic Print Brush

Here's how to create the a graphic print brush:

1. Load the Painter 6 brushes by selecting Library from the drop-down menu in the Brushes: Brush menu. The Painter brush library is located in the same folder that contains the Painter application. (If the Painter 6 brushes are already loaded or you have just restarted Painter, then your Painter 6 brushes are already in place and you don't need to do anything other than selecting the correct brush.)

2. Choose the FX brushes with the Fire variant. Save this variant before you change it. (Choose Brushes|Variant|Save Variant and name it Graphic Print brush.)

3. In the Brush Controls: General palette, you need to make these changes: Change the Dab type to Circular, the Subcategory type to Graphic Print brush, the Opacity setting to 50 percent, and the Grain setting to 0 percent.

4. In the Brush Controls: Spacing palette, change the Spacing setting to 35 percent.

5. In the Brush Controls: Angle palette, change the Squeeze setting to 100 percent and the Angle setting to 27 percent.

6. In the Expression palette, set the Size, Opacity, and Grain fields to respond to the Pressure table and all the other controls to None. Figure 8.15 shows all these changes.

7. Choose Brushes|Variant|Save Default Variant to make these settings permanent.

Using The Graphic Print Brush

Now it's time to see how you can use the brush that you just created:

1. Make the DISCOVRY.PSD image active. Choose File|Clone to create a copy.

2. Select the Brush tool and the Graphic Print brush that you just created.

3. Brush gently over the letterforms and watch as the colors merge and intensify. Add a variable amount of the Graphic Print brush to the image. (Be careful on the letters *R* and *Y* not to wipe out the letters to white as you brush.)

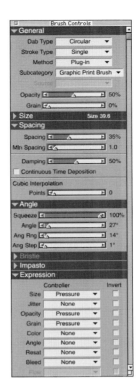

Figure 8.15

You can make a new brush by changing a variety of settings in the Brush Controls palettes.

If you want to use the colors in your color set, you need to convert the lower-color graphic print image to your colors. You can use the Posterize Using Color Set command on the Effects menu to retain the "feel" of the Graphic Print brush. However, I like what happens when you use the Gradients|Express In Image command that's on file. You can make a clone of your image and apply the Posterize Using Color Set command to it. Then you can go back to your work-in-progress and complete this project.

The Graphic Print Brush, Continued

Follow these steps to continue this project:

1. You need to select just the letterforms of the logotype. Choose Select|Auto Select; Using: Original Selection.

2. WebCandy should still be the current gradient. Choose the Art Materials: Gradients|Express In Image command. Set the bias to whatever coloring you like best based on the preview.

3. You might want to outline the text to increase its legibility. Select the 2B variant of the Pencil brush.

4. Choose Select|Transform Selection to make the selection into a path-based selection. Choose Select|Stroke Selection and Select|None.

5. Choose Effects|Tonal Control|Posterize Using Color Set to reduce the image to no more than the 14 colors in your color set. Figure 8.16 shows the finished image.

Notice the difference between expressing the gradation in the image using the original DISCOVRY.PSD image and the one simplified using the Graphic Print brush. Both are eye-catching, low-color images, but they're quite different in character.

Patterns And Texture

You learned how to create paper textures in Chapter 4 and how to create patterns in Chapter 5. When you create repeatable imagery for the Web, the process is exactly the same.

Patterns are used most often on the Web as backgrounds. They can be backgrounds to the entire image or to a particular table cell. If you use cascading style sheets, you can define a pattern as a background to almost any object. When you define a single repeat unit in HTML as a background, the browser will tile it across the user's screen (or across the specified object or area). The advantage to using a pattern tile is that you get a variable-sized background for only the "cost" of a single tile download.

The main problem that exists when using patterns on the Web is that they're usually too strong to place text over them. I very much dislike having to squint in order to read text placed on a wild pattern. The text on the Web page is the important item—not the background pattern. If you forget that, you lessen the effectiveness of your Web site.

Your best design approach is to either keep the background very light and use dark text or to use a very dark background pattern with white text. The key to keeping a background "looking" dark or light is to create a pattern with very little contrast. A pattern that uses white and light green alternating squares is going to look darker than a background that alternates light green and light blue squares of the same value.

The client has decided to select the logotype pictured in Figure 8.11 (the posterized image overlaid with the striped gradient). Discovery selected that logotype because the colors were light but bright, and it retained both the child-like color "feel" of the candy and the hint of the nature-based shapes in the photographic logotype. You now need to create an harmonious pattern to use as a background.

Looking at your color set, the dark yellow and the light orange are the two lightest colors that are closest in color to one another. They seem like a reasonable color choice for the pattern. You can develop any pattern you want for this Web page, but the TULIPS.PSD image embedded in the original logotype might be a good choice.

PROJECT Developing A Background Pattern

This project shows you how to create a pattern and export it as a GIF file. Follow these steps:

1. Open the image TULIPS.PSD on this book's companion CD-ROM. Choose File|Clone to make a copy. Continue your work in the clone image.

2. Select Effects|Surface Control|Express Texture; Using: Image Luminance. Set the Gray Threshold field to 31 percent, the Grain field to 85 percent, and the Contrast field to 400 percent (to leave no soft edges). Figure 8.17 shows the dialog box.

Figure 8.17
You can change an image into black and white using the Express Texture command.

3. Define the image as a pattern, and make it seamless using the technique that you learned in Chapter 5 for creating seamless photographic repeats. (Alternatively, if you're feeling lazy, open the image TULIPAT.PSD on this book's companion CD-ROM.) Figure 8.18 shows the seamless pattern.

Figure 8.18
Seamless tulip pattern.

4. Choose Effects|Surface Control|Apply Screen; Using: Image Luminance. Use gold for Swatch 1 (Apple RGB: 100, 80, 0; Windows RGB: 255, 204, 0). Use light yellow for Swatch 2 (Apple RGB: 100, 100, 0; Windows RGB: 255, 255, 0). Set Threshold 1 to 200 percent. The color in Swatch 3 is not used. Figure 8.19 shows the Apply Screen dialog box with the recommended settings.

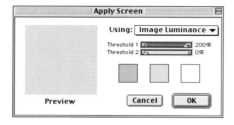

Figure 8.19
Apply Screen dialog box.

5. Select Canvas|Resize and make the image width 100 pixels. You can use a larger pattern size, but I generally prefer to keep the pattern width under 100 pixels unless there's a compelling reason not to. Size is less of an issue in a two-color pattern than the probable number of repeats on a 640 by 480 display.

6. Select File|Save and save the image as TULIPAT.GIF. Select the radio button labeled Use Color Set to export your colors exactly as you've created them.

7. To preview your results in Painter, select the entire image (Command/ Ctrl+A). Choose the Art Materials palette's Patterns|Capture Pattern command. Create a new document (Command/Ctrl+N) that's 640 by 480 pixels. Finally, fill the image (Command/Ctrl+F) using Fill With: Pattern.

The Illusion Of Depth

One of the most common effects you'll see on various Web sites is the illusion of depth. This is most commonly done using a process called *embossing*, and there are many ways to do this. There are actually enough ways to emboss something that one could almost write a book about only that topic—but this is not that book!

I'll confine the discussion here to two techniques chosen from the many possible. One technique is presented because it's a neat trick, and the other is presented because it's something that Painter can do that's not done the same way in Photoshop.

What is embossing? On the computer, it's a technique that makes part of an image look raised and three-dimensional. You can emboss an area to emphasize its contours, or you can emboss an area to create a raised shape from a blank image. Rhoda calls this latter technique *blind embossing*. In either case, it's a process that's quite different than using Photoshop's Emboss filter, which, if used without a selection, raises areas of an image based on that image's luminance.

For this project, you'll continue with the Discovery example. I have consciously referred to the Discovery logotype rather than the Discovery logo because there's another part to the logo that needs to be added. The stylized eye that serves as the *o* in Discovery is not complete. Discovery's logo actually includes "its" special brand—a rooster on top of the world. (All these stylized examples—the eye, the hand, the rooster, and the globe—come from the Ultimate Symbol Design Elements collection, my favorite source of vector art. A generous collection of samples is available free of charge on its Web site at **www.ultimatesymbol.com**.)

You need to emboss the logo design and add it to make a complete logo. The method that you'll use is the Apply Surface Texture; Using: Mask or Using: Original Luminance. Either creates some wonderful embossing.

In order to create the embossed shape and cut it back out of the image, you need to create a mask. The mask needs to be larger than the original shape so that it will include the embossing (which enlarges a shape by several pixels). Because the globe used in the design has holes in the center, you'll need to take some special steps to preserve them when you convert the image from a vector shape into a raster image.

The problem has several solutions—some easier than others. The easiest one that I can find is the one you'll use in the next project.

PROJECT The Great Emboss

The instructions for this project are divided into several sections. You need to first create two masks: one to use for the embossing, and a "fat" mask to use for removing the background from the embossed image. After that, you need to do the embossing to create a raised version of the logo. Finally, you need to extract the logo image from its background.

Come To The Masquerade

When you create an embossed shape, you need a "fat" mask to select the embossed object if you want to place it transparently over something else. You also need a "regular" mask to use when you do the embossing. Here are the steps for creating these masks:

1. Open the image LOGODESN.RIF. Choose File|Clone. Although there are layers in the original image, when you clone the image, everything is flat.

2. Choose Select|Auto Select Using Image Luminance. Then click on the Save Selection button on the Objects: Masks palette. Save the selection to New (which is your only choice anyway). This mask will allow you to emboss your image.

3. Choose the Layer Adjuster tool, press the modifier key (Option/Alt) and click on the selection to copy it into a new layer. Press the right-arrow key one time to move the object one pixel to the right. Click on the Drop button in the Objects: Layers palette to remove the layer.

4. Choose Select|Reselect. With the Layer Adjuster tool, press the modifier key (Option/Alt) and click on the selection to copy it into a new layer. Press the left-arrow key one time to move the object one pixel to the left. Click on the Drop button in the Objects: Layers palette.

5. Repeat Step 4, but this time press the up-arrow key one time.

6. Repeat Step 4 again, pressing the down-arrow key one time.

7. Choose Select|Auto Select Using Image Luminance. Click on the Save Selection button in the Objects: Masks palette. Save the selection to a new mask.

8. Double-click on the first mask name and change its name to Original Selection. Double-click on the second mask name and change its name to Fat Mask. Click on the RGB image to change your focus to the image itself.

9. Save the file.

Adding Surface Texture

Here's a very simple way to emboss in Painter:

1. Start with the file that you saved in the preceding steps.

2. If it's not still open, load the SAFECNDY.TXT color set that you created (click on the Library button on the Art Materials: Color Set palette). Make the strong purple the current color.

3. Fill the image (Command/Ctrl+F; Fill With: Current Color). You've just created a totally purple image.

4. Select Effects|Surface Control|Apply Surface Texture. In the Using box, select the Original Selection mask that you saved earlier. Figure 8.20 shows the Apply Surface Texture dialog box. Set the Softness field to 0; otherwise, the mask might not fit. Do not use any shine. (Shine works best in conjunction with Softness.) Figure 8.21 shows the embossed image.

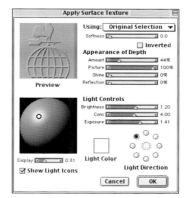

Figure 8.20

The Apply Surface Texture command enables you to emboss an image.

5. Load the Fat Mask as a selection by clicking on the Load Selection button in the Objects: Masks palette.

6. Choose the Layer Adjuster tool and click inside of the selection. Make the Canvas layer active. Choose white as the current color and fill the Canvas layer with white. Now you can clearly see your embossed layer. Figure 8.22 shows the embossed selection layer.

Finishing Up

You're almost done now. Here are the remaining steps for you to do:

1. Open the image LOGOTYPE2.RIF from this book's companion CD-ROM. This image contains the selected logotype. The layer is still active over the background, and the drop shadow is in place.

2. Drag the embossed image into the LOGOTYPE2.RIF image. Place it over the eye shape (as the *o* in Discovery). Figure 8.23 shows this image.

Figure 8.21

Here is the embossed image that you created.

Figure 8.22

The embossed image now has its background removed.

Figure 8.23

Here's the finished logo.

Buttons And Interface Items

Painter contains the best bevel-maker I've ever seen. The Bevel World dynamic plug-in and its results are truly awesome. You can create bevels for square buttons of course—but many other programs can do that as well. You can also bevel uneven shapes, and you can create "settings" for the bevel that, like a setting on a ring, frame the object inside.

◌ Swan Song

In this project, you're going to create a large inset plaque to use as an accent for one of Discovery's pages. You'll take a shape and blind emboss it using the Bevel World dynamic plug-in. The Bevel World dynamic plug-in creates incredible bevels. However, the plug-in doesn't make it obvious what to do if you want to create an embossing that goes *down* rather than up. Because bevels and embosses are visual illusions anyway, you'll learn how to create a critical "down" embossing (useful for rollover effects in which you might want a button to look "pressed in"). Follow these steps:

1. Open the image SWAN.PSD from this book's companion CD-ROM. The image contains a canvas and two layers.

2. You need to fill the objects on each layer with the tulip pattern you created earlier in this chapter. If it's still in your pattern list, fine. If not, open the image PATTDONE.RIF on this book's companion CD-ROM, select the entire image, and capture the pattern.

3. In order to fill the shapes with the pattern, you need to select them first. Because these shapes are a solid color, it's easy. Make the Oval Layer active and then choose Select|Color Select. Figure 8.24 shows the dialog box. Use the settings shown in Figure 8.24 and click on the yellow oval. The entire oval is then selected.

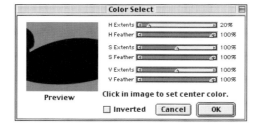

Figure 8.24

You can use the Color Select command to choose a solid shape on a layer.

4. Fill the selection with the tulip pattern (Command/Ctrl+F) and then choose Select|None.

5. It's time to emboss the oval. Select Bevel World from the Dynamic Layers palette in the Objects palette set. Click on the Apply button. Figure 8.25 shows the settings I used. I very carefully cut off the embossing at the edge of the shape (Outside Portion of 0) and discovered the remaining settings by experimentation. I actually liked these settings enough to want to use them as the default. (If you don't want to make these settings the default, write them down before you close the dialog box.) Press OK when you like the bevel you've made.

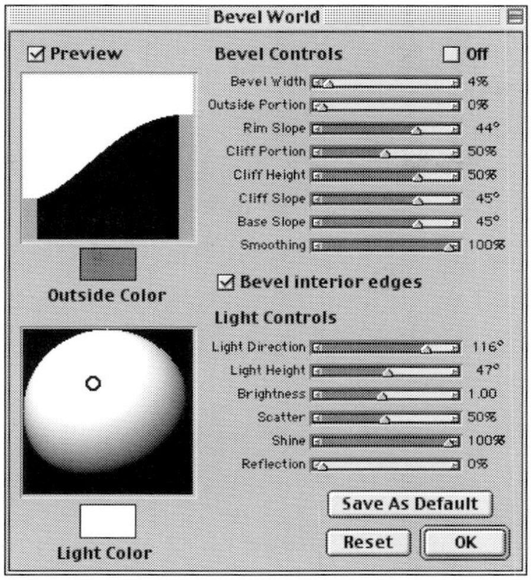

Figure 8.25
These Bevel World settings create a raised shape.

6. Because layers are new to Painter 6, I'll show you how to select the swan using a different method. You can't load the default mask of a layer, but the mask of the layer defines the shape that's visible. Therefore, if you want to select the contents of a layer, the layer mask is actually the item you really *do* want to load. How do you resolve this? You need to copy the layer mask and load the copy. Make the swan layer active.

7. In the Objects: Masks palette, click on the Swan Layer mask. From the drop-down menu at the upper-right corner of the Masks palette, select Copy Mask. Set Copy Mask to New (which is your only option) and click on OK. The mask is labeled New Mask 1. Click on the Load Selection button and load the selection as a new or replacement selection. The entire swan is selected. Make the RGB Swan Layer active in the Masks palette and close the eye icons on the two masks.

8. Fill the swan selection with the pattern (Command/Ctrl+F) and then choose Select|None.

9. Select the Bevel World plug-in in the Objects: Dynamic Layers palette and click on the Apply button.

10. For starters, change the settings so that they're identical to the settings used for the oval. This gives you a lovely matching "double-raised" embossed look. It's not what I am looking for here, but it's a place to begin.

11. The "trick" to creating an inset is to reverse some of the settings in the Bevel controls while keeping the lighting identical. That's why I asked you to repeat your original oval settings as a starting point. Leave the

In Chapter 9, Rhoda shows you how to create text on a curve. I made curved text using Vag Rounded as the font, and I filled it with the same pattern I used on the button. I also reused the settings from the Oval shape in the Bevel World dynamic layer (the "raised" settings). The one change that I made was to drastically reduce the Smoothing setting. Changing that one setting makes all the difference between seeing the embossing and losing it.

Bevel Width and Outside portions the same (in other examples, you can change these settings if you want). The critical settings to reverse are Rim Slope (from +44 to -44), Cliff Height (from +50 percent to -50 percent), Cliff Slope (from +45 degrees to -45 degrees), and Base Slope (from +45 degrees to -45 degrees). Figure 8.26 shows the changed settings. The swan should now be sunk into the oval button. Click on OK when you've made all the necessary changes. Figure 8.27 shows the finished plaque on a patterned background with text surrounding it.

You can get very different effects with the same elements, depending on the colors and the way you create the bevels. Figure 8.28 shows the same swan but uses two solid (and different) colors for each element.

You can also create a very dramatic inset look (although not as sharply shaped) by removing the swan shape from the oval and then beveling the oval with the Bevel Interior Edges button checked. In Figure 8.29, I selected

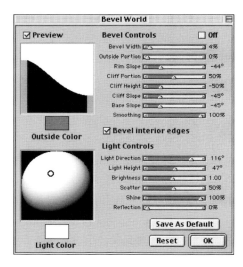

Figure 8.26
You need to reverse a number of settings to create an inset bevel.

Figure 8.27
The finished plaque shows a swan inset into a surrounding bevel.

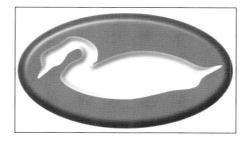

Figure 8.28
The Swan button looks very different in two solid colors.

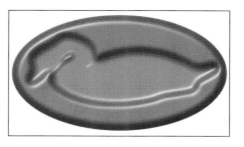

Figure 8.29
This image shows what happens when you remove the swan shape from the oval.

the swan and then deleted the swan shape from the Oval layer (make the Oval layer active once the swan is selected and press the Delete or Backspace key). I also beveled the swan, itself, using the reverse settings. It's a tossup whether the image looks better with the swan on top or the oval on top. I left the swan on top here.

Image Maps

An *image map* is a graphic that combines one or more areas that contain links to URLs into one image. Painter allows you to create GIF or JPEG images that can act as image maps.

In this section, you'll learn how to create an image map, but you might need to consult your Internet service provider to be able to use it. Painter can create both client-side and server-side image maps. A server-side image map requires a CGI (Common Gateway Interface) program that tells the server how to display the image map. Painter writes this program for you, but you need to know whether your server uses a CERN map file or an NCSA map file. This type of technical topic is beyond the scope of this book. Although the client-side image maps are not recognized by every browser, they are supported by the two main browsers in their latest incarnations (Netscape Navigator and Microsoft Internet Explorer level 4 browsers and above). They are much easier to use, so you'll work with them here.

You need to understand a few things about image maps and about Painter's implementation of image maps before you work on this project. In an image map, you define a series of hotspots on which the user can click. The hotspots should not overlap one another. In the event that they do, the spot "on top" wins—that is, its URL is the one that's used when the site visitor clicks on the spot.

WHY TO COPY INTO A LAYER

In this example, I prefer for you to copy the selection into a new layer because Painter has an annoying way of leaving trailing white pixels when it cuts an element from the Canvas layer. By copying the element instead of cutting it, you avoid those unsightly pixels.

Hotspots are allowed to be rectangular, circular, or polygonal. However, Painter doesn't allow you to create polygonal hotspots—the option appears in the dialog box but it's permanently grayed out. Your safest option is to only create rectangular hotspots.

In the following project, you'll create a splash screen for Discovery. You'll use a road that contains iconic symbols as the map (after all, a road is the perfect vehicle for a map). You'll use an existing image that's almost ready to be turned into an image map.

PROJECT A Road Is A Road Is A Road (And Is Also An Image Map)

This project shows you how to create clickable regions using layers. Follow these steps:

1. Open the image ROAD.PSD from this book's companion CD-ROM. Figure 8.30 shows the road. The areas that need to become hotspots are circled. It's immediately apparent that you have a potential problem with overlapping hotspots.

Figure 8.30
ROAD.PSD is waiting to become an image map.

2. You need to select each of the road "tiles" that contain icons and make a layer from the selection. To begin, select the Circular Marquee tool.

3. Drag the marquee around the toucan tiles but make sure that the marquee doesn't overlap into any of the areas occupied by the maple leaf icon. You can move the marquee after you've created it without disturbing any of the underlying data (just wait until you see the crossed arrows cursor when you place the cursor inside of the marquee; then press the mouse to move the marquee). The circular marquee works better for this particular hotspot because you can grab more of the toucan without impinging on the maple leaf. Make sure you keep the Shift key pressed to constrain the oval to a circle as you draw it (oval shapes are changed to rectangles in a client-side map).

4. Using the Layer Adjuster tool, press the modifier key (Option/Alt) and click on the selection to copy it into a new layer.

5. Double-click on the new layer to open the Layer Attributes dialog box. Change the layer name to Toucan, click on the WWW Map Clickable

PAINTER'S LACK OF WARNING

Painter does not prevent you from creating an empty layer from a selection. If you use the Layer Adjuster tool on a selection with an active layer that contains no data in the selected area, Painter creates a *floating object*. It doesn't warn you that you've made a mistake. You can avoid unpleasant surprises by keeping the Layers section of the Objects palette open and visible whenever you're working on an image containing layers.

ROAD BUILDING

You have all the pieces needed to build your own road. I placed a marquee around the area in a "practice" 640 by 480 image that seemed reasonable for a road. I copied the area to a new image so that I had an idea of its size. I then used the Mosaic feature (Canvas|Mosaic) to create the road. I set the height and width as high as possible to make large blocks, and I chose two colors from the limited-color color set to act as road and grout.

I rendered the mosaic to the mask to allow me to more easily select the tiles, and then I adjusted the color to get some variation on the base image. I loaded the mask as an active selection and then cloned the image. In the clone, I grabbed the mask from the original image (Objects: Mask|Auto Mask; Using: Original Selection). I loaded the selection in the clone and transformed the selection to a path-based one. This allowed me to widen the selection by six pixels to get a good "road bed." I saved the larger selection as a new mask.

To get the correct color palette, I used the Effects|Tonal Control|Posterize Using Color Set command. Because I was not happy with some of the tile colors, I individually selected them with the Magic Wand and filled them with a different color from the color set.

I then imported a variety of Illustrator files from the Ultimate Symbol Nature Elements collection (you can download them from the Ultimate Symbol Web site at **www.ultimatesymbol.com**). I changed each one to a layer and reduced its size to fit on the road, and I recolored each one as necessary.

When I had everything the way I wanted it, I dropped all the layers and then used the Apply Surface Texture command (Using: New Mask 1) to get the 3D look on the road. I used a Soften amount of about 4.

MOSAICRD.RIF is included on this book's companion CD-ROM so that you can easily re-create the road should you so desire.

Region box, and enter "http://www.discov.com/sudamerica.html" into the URL field, as shown in Figure 8.31. Select the Oval Inside Bounding Box radio button and click on OK.

6. Make the Canvas layer active. Repeat Steps 3 through 5 for the maple leaf symbol. Use the URL http://www.discov.com/canada.html.

7. Make the Canvas layer active. Choose the Rectangular Marquee tool and create a selection around the lily. Make sure that the selection marquee is the smallest possible size that will allow you to comfortably

Figure 8.31

You can create a hotspot by completing the form in the Layer Attributes dialog box.

Figure 8.32

You can set a default URL for the image map.

select the area. Repeat Steps 4 and 5 and use http://www.discov. com/japan.html as the URL. Select the Rectangle Bounding Box radio button.

8. Make the Canvas layer active. Use the Rectangular Marquee to create a hotspot for the starfish (http://www.discov.com/bermuda.html) and the butterfly (http://www.discov.com/hawaii.com).

9. You can define a default URL for your image map if the site visitor clicks on something that isn't defined as a hotspot. I generally prefer not to do this, but you can if you wish. Choose File|Get Info. Select the WWW Map Default URL checkbox and enter a URL into the large box, as shown in Figure 8.32. Click on OK.

10. Check your layers by closing the eye icon on the Canvas layer. Figure 8.33 shows the defined hotspots.

Figure 8.33

You should check your hotspots for overlap before you save your image map.

11. Make the Canvas layer active. Click on the Load Selection button in the Objects: Masks palette. Load the imagemask mask (I created this for you in the file). This mask selects the entire area in the map that's to remain opaque. You *must* have an active selection if you want to add transparency to your GIF image when you save it.

12. Choose File|Save As. Save the file as ROADDONE.GIF. Although 128 colors should be sufficient, you can decide if fewer is reasonable by looking at the preview. Interlace the file. Click on the transparency button. Choose Background Is BG Color. Select the client-side map radio button. Figure 8.34 shows the Save As GIF dialog box with the options discussed. If you want to make sure all the colors are Web safe, load the default color set before you save the file and select the Color Set radio button.

SETTING THE THRESHOLD FOR TRANSPARENCY

You should set Threshold to 0 for this image when you save it. You can decide which setting you prefer by using the Preview button to see the effect of different Threshold settings for transparency.

Now that you've created your image map, what do you do with it? When you save the GIF file (or JPEG), Painter writes a companion HTML file if you've selected a client-side map. The HTML file is plain text and can be run as if the image map is your entire page, which is an unlikely occurrence, or you can cut the text and paste it into your own HTML document or into the HTML of an authoring program such as FrontPage, GoLive, or DreamWeaver. You can

Save As GIF Options

Number of Colors:
- ○ 4 Colors
- ○ 8 Colors
- ○ 16 Colors
- ○ 32 Colors
- ○ 64 Colors
- ○ 128 Colors
- ○ 256 Colors
- ● Color Set

Misc Options:
- ☑ Interlaced

Map Options:
- ☐ NCSA Map File
- ☐ CERN Map File
- ☑ Client Side Map File

Imaging Method:
- ● Quantize to Nearest Color
- ○ Dither Colors

Transparency:
- ☑ Output Transparency
- ○ Background is WWW Gray
- ● Background is BG Color
- Threshold [_____] 0%

Animation Options:
- Frame Delay: ms

Disposal Method:
- ● Default   ○ Background
- ○ None   ○ Previous
- ☐ Loop   times

[Preview Data] [Cancel] [OK]

Figure 8.34
Use the options shown when you save your GIF file.

also test your code immediately by opening the HTML file in your browser. You should see the link names in the browser status bar when you mouse over the hotspots.

There are some tricks that I've discovered to making the image map work properly in an HTML-authoring program. You need to place the GIF image that's referenced in the image map into the folder or directory that contains your Web site in progress. Open the HTML code in a text editor and copy the text to the Clipboard. Then paste the text into your partially completed Web page. Don't place the GIF image into your page. When you paste the HTML code, the reference to the file is already there, and the image will be displayed. If you also insert the image as you would a normal picture, it will be there twice (and not work one of the times). Figure 8.35 shows the image

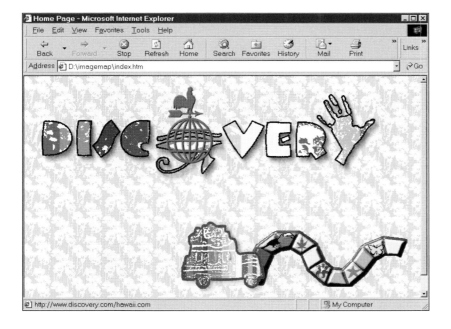

Figure 8.35
The image map works when placed into a browser.

map placed into Internet Explorer. I could not capture the cursor, but it's over the butterfly (as you can see in the status bar).

Images Sliced, Diced, And Rolled (Over)

One of the wonderful new features of Painter 6 is the Image Slicer plug-in. If you've created Web sites already, you'll know that one of the most thankless tasks involves cutting up an image to use it in a layout table. Tables are the best way to make sure that your images display the way you want them to. Although you can use precise positioning in CCS2 (level 2 of the cascading style sheets standards), browser support for CCS2 is limited to the most current crop of browsers and is not implemented the same way by all of them. For the Web designer, tables are still the safest choice.

When you create a table, you need to place your images into specific cells. A number of programs can create image slices, but I really like Painter's implementation. Painter's Image Slicer is much easier to use than image slicing in Adobe Image Ready, and it's eons above the agony of creating a complex table in Microsoft FrontPage.

The complexity in defining a table comes from the fact that the designer usually doesn't want to create even rows and columns in a table. Although you can span a number of columns and make then into one, you still need to determine just how many slices you want first.

Figure 8.36 shows a page designed for a personal Web site. The Web site is called A Candle In The Wind, and the home page features five candles. When you pass your mouse over any of the candles, a flame appears on top of the candle and indicates the page to which you'll be taken if you click on the

Figure 8.36
This is the A Candle In The Wind home page design.

candle. In order to make the rollovers appear, you need to place the image into a table with the rollover areas each in their own cell.

The idea is conceptually simple. Looking at Figure 8.36, you can see that everything should be easy to do. However, appearances can be deceiving; to get the five areas for the rollovers isolated—each into its own cell—requires a table with nearly one hundred cells. Luckily, the process, once you understand it, is really not that bad.

You do need to carefully design your image and leave it in its original layers until you're ready to export it. The image that you'll use, CANDLE-INTHEWIND.RIF, is still in layers, but all the layers that I used to construct the basic image are already grouped and then collapsed to merge them. I've already tested this image to make sure that none of the flames overlap each other and that it's possible to create a grid that will isolate each of the flames. Figure 8.37 shows the image with all the flames lit. Even though the site visitor will never see the image with all the flames lit, you need to make certain that your images contain no areas of overlap when all the rollovers are in place.

If you examine the Layers palette of the image, you'll notice that each flame is in its own layer. When I created the image, I had the flame, the glow behind the flame, and the editable text of the label as separate layers. However, you would not have been able to see the text unless you also had the same font (ITC Wisteria) that I used, so I committed the text layer to a regular layer and grouped and then collapsed the layers that comprised each rollover area.

Some of the glows look as if they are overlapping one another very slightly, but when you cut the image up, you won't notice a few areas of missing glow.

Figure 8.37
This image has been tested to make sure you can create nonoverlapping rollover areas.

PROJECT Slicing Up An Image

I divided this project into a few stages for easier comprehension. This first section of the project shows you how to open the Image Slider plug-in and create the basic slices.

At First Slice

Now, you'll get ready to make the first cuts:

1. Open the image CANDLEINTHEWIND.RIF, which is located on this book's companion CD-ROM.

2. Make the Canvas layer active.

3. Choose the Image Slicer plug-in on the Objects: Dynamic layers palette. Click on the Apply button. Figure 8.38 shows the Image Slicer dialog box.

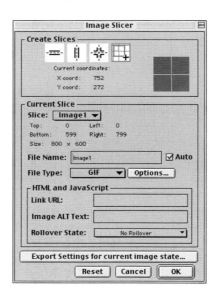

Figure 8.38
The Image Slicer dialog box.

4. Select the Horizontal Slice tool. You need to leave a horizontal slice above and below each flame. Figure 8.39 shows all the horizontal slice lines you need.

5. Choose the Vertical Slice tool. You need to leave slice lines on each side of the five flames. Because the flames don't line up evenly, you might need to slice in the middle of one flame in order to get the top and bottom of another. That is okay because you'll be able to combine sliced areas into one block again. Figure 8.40 shows the vertical slices.

Now that you've created some horizontal and vertical slices, you need to examine the cells very carefully and make some decisions about how you want to group the cells to export them. One of the beauties of using a table is

BREAK TIME

If you need to close the dialog box for any reason, you can do so by double-clicking on the OK button. You may open and close the Image Slicer dialog box as many times as you want with no ill effects.

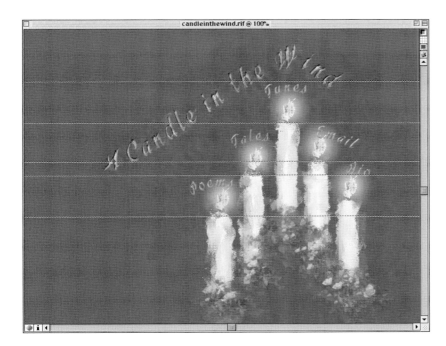

Figure 8.39
These are the horizontal slices needed.

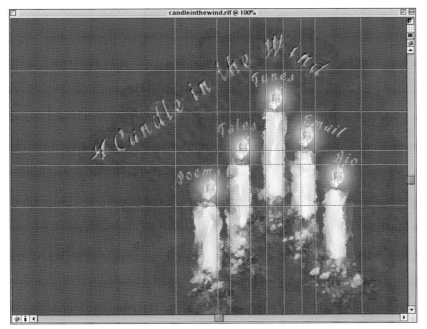

Figure 8.40
You need many more vertical slices than are immediately apparent.

that you don't have to fill every cell in the table, nor do you need to export every cell in the same format.

GIF images are best for areas that contain solid color or that contain low-color artwork. JPEG images work best for continuous color. If you wanted to include regular HTML text in an area of the table, you would not export that area at all. You would let the browser supply the text (by modifying the cell contents in the HTML code after the HTML code for the table is generated).

CORRECTING MISTAKES

You can move a slice line after you've created it by either pressing the Shift key to change the cursor to a double line with arrow heads on each side or by carefully positioning your cursor directly on top of a line so that the double-arrowhead cursor appears. When you see the changed cursor, you can move the line to a new location within the current larger cell (that is, you can't make the slice line jump over another slice line). If you need to remove the slice line entirely, press the Option key on the Mac or the Ctrl+Alt keys on Windows as you click on the line (the cursor changes from a plus sign to a minus sign).

(For Windows readers only: An anomaly exists in this dialog box. If you close and reopen the Image Slicer dialog box, you'll be able to move lines only if the Image Slicer is opened by double-clicking on its icon in the Layers Palette. I was not able to delete slice lines made prior to closing and reopening the Image Slicer.)

If you look carefully at the CANDLEINTHEWIND image, you'll see that with a bit of rearranging, you can create large runs of a single background color. That means that you could either export those solid areas as fast-loading GIF files or not export the areas at all and use the page background color or the cell background color in your table to fill those cells. That would certainly make for a faster-loading page.

The catch (and you knew there would be one, of course) is that the areas of background color might not match when you're done. The GIF and the JPEG file formats will export the background as a slightly different color. This happens to be more noticeable on Windows browsers for this example than it is on the Mac (at least in a comparison between Mac Internet Explorer and Windows Internet Explorer).

One solution is to create more slice lines so that the areas of solid color are chopped as closely to the background texture as possible to minimize the color change. Another solution is to export everything in the same format (although you still need to pick a closely matching background color to compensate for the difference in the site visitor's browser window size). You'll use a combination of the two methods here: chopping the solid areas out of the table as closely as possible and not exporting those slices, and using the same file format for all the slices that do get exported. You'll create the additional slices to isolate the background next.

THE CROSSHAIR SLICER

The third tool in the Image Slicer dialog box is the Crosshair Slicer. This leaves both a horizontal and vertical line at one time. It can be a timesaver for you. I don't use it very much because I prefer to think in only one direction at a time, but you might find it more convenient.

A Chance To Dice

Get out those Ginsu knives and start slicing:

1. Open the Image Slicer plug-in again if you've closed it by clicking on the plug-in icon on the Image Slicer layer in the Objects: Layers palette.

2. Move any lines that you've already created if you need to make them surround a solid area.

3. Use the Horizontal and Vertical Slicer tools to frame additional areas of solid color. Figure 8.41 shows the final slice lines for my image.

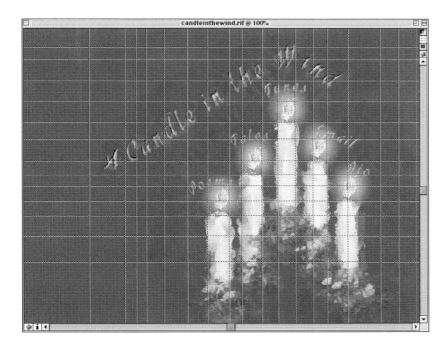

Figure 8.41
Here are the cells for the table before any grouping is done.

Recombinations

Now that you've divided up the image, you need to group the cells to bring some order to the areas for export. Follow these steps:

1. Start grouping cells by creating the groups needed for each rollover image. In the Image Slicer plug-in, select the last tool in the dialog box. This is the Grouping or Selector tool.

2. Locate the first rollover—the one that reads "Poems." Place the Grouping tool in the upper-left cell of the table that contains the word "Poems" and drag diagonally to the right until you've selected all the cells that you want to include in that group (that is, the cells that should be part of the rollover image). When you've selected all the needed cells, release the mouse button. The dividing lines between the grouped cells disappear.

3. Repeat Step 2 for all the rollover image areas. Figure 8.42 shows the combined areas for the rollovers.

4. Next, make the largest possible groupings of blocks to create the solid areas that won't be exported. Figure 8.43 shows these areas.

5. Finally, make groups out of the remaining cells. There is no "right" way to group what is left. Just try for the largest blocks you can create. Figure 8.44 shows my final groupings.

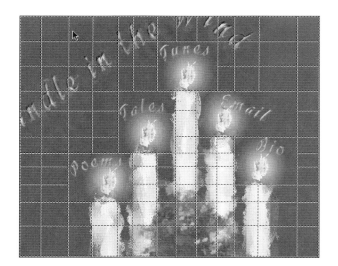

Figure 8.42

Notice the five larger blocks that indicate combined cells.

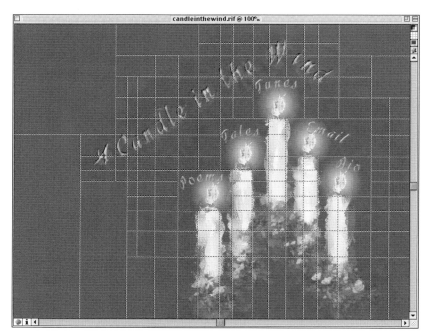

Figure 8.43

You should locate and group the largest blocks of solid color.

Now that you have all the cells determined, what do you do with them? You need to tell Painter how you want each slice exported and what rollover condition should be used to display the slice.

Rollover condition? What's that? Painter gives you several choices for the *state* of the image slice. The exported image slice can have the following states:

- No Rollover

- Mouse Over-Out

- Mouse Over-Out-Click

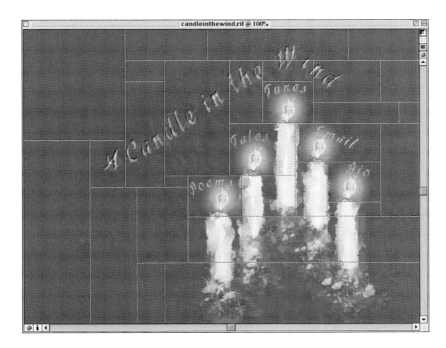

Figure 8.44
Here are the final cells for the table.

This means that you may have up to three images exported for each cell. One image (the No Rollover or Mouse-Out state) is the "normal" condition for the cell. You may also have an image to be displayed when the mouse is located in the cell (the rollover itself—Mouse-Over) or when the image is clicked (the Click state).

Setting Slices

This section of the project shows you how to define the various states for each cell. Follow these steps:

1. Open the Image Slicer plug-in if you've closed it (you can open it again by double-clicking on its icon in the Objects: Layers Palette). Use the Selector tool (the last tool in the dialog box) to locate the first cell in the upper-left corner. The Slice name in the dialog box will automatically read Image 1. I prefer to let Painter name most of my slices. I usually only change the rollover slices so that I can locate them more easily in the HTML code. Set the File Type field to No Export, as shown in Figure 8.45.

2. Locate the remaining solid areas and set the file type for each solid cell to No Export.

3. You can export the remaining slices as either GIF or JPEG. If you export as JPEG, your candles will show a softer and more accurate glow. If you export as GIF, you have a better chance of actually matching the color of the background image. For now, export as JPEG because

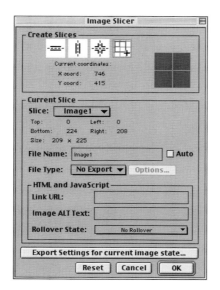

Figure 8.45

Setting the File Type field to No Export keeps the image from being saved as a table image.

it's faster to set the file as there are fewer options. Set the File Type field to GIF for all the images that have no rollovers in them. This will be all the remaining slices with the exception of the five cells that contain the lit candles. For each of these cells, change the File Type field to JPEG and set the Rollover State field to No Rollover.

4. You can now set the conditions for the five rollover areas. Set each File Type field to JPEG. Change the Rollover State field to Mouse Over-Out. I changed the slice name to indicate the menu item (Poems, Tales, and so on). Enter the URL to use as the link. You can use relative or absolute URLs. Enter an ALT text (a text description of the link) for each one as well. Figure 8.46 shows the settings for the Poems slice. Use that as a guide for all five slices.

Exporting The Table

Now that you've set up all of the slices and the conditions, you're finally ready to export your file. Follow these steps:

1. Click on the OK button in the Image Slicer dialog box to close the dialog box. You need to change the visible layers before you can export the file.

2. In the Layers palette, close the eye icons next to the Poems, Tales, Tunes, Email, and Bio layers. You now see the entire image as it should appear during the No Rollover or Mouse-Out state. Figure 8.47 shows the Layers palette set up correctly for the first export.

JPEG OPTIONS

You can set the level of compression in your JPEG using the Options button in the Image Slicer dialog box. I left my settings at the default of 65 percent quality and did not check the Progressive checkbox. This allowed me to quickly assign JPEG as the file type to the various cells. In your own work, you need to make the decision as to which settings you need to use.

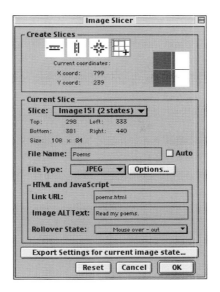

Figure 8.46
Use these settings as guidelines for the rollover slices.

3. Double-click on the plug-in icon next to the Image Slicer layer to re-open the Image Slicer dialog box.

4. Click on the Export Settings For Current Image State button.

5. In the Export Slices Options dialog box that appears (see Figure 8.48), set up the location to use to store the HTML table and the images (I advise creating a new folder to hold both the images and the HTML). I prefer not to have my code in all caps, but you can set it to your liking. Select the Include JavaScript check box. Select the Mouse Out radio button. Click on the Export button.

6. Click on OK to close the plug-in dialog box again. Turn on all the layer visibility icons in your image.

Figure 8.47
Close the visibility icons for the five rollover layers on the Layers palette.

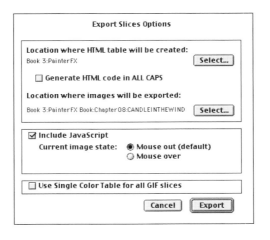

Figure 8.48
Use these export options.

7. Double-click on the plug-in icon next to the Image Slicer layer to re-open the Image Slicer dialog box.

8. Click on the Export Settings For Current Image State button.

9. All your settings are retained from the first export. Simply change the radio button selection to Mouse Over and click on the Export button again. The generating process is now complete. You may close the Image Slicer dialog box.

Look at the images in the folder you created for the table. You should see an _ON.JPG and an _OFF.JPG file for each of the five rollovers in the image. You should also see a text file with an .HTM extension. What's next? The final step is to incorporate the HTML that Painter generated into your Web site.

Here is the top section of the HTML code that painter wrote for this table. As you can see, it contains instructions for cutting up the code and pasting it into another HTML page.

```
<!—

File Created with Painter 5.5 Web Edition
http://www.metacreations.com/

To move the sliced image table and/or JavaScript rollover code to
another HTML document, copy and paste portions as directed below.

—>

<html>
<head>
<title>Untitled</title>

<!— JAVASCRIPT ROLLOVER CODE
    Insert the following block into the
    HEAD section of your HTML document.
    Be careful to paste this outside
    of any existing SCRIPT sections. —>


<!—— BEGIN COPY here for JavaScript rollover code ——>

<script language="JavaScript">
<!—
        // This JavaScript code was automatically
        // generated by MetaCreations
        // Painter 5.5 Web Edition
        // http://www.metacreations.com/
```

```
if(document.images){
mouseOverArray = new Array();
// preload image 1
mouseOverArray["tunes_off"] = new Image(101, 85);
mouseOverArray["tunes_off"].src = "tunes_off.jpg";
mouseOverArray["tunes_on"] = new Image(101, 85);
mouseOverArray["tunes_on"].src = "tunes_on.jpg";
mouseOverArray["tunes_text"] = "Try my Tunes.";
```

The HTML code is so complete that you should probably use this one as the basis of your page and add any other tags that you need to it. If, however, you're only creating a tiny table (a single rollover button, for example, as a single cell table), you can cut and paste as needed. Figure 8.49 shows the resulting table in Internet Explorer 5 for Windows.

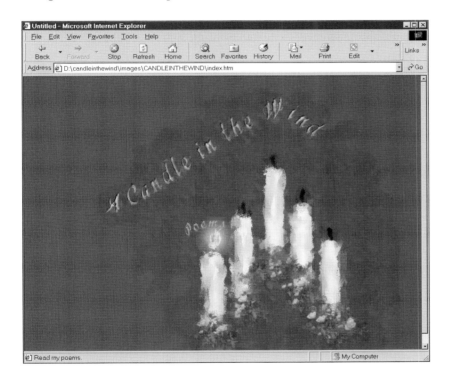

Figure 8.49
The final result of all your efforts is shown in the browser.

Moving On

This chapter gave you a lot of practice in creating items for the Web. You learned how to reduce the number of colors in an image, create a color set, and use many of Painter's Surface Control and Tonal Control commands to keep a limited number of colors in an image. You learned about the various file formats for the Web and how to create a GIF file with transparency. You also learned how to create buttons, image maps, and image slices for JavaScript rollovers. In the next chapter, Rhoda will teach you how to create and work with text in Painter.

DYNAMIC EFFECTS

9

BY

SHERRY

LONDON

In this chapter you'll learn how to create editable effects, such as burned edges, liquid lenses, bevels, and liquid metal.

About Dynamic Layers

Dynamic layers were first introduced in Painter 5 as the dynamic plug-ins. They really are plug-in technology, and, in theory at least, third-party developers can take advantage of the "hook" into Painter to write their own plug-ins. The hallmark of the dynamic layer is that the effect remains live and all of its settings can be repeatedly changed until you decide to make the layer permanent.

Some of the dynamic layers, such as Bevel World, create their effects directly on the selected layer itself. Other dynamic layers, such as Liquid Metal or Liquid Lens, create a completely new layer that sits above the rest of the image.

Unlike the layer effects found in Photoshop, Painter's dynamic layers only allow you to change the settings of the effect. You cannot change the underlying imagery. In Photoshop, after you designate a layer effect (such as a bevel) for a layer, you can draw anything else that you want on the layer and it, too, will get a beveled edge. Painter doesn't do that. You cannot touch anything on your original layer once you've applied a dynamic layer effect directly to it; otherwise, you'll freeze your dynamic settings.

Creating Rice Paper

This section demonstrates a technique that combines the use of several of Painter's dynamic layers. In this section, you'll learn how to create a background image that looks like rice paper with a burned edge. You'll use the Burn and Liquid Lens dynamic layers as well as the Growth Effect.

PROJECT Burning Your Bridges With The Burn Dynamic Layer

Here's a project that lets you experiment with the Burn plug-in. Follow these steps:

1. Open the image BRIDGE.PSD from this book's companion CD-ROM.

2. Select the entire image (Command/Ctrl+A). Click on the selection using the Layer Adjuster tool. This creates Layer 1 and leaves a white background canvas.

3. Select Burn in the Dynamic Layers section of the Objects menu. Click on the Apply button. You'll see the dialog box shown in Figure 9.1.

4. Move all the controls and see whether you can figure out what they do. When you're finished playing, click on OK.

Figure 9.1

You have many options to apply in the Burn dynamic layers.

Here's a brief summary of the controls you can set:

- *Burn Margin*—This sets the size of the burned edges in relation to the size of the layer. A high setting makes the burned object on the layer much smaller.

- *Flame Breadth*—This controls the amount of the object that's colored with the burned edge color.

- *Flame Strength*—This controls how much of the object looks scorched.

- *Wind Direction*—You can change the side of the object that has the largest burn width.

- *Wind Strength*—This sets the amount of burning that occurs on the windward side of the object.

- *Jaggedness*—You can control the irregularity of the edges of the object.

- *Use Paper Texture*—This controls the darkness of the burn area based on the values in the paper texture that's selected. You can best see the effect of this by choosing the Halftone 3 paper texture, scaling it to 200 percent, and setting a 400 percent contrast. As you can see in Figure 9.2, it becomes blazingly clear (sorry) what happens when you check the Use Paper Texture option.

- *Burn Interior Edges*—If your shape is hollow, this checkbox allows it to burn from both the outside and the inside. You need to use this setting carefully because you could finish with your image all burned up.

As you can see, you have a lot of flexibility with the Burn dynamic layer. You can even change the color of the burned area. This flexibility allows you to use this dynamic layer to apply an edge to an area of a layer that you *don't* want to look burned. This is the perfect segue into the next exercise—creating rice paper.

Figure 9.2
You can use a paper texture in the burn areas of your object.

Figure 9.3
This is a simple paper texture with a burned edge.

Growing A Paper

Now that you've "met" the Burn dynamic layer, you can begin to see some of the possibilities of burnt edges. The easiest way to actually create the paper is to make a flat background for the paper first and then use the Burn dynamic layer as your last step.

The simplest possible expression of the concept of paper with a burned and deckled edge would be to create a flat background, add a paper texture, and then burn the edges. It would look like Figure 9.3. However, I have something a bit more interesting in mind.

PROJECT Growing Things With The Growth Command

You're going to the use the Effects|Esoterica|Growth command to add fibers to the paper. This project shows you how the Growth command works. Follow these steps:

1. Create a new image that's 400 pixels square (or whatever dimensions you prefer). I like to work against a white background, but on your own, feel free to use any background color that you want.

2. Choose red as your foreground color.

3. Select Effects|Esoterica|Growth. Figure 9.4 shows the settings I want you to use, but take some time to play with the various settings first and look at the changes that show in the preview (read the "What Are The Growth Brush Controls Doing" section as well). When you're finished, change the sliders to Flatness: 150 percent, Thinout: 53 percent, Random: 100 percent, Thickness: 8 percent, Branch: 9, Max Level: 5, Fork: 1.7, and Fork Ratio: 96 percent. Make certain that both the Hard Edges and Fractal checkboxes are selected.

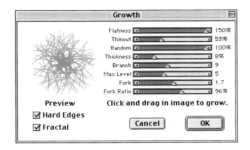

Figure 9.4
The Growth dialog box allows for infinite variety.

What Are The Growth Brush Controls Doing?

As you look at the Growth dialog box in Figure 9.4, it isn't really apparent that the controls are all linked and interrelated in the Growth brush. You might not even realize the extent to which one setting depends on the others when you play with the sliders.

The key control in the Growth dialog box is the Branch slider. If you were to bring all the sliders to the left (that is, in their minimum positions), you would see nothing more than a single horizontal line. The Branch control sets the number of lines that start at the center of the growth brush. The maximum number is 20.

However, the Branch control interacts with the Thickness and the Thinout sliders as well. Thickness controls the base width of the lines. Thinout controls the degree to which the lines get thinner as they move from the center. The slider is counter-intuitive. The line thins out more from the center the lower the slider is set. If the slider is at its maximum setting, lines get thicker as they radiate outward. The first row of effects in the following figure shows this interaction:

1. The only slider that isn't at the left is the Thickness slider, which is set to its maximum of 33 percent.

2. The Thinout slider is moved to its maximum of 150 percent in addition to the Thickness of 33 percent. If the Thickness slider was moved to 0 percent, the Thinout slider would have no effect on the line width at all. You need to use these two settings together.

3. The Branch setting allows you to begin to see a shape. Here it is set to its maximum of 20, with Thinout left at its maximum of 150 percent but Thickness reduced to 2 percent.

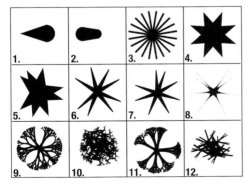

The 12 images shown here illustrate the range of effects you can get with the Growth command.

4. To round out the top row, if you reduce the Branches setting to 8, set the Thickness to its maximum, and set Thinout to 0 percent, you get the quilt star motif shown here. (Tip: By changing the number of branches, the Thinout, and the Thickness, you can create wonderful stars.)

    As you add an element of randomness to the settings, the plot thickens.

5. This example shows the Random setting pushed to the maximum but all the other settings left as they were in image 4. As you can see, the Random setting rearranges the location of the branches.

6. In this example, I changed the Thickness to 10 percent and the Thinout to 20 percent so that you can see the interactions of the Flatness and Max Level sliders in images 7 and 8 more clearly. To recap, in this example, Thickness is 10 percent, Thinout is 20 percent, Branches is 8, and Random is 100 percent. All other settings are at the left.

    The next two settings also work together. Flatness is one of the major settings for the Growth brush, but it has no effect unless the Max Level setting is also moved from the left. The Max Level setting does nothing unless the Random slider is greater than 0. When the Random slider is greater than 0, the Max Level slider changes the random placement of branches (which means that it works better if you have more than one branch).

7. This is the same image as number 6, but the Max Level has been changed to 9. Notice how the position of the spokes has also changed.

8. This image shows what happens when you change the Flatness setting. Here, it's set to 75 percent. The Flatness setting controls the 3D quality of the spokes and works in conjunction with the Max Level, the Thickness, and the Thinout sliders to dramatically change the shapes of the individual spokes.

    The next major change occurs when you begin to move the Fork and Fork Ratio sliders. They both must be moved from the left of the slider if you are to see any change at all from either slider. The Fork slider controls the number of sub-branches on each branch or spoke, and the Fork Ratio controls the number of times and the locations at which the sub-branches branch out. Neither control works without the other, but they will cancel each other out (and make a large blob) if both are set to their maximums.

9. This image shows the Fork slider set to 1.0 and the Fork Ratio set to 100 percent. The other settings are unchanged from number 8.

10. By changing the Fork slider to 2.5, you can create thick brambles rather than plain thorns.

11. By setting the Fork to 0.2 and the Fork Ratio to 150 percent (its maximum), you can create a shape with great complexity at its tips—almost like a delicate sprig of honeysuckle or the single flowers on a hyacinth.

12. If you make the opposite set of changes—changing the Fork to 3.1 and the Fork Ratio to only 22 percent—you can create tangles that are similar to the thorn patterns on a cactus or that look like barbed wire.

4. Once you've changed the settings to your liking (or my specifications), you need to actually "draw" with the Growth brush. (I wish I had a dime for every time I've carefully set up the sliders on the Growth brush and then pressed the OK button, at which point the dialog box goes away, the command is finished, and the canvas is still empty!)

To use the tool, you place your cursor in your image, click and hold the mouse button, and drag out a circular marquee to the size of the brushstroke you want. Painter applies the growth settings within the marquee's area. You need to be aware that you'll always draw the circle from the center, so leave room if you want the entire stroke to appear on your canvas.

For now, you need to draw multiple strokes on your blank canvas with the settings that you selected in Step 4. Overlap the strokes however you want. Get a good coverage of the canvas, but don't place so many strokes that you can no longer see the individual ones. Figure 9.5 shows my example after all the Growth brushstrokes are drawn.

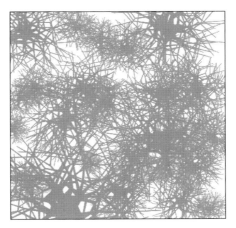

Figure 9.5
Painting with the Growth brush is an organic experience.

5. The next step is to fade the intensity of the color. Choose Edit|Fade and select an Undo amount of approximately 80 percent. This will give your paper a lovely subtlety.

6. Now you can add some specks or threads of bright color to it. Open the Growth brush again (you can press Command+/ on the Mac or Ctrl+/ on Windows as a shortcut). Figure 9.6 shows the new settings to use. Notice that these settings make a more open tangle of color.

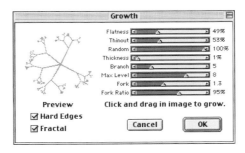

Figure 9.6
Use these settings to create an accentuating Growth brush.

7. Before you paint, you need to change your current color. You may change colors (and settings for that matter) as often as you want while the dialog box is open. Pick a bright yellow in the Color palette. Paint a few small, randomly placed strokes with it and then change to a bright green. These strokes are to provide hints of accent color, so use small strokes and space them widely apart. Make some additional strokes in red, magenta, and orange as well. (I placed the marker in the Colors palette at the tip of the triangle and then just rotated the outside wheel to change the hue.) Figure 9.7 shows the image (although you certainly can't see the color in it). Close the dialog box by clicking on the OK button when you're done.

8. Save your image.

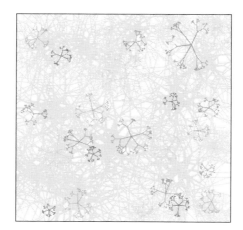

Figure 9.7
The second layer of growth strokes provides a strong color accent.

Once you've applied two levels of the Growth brush, you're ready to put the mixture into a bowl and beat it to a pulp. In other words, it's time for the Liquid Lens.

The Liquid Lens—Or How To Make Pudding From Paper

The Liquid Lens dynamic layer is a layer that's placed on top of all the layers in your image (or on top of the layer that's active when you select the Dynamic Layer command). It allows you to mix up the contents of your image as if you were stirring a batch of cake batter. The Liquid Lens command gives you a variety of egg beaters (each one beats to a different drummer) and also enables you to control the size, spacing, and smoothness of the egg beaters. Unlike mixing a cake, however, if you don't like the taste of this concoction, you can toss it out and suffer no ill effects (and no loss of your original image).

In this project, you'll use the Growth brush image as the batter and beat in the Liquid Lens. It allows both applications of the Growth brush to meld together in the final paper. The Liquid Lens tool is similar to many of the tools in Kai's Power Goo.

PROJECT Mixing Up Some Liquid Pulp

You can mix up the paper texture that you're developing using the Liquid Lens dynamic layer. Here's how:

1. Choose the Liquid Lens dynamic layer in the Objects: Dynamic Layers palette. Click on the Apply button. Figure 9.8 shows the resulting dialog box.

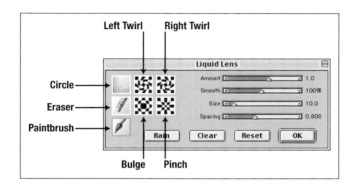

Figure 9.8
The Liquid Lens allows you to non-destructively mix up the colors in your image.

2. You may fiddle with the settings as you please. I used the default settings for this example. I used the Paintbrush and the Left and Right Twirl tools to swirl the colors. You need to be careful that you don't make the accent splotches too muddy. You might want to brush gingerly around them.

3. When you like the swirling results on your image, click on the OK button to exit the dialog box. Figure 9.9 shows my image at this point in time.

4. If you find any areas that you don't like, you have two ways to change them after the fact. First, you can reopen the dynamic layer by double-clicking on the plug-in icon to the left of the layer in the Objects: Layers palette. You can then use the Eraser tool to reverse the transformations on the area as far back as you want. Second, you can use the Layer Adjuster tool to move the layer to a slightly different location. The dynamic Liquid Lens will recalculate its transformations over the new area.

Figure 9.9
The paper-in-progress sports a newly swirled look thanks to the Liquid Lens dynamic layer.

You could drop the dynamic layer at this point and then apply the Burn dynamic layer, but I think that the image doesn't yet look enough like paper. You have a few more effects to apply to it first.

Textures To The Rescue

One of things that the paper lacks most is texture. You'll apply texture to it in two stages. First, you'll use either Image Luminosity or 3D Brushstrokes and then the Paper option in the Effects menu's Apply Surface Texture dialog box.

 To Texture Twice

This portion of the project shows you several ways to apply texture. Follow these steps:

1. Choose Effects|Surface Control|Apply Surface Texture. Figure 9.10 shows the resulting dialog box (which should be familiar to you by now).

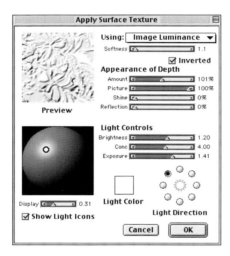

Figure 9.10

The Apply Surface Texture dialog box allows you to add a feeling of depth to your image.

2. There are three controls in this dialog box that are critical. You need to select either the Image Luminance or 3D Brushstrokes option in the Using field. You also need to select an Amount setting and a Softness setting. You should set both Shine and Reflection to 0 percent and Picture to 100 percent (so you don't have a choice for those fields). However, the choices that you make for Softness and Amount will control the success of the texturing step (see the "Is Handmade Paper Really That Lumpy?" sidebar).

3. You may click on the Inverted button if you think this effect looks better. Click on OK when you like the preview. You might want to undo this command several times and try out a variety of possibilities before you make your final decision. Figure 9.11 shows my finished surface texture. Don't panic yet! It won't remain that ugly.

Figure 9.11

The textured Liquid Lens looks surprisingly ugly when it first comes "out of the oven."

4. Use the Edit|Fade command to remove some of the texture if your image is too strong. I used an Undo amount of 48 percent on the image shown in Figure 9.11.

Figure 9.12
You can remove any unwanted areas from your image by using the Eraser brush.

5. The other trouble spot in the textured layer is the embossing that appears around the area that was actually painted by the Liquid Lens dynamic layer. This is easy to fix. Choose the Paintbrush tool in the Toolbox and then choose the Eraser brush in the Brushes palette. Use the Flat Eraser tool. Just wipe away any trace of the unneeded embossing. You can also remove areas of artifacting that you don't like. Remember, your original image is still safely underneath the textured layer and will appear when you use the Eraser. Figure 9.12 shows my "fixed up" texture layer. The texture is still there, but it's much more subtle now.

6. Drop the Liquid Lens layer onto the canvas.

7. Choose the Handmade paper texture in the Art Materials: Textures palette. Now, reopen the Apply Surface Texture command (Mac: Command+/ or Windows: Ctrl+/). This time, choose Paper Texture in the Using field. If you use a Softness setting greater than 0, keeping it less than 1. 0.3 is a good idea. You can leave the Amount setting at 100 percent. Click on OK when you're finished.

8. If the image still looks as if it's composited rather than manufactured, you can apply the same Surface Texture settings again. I faded my second application by 48 percent. You can also apply a bit of smoothing (Effects|Focus|Soften) between the first and second texture application.

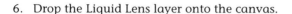

IS HANDMADE PAPER REALLY THAT LUMPY?

Handmade paper can by highly textural. You can actually embed leaves and flowers or threads or onion skins into handmade paper. However, the Apply Surface Texture effect is usually a bit over the top in the realism department. You'll remove some of the texture when you apply a paper texture to whole image. By applying Image Luminance or 3D Brushstrokes texture first, however, you break up the repeating nature of the Apply Surface Texture Using Paper command.

You have some control over the texture as you apply it. The default softness setting of 0 is much too harsh for the paper. The tiny lines in the Liquid Lens layer break up and artifact by gaining ugly black specks around them. By setting the Softness to .5-1.1, you can avoid some of the artifacting. I've found that Softness settings over 1.1 tend to make the texture look as if it had been in an earthquake. However, if you push the Softness even further, up to about 4 or 5, the artifacting and earthquakes disappear and you're left with smooth foothills. The image looks different, but you can work with it. Therefore, you need to use a tiny setting or a medium setting and skip the in-between values for Softness.

You have two approaches you can use for Amount. You can set the effect to 100 percent (or that vicinity) and then fade the effect afterward, or you can use a smaller amount at the beginning. I prefer to fade the effect because that's easier than not adding enough texture. Unlike the old story about "how long do you cook the roast beef?" (the answer to which is "cook it until it burns and then a little bit less"), you *can* "cook" this texture less.

Figure 9.13
The paper is now complete and only awaits its deckled edge.

9. You can also soften the result by adding a new layer to your image. Click on the New button in the Objects: Layers palette. Make white your Current color in the Art Materials: Colors palette. Select Effects|Fill and fill the layer with your Current color. Reduce the Opacity of the layer in the Objects: Layers palette until you're satisfied with the result. I used an Opacity setting of 36 percent. Figure 9.13 shows the finished paper.

10. Drop the white layer onto the canvas.

The paper texture should now look as if it's a complete and unified whole—not a collection of put-together bits.

Controlling The Burn Dynamic Layer

You've seen the deckled edges on handmade paper before. They're the same edges that the Burn dynamic layer creates, but the edges don't look burnt. They look darker and possibly a bit stained. The trick to making a Burn layer look like this is in controlling the attribute settings in the Burn dialog box.

If you use a "flame" that covers too much of your object, the object looks embossed and 3D. "Real" deckled paper would not have a pronounced 3D look to it. Therefore, you need to apply very low settings.

PROJECT Making Deckled Paper

This project shows you how to apply a deckled edge to your paper. Follow these steps:

1. Select the entire Canvas layer (which is also your *only* layer in the image). You can use the Command/Ctrl+A shortcut.

2. Choose the Layer Adjuster tool from the Toolbox. Click on the selected area to change it into a layer (don't hold down the Option or the Alt key—just click). You don't want to leave the original on the canvas; the canvas needs to be white.

3. Choose the Burn dynamic layer in the Objects: Dynamic Layers palette and click on Apply.

4. Turn the Flame Breadth down to a maximum of 3 percent. This immediately removes the embossed look from the paper. Now you can play with the other settings. Once the embossing effect is gone, the other controls can vary however you want them. I raised the Jagged setting to 100 percent, and when I pushed the Wind Strength to 77 percent, I discovered that I needed to reduce the Flame Breadth setting even further (down to 2 percent). Figure 9.14 shows the settings that I used.

HOW CAN YOU COMMIT A DYNAMIC LAYER?

You know that it's possible to commit a crime. Committing a dynamic layer makes no grammatical sense at all! Fear not, when you commit a dynamic layer, you remove the ability to change the settings for the layer and freeze them in their current position. You convert the layer from a dynamic layer into a plain, ordinary layer. You can commit a dynamic layer by selecting Commit from the menu accessed by clicking on the arrow in the upper right of the Objects: Dynamic Layers palette, or you can commit a dynamic layer automatically when you apply another command to it or try to paint on it.

Figure 9.14
These settings create a very narrow edging of burned or deckle on an image.

5. Select a new color for the burn area by clicking on the Burn Color swatch. I picked a slightly darker pink than the texture itself, but one that was very close to neutral gray. I chose Hue: 331, Saturation: 17, and Value: 70. If you try to match my numbers, you should note I was working on a Mac. The Windows Color Picker uses different numbers.

6. Click on OK to view your paper. You can change the edge effect any time until you commit the effect.

7. You're almost done. Handmade paper is sometimes processed in layers so that it acquires a double-deckle on its edges. Here's how to create one. Choose File|Clone. This creates a copy that contains the entire image but only one layer.

8. Choose the Rectangular Marquee tool and drag a marquee that covers the inside of the paper without touching the deckled edge at any point. Make it as large as possible without hitting the deckle.

9. Choose Select|Invert. Use the Layer Adjuster tool, hold down the Option or Alt key, and click on the selection. Just the outer edge of the original image is transferred into the new layer.

10. Apply the Burn dynamic layer again. Immediately turn the Flame Breadth down to 3 percent or less. Then make your other adjustments. The only setting that I changed was to choose the same Burn Color that I used in Step 5. Changing the Burn Margin to a lower number will give you a slightly larger border area. Click on OK when you're pleased with the result.

11. Use the Layer Adjuster tool to drag the layer into your original image. Now you have two dynamic layers that you can adjust if you want. In addition, you can reduce the opacity of the second border layer. I turned it down to 56 percent. Figure 9.15 shows the final result.

Figure 9.15
This paper has been sliced and blended and now has a double-deckled edge.

What else can you do with a handmade paper? I created this London postcard for the introduction of Painter 6, whose theme was "Travel the World." Most of the postcards featured in the Painter manual contain a paint can in them somewhere. In this image, the guard at the Tower of London is wearing the paint can in place of his hat. I built the textured paper using the preceding steps. However, I used a watercolor clone of a collage of London scenes (taken in March 1998 on my first visit to London—a trip I'd dreamed of all my life) as the base for the paper. Figure 9.16 shows the postcard.

Figure 9.16
The queen would probably be surprised if her guards started a new fashion in headgear.

Heavy Metal

Actually, you'll see some very delicate metal in this section. I'd like to introduce you to Kelly Loomis. She's an incredibly talented artist who creates Web interfaces that she releases as linkware. If you've never heard the term *linkware*, it refers to graphics that are free for noncommercial use, but the people who use them must place a link on their sites back to the site that provided the graphics.

In Kelly's case, if you would want to use her graphics on a personal site, you'd have to include her link. Kelly's Web site can be found at **www.7rings.com**. She's fond of the Art Nouveau period, and many of her interfaces are derived from that era. Her interfaces are the most beautiful I've ever seen.

Kelly was kind enough to share her techniques for using Painter's Liquid Metal dynamic layers command. Figure 9.17 shows some of the graphics from Kelly's Aztec Influence set. All the jewelry-like images were created in Painter using the Liquid Metal dynamic layer command. Kelly achieves her

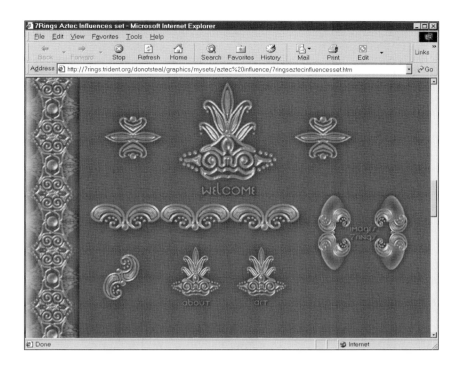

Figure 9.17
Aztec Influences, by Kelly Loomis of 7rings.com, was designed using the Liquid Metal dynamic layer.

effects by creating the original artwork at a larger size than her intended use and by (typically) postprocessing the metal with Flaming Pear's BladePro filter. Let's look at each of these issues.

Why would you create your artwork at a larger size than needed? This has actually been a graphic arts technique for years. Before the advent of computers, many logos were created at, at least, 200 percent and then reduced photostatically. The photostatic reduction got rid of jaggies and hand jitter and generally smoothed things out. Because metallic effects are so reflective, they don't work particularly well on tiny imagery. By creating them at larger sizes, you give the objects a chance to be as exciting as they can be; then you have an increased number of options concerning their new size (such as using them at larger sizes or repurposing them for different publications).

If you haven't used BladePro, you should really try it. It's a beveling filter that creates incredible metallic effects. You can set the texture and the reflection map from thousands of presets or from your own imagery. Flaming Pear's Web site is at **flamingpear.com**. You can download an evaluation copy of BladePro free for 30 days. You'll particularly like this filter if you also have access to Photoshop or PaintShop Pro. Although BladePro does work under Painter, it doesn't work well. It sometimes filters only part of the selection, and on other occasions, it crashes Painter. Kelly always saves the Painter file as a PSD (Photoshop format) file and then brings it into Photoshop for further processing. That's another reason to work at a larger size. BladePro does a better job with larger images than it does with small ones.

Let's take a look at how you might use Kelly's workflow and techniques in a purely Painter-based fashion. You'll have a chance to try both the Liquid Metal dynamic layer and the Bevel World dynamic layer. Figure 9.18 is a design that I created using Kelly's basic techniques. However, I remained in Painter throughout the process and used the Bevel World dynamic layer for postprocessing. In the project, I'll show you how it was done.

Learning Liquid Metal

Why would a dynamic layer be called *Liquid* Metal? Why not just call it Metal? The Liquid Metal dynamic layer is special. Hard metals just stay where they're put, but liquid metal does not. It exhibits *surface tension*, which means that drops of the metal combine and merge together when they get near one another. After you've placed liquid metal in your image (until you commit the layer), you can change the metal and push it around. That's why it's called *Liquid Metal*.

Of course, there's also another reason why it's called liquid metal. By reversing some of the settings in the dialog box, you can also create water. And water, unless it's really cold (or hot), tends to be liquid.

The dialog box for the Liquid Metal dynamic layer is fairly straightforward and easy to understand. However, as with most of Painters tools, it gives you a lot of power and large number of choices. Figure 9.19 shows the Liquid Metal dialog box.

One of the reasons you can continue to mush around the metal, even after you're finished painting, is that the metal is stored as a vector, rather than a raster, object. The Arrow tool is your key to moving around the metal droplets, and, if you wish, you can actually see the position of every droplet by selecting the Display Handles checkbox.

Figure 9.18

Here's a metallic jeweled charm I created with the Liquid Metal and Bevel World dynamic layers.

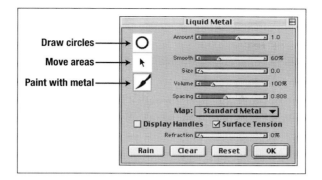

Figure 9.19
The Liquid Metal dialog box allows you to control the form of the metal that you create and to mush it up and order it around.

Painter's manual provides mostly clear explanations of the settings, although the description of the Amount slider ("controls the emphasis of the metal effect...for all droplets in the layer") is not a marvel of clarity. Nonetheless, it usually makes more sense to *watch* what's happening than to read about it. This simple introduction to the Liquid Metal dynamic layer should give you a much better idea of the range of possible effects.

 ## A Touch Of Liquid Metal

This project shows you how to work with Liquid Metal. Follow these steps:

1. Open the image FEATHERDANCE.PSD from this book's companion CD-ROM. Figure 9.20 shows the original image.

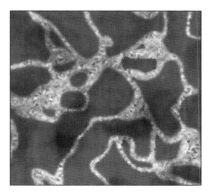

Figure 9.20
Here's the Featherdance image before I added the Liquid Metal dynamic layer to it.

2. Select the Red Roses pattern as your current pattern in the Art Materials: Patterns palette.

3. Select Liquid Metal in the Objects: Dynamic Layers palette and click on Apply. You'll see the dialog box from Figure 9.19.

4. Set the Refraction slider to 0 percent and the Amount slider to 5.0. Set Smooth to 100 percent. Then select the Circle tool.

5. Place your cursor in the center of the image and drag out as large a circle as you can without touching the edges of the canvas. Figure 9.21 shows this step. You see a reflection in a pool of metal.

Figure 9.21
This is the "classic metal" reflective effect.

6. Click on the Surface Tension checkbox to unselect it. As you can see in Figure 9.22, the entire metal blob goes flat. Click on the Surface Tension checkbox to select it again.

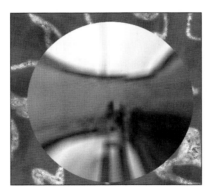

Figure 9.22
The Surface Tension checkbox keeps the metal rounded.

7. Change the Amount setting to -5.0. The reflection flips in the opposite direction.

8. Now, drag the Refraction slider to 100 percent. This is the setting for water. As you drag the Refraction slider to the right, the metal droplet becomes more transparent. At 100 percent, it's fully transparent. The -5.0 setting for Amount magnifies the image area on the layer *beneath* the Liquid Metal (see Figure 9.23). As you can see, the Amount and the Refraction sliders should be adjusted together.

9. Drag the Amount slider back to 0.0. Now you see no effect in your image at all. Slowly drag the Refraction slider toward the left. At 50 percent, you see a muddy, semitransparent droplet. At 0 percent, you see a solid gray disk, as shown in Figure 9.24. You can think of this as

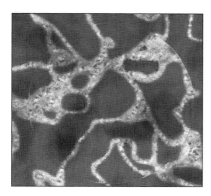
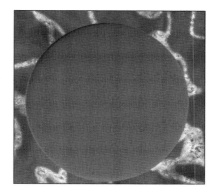

Figure 9.23
(Left) When you reverse the positions of the Amount and Refraction sliders, the effect changes from reflective metal to water.

Figure 9.24
(Right) When the Amount slider is set to 0.0, the Liquid Metal shows color and no reflection if Refraction is also set to 0 percent.

the "neutral" position. Although it's useless for water effects (because they're invisible), it can be a good starting position for metal.

10. You have a variety of metal effects that you can create by changing the option in the Map field. Map defaults to Standard Metal, but you also have the choice of two Chromes, an Interior view, and a Clone Source view (which reflects the current Pattern if no Clone Source is defined). With the Amount slider in the 0.0 position and Refraction at 0, try all the Map options now. Then move the Amount slider to 1.0 and cycle through the list again. Figure 9.25 shows a small example of all five effects. At this setting you can see that you create a mildly reflective metal that's quite pleasant to see (although the Interior Map is not very compelling at a 1.0 Amount setting). When you move the Amount setting to 5.0, the Standard Metal becomes extremely reflective, the Chromes don't change very much, the Interior map acquires a lovely shading, and the Clone source more accurately reflects the rose that you used as the Current Pattern.

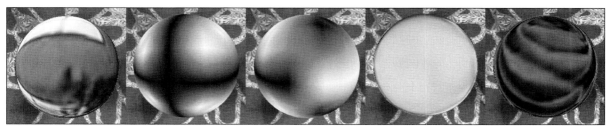

Figure 9.25
From left to right: Standard Metal, Chrome 1, Chrome 2, Interior, and Clone Source. The Amount is 1.0 and the Refraction is 0.

11. Change the Size slider. As you move it around, the large droplet shrinks and grows (but it will never grow as large as its starting position). If you wanted to change the size of either the Brush tool or the Circle tool used in the Liquid Metal dynamic layer dialog box without resizing anything you've already created, you need to select the Arrow tool and click away from all the metal droplets to deselect them. Then move the Size slider.

CHANGING SLIDERS AFTER SOME DROPLETS EXIST

The Smooth, Size, and Volume sliders change the settings for all selected metal droplets and for future droplets. Your last stroke is always automatically selected. If you don't want to change the size of any of these elements, then click away from them with the Arrow tool before you change your sliders. If you want to change some of your previous droplets, use the Arrow tool to select the ones that you want to affect.

12. The Liquid Metal dynamic layer has no Undo command. However, you can "unpaint" metal as well. Deselect the droplet with the Arrow tool and then choose the Brush tool. Press and hold the Option or Alt key and paint over areas of your droplet. The metal disappears from the droplet.

13. You can also create rain. Click the Clear button to remove the large droplet. Change the Refraction to 100 percent and the Amount to -5.0. Change the Size slider to approximately 25. Click on the Rain button. You can stop the rain by clicking on the image when you have enough droplets. Figure 9.26 shows the rain.

14. See what happens when you change the Refraction to 0 percent and set the Map field to Interior. Change the Amount to 2.0. You can also select the entire image by dragging a marquee around it with the Arrow tool and make all the droplets smoother (move the Smooth slider). Figure 9.27 shows this effect (but I lightened the background in grayscale for contrast).

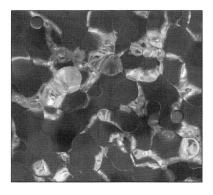 

Figure 9.26
(Left) It's raining droplets!

Figure 9.27
(Right) The Interior map creates interesting metal droplets on rain.

At this point, you should have a very good idea of how to create almost any effect that you want with the Liquid Metal dynamic layer. Here are a few additional tips:

- You can change the Current Pattern while the Liquid Metal dialog box is open, but in order to see the change in the Clone Source map, you need to click on the Reset button in the dialog box.

- You need to exercise some care in selecting an image for the Clone Source map. If you try out different patterns, you'll notice that some of them make the metal flat and dead. A good clone source or pattern has lights and darks that can become reflections.

- Standard Metal uses the pattern called Interior Reflections as its model. The Interior map does not use the Exterior Reflection pattern. (I'm just reporting on this—I didn't design this logic!)

- Try changing the Volume slider. You can make the stroke swell and shrink. If you were to animate the effect, it would look as if the sun came out and dried up all the rain.

- Use the Arrow tool on lines that you've painted to shove them in a different direction or to rearrange their shapes.

- Sometimes the Dynamic Layer dialog box refuses to open again when you double-click on its plug-in icon on the Objects: Layers palette. When this happens, you can reopen the dynamic layer by choosing the Objects: Dynamic Layer menu and then Options.

PROJECT Drawing An Abstract Painting In Metal

Now that you know about Liquid Metal, you're ready to try it out. I'll walk you through the steps for creating an image like the one shown in Figure 9.18, but because this is a totally abstract image, don't worry about trying to duplicate it exactly. Follow these steps:

1. Create a new image that's 400 pixels square with a white background.

2. Choose the Liquid Metal dynamic layer in the Objects: Dynamic Layers palette and click on Apply.

3. Choose the Brush tool. Set Refraction to 0, Amount to 1.0 or greater, and Size to about 3.3.

4. Paint a design in the image. Figure 9.28 shows my "doodle."

> ### WHAT IF YOU DON'T WANT AN ABSTRACT IMAGE?
>
> If you can draw, you can draw whatever you want to in liquid metal. However, if you prefer some help, you can easily place a piece of clip art into your image and use it as the template for your liquid metal painting.

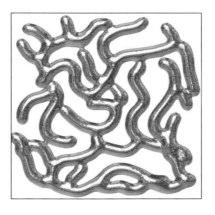

Figure 9.28
You can create an abstract image with the Liquid Metal Brush tool.

5. Use the Arrow tool to pull out some squiggles in the lines.

6. Change the Map to Interior.

7. Click on OK to exit the dynamic layer.

8. Create a second dynamic layer by clicking on Apply in the Objects: Dynamic Layers palette.

9. Make your brush size smaller and set the Map field to Chrome 1. Paint a second layer on top of the original metal.

10. Add a third layer in Standard Metal. This time, paint a tiny line around the outside of some of your abstract lines. I set the Refraction slider for this layer to 71 percent (which made it fairly light). Figure 9.29 shows the effect.

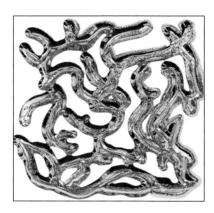

Figure 9.29
(Right) This image contains three layers of Liquid Metal.

Bevel World

The Bevel World dynamic layer (which you used in Chapter 8) provides a wonderful finish to the Liquid Metal metallic effects. You're now going to finish up the creation of the jeweled ornament by adding a variety of bevels and beveled objects to it.

PROJECT A Beveled Ornament

In this project, you'll build an ornament that combines elements from everything you've done in the chapter. The project has several parts.

Beveled Liquid Metal Topping

First, you'll create the top element for the ornament. Follow these steps:

1. Save your Liquid Metal image. Save it again under a new name (you'll use this second copy).

2. Shift-click on the other Liquid Metal layers in the Objects: Layers palette to add them to the selected layers. Click on the Group button in the Layers palette. Then click on the Collapse button to make them a single layer.

3. In the Objects: Dynamic Layers palette, select Bevel World and click on the Apply button.

4. Change your settings to those shown in Figure 9.30. This makes an almost dull-and-pitted-looking metal ingot. The light color is Hue: 60,

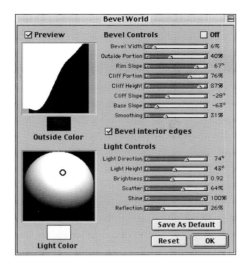

Figure 9.30
Use these settings on the combined Liquid Metal layers.

Saturation: 6, and Value: 100 as chosen on the Mac. It's almost white. This translates to RGB 255, 255, 240.

5. Save this copy. This is the top layer of the ornament, and you'll use it again in a few minutes. But first, you need to build the bottom layer.

Building A Beveled Base

Next, you'll build a base for the ornament. Here are the steps:

1. Open the deckled paper that you created earlier in this chapter (or use mine—DECKLE.PSD on this book's companion CD-ROM).

2. Select Liquid Metal in the Objects: Dynamic Layers palette and click on Apply.

3. Set Amount to 1.0, Map to Interior, and Refraction to 0 percent.

4. Using the Circle tool, create several large droplets that meet and merge.

5. Use the Alt or Option key with the Circle tool to push away some of the metal. Also, create a hole inside of the metal. Use the Arrow tool to reposition the droplets and to select the entire set of droplets so that you can tweak the Smooth and Volume settings. Click on OK when you like the results. Figure 9.31 shows my results.

6. Drop all the layers in the image. Select the entire image (Command/ Ctrl+A). Click on the selection with the Layer Adjuster tool to cut the image into Layer 1.

7. Choose Bevel World from the Objects: Dynamic Layers palette. Click on the Apply button.

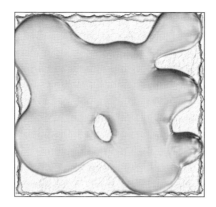

Figure 9.31

I've created some flat metal on top of the rice paper.

8. Use the settings shown in Figure 9.32 to create a steep bevel with a deep lip. The light color is Hue: 60, Saturation: 6, and Value: 100 (Mac), which is also RGB 255, 255, 240.

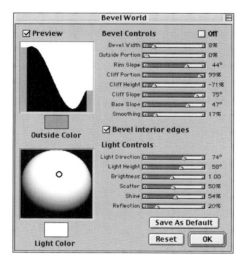

Figure 9.32

These settings create a steep bevel with a deep lip.

9. Drop the layer. Choose Canvas|Resize and change the canvas size to 250 pixels.

10. Click on the window containing your beveled abstract image to make it active. Resize this image as well. Choose Canvas|Resize and set it to 200 pixels square.

11. Choose the Layer Adjuster tool and drag the beveled layer onto the beveled bottom layer that you prepared. Your results should be similar to those shown in Figure 9.18.

What caused the bevel to form the lip? All the controls in the Bevel World dynamic layer are interconnected, but the Cliff Portion and Cliff Height settings were the key ingredients. The Softness setting needs to be set fairly low

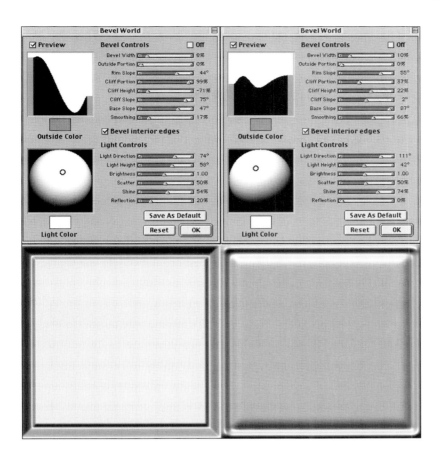

Figure 9.33

Changing the Cliff Portion and Cliff Height settings make dramatic changes in the shape of the bevel.

in order to see the sharp additional ridges. Look at Figure 9.33. The settings are above the bevels.

Finally, you can use the Bevel World dynamic layer or a third-party bevel filter to manufacture jewels to set into your liquid metal. On the left side of Figure 9.34, I filled the layer below the metal with flat areas of color. I then bevel the areas so that they fit into the spaces. On the right side, I used the BladePro filter on the flat color areas to create glass jewels. I then desaturated and darkened the liquid metal for a more dramatic look.

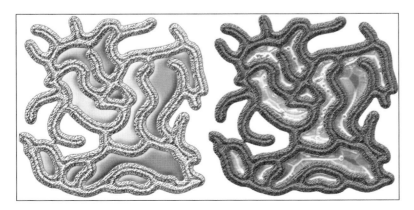

Figure 9.34

You can postprocess liquid metal by making embossed fills for it (Bevel World on the left and BladePro on the right).

Dynamic Layers And Masks

You've learned a lot about several dynamic layers. However, I didn't talk about the need to make selections from them. This is much trickier than it should be, so it's worth a mention.

It's an interesting anomaly that a dynamic layer has no mask. If you need to create a mask for the layer (so that you can use it as a selection) but you still want to keep the dynamic layer in your original image, here's a somewhat convoluted set of steps that will do the trick.

PROJECT Masking An Effect

In this project, you'll learn how to create a selection and a mask from a dynamic layer.

1. Create a new image that's 400 pixels square.

2. In the Canvas layer, draw a circle with the Elliptical Marquee tool. Fill it (Edit|Fill) with the current color or a pattern. As long as it has a color that isn't black or white, you'll see the effect.

3. Select the Liquid Metal effect in the Objects: Dynamic Layers palette. Click on Apply.

4. Use the Brush tool to draw a ring of Standard Metal around the edge of the circle. Feel free to decorate the circle with metal if you want. Click on OK to apply the layer.

5. Let's pretend that you want to color the metal but you're not ready to commit the layer just yet (it's as good a reason as any for this technique). You want to create a selection in the shape of whatever you drew in the metal layer. Make the dynamic layer active. Select the entire layer (Command/Ctrl+A).

6. Copy the layer to the Clipboard (Command/Ctrl+C). Then paste (Command/Ctrl+V) the selection back into the image. This creates a new layer that's also a dynamic layer.

7. Leave the new layer active. Choose Commit from the Objects: Dynamic Layers menu.

8. Twirl down the arrow next to the Objects: Masks palette. Click on the layer mask to make it active (its eye will open as well).

9. Choose Copy Mask from the Objects: Masks menu and select New as the option. The Load Selection command will now be available to you. You can trash the new layer.

10. Click on the New Layer icon to add a new layer above the dynamic layer.

11. Click on the Load Selection button in the Objects: Masks palette and load New Mask 1.

12. Pick a color in the Art Materials: Colors palette that you want to use as a tint for your current color. Fill the selection with the current color. Change the layer's Composite mode to Gel. If you need to further adjust the color, you can use the Effects|Adjust Color command.

Moving On

You've learned a lot of ways to use dynamic layers in this chapter. You've seen how to play with the Burn dynamic layer to create a deckled edge that's not burned (and to create a variety of actual burn effects as well). You've learned the ins and outs of creating liquid metal and water effects. You've also had a chance to try Kelly Loomis's trick of working larger to produce a delicate small metallic jewel. Finally, you've had time to master the Bevel World dynamic layer.

In the next chapter, Rhoda will show you a variety of text tricks—and some of them will use your friend, the Bevel World dynamic layer.

TEXT EFFECTS

BY

RHODA

GROSSMAN

Painter 6 offers two separate ways to create and manipulate text: vector-based shapes and editable Dynamic Text on a baseline that can be curved, slanted, skewed, rotated, distorted, and filled. Did I mention two types of shadow?

Vector-Based Text

The Text tool is grouped with other shape tools on the right side of the Tools palette. There's a rectangle and oval shape tool sharing the same space. The Bezier curve tool, with its pen-point icon, is familiar to users of object-oriented programs such as Adobe Illustrator. See your Painter 6 user guide for instructions on using the Bezier tool to create anchor points and control handles for curves. Sharing the same space with the Bezier tool is the Quick Curve tool, which allows you to draw a freehand shape with anchor points appearing automatically.

Additional tools are provided to alter shapes. The scissors can be used to cut a segment from a shape, and other tools nested under it allow you to add or delete anchor points or convert between smooth and corner points.

Figure 10.1

The word *paint* has been grouped. The group is currently open, so individual letter shapes can be selected.

When the Text tool is selected, the Controls palette gives you choices for font, size, and tracking (letter spacing). Typing on the canvas creates a separate layer for each letter, as shown in Figure 10.1. Each letter has the shape icon next to its name. Notice that the word *paint* has two layers for the letter *i* because the dot over the *i* is a separate shape. The Layer list can quickly become long if you type even a few words, and it's a good idea to group words or phrases to make them more manageable. When the group is closed and selected, you can move, use Orientation commands, or change stroke and fill for the entire word. When the group is open, each item in the group can be selected for alteration.

Staying In Shapes

At some point you might want to paint or add effects to your lettering. This requires committing the shapes to pixel-based layers. Before making that commitment, take advantage of the features that are available only when your text is in shape mode.

PROJECT Strokes And Fills

While your text is a shape, you can assign solid color fills and strokes using Set Shape Attributes in the Shapes menu. Follow these steps:

1. Make a new white canvas that's about 400 by 100 pixels.

2. Click on the Type tool in the Tools palette and choose the font, size, and tracking you want to work with in the Controls palette. I used 94 point Benguiat with tracking set at 0.155

3. Type the capital letter *P* five times. Notice that your Layer list shows each letter as a shape.

4. Select the first letter you typed by clicking on it with the Adjuster tool.

5. Open Set Shape Attributes in the Shapes menu and give the letter a gray fill and a black stroke that's three points wide.

   Figure 10.2 shows the Set Default Shape Attributes dialog box. In this example, a black stroke that's three points wide and a gray fill are being used. Strokes and fills can be turned on or off independently with the appropriate checkbox.

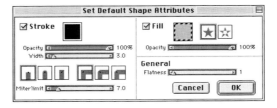

Figure 10.2
The Set Default Shape Attributes dialog box.

6. Select the second letter you typed and give it a black fill and a black stroke. Experiment with the width of the stroke.

7. Give the third letter a dark fill and a stroke in a lighter color. Access the Color Picker by double-clicking on the color swatch.

8. Apply a thin stroke and no fill to the next letter.

9. Finally, apply a thick stroke and no fill to the last letter.

Figure 10.3 has the capital *P* in Benguiat font with a variety of strokes and fills. From left to right, you see a black fill and no stroke and then a black fill and black stroke, which effectively creates a bolder letter. The next sample letter is filled with black and stroked with gray. The fourth sample letter has a delicate look resulting from a thin black stroke and no fill. Finally, you see a wide stroke and no fill.

Figure 10.3
Capital *P* with a variety of strokes and fills.

Font Stylin'

Letterforms can be altered subtly or drastically with the Shape Selection tool (the hollow arrow that pops up when you click and hold on the Adjuster tool). Use the Shape Selection tool to move an anchor point or change the angle of a wing (the line tangent to the curve) by moving the wing's handle. You can select more than one point by Shift-clicking or dragging around the points you want. When points are selected, they're filled with red. Unselected points are hollow. Figure 10.4 shows the capital *P* with four anchor points selected. Also shown is the elegant new letterform achieved when those points are dragged up. Similar transformations to the rest of the Benguiat

Figure 10.4
Capital *P* with four anchor points selected and the stretched letter.

> **Note:** Strictly speaking, you can't really create a font with Painter. However, there are programs, such as Macro-Media Fontographer, that enable you to do this.

> **Note:** You can't select specific anchor points when the entire letter is selected (all points filled with red). You need to deselect the letter first and then click where you want to activate a point.

alphabet could result in an entirely new font, called "Benguiat Stretch," perhaps. Here are the steps to follow:

1. Make a new white canvas that's about 400 by 300 pixels.

2. Use the Type tool and select a font. I'm using Benguiat again.

3. Type the capital letter *P*. If it is too small, don't bother to retype it at a new point size. Just drag from a corner of the marquee with the Adjuster tool, keeping the Shift key down to avoid distortion. You'll distort it in a different way in a moment.

4. Find the Shape Selection tool and use it to select about four points at the top of the letter, as shown in Figure 10.4.

5. Drag the selected points up to stretch the top of the letter and leave the rest of it unchanged. Your results might differ from mine, depending on the style of the font you're using.

You might want to create an entirely new look for all your text or simply distort a few letters for a special effect. As you can see in Figure 10.5, I began with the traditional look of Palatino Bold and transformed the letter *A* into three different styles. The curved legs in the *A* at the upper right gives this letter the bouncy look of a cartoon. I needed to add an anchor point to the thicker leg to make it curve in. The angular "grunge" look on the lower left was easily achieved by moving a few anchor points on the letter's left side. Finally, the reversed out effect was the result of selecting all the anchor points on the left side of the letter and dragging them completely across to the right. All it took was some experimenting with the selection of anchor points and where to drag them.

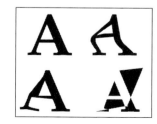

Figure 10.5
Palatino Bold variations.

Making A Commitment

When you begin to apply a brush stroke to text or attempt to use any command in the Effects menu, Painter asks you to commit the shape to a pixel-based layer. Figure 10.6 shows that you have the option to commit, to cancel, or to commit and avoid the warning altogether for the remainder of your work session.

Once you've made that commitment, there's no going back to vector mode, except with Undo. Painter has no feature for converting a pixel-based layer back to a shape. In Figure 10.7, the capital *P* on the far left has a fill, and the letter next to it has only a stroke. Both were committed to pixel-based layers and the Paint Bucket was used to apply a pattern fill to each of them. Notice that the letter that has just a stroke accepted the pattern fill only as a border.

Figure 10.6
The Commit dialog box.

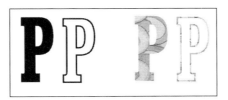

Figure 10.7
Text as shapes with fills or strokes are committed to pixel-based layers. The Paint Bucket fill is restricted to the stroke in the letter without a fill.

Earlier versions of Painter left you without the capability of ever painting or filling the inside of that letter, unless you had enough Undo commands to go back to shapes mode and establish a fill in Set Shape Attributes. Alternatively, you could drop the letter into the canvas and fill it there, thus losing the ability to treat the letter as a separate item. However, Painter 6 introduces a new feature for layers that Photoshop users know, and it's actually given the same name that it has in Photoshop: Preserve Transparency.

With Preserve Transparency enabled, effects and brush strokes are restricted to pixels that already have some color. Turning off the Preserve Transparency function allows you to paint any portion of the entire layer. Your choice depends on the results you want to achieve.

Techniques for embellishing text or any pixel-based layer are provided in the following sections and projects.

PROJECT Esoterica Fills

The Paint Bucket can be used to fill with the current color, gradient, pattern, or weave. There are other ways to create fills—ways that do not require the Paint Bucket. In this project you'll practice using Blobs, Marbling, and Grid Paper from the Effects|Esoterica menu, to produce results similar to those shown in Figure 10.8. Follow these steps:

1. Make a new white canvas that's about 400 by 200 pixels.

2. Type "ABC" in large capital letters in a fat font. I've used a novelty font called Blades.

NOT SO VERY ESOTERIC

Don't let the name *Esoterica* frighten you. This group of effects is not difficult to handle and does not require secret knowledge. I think the folks at MetaCreations must have had an awful time figuring out what to name this diverse set of effects. "Other cool stuff" just didn't seem appropriate. See Chapter 11 for more details on managing these effects.

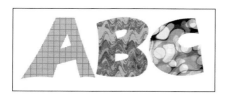

Figure 10.8

Letters with Esoterica fills.

3. Fill all three letters with black. Use a black stroke, too, if you need to fatten up the letters.

4. Select *A* with the Adjuster tool.

5. Find Grid Paper in the Effects|Esoterica menu. Accept the default settings and apply. Your black letter is now white with blue grid lines horizontally and vertically. It might be difficult to read the letter, depending on the design of the font. The next step will fix that.

6. Use Edit|Fade to reduce the fill so that the letter has a gray background but the grid lines are still visible. I used 50 percent.

7. Select *B* with the Adjuster tool.

8. Choose a pattern for filling the letter. I used Celtic Knot.

9. Use the Paint Bucket to fill the letter with the pattern (choose Clone Source in the Fill With pop-up menu).

10. Find Apply Marbling in the Effects|Esoterica menu. You can marble "manually" by choosing a sequence of combinations in the Marbling dialog box. Alternatively, use the Load command to find a recipe that will automatically create a marbling style. I used the nonpareil style.

11. Select *C* with the Adjuster tool.

12. Make white the current color.

13. Find Blobs in the Effects|Esoterica menu. In the Blobs dialog box, choose Current Color. The default settings for size variations and number of blobs are okay when you're filling an entire canvas, but for filling a letterform, you might want to reduce the minimum and maximum sizes. Experiment until you get an interesting fill.

14. Use Edit|Fade to make the blobs medium gray.

15. Repeat the Blobs effect. If you were happy with the settings used in Step 13, there's no need to change them. Randomness is built into the Blobs effect. You can never get the same blobs twice, even if you want to.

16. Fade again, this time allowing the second group of blobs to be lighter gray.

17. Do the blob-and-fade routine once more. Now your *C* should have a bubbly, Lava-Lamp look.

Figure 10.9 shows the word *NUTS* filled with the image of peanuts. The font, by the way, is the truly wacky Basketcase Roman. How can you fill type with an image? You could make a new pattern from a photo or scan of peanuts and use the Paint Bucket to fill the word. Sherry's chapter on pattern effects, Chapter 5, can help you do that. If you don't want a repeating pattern but prefer to use the entire image and have control over exactly where it will show through the text, the following technique will fill the bill. It's not really a fill—it's more like a *reveal*—because it depends on the use of composite methods.

Figure 10.9
Text filled with an image.

Image Fills

Another way to fill your letters is with images. Using the appropriate photographic image to fill type is an effective way to communicate visually. Here are the steps:

1. From this book's companion CD-ROM, open CITYSCAP.tif, John Webster's photo of a landmark San Francisco building reflected in the glass of another (see Figure 10.10).

2. Use the Text tool and type the word "CITY" in a strong sans serif font. I used Magnesium.

Figure 10.10
A cityscape by John Webster.

3. Group the letters.

4. Use Set Shape Attributes to apply a black fill. Add a black stroke if you need to make the letters thicker.

5. Resize the word and move it close to the bottom of the image window, as shown in Figure 10.11.

   The plan now is to make the entire photo a layer on top of the black type and switch the composite method from the default to Lighten. Wherever the white canvas and the photo overlap, white canvas will show (it's lighter than the photo). Where the text and photo overlap, the photo will show (because it's lighter than black).

6. Make the canvas layer active and use Select|All (Command/Alt+A).

7. Click on the canvas with the Adjuster tool, thus making the photo a layer.

8. Place the Photo layer on top of the text group by dragging its name bar to the top of the Layer list. The text is now hidden.

9. Change the composite method of the Photo layer to Lighten.

10. Move the Photo layer around with the Adjuster tool until just the right area is revealed through the text. Your image should look like the one shown in Figure 10.12.

Note: There are two "Select All" commands in Painter. The one you want here is in the Select menu; it selects all pixels in the canvas background. Don't use the Select All command in the Layer menu. That one is used to select all layers except the canvas background.

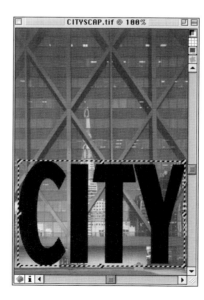

Figure 10.11
(Left) The cityscape with type in place.

Figure 10.12
(Right) The cityscape photo using the Lighten method on top of black text.

Painted Strokes

A wide range of effects can be obtained simply by painting on your pixel-based text. Try the Image Hose with nozzles provided by Painter, or those we created for you on this book's companion CD-ROM. Experiment with combinations of effects.

Figure 10.13 shows text painted with variants of the F/X brush family. The *M* on the left was filled and stroked with black and converted to a pixel-based layer. Then the Neon Pen variant was used to make four strokes with Draw Style in the Controls Palette set to Straight Line. The *M* on the right also began as a black letter, and the Fire variant was used to paint the flames in the Freehand style. Preserve Transparency was turned on so that painted strokes would not spill over outside the letters.

Another pair of letters, shown in Figure 10.14, demonstrates the value of having a choice between freehand and straight-line drawing. The *A* is black with straight white Fine Point Pen lines crisscrossing it. The *B* is white with freehand black scribbles made by a Pencil variant.

Figure 10.13
Text painted with Neon Pen and Fire variants of the F/X brush family.

Note: Freehand or Straight Line are Draw Style options available in the Controls palette when the Brush tool is active.

Figure 10.14
Straight-line and freehand drawing styles.

 ## Quick-And-Dirty Marbling

Here's a way to make a kind of marbling using two F/X variants in tandem:

1. Make a new canvas or just use your current image for this project.

2. Use the Text tool to type a letter or word in the font of your choice.

3. Select the Piano Keys variant of the F/X brush family. Make some test strokes with Piano Keys and, if needed, increase the variation in Saturation and Value until your stroke has a wide range of light and dark striations.

4. Enable the Preserve Transparency feature in the Layers palette.

5. Paint Piano Keys strokes on the text.

6. Switch to the Squeegee variant and scribble over the text until you get the amount of distortion you want. Figure 10.15 shows the letter *N* before and after the Squeegee strokes.

Note: Variability in the Hue, Saturation, and Value settings is controlled with sliders in the Color Variability section of the Art Materials palette.

Figure 10.15
Text painted with Piano Keys and then marbled with the Squeegee variant.

Surface Effects

Some of the brush variants in Painter 6 include surface texture effects—notably the Impasto family. Texture and emboss effects can also be applied with commands in the Surface Control menu. In Figure 10.16, the letter *A* has had Pavement paper added with the Apply Surface Texture command. The letter *B* shows the same paper applied, but the Express Texture command was used.

The Apply Surface Texture, Using Original Luminance, command created the embossed look on the letter *C*. Using Original Luminance delivers a texture based on the grayscale values of the current item in the Pattern palette, unless you've designated some other open image as the clone source. In this case, the Overlapping Waves pattern was used. See Figure 10.17 for my settings in the Apply Surface Texture dialog box. Notice the Light Direction indicator and the application of a small amount of softness.

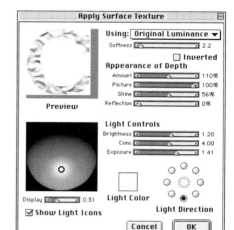

Figure 10.16
(Left) Some texture effects.

Figure 10.17
(Right) The Apply Surface Texture settings for the letter *C*.

3D Effects

All three letters in Figure 10.18 have depth effects made with Apply Surface Texture using the letter's mask. The only difference among them is the Softness setting. Softness at zero gives the *D* some thickness, like press-on type made from vinyl. Increase the Softness setting to about 5 for a beveled look, and raise it to 10 to get the puffy effect.

Serious bevelers will want to use Bevel World in the Dynamic Layers library. See Chapter 9 for details on managing those powerful tools. Figure 10.19 has two bevel effects made by my students. Magda Elshimi altered the shape of the letter *A* by moving anchor points and applying Bevel World settings.

Figure 10.18
Apply Surface Texture using the layer mask and different Softness settings.

Tony Salguero's *H* was given extreme perspective using the Orientation|Distort command. Then he added the bevel. A drop shadow adds to the 3D illusion.

PROJECT Me And My Shadows

Drop shadows are created easily in Painter, and they're conveniently independent of the items they shadow. Shadows can be applied to all the members of a group simultaneously—another convenience. With little effort, you can regroup the shadows for each letter in a word in order to make a new group containing only the shadows. You'll see how handy that can be in this project. Follow these steps:

1. Make a new white canvas that's about 500 by 300 pixels.

2. Type a word in a font of your choice. Use Set Shape Attributes to give it a black fill.

3. Group the letters and create a drop shadow for the entire word by using Effects|Objects|Create Drop Shadow (see Figure 10.20).

   Painter automatically groups a layer with its shadow. Figure 10.21 shows the Layer list at this point. The group W and Shadow is open, so you can see both the letter *W* and its shadow as independent items. In the next few steps you'll reorganize these layers so that all the shadows are grouped together into one.

Figure 10.20
(Left) Drop Shadow applied to the grouped letters.

Figure 10.21
(Right) The Layer list after applying a drop shadow to grouped text.

Figure 10.22

The Layer list after grouping all shadows together.

4. Open all six groups containing the letter and its shadow.

5. Shift-click on each of the shadows to select them all.

6. Group them by clicking on the Group button or using the Group command in the Layers menu (Command/Ctrl+G). Your Layer list will look like the one shown in Figure 10.22.

7. Collapse the group into one layer by clicking on the Collapse button or using the Collapse command in the Layers menu. This will enable you to apply any effects that are not allowed on a group.

8. Use Effects|Orientation|Flip Vertical on your new shadow layer and drag it into the position shown in Figure 10.23.

   Now you have a cast shadow—or at least the beginning of one. A bit more tweaking will enhance the illusion.

Figure 10.23

The Shadow layer flipped vertically and positioned to create a cast shadow.

9. Your shadow layer is still selected. Use Effects|Orientation|Distort to reduce the height of the shadow and skew it to the left or right.

10. Gently spray white with the Digital Airbrush variant to make the shadow appear to fade slightly as it spreads away from the letters.

In Figure 10.24, the word appears to be standing on a flat surface with light coming from the right to cast a shadow toward the left.

Figure 10.24

The cast shadow completed.

Edge Effects

Sherry describes manipulating edges in Chapter 9. The dynamic layers I find especially useful for creating edge effects on text are Tear and Burn. The two letters in Figure 10.25 were given a medium gray fill with Set Shape Attributes. Then Tear and Burn was applied.

Figure 10.25

Tear and Burn applied to gray text.

I discussed beveling as a 3D effect, but it can also be considered in the category of edges. What would happen if you added beveling to a torn or burned letter? Figure 10.26 shows a capital *Z* with Tear applied and then a bevel applied. The final effect looks like eroded canyons or a stone-age carving.

Figure 10.26
Text with Tear and Bevel
World effects.

All Together Now

You've learned a variety of text effects in this chapter. I think you're ready for the final exam. The following project will give you an opportunity to use everything you know and maybe discover some things I never thought of.

PROJECT Alphabet Sampler

A *sampler* refers to a piece of artwork that demonstrates a wide variety of techniques. Think of the needlework samplers of an earlier era. You'll create a complex image from a simple outline alphabet using a different effect for each of the 26 letters.

I'm grateful to Gordon Silveria, head of the illustration department at San Francisco's Academy of Art, for this project. I've found it to be an excellent assignment not only for working with type but also for exploring principles of good graphic design. Before you plunge in, you might want to take a moment to examine solutions by some of my students in the color Painter Studio.

Figure 10.27 shows the alphabet you'll be working with. They're outlines made from a sans serif font in Adobe Illustrator. Painter will interpret these vector outlines as shapes. Here are the steps:

1. From this book's companion CD-ROM, open ALPHABET.ai in Painter, using the Acquire command in the File menu.

2. Look at the Layer list in the Object palette. Notice that each letter is listed as a "compound." Select All in the Layer menu and click on the Ungroup button at the bottom of the palette. Now each letter is listed as a numbered shape. Figure 10.28 shows the Layer list at this point.

GRAPHIC DESIGN BASICS

If you want to accept the challenge of creating a good composition as well as just practicing text effects, keep the following general principles in mind as you work on this project:

- Have a focal point. Make one or two letters more important than the others.
- Create variation. Variation can be achieved through differences in size, color, value, opacity, angle, complexity, and texture.
- Create balance. This can be done through symmetry or with asymmetrical tensions.
- Unify the composition. There are several methods for keeping your artwork from looking like a ransom note. Limit your colors, for example. Be aware of the importance of "negative space" (the shape of empty areas around your letterforms).

Figure 10.27
The alphabet image.

Figure 10.28
Alphabet layers listed as
numbered shapes.

WHO'S COUNTING?

There are 34 shapes corresponding to the 26 letters in
the alphabet because some
letters are composed of more
than one shape. The letter *A*,
for example, has an interior
shape for the hole (called a
counter by typographers). The
letter *B* has two counters, so
it's made up of three shapes.

---

3. Double-click on each item in the Layer list and rename it with the corresponding letter of the alphabet so that you can easily find the item you want to work with.

4. Use the Set Shape Attributes dialog box to apply various strokes and fills to the letters.

   Change the sizes and angles of some letters and experiment with overlapping them.

5. Use the Shape Selection tool to alter some of the letters by manipulating their anchor points and curves.

6. Commit some of the shapes to pixel-based layers or convert them to selections. The following steps refer to methods you can use after committing shapes to pixel-based text.

7. Paint the shapes with Brush variants.

8. Fill some of them with gradients, patterns, weaves, and other images.

9. Add some drop shadows.

10. Apply surface textures using a variety of source images.

11. Create edge effects with Bevel World, Tear, and Burn.

12. Change composite methods (letters must overlap for this to work).

13. Drop some of the letters into the background canvas and then use Effects|Focus commands or Liquid brushes to distort the type.

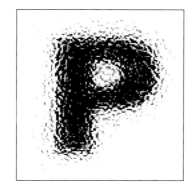

Figure 10.29
Glass Distortion applied to
text that was dropped into
the background.

An example of what can be achieved after dropping a letter is shown in
Figure 10.29. The capital *P* was dropped and the Rectangular Selection marquee dragged around it, leaving some space for the letter to spread.
Effects|Focus|Glass Distortion was then applied using Paper.

Dynamic Text

A major new feature of Painter 6, Dynamic Text, is a member of the library
of dynamic layers, which includes the edge effects used in this chapter—
Burn, Tear, and Bevel. What makes them all "dynamic" is their capability of
having their settings changed at any time, until they're committed to standard layers.

Figure 10.30 shows where to find Dynamic Text, and Figure 10.31 tells you
what I think about it.

When you apply Dynamic Text, you'll create new type in the dialog box
shown in Figure 10.32. This is really three dialog boxes in one. You have
three choices for curve style in the Baseline controls, plus the option of keeping

Figure 10.30
Dynamic Text selected in
the Dynamic Layers section of
the Objects palette.

Figure 10.31
An example of Dynamic Text
on a curve.

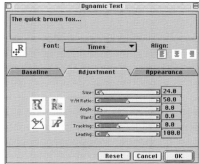
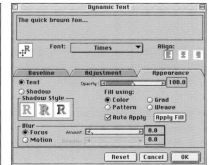

Figure 10.32

The Dynamic Text dialog box has controls for Baseline, Adjustment, and Appearance.

the type on a straight line. It's hard to tell from the icons how the three curve styles differ. Figure 10.33 shows a line of text in each of the three styles.

Use the arrowhead icons to select, add, or subtract anchor points on the baseline, which is a Bezier curve. Figure 10.34 shows the curve being altered by moving the handle on the anchor point's wing.

You can make the text do every contortion imaginable with the Adjustment controls, especially if legibility is not a high priority. One thing you cannot do is mix fonts within the same Dynamic Text layer. Figure 10.35 shows the use of the word *jumps* with a different font and, of course, its own baseline and other controls.

Figure 10.33

Three curve styles for Dynamic Text.

Figure 10.34

Altering the baseline using Bezier techniques.

Figure 10.35

Two Dynamic Text layers in different fonts.

The Appearance controls provide a dizzying array of possibilities. There are the usual suspects for fills: Color, Pattern, Gradient, and Weave. Two kinds of blur and two styles of shadow are available, and you decide whether the fills and blurs are applied to the text or the shadow. Figure 10.36 shows black text with an outside (drop) shadow and light-colored text with an inside shadow.

A bit of experimenting will yield a rich harvest of effects, some of which you might actually want to use.

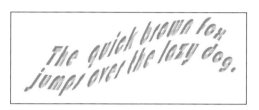

Figure 10.36
Two kinds of shadow for Dynamic Text, outside and inside.

PROJECT **Flaming Type**

Choosing an appropriate font is the first step in creating many type effects. The emotional impact of color needs to be considered. In this project, you'll also take advantage of precise controls for Motion Blur. Follow these steps:

1. Make a new canvas that's about 400 by 150 pixels.

2. Apply Dynamic Text and type the word "Flaming" in the text box. Use the straight-line option for the baseline. I used a novelty font called Metamorph, as shown in Figure 10.37.

Figure 10.37
The word *Flaming* in the font Metamorph.

3. Click the Adjustment tab and change the slant of the type. I used a slant of -80. Adjust the size in this control panel if you need to.

4. Click the Appearance tab.

    The remaining effects will be done in with Appearance controls. You have access to Art Materials sections while the Dynamic Text dialog box is open, so leave it open while you do the following preparation.

5. Establish a bright red as your primary color and black as your secondary color.

Figure 10.38

The Gradients section of the Art Materials palette, with the two-point gradient selected.

6. Choose the two-point gradient in the Gradients section of the Art Materials palette and move the angle ring so that black is at the bottom and red is at the top of the preview swatch (see Figure 10.38).

7. Return to the Dynamic Text dialog box. Make sure the Text radio button is enabled and click on the Grad button in the Fill Using section.

8. Click on the Shadow radio button and choose the outside shadow style.

9. Fill the shadow using color. It should still be red.

10. Enable Motion Blur for the shadow and adjust Amount and Direction to make the word appear to have flames blowing up at the angle you want. Figure 10.39 shows my finished effect, with a Blur setting of 75 and Direction set to 145.

Figure 10.39

A "flaming" effect using Motion Blur on the shadow.

Moving On

This chapter gave you quite a workout manipulating text. Perhaps you also acquired a love for fonts as you practiced these techniques—or at least a healthy respect for typographers. You also had a glimpse of some of the Esoterica effects, which you'll learn from Sherry in greater detail in the next chapter.

11 ESOTERIC EFFECTS

BY

SHERRY

LONDON

*Learn how to create mosaics and marbled images
that give a modern look to some ancient crafts.*

Mosaics

Mosaics are traditionally formed from small, colored pieces of pottery or ceramics. When they're put in place into a grout (or cementing medium) and viewed from a distance, the tiny pieces blend optically and a picture emerges.

Painter contains a wonderful mosaic-creation facility that allows you to simulate this ancient art form. You can work from an image and re-create it from the original colors, from a more limited color palette, or you can create a mosaic with no reference image.

Creating Random-Image Mosaics

Painter allows you to create mosaics by simply "painting" them onto a blank canvas. Each mosaic tile is a vector-based shape. This means that the tile can be reshaped if you wish (actually, it means that you can remove individual tiles and redraw them, and the redrawn tiles will conform to the "hole" that's left for them to occupy). You can also create your mosaic at a small size and render it much larger at no loss of resolution.

Figure 11.1

The Make Mosaic dialog box is your control panel for creating mosaics.

You might not have used mosaics before, so let's take a quick look at the controls for this feature before going any further. Figure 11.1 shows the Make Mosaic dialog box. This dialog box contains all the options for working with a mosaic image. The four boxes that contain an image of tiles and a cursor are the "tools" that you use to create the mosaic. From left to right, they are the Apply Tiles icon, the Remove Tiles icon, the Change Tile Color icon, and the Select Tiles icon.

You can control the size and appearance of the tiles through the "double-duty" sliders at the top of the dialog box. The Settings menu, which now reads "Dimensions," can be changed to control randomness. The Dimensions sliders let you control the length, width, and grout spacing of the tiles. The Pressure slider applies only if you use a pressure-sensitive tablet. It allows you to set the Apply Mosaic tool's sensitivity to pressure. At 100 percent, all the tiles are the same size (or would be if you've elected not to add any randomness to their creation).

When you change the Settings menu from Dimensions to Randomness, the Pressure slider becomes the Cut slider, and it allows you to vary the angle of the tile ends (at 0 degrees, all tile ends are perpendicular to the direction in which you move the cursor). The units on the other three sliders change to percentages, thus allowing you to specify the degree of deviation from your Dimension settings that you'll tolerate. For example, if you specify a length of 10 pixels for your tiles, choosing a Randomness of 10 percent allows the tiles to vary from 9 to 11 pixels. A Randomness setting of 50 percent would allow the tile length to fluctuate between 5 and 15 pixels.

Finally, there's an unidentified menu box in the upper-right corner of the dialog box that pops up to reveal another set of commands, as shown in

Figure 11.2. These commands let you clear all the tiles (Reset), re-render the mosaic to make a "clean" copy (especially useful if you change the size of your image, and render the tile to the mask (which lets you add surface dimension to it later). You can also remove the ability to start a tile at the edge of the canvas (Respect Edge Of Image) and start your rows of tile with a triangular shape (to make it easier to fit rows together). What's more, you can also stroke or fill a selection with tiles.

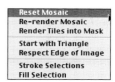

Figure 11.2
The mosaic commands menu allows you to perform additional tasks.

PROJECT Creating A Mosaic Repeat Pattern

Let's see how all these controls work together to create a mosaic. You'll create a tile that's filled randomly and then colored using an existing pattern. The several pieces of this project will ultimately create a background for the image that you'll create later in the chapter.

Tiling Nothing

In this portion of the project, you'll create a mosaic tile that starts with a blank image. Here are the steps:

1. Create a new document (Command/Ctrl+N) 400 pixels square. The paper color should be white.

2. Change your current color to black.

3. Choose Canvas|Make Mosaic.

4. Select the Randomness settings menu. Give all the sliders a value of 20 (20 percent randomness for Length, Width, and Grout, and 20 degrees variation for Cut).

5. Change the Dimensions sliders to a Length and Width setting of 10 pixels, a Grout setting of 2 pixels, and Pressure setting of 50 percent.

6. The first line of tiles that's set is the most important, because it creates the structure for the tiles that follow. Using the Apply Tiles tool, drag your cursor over the canvas as if you were creating a very curvy cloverleaf highway, as shown in Figure 11.3. You don't need to follow my image exactly, but use it as a general guide for shape.

7. Continue to fill in the image with random cloverleaf lines, as shown in Figure 11.4.

8. Finally, fill in the rest of the mosaic image with random scribbles. You can use straight lines for some of the areas and then brush back and forth, or you can literally scribble over the canvas and create more tiles. If you find an area that you really dislike, use the Remove Tiles tool to get rid of it; then refill it with the Apply Tiles tool. Figure 11.5 shows the final image.

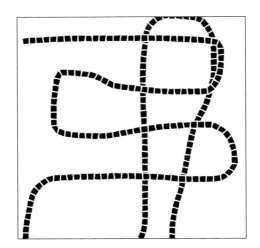

Figure 11.3
This is the start of your random mosaic.

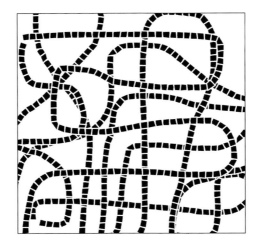

Figure 11.4
Adding more structure lines to the image.

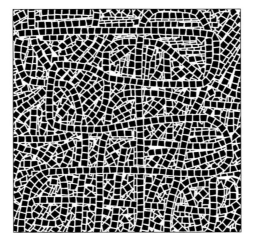

Figure 11.5
Here's the completed mosaic image.

9. Choose the Render Tiles Into Mask option on the mosaic commands menu to place a copy of the mosaic into a mask. This creates a duplicate of the tiles and places it in Mosaic Mask, as you can see in Figure 11.6, which shows the Objects: Mask List palette. Click on the Done button to exit the dialog box. You can reopen it at any time.

10. Save the image.

This random mosaic image becomes the base for a new pattern that you're going to create. Because the new pattern is based on an image that you are going to capture as a pattern, there's no need for you to add color to the mosaic through the Color tool in the Make Mosaic dialog box.

Creating A Background Tile

In this portion of the project, you'll convert a pattern tile into a mosaic image using the mosaic you just created. You'll then color the mosaic and size it so that it repeats properly. Here are the steps:

1. Open the file FLORAL.RIF from this book's companion CD-ROM. Select the entire image (Command/Ctrl+A). From the Pattern menu in the Art Materials: Patterns palette, choose Capture Pattern. Name the new pattern "Floral." Click on the Horizontal radio button and set a bias of 50 percent. This enables the pattern to tile correctly. Figure 11.7 shows the Floral pattern.

Figure 11.6
The Objects: Masks palette shows the new Mosaic Mask entry.

Figure 11.7
This is the Floral pattern.

2. Choose the mosaic image that you created. Select Effects|Fill; Using: Pattern.

3. Choose Effects|Surface Control|Apply Surface Texture. Figure 11.8 shows the settings in the dialog box. They differ from the default settings in only two categories; Shine is set to 100 percent, and Using is set to Mosaic Mask.

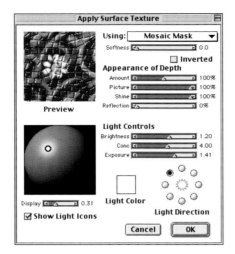

Figure 11.8

Use these settings in the Apply Surface Texture dialog box.

4. The pattern is much too dark at this point. To lighten it, choose Effects| Surface Control|Dye Concentration; Using: Uniform Adjustment. Set the Minimum field to 0 percent and the Maximum field to 19 percent. This lightens up the image nicely, as you can see in Figure 11.9.

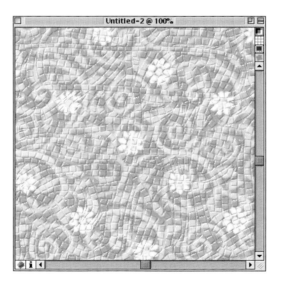

Figure 11.9

Lighten the pattern by using the Dye Concentration command.

5. Choose Effects|Surface Control|Apply Surface Texture again. Change the Shine setting to 0 percent. The application of Surface Texture enhances the 3D look of the image.

6. Choose Effects|Surface Control|Dye Concentration. This time, change Using to Image Luminance. Set Minimum to 114 percent and Maximum to 132 percent.

7. Save the image using a different name (File|Save As).

You're now ready to make the image into a repeating pattern. The Floral pattern, if you check its dimensions in the Art Materials: Pattern palette, is 256 pixels square. One of the things you learned about patterns in Chapter 8 is that you can re-create a seamlessly tiled pattern from anywhere within the repeat so long as you match the exact dimensions. You need to cut the canvas size of the mosaic image down to 256 pixels square.

Repeat Pattern Déjà Vu

In this final portion of the project, you'll learn how to find the specific 256 pixels that you want to use for the repeat pattern and try out the pattern to make sure that you like it. Here are the steps:

1. Choose File|Clone to create a copy of the saved mosaic image.

2. Create a new document (Command/Ctrl+N) that's 256 pixels square. Select the entire image (Command/Ctrl+A). Choose the Layer Adjuster tool and press the modifier key (Option/Alt).

3. Drag and drop the selection, using the Layer Adjuster tool, into the mosaic image clone that you created in Step 1. The new layer, which is 256 pixels square, will help you decide which portion of the image to choose. Change the opacity of the layer in the Controls: Adjuster palette to 40 percent.

4. When you have the layer over the target area, select the Crop tool. If necessary, magnify the image so that you can easily see the area that you want to crop. Drag the Crop tool from the upper-left corner of the white layer to its bottom-right corner. Watch the Controls palette very carefully to make sure that your dimensions are exactly 256 by 256. Click inside the crop marquee to crop the image.

5. Select the entire image (Command/Ctrl+A). Switch to the Rectangular Marquee tool. The Info area at the bottom of the Controls palette should show a size of 256 pixels by 256 pixels. If you don't see this size, undo the Crop command and try again. Click on Layer 1 and then click on the Delete button because you no longer need the white layer.

6. Choose Art Materials: Pattern menu|Capture Pattern command. Name the pattern Floral Mosaic. You need to choose a horizontal pattern with a 50-percent bias to match the repeat of the original image.

   Save the image because you'll use it again in this discussion of mosaics.

HOW DO I KNOW WHERE TO PLACE THE EMPTY LAYER?

You want the pattern to repeat. Look for an area that seems as if it might match on two sides. A good spot to try is somewhere just inside of a vertical line for the left edge or a horizontal line for the top or bottom edge. The structure tiles that you created first can either be an excellent or a very poor choice, depending on how well they relate from side to side. Some seam is inevitable in this technique; the idea is to minimize it. The other, usually good spots to try are the upper-left corner and the center of the image.

Creating Image-Based Mosaics

Although you started exploring mosaics by creating one that was drawn without a source image, it's much more common to use a source image as the starting point. Now that you have an idea how mosaics work, you can create the foreground image for the mosaic composite that's being slowly built in this chapter.

There are several minor differences when you create a mosaic from a source image. First, your foundation lines are even more important, because they give the basic shape and structure to your composition. Next, you might want to change the size of your tiles as you work—to leave large tiles for the foundation lines and large-scale fill-in areas, and to leave smaller tiles for fine details. Finally, accuracy is more important if you want to see a resemblance between your original and the finished mosaic.

It's not as easy to be accurate as it is to be sloppy (surprise!). You'll do better creating the mosaic if you have a stylus and tablet than you will with a mouse. Because the mosaic tiles have a mostly fixed shape and size to them, they have a tendency to appear where they want rather than where you think you're placing them. Although you cannot use the Undo command from the menu when you have the Make Mosaic dialog box open, the keyboard shortcut (Command/Ctrl+Z) works, and it works for multiple Undo instances as well. You will be able to use the Remove Tile tool in the Make Mosaic dialog box as well.

PROJECT Creating A Mosaic From An Image

In this section of the chapter, you'll create a mosaic from an image of a Chinese statue photographed by Ed Scott. Only the statue itself is used for the mosaic, so you can combine it with the background pattern that you created earlier. You'll learn how to color the mosaic, how to render the tiles to the mask, and how to make another mask from the rendered tiles to select only the statue. You'll add the statue to the background and learn how to shift the colors in the statue mosaic to blend with the background colors.

Laying A Foundation

In this portion of the project, you'll create the tiles for the mosaic. Here are the steps:

1. Open the file STATUE2.PSD from this book's companion CD-ROM. Figure 11.10 shows the original image.

2. Choose File|Clone to make a copy of the image.

3. Change your current color to black.

4. Select Canvas|Make Mosaic. In the Dimensions setting box, set the tile width to 10 and the tile length to 8. Set the pressure to about 50 percent, or wherever you're comfortable, and set the grout to 2.

Figure 11.10
STATUE2.PSD is a photograph by
Ed Scott.

5. Change the grout color to a light gray (RGB: 197, 197, 197 or Apple
    System HSL of 288, 0, 77.25). You can change the grout color by click-
    ing on the color swatch in the Make Mosaic dialog box. Your system
    Color Picker appears.

6. Click on the Use Tracing Paper icon to show the underlying image.
    Drag the Apply Mosaic tool over the key lines in the image, as shown
    in Figure 11.11.

Figure 11.11
Create some key lines by tracing
over the source image.

7. Fill in the areas between the major foundation lines by making paral-
    lel lines in the direction of the area or by making curved lines that
    follow the form. When you fill in the face details, make your tiles
    smaller. Figure 11.12 shows the filled mosaic (still in black).

8. Save the image.

Figure 11.12

The filled mosaic image is ready to be colored.

Now you're ready to add color to the mosaic and prepare it for compositing with the background pattern. You might wonder, however, why you were not asked to use the original color (and why you didn't select the Clone Color option). For this example, I wanted to use several key colors, and these colors are not in the original. However, if you want to create a mosaic that uses the colors in the image, you can easily do so by checking the Use Clone Color box in the Art Materials: Color palette. You can also create the original foundation lines and fill-ins in specific colors if you know in advance what you want them to be. The Art Materials: Color palette is accessible to you when you're working in the Make Mosaic dialog box.

Color And Select

In this portion of the project, you'll color the mosaic, render it to a mask, and create an additional mask for selection of the outline of the statue.

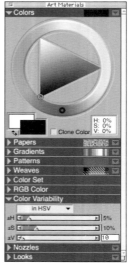

Figure 11.13

Turn down the arrow next to the Art Materials: Color Variability palette to add some randomness to your image.

1. Click on the arrow next to the Art Materials: Color Variability palette to expand it so that you can see the Hue, Saturation, and Value variability sliders, as shown in Figure 11.13. Set the Hue variability to 5 percent and the Saturation and Value sliders to 10 percent.

2. Select the Change Tile Color tool in the Make Mosaic dialog box. Switch back and forth between Color and Tint, as desired, and change and add color to the mosaic tiles that you've already created. You may color this as you wish, but I used reds to browns for the helmet area, golds for the collar, flesh tones for the face (with blue eyes), gray-purples for the gloves, and various greens for the body. Figure 11.14 shows the colored mosaic, but it looks better on the color pages.

3. Choose the mosaic command drop-down menu's Render Tiles To Mask command.

Figure 11.14
The colored mosaic looks better in color than it does in black and white.

4. Click Done to close the Make Mosaic dialog box.

5. Now is as good a time as any to increase your canvas size to allow for a bit more "head room" for the statue. Use the Eyedropper tool to make the gray grout color your current color. Choose Canvas|Set Paper Color. Select Canvas|Canvas Size and add 50 pixels to the top. This not only adds the extra canvas, it adds the canvas in the same gray as your current background.

6. Add a 3D look to the tiles by choosing Effects|Surface Control|Apply Surface Texture; Using: Mosaic Mask. Use the default settings (Amount and Picture settings of 100 percent, Shine setting of 40 percent, and Reflection setting of 0 percent).

7. Now you need to make a mask that selects both the mosaic tiles and the grout. There is, unfortunately, no easy, automated way to do this. Use the Lasso tool to draw around the edges of the statue. When you have a decent selection, choose the Objects: Masks palette's Save Selection command and choose New as the mask. Change the name of the mask to Shape Mask.

8. Select one of the monochrome Web brushes (or create one) that uses the Cover method and the Flat Cover subcategory.

9. Clean up the mask that you saved (make the mask active and leave the visibility icons on for both the mask and the RGB image). Use white as your current color to remove areas of the mask. Use black as your current color to add areas to the mask.

10. Choose Effects|Focus|Soften and use a setting of 1.5 to slightly blur the edges of the mask. This adds anti-aliasing and a bit of softness to the

COLORING TILES

There are five options on the Change Tile Color menu. Color changes the tile to the current color. Darken and Lighten change the tile color about 10 percent in the direction specified. Tint adds a small amount of the current color to the tile, and Vary changes the color of the tile based on the variability settings in the Art Materials: Color Variability palette.

I used the Tint option more than the Color option to keep the tones in the statue fairly subdued. I also colored over the areas to change their colors. You can preselect the tiles, however, by using the Select Tiles tool. Once you have a group of tiles selected, you can tint them by pressing the T key or color them by pressing the C key. Also, you can add color variability by pressing the V key. This allows you a slightly faster means of coloring the tiles.

SWAPPING CURRENT COLORS

You can easily change between white and black as your painting color by clicking on the double-headed arrow below the foreground/background Current Color swatches on the Art Materials: Colors palette.

border of the statue. Look at both the original and the mask (both visibility icons are turned on) to make sure that the contours of the mask are soft and are where you want them to be. Figure 11.15 shows the final mask against the original image. You may prefer to adhere fairly closely to the contours of the tiles rather than smoothing the lines around the statue's left shoulder (on your right side). Double-click on the mask name in the Objects: Mask List palette and change the name to Shape Mask.

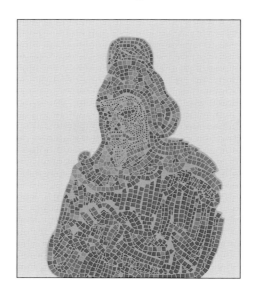

Figure 11.15
Smoothing produces the final shape mask shown here with the original visible.

11. Load the new mask by clicking on the Load Selection button and choosing the mask. Choose the Layer Adjuster tool, press the modifier key (Option/Alt) and click inside the selection. This creates and floats a copy of the selection. Save the image with a new name.

Once you have a layer, you can proceed with the last portion of this project.

Putting It All Together

In this part of the project, you'll add the background that you created and color the statue to blend it in better using a tricky coloring maneuver. After playing with this image and trying to take the sharp color edge off of the statue once it was placed over the mosaic floral background, I finally realized that the best way to tone it is to use the background image itself as the toning element. You'll fill a layer with the background pattern and blur it. You'll then copy a previously made luminosity mask of the original statue to the layer mask. The mask helps vary the intensity of the tonal adjustments being applied to the base image. Finally, you'll change the composite mode to Hard Light to complete the toning effect. Here are the steps:

1. Select the Mosaic Floral pattern in the Art Materials: Pattern palette.

2. Click in the Canvas layer to make it active.

3. Fill the image (Command/Ctrl+F) using Fill With: Pattern.

4. You now need to build a mask that will become the layer mask for the color-blend layer. Select the Objects: Mask menu's Auto Mask command with the Using: Image Luminance setting. This creates a new mask (which should be New Mask 2). The new mask should now look like the one shown in Figure 11.16. Double-click on this mask entry and change its name to Lumi Mask.

Figure 11.16
Make a new luminosity mask that only masks the statue.

5. Make sure that Layer 1 is active. Click on the Drop button in the Objects: Layers palette. This places your statue back onto the Canvas layer.

6. Create a new layer by clicking on the New button in the Objects: Layers palette.

7. Make sure that the layer rather than the canvas is selected; then fill the layer with the Mosaic Floral pattern (Command/Ctrl+F using Fill With: Pattern).

8. Double-click on the layer name in the Objects: Layer List palette. This opens the Layer Attributes dialog box. Change the Layer Visibility Mask attribute in the dialog box to Disabled. This makes the layer mask inoperative.

9. Choose Effects|Focus|Soften. Set the Amount to somewhere between 15 and 21. The idea is to soften the pattern and blur it until it's smooth, but not to blur it so much that the colors—especially the white flowers—are no longer visible at all. Figure 11.17 shows the image at this point.

Figure 11.17
Blur the background pattern on the layer.

10. Click on the Lumi Mask in the Objects: Mask List palette. Select the Objects: Mask menu's Copy Mask command. Copy the Lumi Mask to the Layer 2 mask (or whatever layer name you're using for the blurred floral mosaic pattern layer).

11. Double-click on the layer name in the Objects: Layer List palette. This opens the Layer Attributes dialog box. Change the Layer Visibility Mask attribute in the dialog box to Normal. This activates the layer mask. Change the composite method to Hard Light. Figure 11.18 shows the finished image. Notice (on the color page) how the colors of the original have softened.

Figure 11.18
You've now toned the statue toward background colors.

Marbling

Marbling is a process with a distinguished history. It has been practiced for at least 700 years and seems to have originated in either China or Japan. By the early 1600s, records exist of marbling being done in Persia and Turkey. Marbling has been done on paper and on fabric, and it's prized for the beauty and spontaneity of the work.

Even if you've never tried traditional marbling, you're probably familiar with the concept of marbling, and you may even have tried something similar with cake batter at some point in your life (or watched your mother do it while you licked the bowl afterwards). If you have a batch of vanilla batter and drop spoonfuls of chocolate onto it and then swirl the batter around with a knife, you're marbling (hence the name *marble cake*).

Traditional marbling is done by dropping dyes onto a gelatinous bath. The dyes stay at the top of this bath. You then use a rake or a comb to mix the colors in such a way that they intermingle but do not mix or muddy. You then place a piece of paper or fabric face down in the bath and the dyes are transferred onto it.

Although no two pieces of marbling are likely to be identical, over the years, standard ways of creating specific types of patterns have been developed. Using these "recipes," you can get a fairly consistent look to your marbling.

Painter has the ability to reproduce many of the most common types of marbling patterns. Like Painter's weaving capabilities, marbling is an underused and not-well-understood process for most artists. However, it's a tremendous amount of fun and is easy to do once you master the basic principles. It's also a lot less messy on the computer.

Preparing A Base

In order to begin marbling, you need to have something to mix. You need to start with an image that contains at least two colors in it. Otherwise, you won't see the effect at all. Painter has a wonderful feature called *Blobs* (Effects|Esoterica|Blobs) that drops blobs of the current color, current pattern, or whatever is pasted on the Clipboard into your image. However, unlike simply filling multiple circles with color, the blobs actually mimic the displacement that you see when you drop dye into a gelatin bath. The blobs push aside the image as if it were made of water-soluble inks.

In order to create solid color blobs, you should first have a color scheme. Marbling can get much too complex and ugly if you add too many colors to it. Your best bet is to use three key colors, one neutral, and a "kicker" (my term for a color that is either unrelated to the other colors or of a slightly "wrong" hue). This odd color is used in very small quantities to add a zing to the finished marbling.

I found a wonderful program via the Internet called Palette Picker, by Lightdream (**www.lightdream.com**), that lets you search a database of color schemes based on several criteria and then gives you the RGB or CMYK values of your chosen colors. Figure 11.19 shows the Palette Picker main screen. The program is available for Mac and Windows and is reasonably priced. The second page of the program lets you preview your chosen scheme against white, black, or gray and in various proportions of color. I used this program to develop the color set you'll use for the first marbling project.

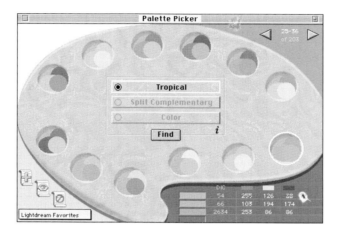

Figure 11.19
This is the Palette Picker interface.

 ## Meet The Blob

This project shows you how to create blobs and apply a marbling recipe to the blobbed image. Here are the steps:

1. Create a new document (Command/Ctrl+N) that's 400 pixels square.

2. Open the color set TROPICAL.TXT from this book's companion CD-ROM (use the Art Materials: Color menu's Load Color Set command).

3. Select aqua (Color 3 in the color set) as your current color. Fill the image (Command/Ctrl+F using Fill With: Current Color). This should be the main color in the image.

4. Select coral (Color 2 in the color set) as your current color. This is the main accent color. Choose Effects|Esoterica|Blobs.

5. Determine the number of blobs you want. For this first pass (for this example), select 35 blobs, ranging in size from 40 to 70 pixels. Leave the Subsample setting at 4 and the Fill Blobs setting at Current Color. Leave the random Seed setting alone and let it generate whatever number it pleases. Figure 11.20 shows the Blobs dialog box (Create Marbling "Stone" Pattern). Figure 11.21 shows the result of this step.

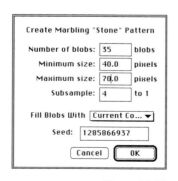

Figure 11.20
Use these settings in the Create Marbling "Stone" Pattern dialog box.

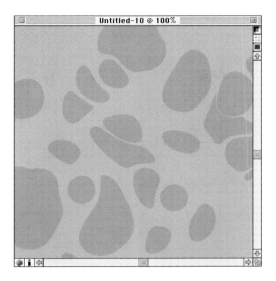

Figure 11.21
This is the first set of blobs.

6. Make light orange (Color 1 in the color set) your current color. Choose Effects|Esoterica|Blobs. Select 50 blobs, ranging in size from 20 to 40 pixels. You want less of this color in the image.

7. Make light gray (Color 4 in the color set) your current color. Choose Effects|Esoterica|Blobs. Select 15 blobs, ranging in size from 25 to 30 pixels. You want even less of this color in the image.

8. The final pass uses the kicker (whichever color you've selected for this). You want only a few spots of this, but if they're too small, you won't see them. Choose Effects|Esoterica|Blobs. Select five blobs, ranging in size from 40 to 55 pixels. Figure 11.22 shows the final blob image.

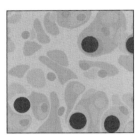

Figure 11.22
The blob image is complete.

9. Select File|Clone to make a copy so that you can keep the original blobs for additional use.

10. Choose Effects|Esoterica|Apply Marbling. Click on the Load button and select the T2B Rake in the list of marbling recipes.

11. Drag the Quality slider to 3.30 and click on the Replace button. Click on OK. Figure 11.23 shows the Apply Marbling dialog box. Figure 11.24 shows the blobs marbled with a top-to-bottom rake.

It's time to regroup for a moment and see what you did. You used solid colors to create the blobs that were used as the basis for the marbling. You could also have used a pattern or a selection to make the blobs. For example, you could capture a section of the original blob image as a pattern and use that pattern as the basis for another marbling attempt. This is an interesting way to "premix" some colors but keep other areas of solid color.

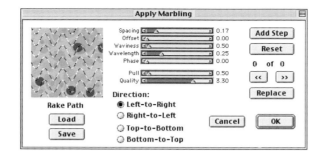

Figure 11.23
This is the Apply Marbling dialog box.

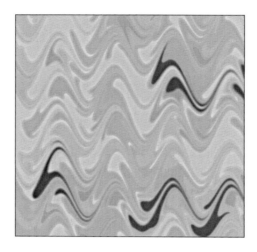

Figure 11.24
The settings in Figure 11.23 produce this first marbling example.

Creating A Get Gel

In traditional marbling, colors are premixed by creating a *get gel* (both words are pronounced with a hard *g* sound). The get gel (which in Turkish means *to come and go*) is the initial combing of the pattern to mix colors. A comb is dragged through the pattern from top to bottom and then from bottom to top, offset by half from the first combing. Then the comb is dragged from left to right, and finally, from right to left. It's dragged in a straight line.

One of the presets in the marbling list is a horizontal get gel (there's also a vertical one). Let's use this to investigate what the marbling engine is actually doing.

PROJECT Recipe For Marbling

In this project, you'll create get gel in steps, breaking apart the recipe to see what each step does. Here are the steps:

1. Make the original blob image active. Choose File|Clone.

2. Select Effects|Esoterica|Apply Marbling. Load the Horizontal Get Gel recipe. It has four steps. Click on the Reset button. This removes all steps but the current one. Figure 11.25 shows the dialog box. It creates

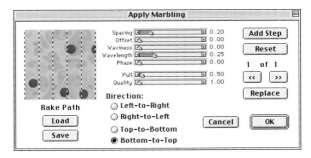

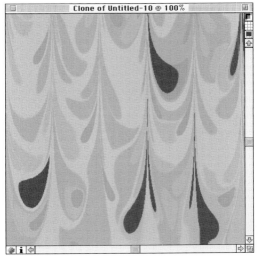

Figure 11.25
This is the first step of the get gel process and its result.

a rake path from the bottom of the image to the top with a spacing of 20 percent. Regardless of the size of your image, this setting will divide it into five sections. Click on OK to apply. Figure 11.25 also shows the result.

3. Select Effects|Esoterica|Apply Marbling. Load the Horizontal Get Gel recipe. Scroll one step forward using the forward-pointing double arrows. Click on Reset to keep only the current definition. The only two changes from the previous step are the Direction setting (now top to bottom) and the Offset setting (now offset 50 percent).

4. Repeat Step 3, scrolling to Step 3 in the Horizontal Get Gel recipe. This step changes the direction to "right to left."

5. Repeat Step 3, scrolling to Step 3 in the Horizontal Get Gel recipe. This final step in the process changes the direction to "left to right" and offsets the marbling by 50 percent. Figure 11.26 shows the result of the four raking steps.

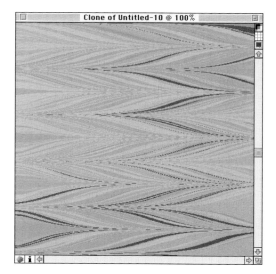

Clone of Untitled-10 @ 100%

Figure 11.26
The finished get gel.

What Can You Do With A Get Gel?

The get gel is not particularly attractive by itself, but it's a good start for other marbling passes. One common pattern is formed by combing a final time with a fine-tooth comb in a straight line. This is called the *nonpareil finish*.

PROJECT Making A Tiny Rake

The nonpareil finish is like drawing in your marble bath with a tiny rake. Here's how to create it:

1. Use the get gel from the previous project as your starting point.

2. Choose Effects|Esoterica|Apply Marbling.

3. This time, you'll create your own tiny rake to save for combing a non-pareil. Set the Spacing field to .02 (it will leave 50 lines in the image).

4. Change the Offset field to 50.

5. Change the direction to "top to bottom."

6. Click on Save and save this step as Tiny Rake. Click on Replace to make the change take effect. Figure 11.27 shows the recipe and the result.

Creating Your Own Pattern

You can create interesting marbling patterns just by playing with the settings. In this project, you'll enter three steps from scratch and create a new recipe. I call this "Double Pull," and it has no comparison in traditional marbling.

WHY CLICK ON REPLACE?

You *must* click on Replace when you change anything in a recipe. If you do not, the marbling effect applies the original recipe. I cannot count the times that I've made this mistake!

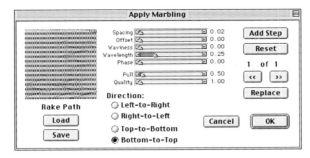

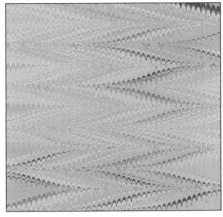

Figure 11.27
Here is a nonpareil finish recipe and its result.

Roll Your Own

You can create your own marbling recipes. Here's how:

1. Open the image WASH.PSD from this book's companion CD-ROM. You'll use this instead of the blobs (by the way, blobs are called *stones* in traditional marbling).

2. Choose Effects|Esoterica|Apply Marbling. Click on the Reset button.

3. Enter the settings in Figure 11.28 and click on Replace.

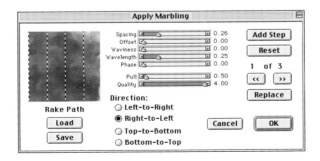

Figure 11.28
Use these settings as the first step in your marbling recipe.

4. Enter the settings in Figure 11.29 and click on Add Step.

5. Enter the settings in Figure 11.30 and click on Add Step. You now have a three-step recipe. Save it as Double Pull. Click on OK. Figure 11.31

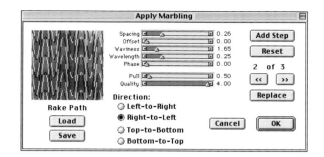

Figure 11.29

Use these settings as the second step in your marbling recipe.

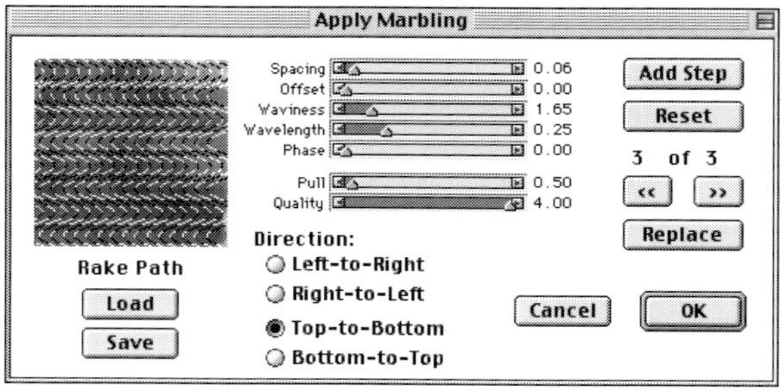

Figure 11.30

Use these settings as the final step in your marbling recipe.

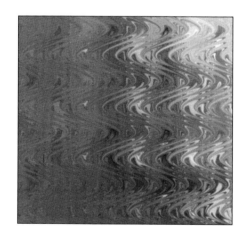

Figure 11.31

This is the Double Pull recipe used on a watercolor-wash image.

QUALITY MARBLING

When you increase the Quality setting, it makes a big difference. A high setting renders a beautifully smooth image. A low setting renders noise. However, the higher the Quality setting, the longer the effect takes to render. If you have a large image and a lot of steps, it could take well over an hour on a fast machine.

shows the result. (Note that because the Quality field is set to 4, you should be prepared to wait. It can take a very long time.)

Moving On

In this chapter, you learned about creating mosaics and marbling. These are both craft techniques with ancient lineages that predate the computer by centuries. Painter enables you to create electronic versions for both techniques that not only keep the original feel of the craft but also expand on it and allow you to take the techniques digitally where they could not go in reality.

In Chapter 12, Rhoda will expand on the idea of traditional art as she discusses fine-art techniques using Painter 6.

12 FINE ART TECHNIQUES

BY

RHODA

GROSSMAN

Learn to draw and paint more skillfully by practicing assignments from traditional art classes. Transfer the skills and styles you have with conventional media to Painter's digital toolbox. If you're a beginner, don't worry—we have ways of making you draw!

The Big Picture

Does the artist determine the nature of the artwork or is the artwork a function of the tools that are used? If I give you a box of crayons, your drawing will look very different from the work you would do with a set of watercolors. On the other hand, the work of Rembrandt or Picasso is recognizable regardless of whether it's a pencil sketch or an oil painting.

This reminds me of the old "nature vs. nurture" controversy: Which factors are the primary predictors of human behavior—environmental or genetic? Let's not fall into that trap. Complex behavior is the result of an assortment of input variables. Art is certainly complex behavior. It's a product of the skill of the artist, the quality of her tools, and the sum total of her experiences as viewed through the prism of the society in which she lives.

Painter is a complex toolbox, and it has a learning curve considerably steeper than a box of crayons—but not nearly as steep as traditional oil painting. Once you've navigated some of Painter's learning curve, your creativity can develop unencumbered by the need to take time for preparing the surface of a canvas or for prying open dried-up tubes of paint. Looking at a blank sheet of expensive 100-percent rag paper wouldn't seem so frightening if you could undo strokes or just start over like you can in Painter. What's more, with Painter, you'll never run out of yellow at a critical moment.

Practice! Practice!

We're all artistic as children. Some of you have forgotten that, some were told by wrong-headed adults that you had no "talent," and many of you were persuaded that art wasn't really important. Drawing and painting are skills you can learn at any age. I was over 30 when I realized my childhood talent was waiting for me to get back to it. (By then, I had gotten over the traumatic episode in high school when I was told I was too intelligent to be an artist.)

Like many skills, drawing is a combination of certain physical or mental aptitudes (commonly called *talent*) and lots of practice. People assume that a virtuoso pianist or violinist works hard every day, plays scales for hours, and wasn't just "born that way." You might never make it to Carnegie Hall, but you know you could learn to play an instrument if you worked at it. My cartoon in Figure 12.1 is a classic gag on the relationship between attitude and aptitude.

Learning To Draw With Painter

This section provides a series of exercises for developing skill and control with Painter's brushes. Like musicians, artists must warm up before a performance. In a conventional drawing class, you'd probably use a sketch pad that's about 18 by 24 inches to give you plenty of room to use your whole arm. If you stand at an easel, your entire body can get into the act. Using the typical 6-by-8-inch

Figure 12.1
A cartoon based on the old joke,
"How do I get to Carnegie Hall?"

graphics tablet will not give you that kind of exercise, so it doesn't hurt to stretch and flex your body before a Painter session and then get comfortably settled at the computer. Launch Painter and open Edit|Preferences|Brush Tracking. Make a scribble or stroke, as shown in Figure 12.2, and click on OK. This establishes the level of pressure sensitivity for the way you work. Now open a new canvas and just scribble for a while.

> **Note:** Painter won't remember your touch from one session to the next, so get into the habit of using Brush Tracking every time you open Painter. Also, you might want to adjust Brush Tracking if you switch to a different style or technique during a session.

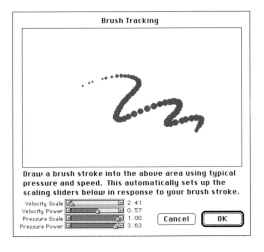

Figure 12.2
Use Brush Tracking to customize the pressure for your graphics tablet.

PROJECT Warm Up

Here are some exercises for developing control of your stylus (you'll practice re-creating the examples in Figure 12.3). Follow these steps:

1. Make a new picture about 600 pixels wide and 200 pixels high at 72 pixels per inch, with a white background.

2. Use the rectangular marquee to select a square about one-third the width of your canvas.

3. Fill the square with black, using either the Paint Bucket tool (with Current Color as the Fill With choice) or the Fill command in the Effects menu.

Figure 12.3

Warm-up exercises.

Note: You can turn your nervous scribbles into a new paper texture using the Capture Paper command in the pop-up Paper menu.

4. Choose the Nervous Pen variant of the Pens group and switch the current color to white.

5. Fill the black square with Nervous Pen strokes, as shown in the left square of Figure 12.3. Use circular scribbles and try to achieve an evenly distributed textured look.

6. Now practice shading control. Select another square in the center of your canvas.

7. Fill the square with a medium gray color.

8. Use one or more of the Airbrush variants to spray Black from one corner, feathering out toward the center of the square.

9. Change the current color to white and spray from the opposite corner. I used the Pepper Spray variant for a coarse-grained look.

10. Now choose the Scratchboard Tool variant of the Pens family, with black as the current color. This time make your square freehand.

11. Draw a series of horizontal lines with increasing pressure as you drag from left to right. Then draw vertical lines with increased pressure as you go down. See how well you can get a smoothly increasing thickness of lines and approximately equal spacing between them.

PROJECT  Shape Up

Figure 12.4 shows a block and a cluster of eggs you can use as subjects for practice sketches. The full color image of these items is included on this book's companion CD-ROM for use as a reference. Both student artists and professional artists can benefit from doing studies of such simple objects from time to time. Beginners can work on getting the proportions correct with pencils and then adding light and shadow. More advanced challenges include using Water Color or Oil variants.

Pastel artists often draw on tinted paper, which can be used to convey the midrange values of the image. They use lighter and darker tonalities to develop the form and create the illusion of three dimensions on a two-dimensional surface. Be aware that the light source (unseen) is above the object. The most well-lit plane is the top of the block. The cast shadow helps the illusion, as does perspective. You know that the block is square, but

USING A MOUSE?

If you're still using a mouse instead of a graphics tablet, it will be more challenging to emulate pressure sensitivity. You can create separate strokes, changing opacity and/ or grain between each stroke. To fade out during a single stroke, adjust the Dryout slider in the Well section of Brush Controls. Another way mouse users can create variation in a stroke is with the Expression section of Brush Controls: Set Opacity, for example, to respond to direction or velocity rather than pressure.

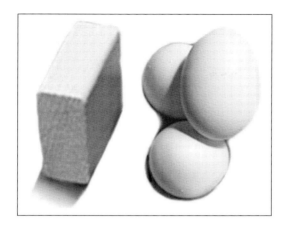

Figure 12.4
Basic shapes for practice sketches.

the largest surface is nearly diamond shaped. Your mind translates this as a square block seen from the edge. My pastel study of the block is shown in Figure 12.5. Here are the steps to follow for this project:

1. Open SHAPES.tif. View the block at 100 percent size.

2. Make a new picture the approximate size of the block, using a medium-gray paper color: Click on the white paper swatch in the New Picture dialog box. When the Select Paper Color dialog box appears, change the Value setting to about 50 percent.

3. Use a darker gray and Big Grain Rough Paper to sketch in the shape of the block with Sharp Chalk.

4. Add color with the Square Chalk or Artist Pastel Chalk and use the Eyedropper tool to get the exact colors from the reference photo.

5. Blend some of the areas, if needed, with the Grainy Water variant of the Liquid family.

Figure 12.5
Pastel study of block on gray paper.

It's a bit more challenging to render a curved object. Look closely at the topmost egg in Figure 12.4. The primary light source is above and to the right. Notice that the darkest shadows on the egg are not at the points most distant from the light source. There's a thin edge of lighter tone beyond that dark shadow. This is due to light reflecting from the other surfaces. Here are the steps for this part of the project:

1. Continue using the SHAPES.tif image as a reference. Erase or delete everything but the topmost egg.

2. Make a new picture about the same size as the single egg. Arrange the two image windows so you can see them both and switch easily between them.

3. Use the Eyedropper tool to choose a color on the light side of the egg.

Note: Access the Eyedropper tool while you're using a painting tool by pressing the Command/Ctrl key. The eyedropper cursor appears. Click where you want to pick up color; then release the key and continue to paint.

4. Switch to a fine-grain paper texture and draw an outline of the egg with Sharp Chalk. It doesn't have to be perfect, but it should be about the same size as the original.

5. Change to a larger Chalk variant and fill in the contours of the egg, starting with the lightest area. Rely on the Eyedropper tool for tonal changes. Fill in concentric ovals and crescent shapes. Five or six shades should do it. Your drawing might look "posterized" at this stage, as shown in the center of Figure 12.6.

6. Smooth out the tonal transitions by blending their edges with Grainy Water.

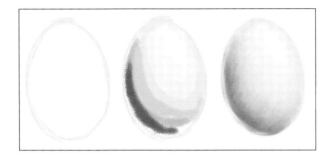

Figure 12.6
Three stages in a pastel drawing of an egg.

Figure 12.7
A complex shape for blind contour drawing—the urn.

PROJECT Line Up

A classic exercise in art school is *blind contour* drawing, the technique of drawing the outline of a complex object without looking at your paper. The idea is to keep your eye on the object and your drawing tool on the paper at all times. As your eye slowly follows the contour of the object, drag your pencil through the same lines and curves. Try it with the urn—the big-handled trophy cup in Figure 12.7. There's a "virtual blindfold" document on the companion CD-ROM that will help you do this exercise without cheating. Here are the steps:

1. Open the images URN.tif. and NoPeekin.rif. Figure 12.8 shows the NoPeekin document with its Layer list.

2. You'll draw under the black layer by leaving the layer visible (eye icon open) but deselected. Deselect it by clicking on the Canvas layer. Now you can draw on the canvas with the black layer blocking your view.

3. Decide where your line will begin—perhaps one of the points where a handle joins the container. Place your cursor in the same relative position on the NoPeekin document.

4. Very slowly move your eyes around the shape of the urn as you drag the stylus or mouse through the same curves. When your eyes have completed tracing the urn, you're done.

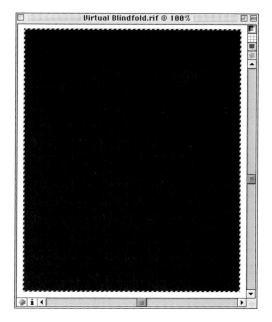

Figure 12.8
The virtual blindfold.

5. Look at your drawing, by closing the eye icon of the black layer. Remember, this is about process, not product.

Figure 12.9 shows two examples of blind contour drawing—one made with the Scratchboard tool and the other with Sharp Chalk using a medium-gray color. Repeat this exercise regularly and save your drawings to see your eye-hand coordination improve.

Figure 12.9
Examples of blind contour drawing.

PROJECT What You See Is What You Draw

You won't want to be "blindfolded" for this project. You'll practice drawing the contour of shapes as accurately as you can. Figure 12.10 shows a black-and-white image called OUTLINE.tif, located on this book's companion CD-ROM. Part of your mind can't help trying to figure out what this is. (No, it's not a camel with attitude!) For the purpose of this project, it isn't anything but a shape made up of lines and curves. Here are the steps:

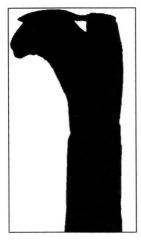

Figure 12.10
An image for practicing outline drawing.

1. Open OUTLINE.tif in Painter.
2. Click on and hold the "i" at the bottom left of the image window to see pixel dimensions and resolution. Make a new picture the same size and resolution.
3. Enable the grid overlay: Click on the tic-tac-toe symbol in the upper right of the image window. You'll probably want to adjust the distance between the grid lines. Canvas|Grid|Grid Options brings up the dialog box for customizing the grid, shown in Figure 12.11. I used 30 pixels between each line.

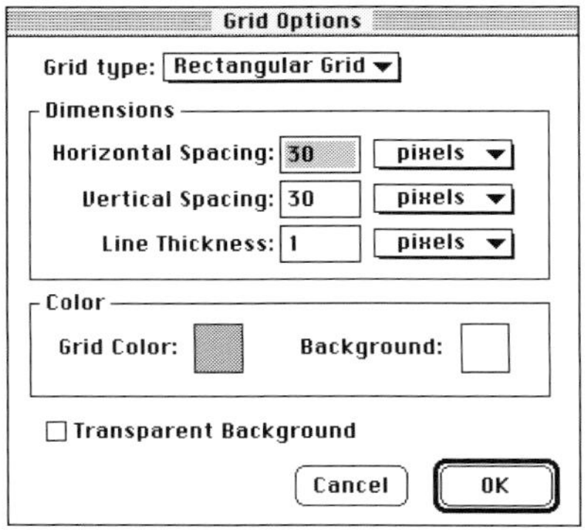

Grid Options
Grid type: Rectangular Grid
Dimensions
Horizontal Spacing: 30 pixels
Vertical Spacing: 30 pixels
Line Thickness: 1 pixels
Color
Grid Color:
Background:
Transparent Background
Cancel
OK

Figure 12.11
Grid Options dialog box.

In Grid We Trust

The Old Masters used wire grids as aids to translate the three-dimensional shapes of their subjects to the two dimensions of paper or canvas. It was also necessary to use a grid over a sketch in order to expand it accurately to a wall-sized mural. Use the grid overlay as "training wheels"—enlarge the space between grid lines a little more each time you practice.

4. With the same grid overlay on both the source image and the blank canvas, begin to copy the outline, square by square. Use a fine-line pen or pencil. Don't worry about errors inside the black shape, because they will be filled in. Figure 12.12 shows the drawing in progress.
5. When you're satisfied with your outline, turn off the grid and fill the shape with black. To stay in the spirit of traditional art techniques, don't use the Paint Bucket tool. Use a non-grainy tool such as the Smooth Ink Pen.
6. To see what the object really is, use Effects|Orientation|Flip Vertical. Then scale it to 50 percent vertical, leaving the horizontal scale unchanged. Figure 12.13 shows the Scale Selection dialog box with the settings needed. Notice that Constrain Aspect Ratio is disabled. Your artwork is a silhouette of a familiar object, as shown in Figure 12.14.

Drawing On The Right Side Of The Brain

Betty Edwards' famous book of the same title addresses the fear of drawing many adults have. It also presents a variety of exercises to help suspend the kind of mental judgments that can get in the way of successful drawing. One of the barriers to accuracy is thinking too much about what an object "should" look like. Edwards found students could copy images better, even complex ones, if they didn't "know" what they were copying. Drawing an upside-down object is one way to trick your brain into getting out of the way, so you can simply draw what you see.

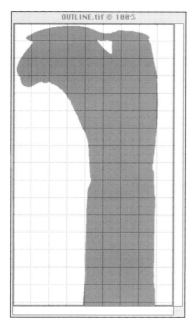

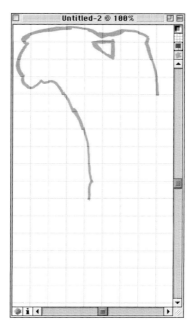

Figure 12.12

Using a grid to copy a shape.

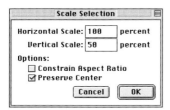

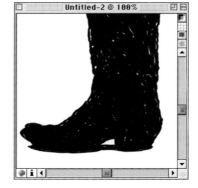

Figure 12.13

(Left) The settings for the Scale Selection dialog box.

Figure 12.14

(Right) It's a boot.

PROJECT Accentuate The Negative

The image shown in Figure 12.15 is more complex than the silhouette of the boot you just drew, but a similar process will be used. You might recognize the image as a "reverse silhouette" of a chair, upside down. You'll copy the black shapes once again, even though it's the white shape that defines the chair. When you focus on drawing everything that's *not* the object, you're working with *negative space*. This is another good way to practice drawing what you *see* rather than what you *think* is there. Here are the steps for this project:

1. Open NEGATIVE.tif from this book's companion CD-ROM in Painter.

2. Activate the grid overlay. It should still have the spacing you established in the previous exercise.

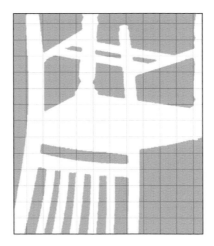

Figure 12.15

Negative space—
upside down chair.

3. Make a clone of the image. You won't be using any cloning or tracing, but this is a quick way to get a blank image the exact size as the original. Choose Select|All and press the Delete/Backspace key. Only the grid lines will remain.

4. Arrange the two image windows so you can see them both.

5. Copy the contour of each black shape as precisely as you can, using black with a fine-point drawing tool.

6. Fill each shape as you go along, using the same brush with sketchy scribbles or crosshatching. Figure 12.16 shows the sketch about half done.

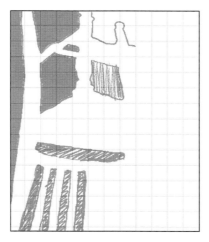

Figure 12.16

Shapes and fills in progress.

7. Finally, flip the finished copy vertically to see how well you've captured the proportions of the chair.

Learning From The Old Masters

Skills can be learned by studying and, yes, copying masterpieces. European art galleries are favorite sites for students who wish to improve their brushwork. The pride of the Prado Museum in Madrid is *Las Meninas* (*The Maids of Honor*) by Velazquez, painted in 1656. Figure 12.17 is a photo of this breathtaking canvas. There it is, right behind the tourists. The Picasso Museum in Barcelona devotes several rooms to dozens of huge canvasses that were inspired by the Velazquez masterpiece. Picasso reduces the complex painting to its basic compositional elements, and does variation after variation. Just imagine how quickly he could have produced all those versions if he had a "Save As" command!

You'll examine a couple famous paintings to learn about composition and the use of light and shadow. Managing these elements effectively is as important as knowing how to draw contours. Realism is not a necessary component of art, although many artists learn the basics of accurate rendering as a jumping-off place to develop their own style. The rules of composition are many or few, depending on who is counting. In any case, the first rule is "do whatever works."

Tonality

One of the traditional ways to begin a painting is to establish broad areas of light, middle, and dark tones (values) at the beginning. This is a good method for working out the composition early. By reversing this technique, reducing a finished painting to its basic tonalities, you can more easily study the compositions of the Old Masters. I scanned a photo of Leonardo da Vinci's *Mona Lisa* in grayscale and then reduced the value range to just a few shades of gray.

Figure 12.17

The Maids of Honor, a composition with tourists.

Painter provides more than one way to accomplish this simplification:

- Clone the scanned image using an enlarged Chalk Cloner to blur detail.

- Smear the scanned image with an enlarged Grainy Water brush or other blending variant to eliminate detail.

- Use Effects|Tonal Control|Posterize with Levels set to 3 or 4. Then smear or touch up with flat color until you have areas of solid tones.

Figure 12.18 shows the result of posterizing to three levels and smearing.

Figure 12.18
Mona Lisa reduced to basic tonalities.

Figure 12.19
Mona at 12.5 percent.

Geometry

I scanned another familiar painting, known as "Whistler's Mother." It's already fairly simple in terms of tonality. I simplified it further by reducing it to geometric shapes as much as possible. Now you try it.

PROJECT Simplifying Shapes

Here are the steps you'll follow for this project:

1. Open WISLRMOM.tif from this book's companion CD-ROM.

2. Make a copy using File|Clone.

3. Choose Select|All and press the Delete/Backspace key. Turn on Tracing Paper so that the original image shows at 50 percent opacity.

4. Re-create the image with simple geometric shapes: Use Shape tools to drag rectangles and ovals, placing and sizing them as needed. You might need to make a polygon or two by clicking on corners using the Shapes Pen.

5. Fill each shape with the appropriate shade of gray, using Shapes| Set Shape Attributes. You won't need more than two or three grays plus black.

> **Note:** Use Edit|Preferences| Shapes to enable the Fill With Current Color feature so you can change to the shade of gray you want before drawing a shape. This is more efficient than adjusting colors afterward with the Shapes Attribute dialog box.

Figure 12.20 is my geometric analysis of "Whistler's Mother." It shouldn't surprise you to learn that the painting's actual title is *Arrangement in Gray and Black*. Figure 12.21 shows a new composition using the same shapes. The Layer list of the shapes used is shown in Figure 12.22.

Analyze other masterpieces or compose your own abstract art using these techniques for simplifying elements. Save your work in RIFF format so the

Figure 12.20
Arrangement in Gray and Black.

Figure 12.21
(Left) Rearrangement in Gray and Black.

Figure 12.22
(Right) Shapes list for analysis of "Whistler's Mother."

shapes will remain independent of the background canvas. You can create a series of variations in the following ways:

- Move shapes around on the canvas by dragging them with the Adjuster tool.

- Reorder items from front to back by moving their names in the Layer list.

- Resize shapes by dragging handles with the Adjuster tool.

- Reshape by dragging anchor points or wings with the Shape Adjuster tool.

- Change fill and stroke colors in the Set Shape Attributes dialog box.

- Make some items invisible by clicking on their eye icon in the Layer list.

Use Your Edge

The edges of your canvas are an important part of the composition. Keeping away from the edges of the paper is a common pitfall for beginning artists. They often make tiny drawings surrounded by a sea of white. Get into the habit of letting parts of each drawing break through at least two edges.

You always know where the edges are when you work with conventional paper or canvas. This is not always true on the computer. Two ways to help you be aware of your edges are shown in Figure 12.23. The image on the left has a border made with the rectangular Shape tool. The shape was given a thin black stroke and no fill and then dropped into the canvas background. The example on the right has a border resulting from simply dragging the corner of the image window out so that there's a rim of contrasting gray around the canvas. Even better, choose Window|Screen Mode Toggle (Command/Ctrl+M) to get a solid gray background for your image, which eliminates the distractions of other windows.

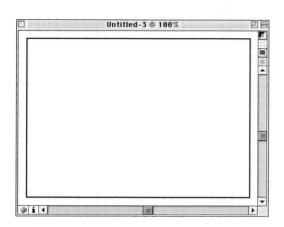

Figure 12.23
Know where your edges are.

Stealing From The Old Masters

I asked a well-known printmaker whether the image in one of his popular posters was borrowed from a painting in Picasso's Blue Period. His response: "Steal with both hands!" Of course, he had reinterpreted the Picasso figures in a contemporary style.

"Inspired by, based on, in the style of, an homage to..." are some of the ways artists acknowledge their debt to the past. To help you decide whether a particular piece is a tribute or a rip-off, see the sidebar. It was contributed by Roy S. Gordet, an artist-friendly San Francisco attorney who specializes in copyrights, trademarks, and multimedia legal issues.

Drawing On Reality

Once you've got some practice painting eggs or apples or portraits by copying them from photographs, the next logical step is to look at a real egg or apple or the person sitting in front of you. Now you'll be translating a three-dimensional subject into a two-dimensional space—the flat plane of your monitor. You won't be able to pick up color with your Eyedropper tool, but all the other techniques you've learned will be useful.

Whether your painting is going to take five minutes or five hours to complete, the first several strokes should establish the basic composition and areas of tonality. You are advised to work the entire canvas so that all elements are at approximately the same stage of development. Avoid getting caught up "noodling" details in a corner while the rest of the image is still blank. If you follow the FTL order—forest, trees, leaves—your drawing should look coherent at every stage. This hierarchy applies to subjects other than landscape, of course.

LEGAL MATTERS BY ROY S. GORDET

Copyright protects expression. Copyright never protects an idea. To the extent you copy only someone else's concept and not the specific expression of it, then you should be safe from copyright infringement charges.

Sometimes it is not that easy to distinguish between what is idea and what is expression. For example, is a graphical user interface an expression or an idea? Is its expression so closely associated with its function that it is considered closer to an idea and therefore unprotectable? This difficult issue was the "core" of the Apple versus Microsoft "look and feel" case.

To be considered protectable expression, the "author" (this term includes artists) must only show some small spark of originality. Then the author has the exclusive right to reproduce, display, distribute, and perform the work, and the exclusive right to create derivative works based upon it.

In order to sue for copyright infringement successfully it is necessary to prove that the person actually copied, and that the two works are "substantially similar." If the accused infringer independently created her own work, then there was no copying. If the accused infringer took some small portion of the work, but the works are not substantially similar (or you cannot recognize the copied portion because it is so small), *the experts are divided as to whether or not this is an infringement.* The use of the portion arguably constitutes the creation of a derivative work, to which the copyright owner has exclusive rights.

A copyrightable work is protected the moment it is created, whether or not it is published or registered for copyright. However, there are significant advantages to registration, most notably that if a copyright is registered prior to some infringing activity, the copyright owner might be able to collect attorney fees from the infringer.

Copyright protection is limited in duration. New legislation was passed in 1998 stating that the copyright expires 70 years from the death of the last surviving author, rather than the 50 years it was under the 1978 act. In the case of works made for hire or works created by a corporation, (Disney, for example) the copyright lasts for 95 years from the date of publication, or 120 years from the date of creation, whichever is shorter. Once a copyright expires, the work is in the *public domain* and is free to all to use. Anyone is free to create derivative works based on the public domain work and to copyright such derivative works.

It is important to realize that there is an immense difference between the tangible piece of art that hangs in someone's living room and the copyright in that piece of art. They are separate. Just because someone purchases a painting from you does not mean that he has the right to begin to use that image in a calendar, unless you also assigned such rights to him. In any projects involving the creation of copyrightable expressions, communicate with all concerned so that everyone is clear on ownership issues. And get it in writing!

PROJECT Still Life Painting

A *still life* is an arrangement of inanimate items used as the subject for a drawing or painting. The term also refers to the drawing or painting itself. Traditional still life studies often included fruit, flowers, or household objects. Any combination of items that have some variety in shape, size, color, and texture will do. Here are the steps for this project:

1. Set up a simple arrangement of two or three objects where you can view them comfortably from your computer. Adjust lighting, if possible, to create strong highlights and shadows.

2. Establish the visual format by choosing the height and width of your canvas.

3. Do a few quick composition roughs. These can be "thumbnails," as shown in Figure 12.24, small enough so you can have several of them onscreen at one time. Be aware of the edges of the drawings and the negative spaces between and around the objects.

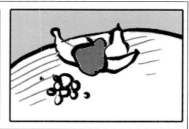

Figure 12.24
Composition thumbnails.

4. Choose the composition you like best and use Canvas|Resize to enlarge it to fit your screen.

5. Use any combination of Painter brushes to develop the drawing. You can refer to the watercolor techniques used in Chapter 2 for the fruit bowl still life, for example, or rely on the Impasto brush family to create a painting with strong texture.

Still Life Using Paper Cutouts

Here's a variation on the still life assignment. You'll create the composition so that it looks like it was constructed with shapes cut from textured paper. Use the same setup as before for your subject or make a new arrangement. Just keep it simple. Follow these steps:

1. Make two or three preliminary sketches to explore possible compositions.

2. Enlarge your best sketch to the size you want to work on.

3. Use File|Clone to make a copy of the image. Choose Select|All and press the Delete/Backspace key. Turn on Tracing Paper. Now you can see the sketch at 50 percent opacity.

    In the following step you'll make a layer for each element in the sketch, using the Lasso as if it were a tool for drawing. Work with the Layer section of the Objects palette open until you're finished with this project.

4. Trace one of the items in the sketch with the Lasso, fill the resulting selection with a solid color, and click on it with the Adjuster tool. Repeat for each item in the composition.

    I used the middle sketch in Figure 12.24 to work on the "cut paper" look. Figure 12.25 shows the clone with three layers selected and filled.

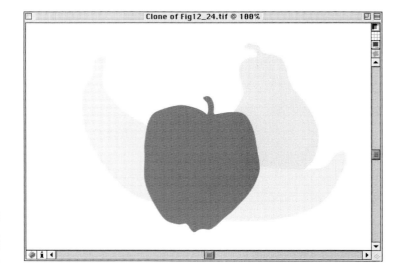

Figure 12.25
Lasso selections for the apple, banana, and pear, filled with solid colors and on separate layers.

Note: Painter automatically creates a group for each layer to which you add a drop shadow. This is useful if you want to make any alterations to the shadow and not to the item it shadows. Figure 12.27 shows the Layer list after a drop shadow has been added to the members of a group.

5. Use Effects|Surface Control|Apply Surface Texture |Using: Paper to add a different texture to each item.

6. Add drop shadows to all the layers with one command: Select all layers and group them. Use Effects|Objects|Create Drop Shadow. The default values for all settings are recommended. Figure 12.26 shows my work at this point.

Figure 12.26
Fruit layers with textures and drop shadows added.

Figure 12.27
The Layer list after a drop shadow has been applied to a group. A new group, called "Apple and Shadow," is open, allowing either the apple or its shadow to be selected.

The cut-paper illusion is complete, but I think something is still needed to hold everything together. I'll add a background element with a torn paper edge in the following steps.

7. With the Canvas layer selected, make a rectangular selection that's just a bit smaller than the fruit composition.

8. Fill the selection with a two-point gradient. I used two shades of blue, with the lighter value at the top.

9. Click on the selection with the Adjuster tool to make it a layer.

10. Apply the Tear effect in Dynamic Layers. Adjust the settings in the Tear Options dialog box. My final art is shown in Figure 12.28, and several more examples are included in the color Painter Studio.

Figure 12.28
Finished fruit still life with paper cutout techniques.

Room With A View

Chances are there are some interesting things you can draw in the room where you're sitting. The room itself, with some of the objects in it, is an excellent (and always available) subject for drawing. Artists often sketch their immediate environment, focusing on a favorite chair or other item. If there's a lot of clutter, you might want to draw only parts of what you see or make the clutter, itself, your subject. When you draw whatever you see from where you're sitting, you might have to deal with perspective, loss of detail as you go back in space, and some decisions about what to emphasize or minimize.

Figure 12.29 shows a sketch I made a couple of years ago with Painter 5. It's the view a few degrees to the left of my work area at that time. The elements are loosely drawn but recognizable, with a focus on the computer and a stack of external drives topped by a shiny apple. The bookshelves in the background are much less detailed and have less contrast than the featured items.

I used three shades of gray plus a few black accent strokes. Square Chalk and Sharp Chalk were used, and some thin lines were made with the Scratchboard tool. Enough white space was left to create a feeling of light. The piece has a

Figure 12.29
The digital artist's studio.

casual look, because the lines and shapes are irregular and laid down quickly. The cables were each drawn with a single stroke of the Square Chalk variant.

Life Drawing

What you learned about drawing still life studies can be applied to portraits and the human figure. It's likely to take a lot longer to develop proficiency at realistically rendering people, because the correct proportions in the human form are much less variable than those of fruit or vegetables. Your sketch of an apple can be inaccurate, but it will still look like an apple. Move your subject's nose a bit to the left or right, however, and there's definitely a problem.

Figure drawing appears to be a combination of left-brain and right-brain functions—drawing what you see *and* what you know. The technical knowledge of anatomical structure is coupled with creativity. When these elements are working together, the artist not only knows what the rules are but when to break them. Experiment with a few rough compositions, in vertical and horizontal format. Then choose between the following two approaches—or combine them:

- *Linear*—Draw the outline of all shapes and then fill them in. Possible fills include flat color, crosshatching, gradients, clone sources, and patterns.

- *Tonal*—Establish major lights and darks. Work from large to small, developing the forms as you go. Add details toward the end.

Life drawing classes generally begin with a session of gesture poses. The model changes position every few minutes, and students have no time to get caught up in details. The idea is to make a few bold strokes to indicate the essence of the pose. I have taken my Powerbook and a WACOM tablet to life drawing workshops. Figure 12.30 shows a three-minute drawing made with the Oil Pastel variant.

Figure 12.30
A three-minute gesture drawing
painted with the Oil Pastel variant.

PROJECT Imitation Of Life

Traditional artists' mannequins are fully articulated, so they can
be posed in just about every position. There are no realistic details, but the
proportions are right. You can acquire some skill at depicting how body parts
are connected by using a real mannequin for this project. Poser software
provides a mannequin body type useful for this kind of practice. Figure 12.31
shows a couple Poser mannequin figures, which you can use in the following steps:

1. Open the file MANIKIN.tif on this book's companion CD-ROM or
   create some mannequin poses yourself in Poser and export them so
   they can be opened in Painter.

2. Use File|Clone and delete the copy. Turn on Tracing Paper (Command/
   Ctrl+T).

3. Working quickly, use the Pencil Sketch Cloner to establish the basic pose.

4. Switch to the Chalk Cloner and rough in the tonalities. A natural
   texture such as Hand Made or Raw Silk Paper is recommended.

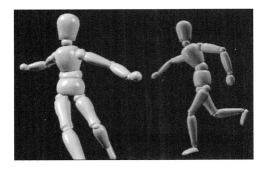

Figure 12.31
Mannequin-style figures made
with Poser.

5. Try the following for dramatically different results (start with a freshly deleted clone each time and toggle Tracing Paper on and off as needed):

- Fill the empty canvas with medium gray, using the Paint Bucket tool. Scribble with the new Nervous Pen variant, using black or white, for an energetic look. A few touches with the Bleach variant from the Eraser family can add highlights for the illusion of depth.

- Choose the Thick & Thin Pencil variant and light gray as the current color. Turn opacity of the brush down to about 60 percent. (Because they use the Buildup method, pencil strokes will get much darker as you go over them.) Concentrate your strokes on the darker areas of the mannequin. Switch to Coarse Smear or Grainy Water to blend strokes and achieve some "quick and dirty" tonal range.

Mannequin forms are gender neutral. You can make a figure look more feminine by emphasizing curves rather than flat planes and angles. Figure 12.32 shows some gesture drawings using the Poser mannequin figures.

Figure 12.32
Gesture drawings, using Poser mannequin figures as the source.

Portraits

John Singer Sargent was a famous portrait painter about 100 years ago. He's honored by the inventors of Painter with a brush variant named for him in the Artists group. Strokes with the Sargent Brush are shown in Figure 12.33. They are luscious and creamy, like Sargent's own style for painting the rich and famous of his time. You can make the Sargent Brush even creamier and more luscious by increasing bleed and decreasing resaturation in the Well section of the Brush Controls palette. Sargent was quoted by an art teacher of mine

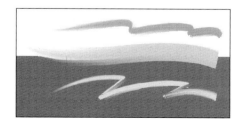

Figure 12.33
Strokes with the Sargent variant of the Artists brush family.

as giving the following definition of a portrait, "It's a painting that has just a little something wrong with the mouth." Whether or not he really said it, we can agree that successful portrait painting is about as challenging as it gets.

PROJECT Portrait Of The Author As A Middle-Aged Woman

You'll avoid some of the problems of achieving a likeness by working with a photograph so that you can focus your energy on style and technique rather than accuracy. The photo of me in Figure 12.34 is what I call my Rembrandt pose, due to its similarity to one of the Flemish master's self-portraits (shown in Figure 12.35).

Figure 12.34
Rhoda's Rembrandt pose.

Figure 12.35
A self-portrait by Rembrandt.

Here are the steps to follow for this project:

1. Open RHODAREM.tif on this book's companion CD-ROM. Notice that the photograph is flawed by some artifacts such as color shift and scratches that were the result of the shot being near the end of the roll of film. This will not be a problem.

2. Darken the tonality in order to make the image more dramatic and to further enhance the similarity to the Rembrandt painting: Use Effects|Tonal Control|Adjust Colors and move the Value slider to the left. I used a setting of -40 percent.

3. Increase contrast with Effects|Tonal Control|Brightness/Contrast. There are no numerical settings in this dialog box, so just "eyeball" it. Refer to Figure 12.36 and its color version in the Painter Studio.

Figure 12.36
Adjusted photo, with Value decreased and Contrast increased.

4. Clone the current version of the photo so you'll have a "safety net" for the next step.

5. Working on the clone copy, use the Grainy Water variant of the Liquid group with Big Grain Rough selected in the Papers section of the Art Materials palette to smudge out the details of the photo. Make strokes that follow the contours of the face and the jacket. Change the size of the brush as needed. You should see a painterly look begin to emerge, as in Figure 12.37. If you want to rework an area, use the Soft Cloner to paint back the previous version (it's the clone source).

Figure 12.37
Details smudged out with Grainy Water.

6. Now you'll add the look of Impasto brush strokes with the Smeary Varnish variant of the Impasto family. This exciting new brush paints with Depth set at 12 percent. It also has Resaturation set at 0 percent and Bleed set at 61 percent in the Well controls. You can change these settings to alter the depth effect or "smeariness," of course. I used the default settings.

Figure 12.38 shows a detail of the image with some of the smearing in progress as well as a later stage with some Smeary Varnish strokes applied. Figure 12.39 is the finished painting.

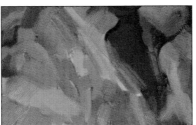

Figure 12.38
Detail of the portrait shows part of the jacket with Grainy Water smears (top) as well as the same area after Smeary Varnish Impasto brushwork (bottom).

Figure 12.39
The finished painting of Rhoda in the Rembrandt pose.

PROJECT Self-Portrait Painting

You're ready to work on your own face now. Find a photo of yourself that you like. A head-and-shoulders pose is fine, or it can include the torso. Now follow these steps:

1. Scan the photograph at the appropriate size and resolution. If the photo is tiny, increase the resolution and/or the dimensions until the combination of settings gives you an image that's big enough to work with.

2. Improve the quality of the image as much as you need to, keeping in mind your purpose is not to perfect the photo but to use it as a reference. Adjust the Brightness and Contrast settings, for example.

3. Select File|Clone to make a copy of the image.

4. Choose Select|All and press the Delete/Backspace key. Enable Tracing Paper so that you can use the scanned and adjusted photo as a reference.

There are many styles and techniques to choose from at this point. You can repeat the smudge-and-varnish method from the previous exercise. Alternatively, try one (or more) of the techniques in the following projects. Examples using each technique are provided in the color Painter Studio.

Trace And Fill

A photo that emphasizes the light and shadow that define the forms of the head and face is the best kind of source image for this method. Follow these steps:

1. Trace the reference image with a Pen Variant and a dark color. Be sure to make solid lines with no breaks. The challenge is to see the

SCANNING BASICS

Scanners have different software interfaces and can use different terminology for the same thing. What's important is to be able to specify 24-bit color mode (also called millions of colors or full color), and to have some control over the resolution and the image dimensions. Changes in size and resolution as well as cropping can easily be done in Painter after you scan the photo.

curves of the face in a way that allows you to translate them into planes and angles.

2. Use the Paint Bucket tool to fill the spaces with solid colors. You can choose realistic skin tones or colors that convey emotion. Figure 12.40 shows this method as used by one of my students, Judy McAlpin.

Note: If your Paint Bucket fills leave some of the edge pixels near the lines unfilled, try increasing the tolerance setting for the Paint Bucket in the Controls palette. If color spills over into additional spaces, you might have to repair the "leaky" lines, small gaps in the drawing that allow Paint Bucket fills to "flow" through.

\ **Figure 12.40**
Self-portrait by Judy McAlpin, using the trace-and-fill method.

Wet And Dry

These steps are basically the same as those for the fruit bowl still life project in Chapter 2. Julie Wyeth's self-portrait, shown in Figure 12.41, makes good use of this technique:

1. Trace the reference image sketchily in Pencil or Pen, without concern about "leaky" lines.

\ **Figure 12.41**
Self-portrait by Julie Wyeth, using the wet-and-dry method.

Note: Take advantage of the separate layers in the wet-and-dry method. You can alter the sketch without harming your watercolor strokes, and your wet work will not harm the sketch. Be sure to save your work in RIFF format until you're ready to "dry" everything.

2.   Paint color with Water Color variants. The watercolor strokes will automatically occupy their own "wet" layer, independent of your sketched lines.

3.   When you have enough detail in the wet layer, use Select|All and press the Delete/Backspace key. Only the dry layer will disappear.

4.   Fade the delete action if you want some of the sketch to reappear while you continue working. You might want to bring back some or all of the sketch to be part of the finished piece.

Mixed Media

The term *mixed media* in traditional art refers to the combining of drawing and painting with the possible inclusion of collage or assemblages of textures and even objects. On the computer, borrowing from a variety of styles or using brushes and effects in unexpected ways can result in a "mixed media" look. Basically, anything goes. Laurie Aubuchon's self-portrait, shown in Figure 12.42, has that kind of bold, experimental quality.

Figure 12.42
Self-portrait by Laurie Aubuchon, using mixed media.

Moving On

You've learned or remembered quite a bit about traditional drawing and painting in this chapter. You had the opportunity to put several skills together and apply them to some challenging projects. Come back to these exercises from time to time and see how much more skill (and talent) you have acquired. This chapter was fun for me, especially because I got to showcase the work of my Painter students.

Sherry and I hope you've enjoyed this book and that you'll keep on making art a part of your life.

24-bit "true color," 185, 187
216-color palette, 186
256-color palette, 185–186
3D Brushstrokes setting, Apply Surface Texture command, 236–237
3D effects, for letters, 264–265
3D-modeling project, 20–21
8-bit grayscale, 19–20

A

Abstract painting, 246–247
Add Grains brush, 83
Adjust Color command, 161
Adjuster palette, 7
Adjustment controls, Dynamic Text, 270
Adobe Image Ready, 214
Adobe Photoshop
    color tables, 188
    contrasted with Painter, 19–20, 228
    Erase To Saved feature, 19, 54
    Fadeout control, 43
    and layer effects, 228
    and masks, 9–12
    and Offset filter, 85
    and patterns, 85, 106–107, 121
    preparing images in, 154
    and Web-safe colors, 187
Airbrush, 53, 298
Aliasing, 149, 189
Alphabet sampler project, 267–269
ALT text, for Web links, 222
Anchor points, selecting, 258
Animation
    abstract, 169
    basic techniques, 164
    and frame stacks, 164, 167
    GIF, 185
    recording scripts for, 173–175
    and rotoscoping, 175
    saving, 175, 185
    splicing, 180

Animation projects
    neon spiral, 169–170
    photo flip-book, 168–169
    purple heart, 170–171
    running child, 176–180
    script creation, 174
    walking cartoon man, 164–167
    worms, 171–173
Anti-aliasing, 149
Appearance controls, Dynamic Text, 271
Apply Brush Stroke to Movie command, 173
Apply Color Overlay command, 135
Apply Script to Movie command, 173–175
Apply Surface Texture command
    and Luminance settings, 19, 91, 236, 264
    restoring default settings, 137
    settings for, 79
    and 3D Brushstrokes, 236–237
Arrange Palettes command, 15
Arrow tool, 242, 246
Art Materials palette
    Color settings, 30–31, 282–284
    new features, 2–4
    Paper Mover, 72
    and pattern creation, 102
    V slider, 59
    Value settings, 30, 59
Artists Brush, and Van Gogh Cloner, 58
Autoclone, 46
AVI files, 175, 180

B

Background, separating image from, 153–155
Background color, 218, 230
Background pattern project, 201–202
Background tile, mosaic, 277–279
Baseline controls, Dynamic Text, 269–270
Beads projects, 27–30
Benguiat font, 257–258
Bevel World dynamic layer, 205–209, 248–251, 264–265

Beveling projects, 206–209, 248–251
Bezier tool, 256
Bias slider
    Capture Pattern command, 108
    Express in Image command, 178
Big Dry Felt Pen Cloner, 65
Big Grain Rough texture, 47, 299
Bird collage project, 155–157
Black and white, in textures, 73–75
Bladepro filter, 241, 251
Bleach variants, Eraser group, 17
Bleed settings, Brush Controls palette, 43
Blending modes, 151
Blind contour drawing, 300–301
Blind embossing, 203
Blobs effect, 260, 287–289
Block repeat, 102–104, 106
Blue gold project, 139
Blur effect, 272
Book jacket collage project, 158–161
Boot drawing project, 301–303
Boys swimming project, 127–129
Branch control, Growth command, 231–232
Brick repeat, 105, 106, 109, 120
Bristle controls, 34–36
Browsers. *See* Web browsers.
Brush anatomy project, 27–29
Brush categories, 24
Brush Controls palette
    Angle settings, 199
    Graininess settings, 28–29
    Impasto settings, 39
    new features, 2–4
    Size settings, 27
    Spacing settings, 19, 28, 199
    Stroke Type settings, 19, 27, 33–34
    Well controls, 42–43
Brush library, 19, 24, 33
Brush Look Designer, 25
Brush methods, 26, 76. *See also* specific methods.
Brush Mover, 16–19, 35
Brush palette, 24
Brush projects
    adjusting smeariness of brushes, 42–43
    creating watercolor still life, 40–42
    experimenting with brush variants, 24–27
    using Bristle controls, 35–36

    using Brush Controls, 27–29
    using Expression Controls, 29–30
    using Impasto controls, 38–39
    using Look Designer, 25–26
    using Piano Keys variant, 30–31
    using Rake Controls, 33–34
    working with dab types, 27–29, 32, 36–38
Brush Tracking command, 15–16, 297
Brushes. *See also* specific types.
    and Chalk Cloner, 48
    changing size of, 27, 48, 64
    controlling bristle characteristics, 35–36
    controlling pressure applied to, 29–30, 53, 297
    converting to cloners, 61
    copying, 17
    creating, 198–199
    creating new icons for, 18
    and Felt Pen Cloner, 64
    and masks, 9–10
    Methods and Grainy subcategories for, 76
    new features in Painter, 2, 14, 31, 77
    restoring default settings, 31
    saving, 17, 31
    Stroke Type settings, 19, 33
    and textures, 73
    and Van Gogh Cloner, 58
Brushstrokes
    animating, 171–173
    controlling, 27
    previewing, 27
    recording/playing back, 170–173
    types of, 33
Buildup methods, brush
    and masks, 9–10
    and paper textures, 74–76
Bulge brush, 83, 96–98
Bulging paper textures project, 96–98
Burn dynamic layer, 228–230, 266–277
Burn tool, 17
Butterfly projects, 103–110, 117–120
Buttons, beveled, 205

C

Cable modems, 185
Calligraphy pen, 27–28
Camel Hair effect, 51

"Candle in The Wind" Web site project, 214–225

Canvas

    breaking through edges, 308–309

    squaring, 116

Canvas paper, 52

Canvas|Dry command, 40

Canvas|Mosaic command, 211

Capture Brush command, 36, 37

Capture Paper command, 97, 298

Capture Pattern command, 97, 103

Captured Brushes library, 43

Captured dab type, 36–38

Cartoon animation, 164

Cascading style sheets, 214

Caterpillar animation project, 171–173

Cats collage project, 158–161

CCS2, 214

Cel animation, 164

CERN map file, 209

CGI program, 209

Chalk brushes, 33, 74, 75, 299–300, 313–314

Chalk Cloner, 46–48, 72, 90

Chalk Grain setting, 74

Charcoal brush, 33, 74, 75

Child running project, 176–180

Chinese statue mosaic project, 280–286

Chrome effects, 245

Cityscape image fills project, 261–262

Client-side image map, 209, 212

Cliff settings, Bevel World dynamic layer, 250–251

Clone brushes, 128

Clone Color variant, Color palette, 61

Clone command, 54

Clone source, 104

Cloner brushes, 46–48, 60

Cloners, 46, 67. *See also* specific cloners.

Cloning

    advanced techniques, 60–67

    basic techniques, 46–60

    contrasted with filtering, 46

    single vs. multipoint, 57

Cloning methods, for brushes, 76

Cloning projects

    colored pencil drawing, 52–53

    felt marker sketch, 64–66

    Melt Cloner, 50–51

    oil painting, 51–52

    pastel drawing, 47–48

    scribbling, 49–51

    selective elimination, 55–56

    selective reverting, 54–55

    still life and Impressionist Cloner, 66–67

    sunflowers and Van Gogh Cloner, 58–60

    two-point cloning, 57–58

    watercolor study, 61–62

    watercolor wash, 63–64

Coarse Smear variant, Liquid brushes, 48

Coin projects, 134–143

Collage

    and composite methods, 151–153

    derivation of term, 147

    layers, hard-edged vs. seamless, 158

Collage projects

    hands, 148–151, 153–157

    mystery novel cover, 158–161

    surrealist poster project, 153–157

Collapse button, 7

Color

    hex values, 187

    and marbling, 289–290

    RGB values, 187, 191, 193, 197

    and Web design, 185–191, 218

Color high pass project, 139

Color indexing, 184

Color palette, 61, 185–186

Color Picker, 196

Color Select command, 206

Color sets

    contrasted with Photoshop color tables, 188

    and posterization, 186

    projects involving, 189–193

    purpose of, 188

Color settings, Art Materials palette, 30–31, 282–284

Color tables, Photoshop, 188

Commands. *See* Keyboard shortcuts, specific commands.

Commit command, 238, 240, 259

Composite methods. *See also* specific methods.

    and collages, 151–153

    Photoshop considerations, 20

    proprietary, 20

Composition, rules of, 305–309, 314

Compound patterns, 102

Compression, file, 175, 187–188, 222

Computer art, flatness of, 70
Confusion variant, F/X brush, 122–124
Contrast, paper texture, 83
Controllers, expression, 30
Controls palette, 7
Copy command, 17
Copyright laws, 309, 310
Cover methods, for brushes, 74–76
Crackle paper texture, 93–94
Crayon brush, 33, 74, 75
Crinkly texture, 81–82
Crop tool, 86, 97, 114–115, 279
Crossfade, 95, 102
Crosshair Slicer, 218
Crosshatching, 47, 52
Current grad. *See* Gradient.
Curve tool, 256
Customization
    of icons, 17–18
    of libraries, 16–17

D

Dab types, 31. *See also* specific types.
Dabs
    composition of, 27
    projects involving, 27–29, 32, 36–38
Dancers project, 98
Darkener variant, Eraser group, 17
Dear Teacher font, 95
deBabelizer, 187
Deckled paper project, 238–240, 249
Define Pattern command, 119, 127–128
Depth Equalizer variant, Impasto group, 51
Depth Rake variant, Impasto group, 33
Depth Smear variant, Impasto group, 51
Diaper pattern, 109–110
Diaper repeat project, 110–118
Difference composite method, 151–153
Diffuse Water variant, Water Color brushes, 40
Discovery Web projects, 188–189
Disk storage
    and Image Portfolio library, 13
    and QuickTime/AVI files, 175
Disposal Method, animation, 185
Dissolving coins project, 137–138
Distort Cloner, 57

Dithering, 186, 192
Dodge variant, Eraser group, 17
Doors project, 60–64
Double circle project, 141
Double repeating pattern project, 111–114
Drag and drop, 136, 139
Drawing projects
    blind contour drawing, 300–301
    life drawing, 20–21, 315–322
    outlining, 301–303
    pastels, 47–48, 298–300
    pen-and-ink, 63
    reverse silhouette, 303–304
Drawing skills, 296, 302, 305, 309
DreamWeaver, 212
Drip methods, for brushes, 76
Drop button, 7
Drop patterns, 105, 107–110, 146
Drop repeat, 70
Drop Shadow effect, 13–14, 156, 265–266
Dry brush, 125–126
Dry command, 40
Dry Ink variant, Brush group, 34–36
Dry Media brushes, 33, 74
Dryout settings, Brush Controls palette, 43
DSL, 185
Dye Concentration command, 135, 278
Dynamic Layer command, 234
Dynamic layers. *See also* Layers.
    committing, 238, 240
    contrasted with Photoshop layer effects, 228
    editing, 228
    and masks, 252–253
    purpose of, 14, 228
Dynamic Layers library, 264, 269
Dynamic Layers projects
    creating beveled ornament, 248–251
    creating rice paper, 228–240
    masking an effect, 252–253
    working with Liquid Metal, 243–248
Dynamic plug-ins, 14, 228. *See also* Dynamic layers.
Dynamic Text, 269–272

E

Edge effects, 266, 269
Edges, canvas, 308–309

Edwards, Betty, 302
Egg pastels project, 298–300
Embedded palettes, 2–3
Embossed color project, 139
Embossed image project, 203–205
Embossing, 63, 71, 72, 202–203
Enable Impasto icon, 38–39
Engineered texture project, 77–85
EPS files, 19
Equalize command, 81, 194–195
Erase To Saved feature, Photoshop, 19, 54
Eraser group, 17
Eraser methods, for brushes, 76
Eraser tool, 12
Esoterica fills project, 259–261
Export Slices Options, 223–224
Express in Image command, 177–178, 197–198
Express Texture command, 82–83
Expression controls, for brushes, 29–31
Eyedropper tool, 299–300

F

Fade command
    as alternative to Tracing Paper, 67
    and embossing, 63–64
    and Wet Eraser, 40
Fadeout control, Photoshop, 43
Fairy Dust brush, 173
Featherdance project, 243–247
Features, new in Painter, 2–5, 14
Felt marker sketch project, 64–66
Felt Pen Cloner, 64–66
Fence movie project, 165–167
Fiber Cloner, 49, 179–180
Figure drawing. *See* Life drawing.
File formats. *See also* specific file formats.
    image map, 209
    image slice, 221
    indexed color, 184, 186
    Painter-compatible, 19
    Painter's native, 13
    Web, 186
Fill command, 10, 124, 133
Fill pattern, 104, 124
Fills and strokes project, 256–257
Filters, 46, 85, 241, 251

Fire variant, F/X brush, 122–125, 263
Flame Breadth settings, 238
Flaming Pear, 241
Flaming type project, 271–272
Flat Cover method, paper textures, 74
Flip-book animation project, 167–169
Floater Portfolio library, 5
Floaters, 4–5, 38
Floating color project, 91–92
Floating object, 9, 210
Floral background tile project, 277–279
Font-creation programs, 258
Font styling project, 257–258
Font textures, 95
Fontographer, MacroMedia, 258
Fork controls, Growth command, 232
Four-way repeat project, 129–132
Frame Delay, animation, 185
Frame stacks, 164, 167, 172
Freehand, 19
FrontPage. *See* Microsoft FrontPage.
Fruit layers projects, 5–6, 8, 11–14
Fruit still life project, 310–313
FTL order, for drawings, 309
Furry Cloner, 50–51
F/X brushes, 33, 122–125, 173, 263

G

Gel composite method, 151, 159–161
Geometric shapes, simplifying, 307–308
Gesture drawings, 316
Get gel, for marbling, 290–292
GIF files
    and animation, 185
    and color considerations, 186–188, 217
    and image slices, 221–222
    interlaced, 187
    transparent, 212
    and Web graphics, 184–188
Glass Distortion effect, 54, 180, 269
Gloopy variant, Impasto group, 39
Goats project, 82–85
GoLive, 212
Gooey brushes, 16–17
Gordet, Roy S., 309–310
Grabber Hand cursor, 59

Grad Pen variant, Pens group, 171

Gradation, linear, 129–132

Gradient
and animation, 169, 177–179
defined, 121
and Pop Art fill, 195–196
and seamless pattern, 122–125

Gradient library, 171

Gradients palette, 3

Grain settings, 73, 74

Grainy subcategories, for brushes, 26, 76

Grainy textures, 52, 74, 76

Graphic design, general principles for, 267

Graphic Paintbrush variant
Brush group, 32–33
Impasto group, 38

Graphic Print brush, 198–200

Graphics, Web, 184

Graphics programs, 2, 19–20. *See also* Adobe Photoshop.

Graphics tablet
adjusting sensitivity of, 15, 297, 298
using mouse in place of, 298

Gray tones
in masks, 10
in textures, 73, 76–77, 87, 151–155

Grayscale mode, 8-bit, 19–20

"Greeking in" type, 94–95

Grid lines, as drawing aid, 302

Grid Paper effect, 260

Grouping
of brush variants, 18–19
of cells, for rollover image, 219
to form patterns, 71
of layers, 7, 312

Grouping tool, 219

Growth brush, 231–234

Growth command, 230–234

H

Hair Scale sliders, Bristle controls, 35

Half-drop repeat, 70–71, 105–110, 119–120

Halftone texture, 47

Handcuffs project, 36–38

Handmade paper, 53, 237, 238–239. *See also* Rice paper projects.

Hands collage projects, 148–151, 153–157

Hard Cover method, paper textures, 74

Hard Light composite method, 151

Hard view, brushstroke, 27

Hex values, color, 187

Hide Marquee option, 15

High pass project, 138

Horizontal Slice tool, 216, 218

Hose brushes, 19, 33

Hotspots, 209–212

House collage project, 158–161

HSL Color Picker, 197

HTML
authoring programs, 212–213
Color Picker, 197
files, 212–213, 224
JavaScript rollovers, 224–225

Hue, 30, 161

I

Icons, customizing, 17–18

Illustrator, 19

Image Hose brush, 119, 125–126, 172, 180, 263

Image Luminance settings, Apply Surface Texture command, 236

Image map, 185, 209–214

Image Portfolio library, 5, 12–13

Image Slicer plug-in, 214–225

Images
cloning, 46, 53–54
color considerations, 185–186
combining in collage, 148–150, 153–161
determining size and resolution of, 176
displaying paper textures in, 71–72
dragging and dropping, 136, 139
embossing, 202–203
file compression considerations, 187–188
posterizing, 192–195
previewing before applying effects to, 59
separating from background, 153–155
sources of, 5
using as fills, 261–262

Impasto brushes, 14, 33, 38–39, 76, 96, 264

Impasto Impressionist Cloner, 67

Impasto layer, 38

Impasto palette, 51

Impressionist Cloner project, 66–67
Impressionist landscape project, 125–126
Impressionist variant, Brush group, 37
Indexed color, 186–187
Insert Movie command, 180
Interlaced GIF files, 187
Internet Explorer. *See* Microsoft Internet Explorer.
Invert Grain setting, Paper palette, 73

J

JavaScript rollover code, 224–225
JPEG files
    and color considerations, 186–188, 217
    and compression, 222
    and image slices, 221–222
    and Web graphics, 186–188
Jungle dance animation, 180–181

K

Keyboard shortcuts
    changing brush size, 48
    copying to Clipboard, 108
    creating new document, 15
    filling with color/pattern, 73
    hiding "marching ants," 15
    hiding palette, 15
    opening palette, 24
    repeating command, 52
    rotating page, 64
    selecting image, 80
    turning on Tracing Paper, 89
Kimono project, 144–145

L

Landscape project, 125–126
Lasso tool, 12
Layer Adjuster tool, 7, 83, 85, 91, 210
Layer floating object, 9
Layer mask
    blocking out pixels in, 12
    and collage projects, 154–155, 158
    and floating color, 92
Layers. *See also* Dynamic layers.
    activating, 9
    blending, 151, 158

contrasted with floaters, 4–5, 38
creating/editing, 5–6, 228
deleting, 7
and Fill command, 133
grouping/ungrouping, 7, 13, 312
hiding, 13
and masks, 9–11, 158, 160
merging/moving, 7–9
naming/renaming, 12, 150
and paper textures, 89, 91–94, 97
and patterns, 136, 144
preserving transparency of, 10, 150
and rollovers, 215
saving, 19
and Select All command, 262
tips for avoiding problems with, 210, 228
Layers projects
    creating layers, 5–6
    creating masked objects, 11–14
    manipulating/moving layers, 8
Leafy brush, 43–44
Leaky Pen brush, 173
Legal issues, 309, 310
Lemon mask project, 11–14
Letters. *See* Text, Text effect projects.
Libraries, 16–17. *See also* specific libraries.
Library Mover, 13
Life drawing
    projects, 20–21, 315–322
    techniques, 313
Lightdream Palette Picker, 288
Lighten composite method, 151
Line drawing, 19
Linear gradation project, 129–132
Linked motif pattern project, 119–120
Links, rollover, 222
Linkware, 240
Liquid brushes, 33, 48, 83, 96, 173
Liquid Lens dynamic layer, 234–235
Liquid Metal Brush tool, 246–247
Liquid Metal dynamic layer
    default settings, 242
    projects, 243–248
    purpose of, 242
    tips for working with, 246–247
Litmus pattern project, 124, 134–143
Load Library command, 35

Load Selection command, 153
Logo, embossed, 205
Look Designer project, 25–26
Loomis, Kelly, 240–242
Loop
    animation, 168, 185
    pattern, 114
Lossy compression, 187
Luminance settings, Apply Surface Texture command, 19, 91, 236, 264

M

Macintosh
    Color Picker, 196, 197
    and editing of dynamic layers, 228
    Web browsers, 218
MacroMedia Fontographer, 258
Magic Combine composite method, 151
Magic Wand tool, 149
Make Mosaic command, 274–275, 280
Make Paper command, 77–78
Man walking project, 164–167
Mannequin drawing project, 315–316
Map field, Liquid Metal dynamic layer, 245
Marbling
    altering recipes, 292
    creating get gel for, 290–291
    history of, 287
    premixing colors, 290
    preparing base, 287–288
    Quality settings, 294
    and text effects, 260, 263–265
    traditional vs. Painter, 287
Marbling projects
    creating blobbed images, 288–289
    creating get gels, 290–292
    creating new recipes, 293–294
    making a rake, 292
"Marching ants," 15
Marquee, hiding, 15
Mask List palette, 144
Masked fruit project, 11–14
Masked litmus project, 139–141
Masks
    basic principles for working with, 10–11
    and dynamic layers, 252–253

    and embossing, 203
    and layers, 9–11, 92, 154–155, 158
    and patterns, 14, 135, 142–143
Masters. *See* Old Masters.
Media effects, 23. *See also* Brush projects.
Melt Cloner project, 50–51
Memory, conserving, 55
Metallic effects, 241, 245. *See also* Liquid Metal dynamic layer.
Methods, brush, 26, 76
Mexican dancers project, 98
Microsoft FrontPage, 212, 214
Microsoft Internet Explorer, 209, 218
Mirror Cloner, 57
Mixed media, 322
Modems, 185
Mona Lisa, and tonality, 305–306
Mosaic feature, Canvas command, 211
Mosaic projects
    creating background tile, 277–279
    creating image-based mosaic, 280–286
    creating repeat pattern, 275–277
    cropping and testing pattern, 279
Mosaics
    coloring, 282–283
    controls/settings for, 274
    image-based, 280–286
    random-image, 274–277
Motif, pattern, 102–103, 118–119
Motion Blur effect, 272
Mountain landscape project, 125–126
Mouse, using in place of graphics tablet, 298
Mouse Over-Out states, 220–222
Movers, 16–17. *See also* specific movers.
Movies. *See* Animation.
Multi-stroke brushes, 19, 33, 35
Multiply Composite method, 93–94, 151
Multipoint cloners, 57
Museums, 305
Muybridge, Eadweard, 176
Mystery novel collage project, 158–161

N

Navigator. *See* Netscape Navigator.
NCSA map file, 209
Negative space, 177, 178, 303–304

Neon Pen variant, F/X brush, 263
Neon spiral project, 169–170
Nervous Pen brush, 173, 298
Netscape Navigator, 186, 209
Novel cover collage project, 158–161
Nozzles, Image Hose, 125, 172, 180, 263
Nozzles palette, 126

O

Objects palette, 2, 4, 7
Objects: Layers palette, 7, 9
Objects: Mask palette, 11–12
Offset, pattern, 102, 105, 108
Offset cloning, 54
Offset filter, 85
Offset Slider project, 105–106
Oil Brush Cloner, 51–52
Oil painting project, 51–52
Oil Pastel variant, Dry Media group, 42–43
Old Masters
    and geometric shapes, 307–308
    and grid lines, 302
    "stealing" from, 309
    and tonality, 305
Onion skin, 164–165, 175
Opacity
    and felt marker sketch, 64
    and layers, 150
    and textures, 73
    and watercolor wash, 63
Opacity slider
    Brush Controls, 53
    Layers palette, 150
Organization tips
    for brushes, 18–19
    for palettes, 14–15
Outline drawing project, 301–303
Overlays, pattern, 139

P

Paint Bucket tool, 166, 259–261, 321
Painted patterns, 121–126, 145
Painter 6
    contrasted with Adobe Photoshop, 19–20, 228
    new features, 2–5

Painting projects. *See* specific types of painting.
Painting skills, 296, 305, 309
Palette Picker, Lightdream, 288
Palettes. *See also* specific palettes.
    hiding, 15
    new features in Painter, 2–4
    organizing, 14–15
Paper color, selecting, 6
Paper Mover, 16, 52, 72
Paper texture projects
    bulging textures, 96–98
    combining textures, 88–94
    creating textures, 77–85
    "greeking in" text, 94–95
    randomizing textures, 98–99
    repeating textures, 86–88
Paper textures
    black-and-white vs. grayscale, 73, 76–77, 87,
        151–155
    and Burn dynamic layer, 229–230
    and Chalk Cloner, 46–48, 72
    changing names of, 52
    combining, 88, 135
    contrasted with patterns, 102
    controlling contrast and brightness, 83
    creating your own, 77–82, 94–95
    function, 73–75
    and Impasto features, 96
    multiplying, 93–94
    and Oil Brush Cloner, 52
    saving, 144, 152
    sources of, 72
    terminology, 70–71
Pastel drawing projects, 47–48, 298–300
Pattern file
    contrasted with Offset filter, 85
    limitations of, 121
    masking, 135
    projects, 122–126
Pattern Fill command, 10, 124
Pattern-generating unit, 102, 106
Pattern library, 30, 117, 166
Pattern Pen brush, 14–15, 145
Pattern projects
    double-motif repeat, 110–118
    four-way repeat, 129–132
    half-drop repeat, 107–110

Kimono composition, 144–145
linked motif pattern, 119–120
mosaic repeat, 275–279
offset repeat, 105–106
pattern file, 122–126
pattern/texture combinations, 134–143
patterned text, 132–133
seamless pattern, 122–126
seamless repeat, 127–129
simple block repeat, 103–104
single-motif repeat, 103–120
Pattern seam line, 122
Pattern unit, 70
Patterns. *See also* Pattern projects.
adding to text, 132–134
changing scale of, 104, 105
contrasted with paper textures, 102
editing, 137
interlocking, 132
and layers, 136, 144
limitations of, 121
masked, 14, 135, 142–143
mathematical component, 107
object-proportion considerations, 110, 118
painted, 121–126, 145
photographic, 127–129
rules for varying, 135
saving, 108, 117, 144
scaling, 137
seamless, 85–86, 102–103, 119–121, 127, 129–132, 134
sources of, 103, 121, 127
spacing considerations, 114
terminology, 70, 102–103
tips for applying, 144
and Web design, 200–201
Patterns palette, 117
Pen-and-ink drawing, 63
Pen brush, 145
Pencil Sketch Cloner, 52–53
Pens brush family, 298
Pepper Spray brush, 298
Perspective, 313
Photo Brush group, 17, 33
Photo flip-book project, 168–169

Photographic patterns, 127–129
Photographs
creating texture from, 86–88
file compression considerations, 188
flatness of, 70
Photoshop. *See* Adobe Photoshop.
Piano Keys project, 30–31
Piano Keys variant, F/X brush, 173, 263
Picasso Museum, 305
Picket fence movie project, 165–167
PICT files, 19
Pixels
avoiding unwanted, 149
cropping images by, 115
and pattern repeats, 107
Playback Script command, 173–174
Playback Stroke command, 170–171
Plug-in method, for brushes, 26, 43–44, 76
Plug-ins, 14, 214, 222–225, 228
Point-to-point cloning, 54
Pop art fill project, 195–197
Portrait painting projects, 317–322
Poser, 20–21, 315–316
Postcards, 240
Posterize command, 193
Posterize Using Color Set command, 186, 192–193
Posterizing projects, 192–195
Prado Museum, 305
Preserve Transparency settings, 133, 259
Pressure, brush, 29–30, 53, 297
Preview, image, 59
Projects. *See* specific types of projects.
Prose, patterned, 132–134
PSD files, 187
Pseudocolor composite method, 91, 151
Pure Water variant, Water Color brushes, 40
Purple heart animation project, 170–171

Q

Quality settings, marbling, 294
Quantize methods, 186, 192
Quick Curve tool, 256
QuickTime/AVI files, 175, 180

R

Rake brushes, 19, 33–34, 35
Rake project, 292
RAM, conserving, 55
Random-drop patterns, 146
Random-image mosaics, 274–277
Randomizing textures project, 98–99
Raster objects, 4
Raw Silk paper, 52
Realism, 305, 309
Recipes, marbling, 290–294
Record Script command, 173–174
Record Stroke command, 170
Recorded stroke F/X animation project, 170–171
Rectangular objects, for patterns, 110, 118
Rectangular repeat. *See* Block repeat.
Reference pixel, for patterns, 107
Refrigerator art project, 24–25
Regular Fine paper, 53
Rembrandt, 317
Repeat unit, 70, 85, 102
Repeating pattern projects. *See* Pattern projects.
Repeating textures project, 86–88
Resize Cloner, 57
Restore Default Variant command, 31
Retouching, and Soft Cloner, 55
Reverse Out composite method, 151
Reverse silhouette drawing project, 303–304
RGB values, 187, 191, 193, 197
Rhino texture project, 86–88
Ribbed Pastel texture, 47
Rice paper projects
    adding fibers, 230–234
    adding texture, 236–238
    creating burned edge, 228–230
    making deckled paper, 238–240
    mixing liquid pulp, 235
RIFF files, 13
Road image map project, 210–214
Rollovers, 215, 219–221
Rose collage project, 158–161
Rotate Cloner, 57, 58
Rotate Page tool, 64
Rotoscoping, 175
Rules, pattern variation, 135
Running child animation project, 176–180

S

Sampler alphabet project, 267–269
Sampler effect, avoiding, 88
Sargent, John Singer, 316
Saturation, 30, 87–88, 161
Save Paper command, 152
Save Selection command, 153
Scale Cloner, 57
Scale Selection command, 303
Scaled pattern project, 137
Scanners, 320
Scissors tool, 256
Scratch pad, 15–16
Scratchboard Rake variant, Pens group, 33–34
Scratchboard tool, 298, 301, 313
Screen composite method, 151
Scribbling, 47, 49–51, 180
Scripts, animation, 173–175
Seamless pattern/texture, 85–86, 102–103, 134.
    See also Pattern projects.
Seashell projects
    cloning, 49–53
    collage, 153–157
Select All commands, 262
Selective elimination project, 55–56
Selective reverting project, 54–55
Selector tool, 219, 221
Self-portrait painting project, 320–322
Server-side image map, 209
Shadow effect, 156, 265–266
Shadow Map composite method, 159
Shape Selection tool, 257–258, 268
Shape tools, 256–257
Shapes, simplifying, 307–308
Shapes command, 133, 307
Shear Cloner, 57
Shell projects. *See* Seashell projects.
Shortcuts. *See* Keyboard shortcuts.
Silhouette drawing project, 303–304
Silveria, Gordon, 267
Simple Water variant, Water Color, 61, 62
Single-motif repeat projects, 103–120
Single-stroke brushes, 19, 33
Slice tools, 216, 218
Small Forest nozzle, 126
Smeariness, brush, 42–43, 179

Smiley face animation project, 174

Soft Cloner, 53–56

Soft litmus mask project, 141

Soft view, brushstroke, 27

Source menu, dab types, 32

Spacing, pattern, 114

Spatter Water brush, 173

Spiral animation project, 169–170

Splash screen, 210

Splattery brushes, 173

Splattery Clone Spray effect, 49–50

Splicing movies, 180

Square Chalk Dry Media brush, 75

Square objects, for patterns, 110, 118

Squeegee variant, F/X brush, 263

Standard Metal effect, 245, 246

Start loop, pattern, 114

States, rollover, 220–222

Static Bristle dab type, 34–35

Statue mosaic project, 280–286

Still life projects, 40–42, 66–67, 310–313

Stone circle project, 142

Storage space. *See* Disk storage.

Straight Cloner, 53

Strawberry mask project, 11–14

Stroke Type settings, for brushes, 19

Strokes and fills project, 256–257

Study, contrasted with rough sketch/rendering, 61

Styling fonts project, 257–258

Stylus control project, 297–298

Subpalettes, 2–3

Sunflowers project, 58–60

Super Cloners, 57

Surface tension, 242, 244

Surface texture. *See* Apply Surface Texture command, Paper Textures.

Surrealist poster project, 153–157

Swan plaque project, 206–209

Swimming boys project, 127–129

System Picker, Windows, 197

T

Tables, and Image Slicer plug-in, 214, 222–225

Tablet. *See* Graphics tablet.

Taxi project, 111–117

Tear dynamic layer, 266–277

Tear effect, 266–277

Text

   adding pattern to, 132–134

   beveling, 208, 266–277

   creating paper textures from, 94–98

   dynamic, 269–272

   and edge effects, 266–277

   "greeking in," 94–95

   and Impasto features, 96

   and 3D effects, 264–265

   vector-based, 256

Text effect projects

   applying drop shadows, 265–266

   assigning fills and strokes, 256–257

   creating alphabet sampler, 267–269

   creating Esoterica fills, 259–261

   creating flaming text, 271–272

   filling letters with images, 261–262

   marbling with F/X variants, 263–265

   styling fonts, 257–258

Text tool, 256

Texture projects. *See* Paper texture projects.

Textured surface, 70

Textures. *See also* Paper textures.

   anatomy of, 70–72

   black-and-white vs. grayscale, 73, 76–77, 87, 151–155

   combining, 27, 88–94, 135, 141, 235

   creating with Make Paper command, 155–160

   factors affecting, 151

   randomizing, 98–99

   repeating, 86–88

   using text for, 94–98

Thickness/Thinout controls, Growth command, 231–232

Thumbnails, 311

TIFF files, 19

Tile, pattern, 102, 129–132

Tile Color menu, 283

Tiles, mosaic, 274–275, 277–279, 283

Tonality, 305–306

Tools palette, 25, 256

Trace-and-fill method, for self-portrait, 320–321

Tracing Paper feature

   contrasted with Fade command, 67

   when to use, 46, 89–90

Trademarks, 309–310

Transparency, preserving (for layers), 10, 133, 259
Transparent GIF files, 212
Triangle paper texture, 78
True color, 24-bit, 185
Tulip pattern project, 201–202
Turbulence variant, Liquid brush, 171, 173
Type. *See* Text.
Type tool, 94

U

Ultimate Symbol Design Elements collection, 203, 211
Undo command, 55
URLs, and rollovers, 222
Urn drawing project, 300–301

V

V slider, Art Materials palette, 59
Value settings
    Adjust Color command, 161
    Apply Surface Texture command, 79
    Art Materials palette, 30, 59
Values, texture, 73, 151
Van Gogh Cloner, 46, 58–60, 180
Van Gogh variant, Artists group, 35
Variants, brush, 18–19, 31
Variation rules, pattern, 135
Vector art, 203
Vector-based text, 256
Vector files, 19
Vertical double-repeat project, 113–114
Vertical offset repeat, 105
Vertical Slice tool, 216, 218
Vignette, 48
Visibility masks, 11, 158, 160

W

Walking cartoon man project, 164–167
Wallpaper, textured vs. patterned, 70
Wash, watercolor, 41, 63
Water buffalo project, 89–94
Water Color brushes, 39–42
Water Color Cloner, 60–63
Watercolor effect, 50–51

Watercolor projects
    still life, 40–42
    study, 61–62
    wash, 63–64
Web
    color considerations, 185–189, 218
    embossing effects, 202–203
    graphics, 184
    pattern and texture considerations, 200–201
    recommended books about, 184
Web browsers
    color considerations, 185–186, 218
    and image maps, 209
    Macintosh, 218
    Windows, 218
Web projects
    beveling, 206–209
    creating background pattern, 201–202
    creating Graphic Print brush, 198–200
    creating image maps, 210–214
    creating a Web-safe color set, 189–191
    embossing images, 203–205
    pop art fill, 195–197
    posterizing images, 192–195
    slicing up image, 216–225
    using Express In Image command, 197–198
Web-safe colors, 186–191
WebMedia brush library, 189–190
Well controls, Brush Controls palette, 42–43
Wet-and-dry method, for self-portrait, 321–322
Wet Eraser variant, Water Color brushes, 39–40, 61–62
Wet layer, 39–42
Wet method, for brushes, 39, 76
Wet Paint effect, and watercolor wash, 63–64
"Whistler's Mother," geometric analysis of, 307–308
Window Shade feature, Mac, 14–15
Windows
    Color Picker, 196
    System Picker, 197
    Web browsers, 218
World Wide Web. *See* Web.
Worms animation project, 171–173

X

xRotate Cloner, 58
xScale Cloner, 57

COLOPHON

From start to finish, The Coriolis Group designed *Painter 6 f/x and Design* with the creative professional in mind.

The cover was produced on a G3 Macintosh using QuarkXPress 3.3 for layout compositing. Text imported from Microsoft Word was restyled using the Futura and Trajan font families from the Adobe font library. It was printed using four-color process and spot UV coating.

Select images from the Painter Studio were combined to form the cover montage art strip, unique for each Creative Professionals book. Adobe Photoshop 5 was used in conjunction with filters to create the individual special effects.

The Painter Studio was assembled using Adobe Pagemaker 6.5 on a G3 Macintosh. Images in TIFF format were color corrected and sized in Adobe Photoshop 5. It was printed using four-color process.

The interior layout was built in Adobe Pagemaker 6.5 on a G3 Macintosh. Adobe fonts used include Stone Informal for body, Avenir Black for heads, and Copperplate 31ab for chapter titles. Adobe Photoshop 5 was used to process grayscale images, lightening the original files to accommodate for dot gain. Text originated in Microsoft Word.

Imagesetting and manufacturing were completed by Hart Graphics, San Antonio, Texas.

If you like this book, you'll love these...

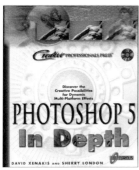

WHAT'S ON THE CD-ROM

The *Painter 6 f/x and Design* companion CD-ROM contains elements specifically selected to enhance the usefulness of this book, including:

- All of the project images mentioned in the book. These images allow you to work through each chapter's projects and master various techniques.
- A custom brush library that contains brushes not included in the Painter 6 installation set.
- Additional color sets to provide you with different palette options.
- A gradation library containing some of the authors' favorite gradients.
- A multitude of free seamless and tileable patterns.
- A number of free seamless papers for you to use.
- A collection of Image Hose nozzles.
- A variety of objects in an Image Portfolio library.
- A Selection Portfolio, containing some interesting selection shapes.
- Animations made with Painter 6.
- Artworks by Painter students and children to inspire your creativity.

System Requirements

Software

PC

- Painter 6
- Windows 95, 98, NT4, or higher
- A Java-compatible Web browser (to produce rollovers using the Image Slicer plug-in)

Macintosh

- Painter 6
- System 8 or higher
- A Java-compatible Web browser (to produce rollovers using the Image Slicer plug-in)

Hardware

PC

- An Intel (or equivalent) Pentium processor (with as fast a speed as you can afford is recommended)
- At least 32MB RAM (64MB or more of RAM is recommended)
- At least 300MB of disk storage space (for the Painter 6 application)
- Color display (24-bit recommended)
- CD-ROM drive

Macintosh

- A Power Macintosh (with as fast a processor speed as you can afford is recommended)
- At least 32MB RAM (64MB or more of RAM is recommended)
- At least 300MB of disk storage space (for the Painter 6 application)
- Color display (24-bit recommended)
- CD-ROM drive